Dead End Kids

The University of Wisconsin Press
1930 Monroe Street
Madison, Wisconsin 53711

3 Henrietta Street
London WC2E 8LU, England

www.wisc.edu\wisconsinpress

7   6   5   4   3

Printed in the United States of America

Library of Congress Cataloging-in-Publication Data

Fleisher, Mark
    Dead end kids : gang girls and the boys they know /
Mark S. Fleisher.
        290 pp.   cm.
        Includes bibliographical references and index.
        ISBN 0-299-15880-2 (cloth: alk. paper)
        ISBN 0-299-15884-5 (pbk. : alk. paper)
        1. Delinquent girls—Missouri—Kansas City—Case studies.
    2. Gang members—Missouri—Kansas City—Case Studies.
    3. Problem youth—Missouri—Kansas City—Case studies.
    4. Gangs—Missouri—Kansas City.
    5. Juvenile delinquency—Missouri—Kansas City.
    I. Title.
    HV9106.K2F54   1998
    364.36'082'09778411—dc21   98-15537

Mark S. Fleisher

Dead End Kids

*Gang Girls and the
Boys They Know*

The University of Wisconsin Press

To Red,
thirty years, always there,
"cut man," teacher, friend
love, s

Contents

Acknowledgments

A special thank you is due a number of colleagues and friends (my "homeboys" and "homegirls") who hung with me over many years while I did fieldwork and wrote this book.

Jim Gallison, John Shaw, Al and Diana Marshal, Philippe Bourgois, Kathleen O'Brien, Dale Welling and the executive staff and members of the National Major Gang Task Force, Gery Ryan, Devon Brewer, and Marcellus Andrews made contributions to this book by allowing me to talk ceaselessly about the Fremont Hustlers. Each of you had a different perspective on what I said, and together you helped me create *Dead End Kids*.

Scott Decker and Dave Curry have supported and encouraged my Kansas City research for years and have offered me opportunities to voice my ideas at the University of Missouri–St. Louis. Scott and Dave have always had insightful opinions and good constructive criticism about my interpretation of these ethnographic data.

While I sat with Jeff Fagan at breakfast in Lisbon, Portugal, in April 1996, he suggested that I write a natural history of a youth gang. Then in May 1996, while enjoying a sunny afternoon overlooking the fishing fleet in the northern Spanish city of San Sebastian, James B. James, encouraged me to write a book geared to students and a general reading audience. Jim said the problems of youth gangs and the social, economic, and political issues underlying them are so important that these issues must be broadcast well beyond the academy. I took Jeff's and Jim's good advice and tried to write a natural history of a youth gang for a wide reading audience. I trust that my effort has been worthy of their good advice.

Irv Spergel allowed me to participate in the Comprehensive Community-wide Approach to Gang Prevention, Intervention, and Suppression Program, a remarkable community-mobilization program funded by the Office of Juvenile Justice and Delinquency Prevention. Working with Irv has been a distinct pleasure. He is kind and generous, energetic and very smart, and his passion to remedy the lives of gang kids is endless. The Spergel Model of community mobilization has influenced the policy suggestions offered here. I am hopeful, Irv, that I have been a good student and have used your ideas in a thoughtful and kind way.

In April 1996, President Lois DeFleur, Dean Linda Biemer, and Dr. Kevin Wright invited me to delivery the annual criminal justice address to the School of Education and Human Development, Binghamton University. This university is my alma mater, and an invitation to lecture on campus about the Fremont Hustlers was an honor. I was given an enormous auditorium, 90 minutes, and an audience of outstanding university faculty and staff members, as well as the members of the local law enforcement and social service communities. The hospitality and encouragement graciously extended to me at Binghamton University were appreciated.

Nancy McKee offered constructive criticisms about the content and tone of this manuscript long before it was ready for public consumption. Your continual willingness to read crude drafts and offer thoughtful, honest opinion is sincerely appreciated.

Phil Olson and I met in 1992, and immediately Phil treated me as though I were a long-lost friend. Between 1992 and 1994, Phil introduced me to the neighborhoods of Kansas City and many of the professionals who are trying hard to make positive changes in the impoverished neighborhoods of Kansas City's east side. Phil arranged for me to teach a summer course in urban gangs in 1994, during which I met Wendy, one of the founders of the Fremont Hustlers. Over the years when I was involved with the Fremont Hustlers, Phil always asked how he could help me, and more important, he wanted to help the gang kids who Kansas City has forgotten. Without your help and support, Phil, I doubt if I would have finished *Dead End Kids*.

Illinois State University does something extraordinary: it supports faculty with university research grants, which often lead to high-quality off-campus research. I want to thank President David Stand, Vice President of Academic Affairs and Provost John Urice, and ISU's administrators who preserve the funding programs to support faculty researchers.

Special thanks go to my colleagues and friends Tom Ellsworth, Ralph Weisheit, and Ed Wells for listening to my accounts of gang life and offering good opinions. Ralph, thanks for keeping your eye on the newspaper and World Wide Web and passing along articles relevant to my research. Your thoughtfulness is sincerely appreciated.

Over the course of my Fremont research I harassed Tom Ellsworth, chair, Department of Criminal Justice Sciences, about bailing me out of

Kansas City's jail should the necessity arise. Tom told me that I was on my own in Kansas City and maybe I'd better stay out of dangerous places. Advice well taken, Tom. However, he did much more than give advice: he arranged my course schedule, which allowed me to spend more time in Kansas City, and he was always patient with the absence.

John J. DiIulio, Jr., has encouraged and supported my ethnographic research over many years. I have been pleasantly surprised on many occasions to open a newspaper or a policy journal or to read a book chapter authored by John and find that he used street ethnography reported in *Beggars and Thieves* as support for his cutting-edge policy recommendations. John, I appreciate your support and am hopeful that this book, too, will encourage lawmakers to pay attention to the fate of America's children.

Karen Colvard and the Harry Frank Guggenheim Foundation have supported two of my long-term ethnographic research projects. *Beggars and Thieves* and *Dead End Kids* were written because Karen and the H. F. Guggenheim Foundation saw intellectual and practical value in street ethnography. I know well that there are many outstanding scholars worldwide who vie to obtain the support of the Guggenheim Foundation; I am honored that it chose to support my ethnographic efforts.

Three reviewers poured over the original proposal for this book and offered constructive comments. Then two senior scholars, one an anthropologist, the other a criminologist, read and reread every word of the first draft. Some parts they liked, others they didn't, and in the end, their extensive knowledge of youth gangs, adolescent deviance, gender and crime, ethnography, and good writing helped me prepare the final manuscript. Long ago, my mentor Russ Bernard taught me that critics are our best friends. As always, he's right.

Dr. Rosalie Robertson, senior editor, University of Wisconsin Press, waited patiently while I finished this book, about nine months late. Thanks, Rosalie. The staff of the University of Wisconsin Press has been exceptionally kind and generous to me, and it's wonderful to work with people who know so much about making books better.

Robin Whitaker, my editor at the University of Wisconsin Press, toiled over nearly 1,000 manuscript pages in *Beggars and Thieves* and *Dead End Kids*. Robin tended to my texts as a gardener toils over early spring plantings. Her talent and concern for the literary quality of these texts transformed my manuscripts into books of better quality. Thanks, Robin. I will not publish a book without you.

Doing this research has taught me a lot, and paramount among the things I have learned is that I am a self-absorbed street ethnographer who doesn't know how to stay out of other people's business. Such behavior takes time. My wife, Dr. Ann McGuigan, put up with my long fieldtrips to Kansas City and cared for our home and kids and her own career while I was hanging out on Fremont. I cannot adequately acknowledge the years of support she has given me, but I can begin with something simple: Thank you, Ann. You have made my life rich.

To my children, Emily and Aaron, thanks for enduring my impatience and irritability after long stretches in Kansas City, marathon writing sessions, and nearly three years of incessant talk about Cara, Wendy, and the Fremont Hustlers. By understanding how important it was for me to write this book, you have made a serious contribution to enhancing the lives of all those Kansas City kids who called our house late at night over so many years.

Dead End Kids

Introduction

Dead End Kids is a firsthand account of the lives of adolescents in a youth gang called the Fremont Hustlers in Kansas City, Missouri. I describe the social and economic pressure on these youngsters and the social arrangements and economic adaptations caused by that pressure. More specifically, I explore how parental neglect, household poverty, crime, and drug addiction induce social and emotional malignancies in these adolescents' lives. Aggravating and intensifying these youngsters' anguish and real-life problems is the neglect of an entire midwestern city, whose law enforcement and civic leaders have overlooked their moral obligation to safeguard children's well-being and have instead pursued an aggressive strategy to lock away disruptive children and keep them out of sight.

Dead End Kids offers an insider's perspective and views youth-gang life through the eyes of a teenage gang girl. I call her Cara. Cara's life is a weave of drugs and guns, shootings and assaults, boyfriends and pregnancies, ratty apartments, broken-down cars, minimum-wage jobs, strained relationships with family members and peers, dodging the police, and praying for peace. You'll take a close look at Cara's world and meet other gang girls and the boys they know. These boys are cold. They abuse the girls, father their children, and then abandon them and the babies until they again need something from the girls.

My bond to Cara was long and personal. Our relationship is a central theme in her story. I tried my best to "save" Cara and pull her off the street. I opened the doors to a private high school and led her in a direction I thought she wanted to go. In the end, however, Cara chose her own path, and it took her back to the street and to girls like her close companion Wendy.

Cara's story isn't complete without Wendy, who is one of the Fremont Hustlers' founding members, a girl who described herself to me in our first conversation in July 1994 as a "straight G," a girl who succeeds in the gang life by doing the things boys do.[1] Cara and Wendy's world is filled with anguish and fear, joy and anger, frustration and rejection, and fantasies of gingerbread houses and lovers who'll rescue them from poverty, lousy jobs, jalopies, and broken promises.

Nearly all Cara's teenage years were spent as Wendy's companion. In a real sense, these teenage girls have been sisters in the street struggle. By the end of my research, they had lost small battles against the street and couldn't find the strength to forsake its dead-end lifestyle. However, they each fought with a never-ending zeal and a remarkable sense of optimism.

In *Dead End Kids,* Cara and her male and female companions are called kids. Had they attended school, they'd have walked through locker-room doors labeled "boys" and "girls." Let's not lose sight of that as I take you into the dark world of a youth gang, where these kids are pursued, arrested, and labeled as gang members, juvenile delinquents, drug dealers, drug addicts, burglars, thieves, and, in some cases, killers. Indeed, these labels fit the Fremont Hustlers, but I'll show you that these kids are much more than those labels.

Dead End Kids isn't specifically about the mistreatment of young children; however, I can't tell the story of the Fremont Hustlers without talking about the horrors of family life. Family abuse and neglect for Fremont kids has happened over at least two generations. The kids I studied have been neglected and/or abused, and now they abuse and ignore their own kids with the ease and thoughtlessness of selling $10 bags of marijuana.

Fremont research reaffirms *Beggars and Thieves*'[2] child-protection policy, which argues for the development of a national, federally funded network of group homes or orphanages in which children can grow up in a healthy and safe environment. *Dead End Kids* argues for safe havens for gang girls and their children. Fremont research shows vividly that teenage gang parents don't rear their children safely. The rearing of children inside a youth gang and the socioeconomic functions that are imputed to pregnant teenagers and their babies are this book's two most important issues in our consideration of gang prevention and intervention.

"Children having children" and rearing them in vile and dangerous places is a scene beyond your wildest nightmare, as you'll see. But a solution may be simple and relatively inexpensive compared with the costs and implications of ignoring poverty, youth gangs, and the rearing of children in dangerous households.

Dead End Kids is uncomfortable to read. You may want to close it or say to yourself, "These things can't really be happening in Kansas City." But the things you'll read here did happen and continue to happen to kids in Kansas City and other cities around the United States. In response to the awful lives gang kids lead, I have offered simple, feasible recommendations which will, first, protect teenage mothers and their children and, second, weaken the underlying social and economic processes of a youth gang, at no extra cost. Safe havens for teenage gang-affiliated girls can be implemented with moderate planning and a relatively low budget. I implore communities to develop supervised residential centers for gang girls, especially for those who are pregnant and those who are young mothers.

To work effectively, these community residential centers must engage in a financial commitment with state and federal lawmakers. Such a "street-level" program offering immediate material care to adolescents and children shouldn't have to wait until federal and state legislators create yet another costly government program. Communities rallying to protect young children and their adolescent parents should be the first major step in the best direction we can take to resolve the youth-gang problem.

Dead End Kids shows that gang behavior doesn't happen because a 14-year-old is bored after school and needs something to do. A youth gang isn't an after-school play group. Rather, the label "youth gang" is a metaphor for a number of behaviors, including truancy, school failure, kids' disenfranchisement from parents and the mainstream community, drug use, drug selling, street violence, and teenage pregnancy and parenthood. However, every behavior has a cause and a context, and it was the search for the causes and socioeconomic contexts of youth-gang behavior that was the purpose of the Fremont research.

Law enforcement and social service officials must cope with the surface manifestations (drug use, drug selling, street violence) of youth gangs. However, policy makers have a far more difficult responsibility, which is to locate and remedy the causes of youth-gang behavior and the contexts in which it occurs. Fremont research shows that the causes of gang behavior are often invisible and run deep inside the social dynamics and economics of gang kids' families, neighborhoods, and communities.

The research findings about the socioeconomics of, and the crime linked to, the Fremont Hustlers, as well as Kansas City's reaction to this youth gang, aren't unique to this city.[3] My conclusions about the Fremont Hustlers are corroborated by decades of gang research in other cities, and other communities' aggressive and suppressive responses to juvenile crime are illustrated by national juvenile arrest data. This isn't to say that youth gangs aren't a problem to communities. They are. However, the issue is the nature of communities' responses to youth gangs and the effectiveness of those responses.

Measuring Gang Crime

Recent research shows that 91.1 percent of 79 cities in the United States with populations in excess of 200,000 have a so-called gang problem.[4] Additional estimates suggest that between 800 and 1,000 towns and cities have troublesome gangs.[5] National Institute of Justice (NIJ) data show 555,181 gang members in 16,643 gangs as having committed 580,331 gang-related crimes in 1993.[6] These can only be estimates of the number of gangs, gang members, and gang-related crimes. Although property crime is the major offense committed by gangs, gang-related violence represents a disproportionate percentage of adolescent violent crime.

The Office of Juvenile Justice and Delinquency Prevention in the Department of Justice reported that in 1993 there were nearly 1.5 million delinquency cases processed by juvenile courts.[7] These cases were classified into the following categories: 54.2 percent were property crimes (burglary, larceny, vandalism, among others); 21.4 percent were crimes against persons (robbery, aggravated and simple assault, rape); 18.3 percent were public order offenses (obstruction of justice, disorderly conduct, weapons offenses, among others); and 5.9 percent were drug law violations. Some undetermined percentage of these juvenile court cases were likely related to gangs. However, for a number of reasons, we don't know that percentage.

First, gang researchers and law enforcement agencies use no national definition for what constitutes a gang. The different criteria used to estimate the number of gangs and gang members are unclear; thus, estimates among cities or police departments are often unreliable and may be inflated to boost police agency budgets.

Second, with no national definition of gangs, there is so much variation in the criteria used to classify juvenile crime into categories, such as "gang" crime versus "gang-related" and "non-gang-related" crime, as well as variations among the categories themselves, that such classifications are unreliable.

Third, if police departments can't accurately determine whether a juvenile crime is a gang-related or a non-gang-related crime, it will also be difficult to distinguish a gang-related crime from a similar crime committed by a gang member acting outside his or her gang or by a group of delinquents who are pretending to be a gang or are misidentified by police as such. Confusion over these issues has led some police departments, including Kansas City's, to stop classifying street crimes as primarily gang or gang-related crimes.

Fourth, the absence of a national database on gang crimes and gang members prevents local, state, and federal law enforcement agencies from sharing data on street crime and criminals that are likely to be linked in some way to gangs or gang members.

The confusion over gang definitions, problems with interagency data sharing, and uncertainty about the most effective short- and long-term strategies for managing youth gangs within communities have created the political shadows necessary for control-minded lawmakers to support oppressive law enforcement rather than creative community responses to youth gangs.

Emergence of a Gang Industry

Confusion over definitions is a nightmare to researchers, but confusion has been a boon to lawmakers and city government officials, who can use the fuzziness of gang crime data in politically motivated under- or overestimates of street crime.[8] To keep citizens calm, police agencies can offer data to show relatively few gangs or can manipulate crime data near an election to indicate that a "tough on crime" stance has reduced gang crime. To boost police department budgets, city officials can claim that their city's gang problems are growing more menacing, thus frightening legislators and federal agencies into dishing out tax dollars to hire gang detectives, develop gang task forces, buy gang-intelligence computer hardware and software, procure gang detectives' cruisers, and load up on antigang guns and bullets. This is the gang industry.

Despite aggressive police control over disruptive adolescents, no one can say with certainty that this type of response will resolve the so-called youth-gang problem by either discouraging adolescents from affiliating with gangs or by remedying the underlying social and economic dynamics inside families, neighborhoods, and communities which lead adolescents to gangs in the first place. What's more, no one has argued convincingly that aggressive police control is the most cost-effective, long-term strategy to cope with the community safety issues caused by youth gangs.

Kansas City's law enforcement officials link street violence to an increase in gang activity. Violence, officials say, includes drive-by shootings, drug-related violence, violent gang initiations, and revenge killings. Official reports note that the frequency and the number of victims of KC drive-by shootings have increased in a short time: in 1988, there were 10 victims; by 1989, there were nearly 20 victims; in 1990, there were 297; and in 1991, there were 316.[9] More recent gang-violence data were unavailable.

In 1996, Dr. Phil Olson, a community development expert and professor of sociology at the University of Missouri–Kansas City, and I met with KC gang detectives. We asked for gang-crime data and were told such data were unavailable. Either the KCPD did a remarkable job reducing the occurrence of gang-related street violence between 1993 and 1995, or they redefined how they tallied gang versus nongang violent incidents. Perhaps the KCPD stopped reporting street violence as gang crime no matter who committed those crimes. Such a strategy might quell growing community fear about crime and gangs. Reporting a homicide or a carjacking as a street crime is one thing, but calling such incidents gang crimes terrifies voters.[10] As you'll see for yourselves, occasional youth-gang crime is far less shocking than the abhorrent daily lives of teenage gang members and their preschool children and the neighborhoods in which they must survive.

A Reader's Guide[11]

Dead End Kids is the story of a number of girls and boys caught in the lifestyle of chronic delinquency and youth gangs. Cara and Wendy are the principal female personalities. The text poses unstated questions (will they make it off the street, or will they always stay a few feet ahead of the police?) as guides to help readers pass through the maze of people and events which composed these girls' family, gang, and street life over nearly two years.

Generally speaking, this story shows how the facts and incidents of their lives, as well as those of other Fremont Hustlers and Northeast Gangstas, are altered by a number of major conceptual issues. However, I haven't used labels, such as "race," "poverty," and "social control," as the basis of the chapters. Nevertheless, these, as well as family dysfunction, the role of community social service and law enforcement agencies in the neighborhoods and their households, and, more generally, the (in)effectiveness of government as a means of directed social change, are *Dead End Kids'* bedrock conceptual notions. The lives of Cara and Wendy and the other kids have been permanently altered by the power of these concepts, but I explicitly kept them in the background so the spotlight never veered away from these gang girls and the boys they know.

Read this book as you would a novel, but remember there's no fiction on these pages. To bring you into the lives of these ghetto kids and their families, I have used direct quotations taken from my conversations with them, and for the most part I have retained the "natural" social settings, that is, the actual social context, in which these conversations occurred. I did this for two reasons. First, there is a theoretical basis for doing it, which I explain in Chapter 15. Second, natural conversations let you listen to Cara, Wendy, and the others talk about a wide range of issues, including the bedrock conceptual notions, in a number of settings with dozens of people over a long time as their lives shift and twist and change direction.

You'll hear kids anguish over decisions about drug selling and use, violence on the street, struggles with parents, and the best way to leave gang life behind. However, it's what these kids don't talk about that makes them so different from "normal" teenagers. Fremont Hustlers and Northeast Gangstas don't talk about high school graduation, college entrance exams, college majors and careers, proms and homecoming parades, and visits to the orthodontist. Rather, these street kids worry about drive-by shootings, pregnancy and abortion, drug raids, family violence, getting cash to buy diapers and baby food, visits to prison to see old companions and boyfriends, the length of prison sentences, bail money, court dates, and KCPD's open investigations of gang murders.

Dead End Kids' natural conversations show that these kids are ill-prepared for mainstream work and social life. They use profanity anywhere, anytime, and don't care how they are perceived by others. Sitting in the Pizza Hut or McDonald's or walking around a convenience store, these kids have no compunction about cursing profusely in raucous voices, bragging openly about bloody fistfights and drive-bys, or discussing the details of feminine hygiene or sexual relationships.

These conversations are linguistic cues that tell us about these kids' family life and hint at difficulties awaiting them in the future. Such conversations show these kids are quite adequately socialized for life on the street but, for the most part, no place else. And these conversations suggest to us how difficult it would be for these kids to move successfully from street life into mainstream society without intensive intervention.

Dead End Kids' single most important policy concern is the ineffectiveness of government to direct social change through bureaucracies. Granted, this research covers a period of only 21 months in one city and isn't directly a study of social and law enforcement agencies. Rather, the lives of Cara, Wendy, and the others tell us how social and law enforcement agencies acted toward them, to their detriment or to their benefit.

At times, I am very critical of Kansas City's ability to remedy *Dead End Kids'* bedrock conceptual issues. Maybe Kansas City officials have done the best they can. After all, America has created cumbersome bureaucracies and empowered anonymous bureaucrats to effect constructive social and economic transformations of neighborhoods and households. Perhaps if I hadn't spent so many years seeing family dysfunction, drugs and violence, and poverty and neighborhood disintegration, I might have conceivably felt differently and perhaps better about local government agencies.

I didn't write this book to be an apologist for government functionaries. *Dead End Kids* is about adolescents surviving on the streets without adult support, and it's about babies and preschoolers living in smoke-filled drug houses and being reared by their foul parents in the company of apathetic gang members, firearms, and illegal drugs. I watched these and other dreadful street and household scenes over 1995, 1996, and 1997 and felt the distant company of some 75,000 fans cheering the Kansas City Chiefs, celebrating football Sundays in the fall and winter, only a few miles to the south and east. Assembled masses at Arrowhead Stadium spent hundreds of thousands of dollars on Sunday afternoons watching wealthy athletes chase one another around an acre of grass. At the same time inside houses on Fremont, preschoolers' eyes were being blackened by angry young gang members, and pregnant teens smoked cigarettes and used drugs with virtually no thought about the life inside them.

I thought if a portion of the money spent on beer and hot dogs at Arrowhead could find its way into the ghetto, the lives of these children could be materially improved. But how many fans, I asked myself, would forgo a Sunday-afternoon Chiefs game and donate the price of a football ticket and a few beers to help kids being reared in gang neighborhoods?

The poverty on Kansas City's northeast side and the wealth exhibited inside the city's grandiose palaces of entertainment, its sports arenas and gambling halls, illustrate to me an important lesson: the rich are miles away from the poor in physical distance, but lightyears away in empathy. As an anthropologist, I asked myself, What is the nature of a culture that allows children to live in life-threatening environments while adults avert their gaze and entertain themselves nearby?

Sociological research has for decades shown us that the poor want what the rich have. Real life in poor neighborhoods tells us that for the most part the rich don't want to share wealth with the poor. The imbalance between the rich and the poor is, of course, controlled by the rich. However, in a humane society, citizens charge government officials with the mission and the moral obligation to mediate the link between the rich and the poor. From my perch in Kansas City's poorest neighborhoods, I couldn't help but conclude that government officials have failed in their mediation function.

Evidence of such failure includes the children and adolescents you'll meet in *Dead End Kids*. It doesn't matter to me if government officials say they are doing the best they can, nor do I care if Chiefs' fans discuss how to resolve the problems of race and economic inequality in their city while they enjoy tailgate parties. What truly matters to me is the actual resolution of these problems and the material improvement of kids' lives.

The responsibility for children's suffering rests squarely on the shoulders of the voters supporting elected officials who find the widening gap between the rich and the poor acceptable. When government agents deliver services to the poor and the helpless with the zest, speed, and dedication of beer sellers at Arrowhead, I may be kinder to bureaucrats and elected officials. And the measure of such dedication will be an increasing number of children from the poorest households who arrive at kindergarten happy and healthy.

Major Players

Dead End Kids talks about a lot of kids and adults. To facilitate your reading, I have assembled a list of major players and a key fact or two about each one:

- *Cara,* core member of the Fremont Hustlers
- *Cathy,* Cara's mother
- *April,* Cara's youngest sister
- *Melanie,* one of Cara's two elder sisters

- *Wendy,* a founding member of the Fremont Hustlers
- *Robert* ("chubby-faced Robert"), Wendy's brother
- *Jackie,* Wendy and Robert's mother
- *Mike,* Wendy's father
- *Jerry,* Wendy's uncle; Jackie's brother
- *Bobo,* Wendy's guard dog

- *Janet,* core member of the Fremont Hustlers
- *Steele Bill,* resident in Wendy's house; father of Janet's daughter, Briana; Cara's long-standing lover
- *Afro,* core member of the Fremont Hustlers
- *Rosa,* Afro's girlfriend
- *Chucky D,* core member of the Fremont Hustlers; close companion and protector of Cara
- *Joanne,* mother of Chucky D's daughter, Charlene, and Charles B.'s daughter, Sequoia
- *Tamara,* one of Chucky D's girlfriends
- *Taffy,* Fremont neighborhood resident and caregiver to Fremont kids
- *House of Pain,* core member of the Fremont Hustlers
- *Cheri,* close companion of Wendy and Cara
- *Dante,* Cheri's elder sister; close companion of Janet
- *Angie* ("Poodle Bitch," "Poodle"), companion of Wendy and Cara; elder sister of Roger

- *Roger,* Angie's brother
- *Wayne,* Angie's boyfriend

- *Teresa,* mother of the preschoolers Amy and RoniRo, infant Kevin, Jr., and an adolescent boy, Jeffrey; outsider with a strong involvement with Fremont members
- *Donna,* Teresa's younger sister; marginal member of the Fremont Hustlers
- *Netta,* Teresa's youngest sister; member of the Fremont Hustler; close companion of Poodle
- *Kevin,* most current of Teresa's lovers; father of Kevin, Jr.

- *Bernard* ("B"), a leader of the Northeast Gangstas; close companion of Wendy and Cara
- *Northeast TJ,* Bernard's younger brother; core member of the Northeast Gangstas
- *Carmen,* homeless teenager befriended by Cara
- *Chris,* core member of the Northeast Gangstas
- *Dusty,* core member of the Northeast Gangstas
- *Snoop,* core member of the Northeast Gangstas; Steele Bill's cousin
- *Thomas Cook,* core member of the Northeast Gangstas; convicted of shooting Cara and Wendy in a walk-by shooting
- *Eddie Solo,* member of the Northeast Gangstas; close companion of Chucky D
- *Carol,* known as the Gangsta Mamma in Cara's neighborhood on the northeast side
- *Joe,* Carol's live-in boyfriend; Missouri parolee

All the people, facts and events, and conversations in *Dead End Kids* are real. However, there were times when I was forced to modify or omit the details of particular scenes to ensure the anonymity of gang kids and the people associated with them in the event of criminal investigations. All the personal names, whether legal or street names, are pseudonyms. I chose alternate names which retain a sense of integrity and the tone of each person's real name. When referring to several colleagues in Kansas City, I have used their real names with their permission.

1
The Call

On December 18, 1996, at 10:15 P.M., while my 18-year-old daughter, Emily, baked Christmas cookies, and my 15-year-old son, Aaron, practiced the cello, the phone rang in the kitchen of my house in Normal, Illinois. Emily grabbed it and yelled, "Dad, it's for you." I walked from the dining room into the kitchen to get the phone. Emily covered the mouthpiece and whispered, "Sounds like one of your gang girls."

Only Cara called me at this time of night.

"Hi," I said, knowing it was her.

"Hiiiy." The low, drawn-out vowel let me know it was Cara. She sounds as if she grew up in the South, but she's a KC girl, a product of The Paseo projects and many other poor places.

Hearing from Cara and other Fremont kids was a treat. I have a residential 800 number, and I'd given it and the access code to Fremont and other gang kids too, telling them to call me if they needed me or just wanted to talk. These kids never just wanted to talk. Whenever they called, they needed something: money or counsel on a legal case, but most often companionship and advice, the kind fathers are supposed to give their kids.

"Hey girl, wha's up with you? I was getting worried about you. You know when I don't hear from ya I get worried." She laughed quietly. I hadn't heard from her in nearly a week. "Where are ya?" I asked.

"At my mom's. It got so cold here last night. It was 20 below last night."

"Yeah, it's cold here too." I paused before asking, "So what else is going on?" I knew there was more to this call than chitchat. When Cara called there was always a reason.

She paused. I heard her take a deep breath. "I'm pregnant."

"Yeah? Great," I exclaimed, but that's not what I thought or how I felt. "How pregnant are you, girl?"

"Five weeks."

"Five weeks. I guess you haven't been working as many hours as you said you have been, huh?" She laughed. I tried to lighten the moment.

"You going to handle that Taco Bell job OK when you get a big belly?" I asked with concern in my voice.

"Yeah," she whispered.

"Who's the father?" I already knew the answer.

"Biyll," Cara lengthened the vowel again, so the word *Bill* sounded like "peel" pronounced with a *b*. Steele Bill, a former Crip, was the Fremont Hustler's "weight man" before the big drug bust in August 1995. Now Steele Bill sells weed on his own. He's a quiet teenager and the father of infant Briana, born on September 16, about 90 days earlier. Janet, Briana's mother, is one of the original Fremont Hustlers.

"Pregnant again," I said. She laughed nervously. I should have kept quiet but I couldn't. Cara, I thought, is my daughter's age, and this is her fourth pregnancy. "Hey girl, next time I come over, let's talk about how girls get pregnant, huh?" She was quiet. "What's your mom think about it?"

Cara yelled, "Ma, Mark wants to know what you think about the baby."

The question interrupted the clanging of stuff in the kitchen and lots of loud chatter and laughter and talk. I heard the answer over the noise of Cara's two sisters' talking.

"She's too young," said Cathy, Cara's mom. An interesting answer, I thought, coming from a woman who had had two children by the time she was Cara's age.

"Hear dat?" asked Cara.

"Yeah. How do *you* feel about it?"

"Goood," she lengthened the vowel.

I switched into my father voice, which Cara has heard many times. I told her she needed to see a doctor as soon as possible, sleep and eat properly, and above all, "no smoking, and that means no cigarettes, no blunts, no joints."

Cara laughed. "I ain't smoked in weeks. No mo' weed, promise."

She said she had an appointment at Truman Medical Center in early January, and that she'd soon tell her probation officer about the pregnancy and ask the PO to help her get a social worker, medical aid, and HUD housing.

"Well," she paused, "I'm gonna have a shower in the spring, and you'd better come."

"Hey, I'll be there. Have I ever let you down when you needed me?"

"Naw," she said quietly. "I love you," she said as a child to a parent. "Mark, you're the only dad I've ever had. I guess you're gonna be a grandpa."

2

Fremont Hustlers

Interstate 70 crosses I-435 on the east side of KC near the Truman Sports Complex, the stadiums of the Kansas City Royals and the Kansas City Chiefs, and cuts through the downtown and metropolitan KC. I-435 wraps metropolitan Kansas City in a ribbon of concrete. A mile west of the sports complex, I-435 extends north toward KC's international airport and south and then west toward Johnson County, Kansas, known to locals simply as Johnson County. The way Kansas Citians say that name lets you know it's "the place to be."

Johnson County is a collection of chain stores sustained by an interminable queue of balding men with bulging bellies, wearing tasseled loafers and weekend Dockers. Mall parking lots are filled with vans packed with kids wearing hats turned backwards and baggy athletic clothes on their way to soccer games. The vans are driven by aging, tanned women who have had so much facial cosmetic surgery that the skin on their cheeks resembles potato chips. Folks in some parts of KC aspire to this way of life. Overland Park, a large community in Johnson County, is the epitome of generic upper-middle-class America. Plywood and sheetrock homes, much too expensive for their construction quality, strip malls, car dealerships, and chain restaurants cover the landscape and offer economic opportunities for business people and employees who drive to this distant southwest corner of metropolitan KC.

About 15 miles east and north of Overland Park is the Fremont Avenue neighborhood, home of the Fremont Hustlers. I-70 dissects Kansas City, first cutting through KC's east side. The Fremont Hustlers sometimes call themselves the Eastside Fremont Hustlers, but nearly always they refer to themselves as Fremont. A Fremont boy known as House of Pain wears a stocking cap with the word *Eastside* embroidered on it. The east side isn't a garden spot, but, to me, it and its residents are more interesting than Overland Park and anyone who lives there.

15

I-70 has eastside exits to Van Brunt Boulevard, Independence, Truman, Troost, and The Paseo. The Paseo was once a north-south thoroughfare lined with fashionable two-story apartment houses. It now marks the imaginary checkpoint separating low-crime, westside, white areas from high-crime, eastside black, white, and Mexican neighborhoods.

Folks who can afford vans and tasseled loafers and skin-tightening surgery don't go east of The Paseo. Fear, promulgated by reports of eastside gangs and street crime in the *Kansas City Star* and on local news channels, has needlessly frightened folks with money, and they now stay away. Longtime Kansas Citians would likely deny it, but years of full-time residence in KC told me that there exists in KC's upper-middle and upper classes a subtle but palpable sense of white racial superiority, which makes the poverty and economic underdevelopment of the east side even easier for dominant Kansas Citians to accept.

The I-70 exit to Van Brunt Boulevard leads to a pleasant narrow lane that's wrapped by 50-year-old trees whose branches overhang the road, casting cooling shadows in the hot humid summers. In winter the city plows Van Brunt because it's a busy thoroughfare leading to and from I-70 as well as downtown Kansas City. If you drive north on Van Brunt for three blocks from the I-70 exit, you'll find Cathy's apartment. Cathy is Cara's mother. Cara, you'll remember, called me at Christmas 1996 from her mother's.

Cathy's apartment is on the first floor of a two-story apartment house that has a dozen units. Cathy's neighbors to the left are "smokers" (rock cocaine smokers) and drinkers who leave empty "forties" (40-ounce bottles of beer or malt alcohol) and generic filter-cigarette butts squashed on the concrete porch.

Cathy's apartment is small and tidy and livable for the $80-a-week rent she paid in 1996. There's a living room with two couches, which also serve as beds. Cathy has one bedroom. April, Cara's younger sister by two years, has the other one. Cathy and April are full-time residents; Cara and 22-year-old Melanie, Cara's second eldest sister, come and go. When the couches are occupied, bodies flop on the floor between the color TV and VCR and the wooden coffee table which always has lots of cigarettes on it, a plastic ashtray full of butts, and of course the phone. The phone is always the centerpiece in any place that Cara stays. The phone, pagers, cell phones, and pay phones are lifelines to the social world of young gangsters.

The kitchen is tiny, large enough for two people to stand in at one time, one on either side of the small formica-top table that separates the sink on one side of the room from the stove on the other. A small bathroom next to the kitchen has a tub and shower, and in the back are the two bedrooms, each about eight by ten. April's bedroom, on the left side, has a door leading onto a small, enclosed back porch. Two other apartments' rear doors exit onto that porch, including the smokers'. When Cara doesn't want Cathy to know what she is up to, she uses the back porch to bring weed into the house. April's room serves as a spot to divide up plastic bags of weed into smaller portions for use and sale. The back porch is the spot where Cara and her companions smoke weed. Cathy would go ballistic if she were aware of her daughters smoking and selling weed inside her apartment.

When Cara called at Christmastime 1996 I heard April, Melanie, and Cathy chatting and laughing. Cathy's fourth and eldest daughter, Mary, is married with a toddler and lives in Atlanta. Melanie works up the street at a laundromat, handing out change and tidying up things. Melanie says she loves doing laundry. I told Cara it's the only laundromat I've ever seen that has a full snack bar, with cigarettes, sodas, and hot dogs for sale. I'll bet you can buy a joint if you ask politely. Cara laughed and said laundromats in ghettos always have a snack bar.

In October 1996, Melanie was walking home by herself near midnight and was robbed by a neighborhood junkie. He scared the hell out of Melanie, took her purse, but didn't hurt her. The purse had a wallet with a few dollars and Cathy's apartment key. Police didn't investigate the robbery. The junkie never used the apartment key. I asked Cara, in front of Cathy, if she'd ask Chucky D, the most charismatic and violent Fremont Hustler, to "handle" the junkie-robber. Cara knew I was teasing. "No," said Cathy with a smile, "he's got too many others to kill to mess with him."

Cara's mother and the kids moved to Van Brunt from a larger, more elegant duplex on Gladstone, in a quiet eastside neighborhood about 10 blocks north of Independence Avenue and close to its intersection with The Paseo. The duplex had large rooms—a dining room, living room, big kitchen with a Krups espresso machine on the counter, and bedrooms eight by ten and larger, one for each daughter. One block up the street was one of Kansas City's beautiful fountains. On hot summer days, Fremont kids would pack into cars and drive to Cara's, and they'd romp in the fountain to the chagrin of neighbors.

This fountain is in the eastside territory of the Northeast Gangstas, known on the street as Northeast. Northeast and Fremont are arch-enemies. Some days at the fountain were uneventful. But other times, Northeast kids would drive by and see Fremont kids, and hell would break loose, according to Fremont kids. I never saw that happen.

Cara's mother said she left that duplex because she wanted something cheaper. But Cara said frequent visits by the KCPD from late August to December 1995 pissed off the landlords so much that the family was evicted.

Cara said the two landlords were criminals. She told me they owned a funeral home and were arrested, prosecuted, and imprisoned for tossing several dead infants enclosed in garbage bags into a dumpster. I heard about that case on the KC radio but didn't follow up to be sure Cathy's landlords were the culprits.

Van Brunt heads north and passes East High School, winds around a tree-lined hill, and then heads down the hill to intersect Truman Avenue. On the northwest corner is a massive old cemetery. Drive north (straight ahead) on Van Brunt for another half mile and you'll find yourself at the intersection of Van Brunt and Independence Avenue. Northeast residents call it simply The Ave. Turn left on The Ave and drive west about a mile, and off to the north is the central territory of the Northeast Gangstas.[1]

If you turn right off Van Brunt and onto Truman and drive a half mile, you'll see on your left a mom-and-pop grocery store. The first left after that store is Fremont Avenue. Turn left onto Fremont, drive down three blocks, and you'll find yourself at Fremont and 13th Street, the home of the Fremont Hustlers.

If you stay on Truman and go two more blocks, you'll see on your right a QT (Quick Trip gas station–convenience store). In hot weather the giant, iced, 99¢ drinks are a magnet for the Fremont, as well as other kids in the area.

Fremont and 13th is only a five-minute walk away, but it's uphill. Fremont kids always wanted me to drive them there in the air-conditioned comfort of my 1986 Acura. It's a small car, and they'd pack in, sit on top of one another, smoke cigarettes, turn the radio to the rap-music FM station, 103.3 JAMS, and sing along. The girls love romantic ballads and tales about "gangs, crime, and love."

Hanging on a telephone pole on the north side of Truman across from QT during a number of my trips to Fremont was an 8½ × 11 sheet of yellow paper that had been posted by a movie company in June 1995. It hung there lazily until the wind finally ripped it off.

I showed its advertisement to a few Fremont girls. "Hey look, they'll make you famous," I joked.

"Hey, nothin' but dumb ass mothafuckas go down dere. And how we supposed to get dere—bus? Fuck dat," said Wendy. "When you get dere, they arrest yo fo' warrants. Shit."

WE'RE LOOKING FOR
STREET GANGS
IF YOU'RE BETWEEN THE AGES OF 17 AND 25
we are holding a casting call for a movie
that will be produced in Kansas City.

OPEN AUDITIONS for speaking and non-speaking roles.

BE AT: KEMPER ARENA
ON: Friday, July 21   12:00 Noon to 6:00 p.m.

OR

Saturday, July 22   12:00 to 6:00 p.m.

PROFESSIONAL ACTORS NOT DESIRED
We are only looking for people with
street gang experience.

At QT, Fremont kids asked me politely and demurely if I'd buy them chips, cookies, and ice cream, too. I couldn't say no to kids who had no one to feed them.

Whenever we went there, Wendy, Cara, Cheri, or another girl in the car would see some kid who resides a few blocks off Fremont, and inevitably, shouting, screaming, and threats would be uttered back and forth in the steamy air. Wendy was always the most publicly aggressive girl. Generally speaking, Fremont girls are more willing to engage in public outbursts than the Fremont boys are.

One Saturday afternoon, a week after I first joined the Fremont kids, I sprang for sodas and chips and was backing up to head back down to Fremont. Wendy yelled, "Stop the fucking car. I'm gonna kill that fucking bitch."

She threw open the back door, jumped out of the back seat, and ran over to the curb and stood there howling at a girl walking with a boy across Truman.

"Bitch." She said it was a short vowel, not drawling it as Cara and others do, as if the *i* sound were a piece of taffy being dragged out and enjoyed. Kids do enjoy playing with vowels.

The target of Wendy's aggression, a thin girl with shoulder-length hair who was dressed in loose jeans, turned her head and kept walking. She looked back over her shoulder as Wendy screamed.

"Come on back here, BITCH. I'll kick your fucking ass. Whore. 'Ho'e bitch. If I see you near Fremont I'll kill you, bitch, you fuckin' bitch. What'ya you lookin at? Fuck you."

The tirade ended; she got back into the car. "She a fucking 'ho'e. You know she's fucked every guy up here, and she's only 15. White trash."

That's Wendy, always ready to fight, scream and howl, and protect her territory, which she drags around with her.

Standing at the intersection of Fremont and 13th Street, an east-west street just a half block south of Wendy's, you can see nice homes to the north, off in the distance. One block to the west on White and 13th, Cara and Wendy were ambushed in a walk-by shooting in August 1994. A few miles to the west are the towers of KC's business district.

The neighborhood surrounding Fremont and 13th is poor.[2] Compared with Overland Park, Fremont looks like an extracted chunk of a Third World country that's been dropped on KC's east side. Old cars and rusty pickup trucks sit in the driveways of small wood-frame houses. Many of the residents here are proud of what they have. Lawns are cut and tidy in the summer, leaves raked in the fall, snow shoveled in winter, garbage on sidewalks or street kept to a minimum. In contrast, a number of houses at and near the corner of Fremont and 13th are the disheveled, untended hangouts of Fremont kids.

In July 1994, I visited Fremont once with Wendy's uncle Jerry. He had enrolled in a course on urban gangs, which I taught that summer at the University of Missouri–Kansas City (UMKC). Jerry offered to introduce me to his niece Wendy, who he said had started a gang in Kansas City. In June 1994, Wendy and her then close companion Janet had appeared on a segment of the "Geraldo Rivera Show" about girls in gangs. Jerry called Wendy, told her about the class, and she agreed to attend class with Janet and answer students' questions for three hours. That's how I met Wendy and Janet and how this research started.

The weekend after Wendy and Janet had appeared in class, Jerry asked me if I wanted to see the Fremont neighborhood. We stopped for barbecue beef sandwiches and french fries at Gate's Barbecue on 12th, a few blocks east of The Paseo, on the way to Fremont. There are a number of Gate's restaurants in high-unemployment neighborhoods. Gate's restaurants are legendary in the city, and folks of all colors flock to them. Gate's sells very good food and has the right formula for inner-city development: sell products that people with money enjoy, and they will come. They do. Bill Clinton enjoyed Gate's Barbecue, said a story in the

Kansas City Star, framed and posted on a wall of The Paseo store. Gate's are known for their counter servers screaming, "Hi, may I help you?" When you're hungry it's the sound of relief.

When Jerry and I got to Fremont we stopped in front of Wendy's house. It was midday and there wasn't a soul on the street. But no one has to be outside to let you know where you are. Fremont Hustlers' territory is marked with FH graffiti on houses, sidewalks, and stop signs. There's nothing remarkable about gang graffiti, I thought. Middle-class folks mark neighborhoods too, but they use NEIGHBORHOOD WATCH signs. On Fremont, the graffiti do the same thing. They tell other gangsters to watch out. They also tell the cops that this is a place to watch.

Jerry said the Fremont kids were "fuck ups, real thugs." An ironic comment, I thought. Jerry was in his early thirties, on parole from the Missouri Department of Corrections, having served a 60-month sentence for commercial burglary. Visiting Fremont with Jerry at noon was easy. Going there alone for the first time on June 8, 1995, was, well, down-right scary.

I remembered the way to Fremont and 13th and recognized Wendy's house. More FH graffiti and names of kids had been spray-painted on shanties downhill from Wendy's house and on the sidewalks and drive-ways since I had been there a year earlier.

I stopped in front of Wendy's, parked, and had to make my first big decision: should I lock the car doors? I sat for a moment thinking about it. If I had to get out of there in a hurry, I thought, I didn't want to stop, take out my key, insert and turn it, before I could drive away. I thought I could be killed taking all that time. Anyway, locking a car door is a silly thing to do in such a neighborhood. A brick thrown through the window or a handgun behind my head would surely give someone access to the car.

I sat a while thinking about locking the doors. Now as I think back on that day, the decision to lock the doors is like pulling up in front of a house and deciding whether you want to go on a blind date. Once I knock, I told myself, the game starts. Whether it turns out good or bad, I'll see it through to the end. That's the way I am.

Closing the windows and locking the doors, I decided, would make me feel as if I were afraid of the Fremont kids, and if that were the case, I'd better just go home. I left the windows down, stepped out of the car with a notebook tucked into the back of my jeans, and climbed the dozen broken concrete steps leading to the front porch. It was a long climb. With each step I felt the need to turn and drive away. What, I thought, have I gotten myself into this time? When I left the streets of Seattle in late 1990 after years of hanging out with young gangsters and adult criminals, I felt more at home on street corners than I did in my university office, but that was years ago. The familiarity with those people and places had faded. The newness of this neighborhood told me this could be a dangerous place, and for now, I wasn't part of it, which made it all the more hazardous.

A broken concrete driveway, overgrown and unused, traversed the steep hillside on the left side of Wendy's house. At the driveway's far end was a dilapidated white garage with side-hinged doors that looked as though they were never closed. To the left of the garage and 10 feet nearer the street, a wall of trees and bushes grew. That bushy wall blocked the line of sight from the street to a picnic table on the uphill side of the garage.

Four unpainted wooden steps led up to the raised front porch of unpainted, cracked and broken two-inch boards. I stared at the front door and searched out a doorbell. That's a middle-class thing to do. The door was slightly ajar. I knocked lightly, hoping a low noise wouldn't piss off anyone inside as much as a loud noise would.

I waited to see who'd answer my knocks and noticed three holes the size of .38s in the metal front door. The holes were on an uphill bias, as if they had been made by bullets someone fired while moving downhill along the street.

A women in her thirties stuck her head around door. She pulled it open slightly more. She stared at me and said nothing. Her eyes darted from my face to the street and back again—a nervous glance, quite justified, especially when confronting a stranger who had just appeared out of the blue at her front door at noon on a Saturday.

"Jackie?" I asked politely. She nodded. Wendy knew me by sight, Jackie didn't.

"I'm Mark. We've spoken many times on the phone. Nice to meet you finally." She nodded again. A crease crossed her face, not quite a smile but at least a small sign of recognition.

For the past six months I had called Wendy every couple weeks. But Wendy never answered the phone. Always Jackie answered or a young voice who never offered a name. Each time Jackie answered, I tried to engage her in conversation. A number of times I succeeded. On those times I asked her questions about herself, Wendy, and what she thought about Wendy's involvement with the Fremont Hustlers. I asked, "Aren't you concerned about your daughter's safety? Why do you let her get involved with a gang?" Little did I know how stupid those questions were.

"I'm here to see Wendy. She knows I coming."

"Upstairs on the right. First bedroom is hers."

Inside the front door to the left were three small bodies. One lay covered with a thin blanket on a three-cushioned sagging couch with broken springs; another lay on a two-cushioned, padded couch; the third was hidden away under a blanket in the center of the floor.

Upstairs rooms were accessible by a stairway to my right. From the bottom the staircase went straight up, then midway it bent to the left. Fourteen stairs brought me to a short hallway. To the right was a bathroom with a toilet, a tub and shower, a sink. Wendy's room was next to it. The narrow, dim hallway was lined with a threadbare carpet. Across from Wendy's room was a thin wooden door, tightly closed. All the upstairs doors were off-white, because the paint was old and dirty and stained by nicotine. At the hall's end, 10 feet from the staircase, was a third bedroom, with its door half open. Old furniture, clothes, and shoes had been tossed in there and lay in a three-foot-high midden across the entire floor.

An odor lingered in the hallway. It was a mixture of cigarettes and sewage that instantly made me smile in recognition. I had smelled a similar odor in Seattle in the late 1980s, when I hung around in apartments rented by the Rollin' 60s Crips and the Black Gangster Disciples.

The stench flowed from the bathroom into the hallway. I peeked in. Linoleum had peeled up at the edge of the tub and around the toilet and along the walls. There was a handwritten sign posted over the toilet, in black and red block letters.

Don't Wipe Your Ass on the Towels.
That Means You, Motherfuckas.
The Management

I slowly opened Wendy's door, walked in, and stood over a body in the sagging bed.

"Wendy, Wendy," I said in a direct but apologetic tone.

I leaned over and tried to awaken the body wrapped in a thin wool blanket. The room was dark, although some shadowy light came through the small window. The blades of an old metal fan scraped at the stale air, creating a whizzing noise.

"Wendy, Wendy, it's Mark," I said again.

The body shifted position a bit but, to my relief, not too much or too suddenly. Truth is, I was wary of pissing off whoever was lying there. I knew guns had to be around somewhere.

I waited. The body, lying face-down, moved slightly, its right side rolling upward. A hand and a forearm emerged, pulling the blanket off the head of a young blonde with squinting eyes.

"Who the fuck are you?" she asked with surprise.

"I'm Mark, a friend of Wendy's. She told me to be here at noon. It's noon."

She stared, eyelids drooping, face sleep-creased.

"Well, she ain't here. Got a cigarette?"

"No, I don't smoke."

"Shit, I really need a fucking cigarette."

"Hey, Cheri, Cheri, wake the fuck up. Go get me a cigarette, biytch."

In the far left corner, wrapped like a cocoon in a sleeping bag and curled up in a padded rocking chair that had lost its rockers, another body stirred. I hadn't recognize the lump as a body when I walked in. A three-cushioned couch sat next to the chair. The darkness concealed the filth and the kids.

"What? What? You want a cigarette? Fuck you. Get it yourself, bitch."

This was Cheri, a 15-year-old girl with an unmistakable smile. Her upper right medial incisor was broken on a diagonal, leaving a jagged point on the right inside cutting edge.

"Bitch, get me a cigarette. *Pleeeease,*" said the blonde, purposely drawing out the word.

Cheri moved slowly but got up and walked out of the room without saying a word to me. She stared at the girl on the bed but said nothing to her either. I heard her knock on a door across the hallway.

Minutes passed. I made small talk with the body in the blanket.

"Whad'ya say your name was?" she asked.

"Mark."

"Where ya from?"

"Illinois, south of Chicago."

"What da fuck you doin' here?"

"I'm a writer."

"A what? A writer? What do you write?"

"I write about kids on the street, gangs, folks who sell drugs, shit like that."

"You here to write a book?"

"I'd like to. Wendy said she'd help me. I met her about a year ago at UMKC," I explained.

I told the body in the blanket how I had met Wendy and Janet and about the phone calls to Jackie. I was honest about everything. I learned long ago that hanging around such places requires honesty about what you say, but you don't have to say everything at once. Cardinal rule number one of street fieldwork is: Never say anything you don't want repeated to everyone. That means temporary selective concealment is often necessary. Years on Seattle's streets had taught me that kids like these know lies and liars. They are highly suspicious of strangers who just show up and ask questions about guns, drugs, and crime.

"That's cool. Can I be in your book?"

"Sure. What's your name?"

"Cara."

Cheri shoved open the door with a vengeance. It banged when the knob bounced against the wall, which had already cracked in that spot.

"Hey bitch, here's ya fuckin' cigarette." Cheri smiled exposing her upper teeth.

"Thanks, biytch." At least Cara said it sweetly, lengthening and exaggerating the vowel until it sounded like "biy-yitch." Said in the right way, at the right time, to the right person, *bitch* is a term of affection and endearment.

Cheri looked at me. "I don't smoke cigarettes. They'll kill ya. But I do like bud [marijuana, weed]." She smiled and exaggerated the *u* in *bud* till the word sounded like "buuuud." These girls took pleasure in saying the word.

Cara looked askance at Cheri. "Now why you be tellin' some dude you never met befo' that you smoke bud? You a dumb mothafuckin' biytch." Cara smiled.

"Cara-mel," Cheri asked, politely, "you got a joiynt?"

Cara shook her head side to side. A brief pause, then excitedly Cara remarked, "Bet Bill does. Go see, biytch." "Bill" refers to Steele Bill. He rents the room across the hall.

"Fuck you," said Cheri. She smiled at Cara and at me, and walked out and closed the door firmly. I heard a knock on Bill's door.

"They call you Cara-mel. Why do they call you that?" I asked.

"'Cause I'm sweet, like candy. Cara-mel candy," she exaggerated the middle syllable. She smiled at me and hollered to Cheri through the closed door. "Hey biytch, where's da bud?"

Wendy walked into her room at 1:15, out of breath from running up the stairs. She shook hands; she apologized for being late. She told Cheri and Caramel that she'd been out with Glen and didn't get to sleep till 5:00. The girls smiled.

Wendy, Cara, and Cheri listened when I said I wanted to hang out with them. "How long you be here, a week?" Wendy asked.

"Nah, I don't work that way. I'll be here a year, maybe longer," I answered.

"That's cool," Wendy responded.

"But I need your help," I said. "How about introducing me to everyone, and I'll tell them what I'm doing. Is that OK?"

"Yeah. But if yer gonna be aroun' here, you need to meet Chucky," said Cara.

"Yeah, an' Afro too," Wendy added. "Chucky, he'd be cool wid it, but 'Fro, I don't know if he'll like it. You bes' be cool wid him."

I wasn't the first outsider to hang out with the Fremont Hustlers. A television crew from Chicago's "Rolanda" show had spent 24 hours filming a day in the life of a youth gang.[3] "They followed us everywhere, and shit, they showed 15 seconds of it on TV. Bitches," Wendy said with displeasure in her voice. "We showed them all kinda shit and, look at that, they hardly showed us at all."

Within 90 minutes of walking into Wendy's house, I was collecting data. I asked Wendy to give me a complete list of Fremont members. A bold move, I thought. I was at first reluctant to ask for such a list, thinking she would be suspicious of my meddling too quickly. But what's the right time? A day, a week—what? Cardinal rule number two of street fieldwork is: If you don't ask, you don't get answers. If she said no, I'd ask her again later.

I handed Wendy a notebook and a pencil for her to list all the members of the Fremont Hustlers. She sat at a wooden table in the room while she wrote the list. Cara looked over Wendy's left shoulder; Cheri, her right. Then together the three of them discussed each of 72 kids on the list. I was excited.

Wendy and Cara and Cheri told me how the Fremont Hustlers had started one day in August 1992. While sitting on Wendy's front porch one afternoon, Fat Sal (age 15), Fremont TJ (12), Buck (14), Janet (16), Frosty (15), and Wendy (16) decided to become a "gang," Wendy told me. She picked Fremont's color, green. Green stands for cash and for marijuana, the two things "Fremont's about," Wendy said. She also created a street name for herself, "G-Love." G symbolizes green, money, and weed; *Love* stands for Wendy's love of cash and weed. Cara added with explicit force: "Yeah, and Northeast started fuckin' wid us, so Fremont got its shit together."[4]

The first kids to spray-paint Fremont Hustler graffiti were Fremont TJ, Wendy, Dante (Cheri's older sister, then 14), and Sal C (16). Wendy takes credit for "bringing" Afro, Snapper, and Chucky D to Fremont. "They were hanging with Eastside, and I brought 'em up here," she said with pride. "Now we cayn't get rid of them mothafuckas." She laughed.

Wendy claimed that Fremont Hustlers are a "Folks" gang and drew a picture to show pitchforks pointing upward, interlocking triangles, and the number six. I asked her why Fremont was Folks. "I don' know. I like to draw pitchforks," she said. No one else ever said anything about Fremont as Folks. It was Wendy's fabrication that no one else shared.[5]

Cheri joked about Fremont. "No gangsters around here, no, no, never, no," she said with excitement in her voice. Later that day, I met House of Pain and told him I would be around a long time because I was interested in studying kids in a youth gang. "There is none of them around here," he said. "We don't believe in them [gangs]. We go to church every Sunday morning, every Wednesday. It's great."

I spent the first afternoon looking around, trying to remember names and put them with faces. I wandered into and out of Wendy's, trying to make myself look as though I belonged there. I found that Wendy's 9-year-old brother, Robert, and his 14-year-old companion, Ryan, had been two of the three bodies asleep in the living room when I walked in; Robert and Ryan were crime partners. I watched the fuzzy color television with them and sat quietly.

I walked around the houses next to Wendy's and down the sidewalk, looking at the trash littered all around. Cigarette butts and packages, broken bottles, dozens of squashed QT one-liter cups, broken gray metal folding chairs, disheveled and tattered overstuffed furniture with broken joints, empty packages from roll-your-own cigarette papers. But it was the chunks of opaque glass the size of cinnamon rolls that caught my eye. What's that stuff? I thought. I looked around but didn't see a source of heavy opaque glass. Then, looking up, I spotted a shattered street light at the top of a power pole directly across the street from Wendy's. I first thought the kids must have shattered it with rocks. How naive.

I watched each car that drove up and down Fremont, asking someone near me about each one and its driver and passengers. That was easy, because there were few cars on Fremont. One thing's for sure, I thought, no one comes here unless they have to.

To my surprise an ice cream vendor, with his bell ringing, came west on 13th Street.[6] Robert ran inside, asked Jackie for money, and came out empty handed. A half dozen kids ran to the truck at the corner of Fremont and 13th.

"Gonna get some ice cream?" I asked Robert. I knew by the expression on his face that Jackie had stiffed him. "Here, Robert, take this." I handed him a dollar.

"You givin' dis ta me?" he asked in a rather puzzled way.

"Yeah."

"Why? What do I have to do for it?" he responded.

"Nothing, Robert. What you have to do is buy ice cream before the truck leaves. Go ahead." He ran over and joined the other youngsters at the truck, bought an ice cream on a stick, and for that moment he looked like a healthy nine-year-old who happened to live in a gang-operated drug house.

Cara walked over to the truck too. Her feet were bare, and she had on a short dress that fell to midthigh. It was lightweight and floated as she moved. Her light-colored hair caught the sun, creating a luminescent band. I walked behind her slowly, giving her distance.

Cara bought an ice cream on a stick, vanilla covered with chocolate, like Robert's, but Cara also bought a "special" treat, a two-dollar joint. Ice cream in her left hand, a joint in her right, a warm summer day—how delightful, I thought. Slowly driving east on 13th toward Fremont came a KCPD cruiser with three officers inside.

The ice cream salesman started his truck and drove off without ringing his bell, turned uphill onto Fremont, and disappeared. The driver didn't speed away, but neither did he make an effort to sell any more ice cream—or marijuana. I backed off too and walked downhill slowly, looking over my left shoulder, staying within earshot. I was surprised the cops didn't look at me more suspiciously, but I wasn't holding notebooks, a camera, or a tape recorder, and there were other adults on the sidewalks too. A Mexican man who lived across the street from Wendy's was watching his preschool daughter ride her tricycle. And a fellow from North Fremont was hanging out in front of Wendy's too. I guess in the cops' eyes I was another middle-aged bald guy with two days' beard growth, just another Fremont relic.

Cara saw the cops, waved her left hand at them, and as they exited the cruiser, she slowly dropped her right hand to her side, opened her fingers and let gravity pull the joint to the ground. As soon as it hit, she slowly, smoothly, nonchalantly raised the outside edge of her right foot and covered the illegal weed. She did it all without taking her eyes off the cops. She's smooth, with practiced maneuvers.

"Hi ya," she said in her sweetest voice. She is charming when charm can be useful to her. Cara has worked as a dancer in a teenage dance club; her lithe body inside her short dress seemed to catch the officers' attention more than the slight shift of her right foot.

The officers moved closer; she chatted and bubbled and bounced and kidded with them. "Looking for bud, huh?" she said and then chuckled. The officers were humorless, but they knew Cara. They weren't aggressive or interested in shaking down anyone or hassling the kids, maybe because there were too many citizens like me, the Mexican, and the fellow from North Fremont watching.

Cara bit at her ice cream, one cop lit a smoke, the others looked bored. In 10 minutes they drove away north on Fremont. Cara waved and smiled at them as they passed. When they were a block away and out of earshot, she yelled at them, "Dumb motherfuckers." Her wave turned into the finger.

By my second day on Fremont I had met Afro. Wendy introduced us on the sidewalk in front of her house. We shook hands. "Wha's up?" he said, then quickly ran off to his house, the one next door to Wendy's on the downhill side. Afro put up with me. It took more than eight months for him to become comfortable enough with me to have a conversation.

In the middle of the second afternoon, I met Chucky D. Listening to kids talk about Chucky D, I thought he must have magic power. If Fremont had a spiritual leader and a protector when I met them in 1995, it was Chucky D. He knew how to exploit others' fear and their need to have him around. Fremont kids mythologize Chucky D. The day before I met Chucky, I heard boys and girls say, "Fuck 'em. If Northeast comes by, Chucky'll get them mothafuckers."

The longer I stayed on Fremont, and later when my research extended to the Northeast Gangstas, I found Chucky D's reputation to have spread over the streets. He is the Paul Bunyon of Fremont and Northeast. He is a charismatic boy, a protector and warrior. In fact, in the early days of my Fremont research, Chucky D was a key link between drugs and drug customers. If he were to work for State Farm Insurance, he'd have a corner office on the top floor.

When the moment of reckoning came, I was sitting in Wendy's room, talking to Cheri, Angie, Wendy, and Cara, and others as they wandered into and out of the room. Wendy didn't like too many people in her room. This was private space and she carefully protected it. There's little seclusion in communal living, and girls in particular treasure privacy.

Wendy permitted a few boys to enter her room—Chucky D, Steele Bill, Glen (her boyfriend from 1995 to 1997), and a few others—if they respected her rules. She called them "my boys." Afro never entered Wendy's room. Wendy and Afro were lovers when she was 14 until she was about 17.

Girls awakened in Wendy's room or, if they'd slept someplace else the night before, they congregated there later. They'd shower or take a bath, do their hair, listen to music, talk and laugh and gossip, and share clothing. They call this getting ready. Ready for what? I wondered for quite a while before discovering that it was getting ready to hang out, party, make love, do whatever they wanted to do.

Angie had just taken a bath, her long brown hair wrapped into a towel turban. She sat cross-legged, wearing baggie sweatpants and a lightweight sweatshirt, in front of a narrow full-length mirror leaning against a wall.

Cara walked over to the closet, found the shirt Angie wanted, and handed it to her. Angie stood up and nonchalantly turned her back toward me, removed her sweatshirt, and put on the shirt. I felt embarrassed.

Angie is Fremont's narcissist and enjoyed telling me tales about her sex life and how much boys "wanted" her. Her thin body and pretty face are a boy magnet, but boys dare not get too close too fast. Angie has the temperament of a viper. Kids also call her Poodle or Poodle Bitch, because her wavy hair reminds them of poodle fur.

"Chucky's here, downstairs. Wanna meet 'im?" Cheri asked me, walking into Wendy's room and closing the door. Even with heavy in-and-out traffic, Wendy protected her space by ensuring that her door stayed closed.

"Yeah."

"You wanna go down or should he come up?"

"Ask him to come up." I didn't want to seem too anxious to meet him.

A few minutes later, the door opened. There he was: five-ten, 160 pounds, a sculpted torso resembling Michelangelo's *David*. Not a tweezer's worth of flab lay on his shirtless upper body. His jeans hung low on his narrow hips, but not ridiculously low; only a few inches of white underwear protruded above his beltline, which fell several inches below his navel.

He looked directly into my eyes and extended his hand. I stood up, looked into his eyes, and extended mine. We shook hands, looking at each other as we spoke.

"I'm Mark."

"I know. I'm Chucky."

"I've heard a lot about you," I said.

He smiled and turned his head side to side as if to point out to the girls sitting on floor doing their hair that even an outsider knows the legend of Chucky D. He got right down to business. "So wha's up?" he asked in a matter-of-fact way. Chucky D has an enveloping glow that broadcasts security.

I explained my purpose on Fremont.

He listened, nodded, smiled. "That's cool. Yeah, I help ya."

"How about an interview?"

"What'ya wanna know?" he asked calmly.

"I wanna know about you."

"You wanna know about drugs?"

That surprised me. "Sure, if you wanna tell me."

"That's cool. I'll tell whatever ya wanna know."

"When?" I asked.

"I busy now. Tomorrow this time."

"I'll be here."

Chucky D just blew off the interview, I thought. I figured I'd never get this kid to tell me about his drug business on tape. I was wrong.

The next day Chucky D drove up with his latest girlfriend, Tamara. He stayed with her at her place in Independence, a 20-minute ride to the east. Chucky D and I talked at the picnic table behind the bushes next to Jackie's house. Chucky D and Wendy sat directly across from me and faced the street, with Tamara and Johnny, humming on a harmonica, next to them. Chubby-cheeked Robert, his straight hair hanging down over his forehead to just above his eyebrows, sat in the dirt near the table. Robert was always included in activities inside and outside the house. Cheri, Roger, and Gordy sat with me on the other side of the table.

Chucky was shirtless, of course, his white tee-shirt draped over his left shoulder. It was a hot, humid day and perspiration put a sheen on his skin, further outlining his upper-body muscles. Years of pumping iron in prison had done wonders for his body. A gold earring highlighted his left earlobe. His brilliant smile showed teeth as bright as polished white piano keys.

I sat with my tape recorder in my left hand, my notebook open on the table. Chucky D nonchalantly told his tale. No one interrupted, no one asked questions except me. In part, this is what he told me that day:

Chucky D joined the LCBs (Latin Count Brothers), at 17th and Lister, near Cathy's Van Brunt apartment, when he was 12 years old. Chucky said the LCBs were "bad apples." His eldest brother, Tommy, was a 24th Street Crip, a gang which is now known as the Grape Street Crips. Chucky claimed that one of his cousins brought the LCBs to KC from Chicago, but he didn't know when.

When Chucky joined the LCBs as an early teenager, they were run by older boys in their middle to late teens. In those days, Chucky D said, the LCBs required an "ass kicking" for initiation into their gang. "Why?" I asked him. "'Cause it was fun to beat some mothafucker. And if dey squealed like a bitch, I beat 'em some mo'." If they fucked up and violated one of LCBs unwritten rules, he'd "beat 'em and beat they ass agin."

LCBs committed burglary and robbery and dealt drugs. These crimes resulted in the arrest and imprisonment of the LCB leaders. By 1990 with these leaders imprisoned, Chucky said, the LCBs were nearly finished as a gang, that is, until he slid into the leadership role, rejuvenated the gang, and then started the LCSs, Latin Count Sisters.

Chucky D altered initiation rules and dropped the violence. He said that "anybody who had heart and was thorough" was eligible for membership in the LCBs and LCSs. "By the end of the first day, I had maybe a dozen guys. By the end of the week, there was about 50."

In several months, the LCBs were solidly under the leadership of 14-year-old Chucky D and were in the rock cocaine business, with cash garnered from robberies and burglaries. LCBs were breaking into homes to steal guns, which they sold and used on the street. They also "jacked fags" in a KC park where homosexual men gathered at night for liaisons. LCBs assaulted these men with fists and baseball bats, stole their wallets and car keys, and, in the victims' vehicles, drove to their addresses and burglarized their houses. Chucky D said they took in up to $500 a night. But his real pleasure was fighting and "shooting people."

Beginning at age 14, he was repeatedly arrested and imprisoned. First he was arrested for two auto thefts, carrying a concealed weapon, and second-degree robbery ("jackin' fags"). For these offenses, he did six months in juvenile detention. There were many other arrests and short stints in treatment centers, the same places where Fremont's as well as Northeast's members were sent for treatment. He escaped from the nonsecurity institutions, and during one such escape he was arrested for carrying a concealed weapon and for grand theft auto. At age 15 he was certified as an adult to stand trial in adult court. He celebrated his 16th birthday at Jackson County Detention Center, known to street folks as Cherry because of its location at 1300 Cherry Street, in downtown KC. At 16 he transferred to adult court and then served 28 months of a 60-month sentence in a number of Missouri state adult prisons.

Cara said Chucky D had been the principal suspect in 7 murders, 12 assaults and robberies, and too many carjackings to remember. And recall, Chucky D hasn't even been on the street very often since he was 15.

In a week, when I was sure most Fremont kids had seen me, I walked up to Wendy's freely at any time and perched on the front porch. I always had a notebook and tape recorder. I hid nothing. Hiding would likely lead to trouble I couldn't fix. If the kids were to refuse to speak to me and include me in activities, I would be a figuratively dead ethnographer. And there was an element of real danger, as well. I'd rather have a kid ask me why I am taking notes, ask to see the notes, ask how I use the notes and why I have a tape recorder running, than have Afro, Chucky D, and House of Pain believe that I'm sneaking around trying to get information they didn't want me to have. That's dangerous, and then I might end up a literally dead ethnographer.

Sitting around had other benefits too. Kids saw me day in and day out. That's cardinal rule number three of street fieldwork: Be there all the time. These kids don't trust adults. When I told them I'd be on Fremont a long time, they didn't believe me. So being there all the time paid off. I had an opportunity to see different incidents and hear kids talk and react to a number of highly stressful situations over a long period of time.

As the weeks passed, they came to think of me as "oh, that's just Mark" or as "the guy writin' a story about us" or "the guy who hangs out with Cara and Wendy." That was fine with me. No one questioned why I was there, and on some occasions kids even looked pleased to see me, especially when I had Newports and Salems.

Whenever I drove to Fremont, I bought cigarettes at the "cheap cigarette store" on the way—a truck stop west of St. Louis. Cigarettes do on the street what they do in prisons: create a sense of reciprocity and sharing. I don't smoke cigarettes, so the kids knew I bought Newports and Salems for them. Folks who smoke marijuana enjoy menthol cigarettes because these feel cooling on irritated mucous linings.

On weekdays and weekends, different things go on at different times. It's not that there's a daily agenda, but activities fall into a pattern. There are parties on Friday and Saturday nights, something even a "hotel party," paid for with drug money. A hotel party happens when a kid rents a room or two at a local hotel which has a pool and recreation facilities, like the Holiday Inn Holidome. Fremont kids and others too gather to swim, use drugs, and, if drug sales have been good, order lots of food from room service. It was after such a hotel party in July 1994 that a boy called T-Man was murdered on Fremont. You'll come to see how the effect of that murder lingered for years.

Fremont social life generally happens at "chill spots." These are houses on Fremont where kids spend time sitting around and, in some of those places, sell drugs. During the early stages of my research, there were four chill spots—two had "Fremont moms" ("They're the ones that are always there if we need something," Cara explained), two didn't.

There was no mom at Afro's. Afro's house, an abandoned shanty, was a chill spot he occupied with Rosa, his 15-year-old girlfriend. Afro had jerryrigged city utilities and got away without paying for the service. On the right-hand side of the shanty's back wall, someone had sprayed FH graffiti and the names "Christina" and "Lucky" in black. An old cloth couch was the only furniture in the living room. Another couch filled a tiny room that would have been the dining room if there had been a table in it. The couches were the kind you see on the curb after college students leave campus in the spring. There were also a few old, rusty, metal kitchen chairs. On the outer wall of the dining room was a stereo with four-foot-high speakers. Afro and Rosa slept on a mattress in the basement, well away from the windows and thin walls, easily penetrated by bullets.

Kids congregated at Afro's to party, and on occasion a kid dropped in to stay a few days. Shawn was tossed out of his parents' house on his 17th birthday and never returned. He took a stash of clothes to Afro's and slept there until he made other plans. On party nights music blasted through the speakers, and kids sat around on the musty couches and rusty metal chairs, stood against the walls, wandered in and out of the kitchen past its unpainted, paper-thin wooden door.

When music played, Cara danced in the middle of the group and reached for a wallflower to dance with her. I saw other girls, too, try to pull boys off their butts to dance in the fog of marijuana smoke filling the dark rooms. Joints were passed, a blunt got rolled, kids got high. These parties lasted till someone got bored and left, convincing others to go too. Leaving the neighborhood was hard, though. None of the kids had cars, except Chucky D, and he never hung out at Afro's house.

Across the street from Wendy's on the northeast corner of Fremont and 13th was the second chill spot without an acting Fremont mom. House of Pain, his brother Cain, their teenage sister, and parents reside there. "[Their parents] don't like us hanging out in front, because Northeast or La Familia come by and shoot up the house. When we go there, we stay inside," Cara says.

Chill spots have been targets in drive-by shootings. "Northeast would just roll by and shoot up one of the chill spots, so we always had people protecting each house, 'cause we knew which one they was goin' to hit up," Cara told me. Wendy's house had been the target in three drive-by shootings, thus, the bullet holes in the metal front door.

House of Pain said his mother didn't allow more than a few youngsters to stand on the front porch or on the lawn. "She doesn't want anyone to think we hang out there, 'cause they'd shoot up the place." There was one drive-by shooting between June 1995 and February 1997.

One block uphill from Wendy's, on Fremont's west side was Taffy's. "Taffy, she's a mom. She's got [three] kids and everything and is like the mom of the family," said Cara. Taffy's husband is a plumber and goes to work every day. Cara says he knew little of Taffy's deep involvement with the Fremont kids. "Taffy's close to Dwayne, TJ, Chucky D, and Clint. She's one all the boys write and call from prison. If any of us go to jail, we always call Taffy's house." Cara laughed. Taffy's phone bill sometimes reached over $300 a month. Chucky D called at least four times a day, seven days a week; others called too, always collect. Cara said Taffy hid the cost from her husband.

Taffy cared for Fremont kids who had run away from or were thrown out of their parents' homes. Fourteen-year-old Fremont TJ, also known as Cyco, shot Tyler, the son of KCPD officer, in Taffy's living room in

1994. It was a horrible scene, Taffy said; she didn't want to discuss it, except to say she had given Tyler mouth-to-mouth resuscitation. TJ was held on a $500,000 bond. It was an accidental shooting to the head, Taffy said, boys playing with a loaded .45 handgun. TJ stood trial for murder and was acquitted; then he stood trial on a double homicide and was acquitted. No one ever paid his bail, so after more than three years on Cherry, TJ was finally released from jail in late spring 1997.

Wendy's house was the biggest, most popular chill spot with a Fremont mom, Jackie. Wendy and Jackie operated a thriving drug business from their house. Afro called it the "dope house," and Wendy's room, the "dope room." Even so, "Jackie lets everyone chill there, 'cause kids got nowhere else to go," Cara told me. A lot of Fremont Hustlers hanging around were also good protection.

Jackie didn't let kids traipse around and make noise inside the house. Her rock smoking made her jittery and paranoid. Some kids would come inside to watch TV, but few had access to the upstairs rooms, where there were drugs, guns, and cash.

Wendy's house could be entered through the garage. A door led into the kitchen and a back room. Jackie used the back room as a bedroom, and she kept her drugs there. The hissing sound of air being pulled through a tubular rock cocaine pipe came from Jackie's room, day and night.

The garage entrance was guarded by Bobo, a black hybrid dog who looks and sounds vicious. But he isn't really, if he knows you and you don't threaten him. Bobo and the Fremont Hustlers are alike in that way.

Bobo watched the street and guarded the kitchen entrance when Jackie was open for business. Jackie sold rocks out of the back of the house. A customer who didn't know Bobo or who knew Bobo wouldn't recognize him or her wasn't likely to walk into the garage. Bobo was also supposed to keep undercover drug and gang detectives out of the garage. Kids said Bobo smells cops. When Jackie was sleeping or out of the house, Bobo wasn't out there watching. It was simple, once you knew the routine.

Kids tell stories about Bobo, and one of them is that Bobo won't hurt you. Sure. None of them went over and played with Bobo though, except young Robert.

There are a lot of "how I shot Bobo" stories. Kids said that someone would just get pissed off with Bobo's barking or Bobo scared one of them, and then it happened. Out came a .22 and Bobo got blasted. Bobo never dies. "He's got nine fucking lives, or even more," Robert said.

When Bobo got shot, the story goes, he would wander off and lie down for a few days, lick his wounds, and then head right back to his spot in the front of the garage. Fremont kids are like Bobo in this way, I thought: They get tired or hurt and wander off for a while, sometimes a day or two, maybe even a week or two, rest and take it easy and get out of "the shit." Then they're ready for more.

A Friday night at 11:00, I pulled up in front of Wendy's, left my windows down, and got out of the car. I walked up the concrete steps, past a dozen or so boys and girls sitting in the dark on Wendy's front steps and porch, and into the house to find Robert lounging on the two-cushioned couch. His eyes pulled away from the fuzzy images on the television long enough for him to ask, "Got 50 I can borrow?"

"Are you kidding? What'ya want $50 for?" I responded, already knowing the answer.

"I need a smoke, real bad. Ya got a dime?"

Smoke refers to weed; *dime* means $10. Even though sister Wendy and mother Jackie were in the drug business, Robert had to pay his own way. Robert was a habitual marijuana smoker. In fact, he smoked so much weed that Fremont kids teased him about it. "That li'l mothafucka won't have no brain if he keep smokin' that much," said Chucky D. "Shit," Cara said, "he smokes more than we do."

"What for?" I asked Robert again about his request for money.

He shook his head in disgust. We played this game when he asked me for weed money. "A dime bag," he replied. "Even *I* need a joint."

"Nah," I said. "Here, have a cigarette." I handed him a Salem.

Before you get too upset about my giving Robert a cigarette, you should know that Jackie had already bought him a "one-hitter," a marijuana pipe used to smoke "roaches" (the tiny ends of smoked joints), for his ninth birthday. Everything's relative on the street. Robert proudly told me it had cost her $10, but he lost it in the parking lot of Price Chopper on The Ave. He said he and his mom had gotten a ride to the grocery store, and she told him to leave it outside. He did, and someone took it. He was very upset, so we went back there together and looked for it, but we couldn't find it.

Later that same Friday evening, about 11:30, Chucky D, Steele Bill, and several other younger boys and a few girls were shooting craps in the garage. Kids who sell drugs earn lots of cash. A favorite pastime is gambling. Craps is the game of choice. Bobo was there too. Steele Bill spread a black bath towel on the concrete floor to catch the dice. Chucky D kept a wad of tens and twenties in his hand; Steele Bill tucked away his folded roll of twenties in his right rear pocket. Twenties were won and lost as if these bills were Monopoly money. A hundred dollars lost tonight, 200 tomorrow night; no one cares when rocks and bud sell well.

Chucky D was down $60 and was rolling dice when the kitchen door popped open. Robert walked out holding a $10 bill.

"My mom said to get a dime bag, Chucky. Got one? A nice fat one?" A smile creased his round face.

"Lateh, boy, lateh. Cayn'cha see I'm in da middle of somefin'." He threw down two twenties and rolled the dice.

Robert looked disgusted but said nothing. No one argued with Chucky D. Cara said quietly more than once that "Chucky's evil." But she smiled when she said it.

A moment later the back door flew open again. It was Jackie. "Chucky, I need to see ya before you go," she said sternly.

"Yeah, yeah, OK," he replied impatiently. Chucky D never missed a sale.

Fremont territory doesn't frighten away outsiders. Kids who know kids on Fremont, and kids who know kids who know kids on Fremont, hung out at Wendy's too, most often on weekend evenings and Sunday afternoons.

Sitting on Wendy's porch one Sunday afternoon in July 1995 was a young man I hadn't seen before, nor did I see him again after that day. He caught my attention because he was older than the other kids. He had a distant stare and eyes as expressionless as pieces of coal. I sat next to him on his right side. "Hi, my name's Mark. I haven't see you before." He didn't ask me who I was or what I was doing, but I told him anyway.

He said his name is Robert and that he was 22. He reached into his back pocket and withdrew his wallet to prove it. He showed me his Missouri driver's license, an identification card from a local psychiatric hospital, the business card of his psychiatrist, and a prescription for a drug administered to calm violent behavior. This young man sat quietly and still, as if encased in glue.

Robert was a companion of Chucky D's. That gave him access to Fremont. His short-sleeved shirt exposed tattoos of a long-bladed knife wrapped by a dragon. The ink covered his left forearm and upper arm above the elbow. He had no tattoos on his right arm. We talked for nearly an hour. Robert had no qualms about telling me his story.

He said Chucky D and he had met years earlier and were members of the LCBs. Chucky D's path led from the LCBs to prison; Robert's, from the LCBs to a satanic cult. There were some 26 members in the cult, kids ranging in age from 14 to 16 who slept in abandoned houses around KC's magnificent Nelson Museum and Gallery and in drainage tunnels on KC's Brush Creek (this waterway crosses midtown KC from east to west and is the southern boundary of KC's well-known upper-end shopping and restaurant area known as the Plaza).

Robert's cult, Sons of the Vampire, killed dogs, cats, and cows and drank their blood. The cow was especially significant to them because it symbolized "power," and cult members believed that ingesting the blood would infuse the cow's DNA into their own.

Robert had been arrested many times, which led him into psychiatric care. His inner world was filled with demons and violent attacks against himself. He had fantasies of kidnapping and torturing humans till they screamed and writhed endlessly in agony. In each fantasy he stopped short of killing his victims and ending the pain. To himself the punishment was equally horrible. He had visions, a kind of virtual reality, during which he imagined himself running fishhooks into his flesh and slowly and painfully tearing off his body's skin. (He had scars on his forearms reminiscent of scars I've seen on prisoners who used knives to score their skin. I didn't ask how he got those scars.)

I always ask kids about their parents. Robert responded reticently and briefly, offering only these words: "My parents were Jehovah's Witnesses." He paused and drifted off to a place inside himself, finally adding, "I'd rather die than go home."

Fremont Hustlers' territory is a sanctuary. This disheveled neighborhood has as much hope of economic development as Bobo has of learning to speak English. Nevertheless, Fremont kids and kids who, like Robert, have nowhere to go can sleep on a couch or in a corner and find a moment's peace on Fremont, and they may be able to make some money.

On Fremont kids come and go as they please without judgment and criticism. No one on Fremont cares about grade-point averages. No one cares what brand of clothes and sneakers they wear. No one cares if or how many times a kid has been to juvenile detention. No one cares if he or she has been hospitalized for emotional disorders, as Cara and Wendy have been, or if he or she has punched his or her mother in the face, as Angie has. No one cares if a kid uses words like *motherfucka* outloud in public. But these kids also live without the guidance necessary to find a path into mainstream life.

The measures of status and prestige used by kids in Overland Park are absent on Fremont. What matters to Fremont kids is that outsiders don't threaten or hurt them and that they, the kids, take only what's coming to them. On Fremont, material goods (drugs) and access to them, through kids like Chucky D and Wendy, are survival sources. If the balance between material goods and social ties is disturbed, there's likely to be highly aggressive outbursts and sometimes violence.

The Fremont neighborhood is a relatively safe spot; however, there is a bitter irony in the Fremont scene. Life inside the Fremont Hustlers rests on a paradox: the gang affords kids short-term social and economic survival, but gang life over the long term is a social and economic dead end.

3
Inside

"Membership" in the Fremont Hustlers is a peculiar idea.[1] Wendy, Cara, and Cheri listed 72 males and females on the Fremont Hustler membership roster; however, Fremont kids don't refer to one another as members, nor do they think of themselves as having "joined a gang."[2]

"Member," "membership," "join," and "gang" are static notions which fit neither the natural flow of Fremont social life nor the perceptions of Fremont kids. Even the question, Are you a member of the Fremont Hustlers? doesn't match these kids' sense of social logic. The question, Do you hang out on Fremont? makes sense to them, but this question didn't bring me closer to understanding the kids' meanings for "joining a gang" and "gang membership." Fremont kids' perceptions of these issues are more complex than I had imagined.[3]

The social boundary between the Fremont Hustlers—the youth gang—and outsiders is open.[4] Fremont has no formal set of written rules (a charter) specifying what prospective members must do to be admitted and to sustain membership. There are no rules of decorum and, thus, no sanctions for violating those rules. Younger Fremont kids are not required to learn and recite a gang pledge of allegiance or attend lectures given by older members about "proper" behavior. There is no rule preventing drug sellers from being drug users. There is no rule requiring a portion of drug sale profits to be returned to a communal gang bank account or paid as tribute to the leader. There is no leader, no boss, no hierarchy that pulls all 72 kids into coherent organization.[5]

Fremont has no initiation. No one is "beaten in" or "courted in" or ordered to commit violent acts. That behavior, kids said, attracts the cops, and cops are bad for business. Cara said violent initiation is "fucked up and stupid. Who wants ta hang out with niggahs who beat ya ass?" By hanging out and establishing ties with Fremont kids, an outsider is slowly assimilated into the social life at a chill spot.

To these kids, Fremont is defined by the interaction of social histories of families; current and former love relationships; boy-boy, girl-girl, and boy-girl hostilities; envy and bitterness over possessions; current and past crime partnerships; arrests and imprisonment in jails, detention centers, and juvenile treatment facilities; histories of prior gang affiliations; and length of interpersonal affiliation. Kids who have known each other a long time, such as Cara and Wendy, stick together, although there were times when they'd vow never to speak to each other again, but that's typical among adolescents.

Kids' vocabulary helps to describe how they perceive Fremont's social arrangements. Generally speaking, Fremont kids differentiate themselves into one category defined by "time" and another by "tightness." *Tightness* refers to the intensity of a relationship. Kids who hang out together much of the time are said to be tight, and kids who are tight "do shit" (commit crimes, use drugs) together.

Tight also implies to some degree a shared social history. Most Fremont kids were members of other Kansas City youth gangs before joining the Fremont Hustlers and were together in juvenile detention and treatment facilities; however, being tight doesn't necessarily imply a long-term relationship. Kids can be tight for two weeks or four months and then become bitter enemies. Such volatility is most common among girls.[6] In July 1994, when Wendy and Janet and I met at UMKC, they had been tight for years and said they were inseparable and swore a mutual allegiance forever. Over the next year, Janet and Wendy vied for Steele Bill's attention. Janet won Bill, lost Wendy, and they haven't spoken to each other since then.

Time refers to the hours, days, weeks, and years a kid spends on Fremont. Time spent hanging out on Fremont differentiates kids into four groups. Kids who hang on Fremont most often have established closer ties than kids who don't. Those who don't hang around much are marginal to the gang's principal economic behavior, drug selling.

Kids use expressions for different time categories; I've noted in parentheses the number of days of hang-out time in each category: "here all the time" (six or seven days a week), "here a lot" (three to five days a week), "comes around" (one or two days a week), and "will be here if we need him (or her)" (several days a month). The last group includes kids who didn't appear even once on Fremont between June 1995 and February 1997, but hung out there at some time in the past. These kids are still considered to be Fremont. Fremont Hustlers who have been killed continue as members. The children of Fremont girls are Fremont, too.

A kid who is "here all the time" also is said to be in the "everyday" group. It's common in natural speech for kids to refer to the everyday group as kids "who's in the shit everyday," said Cara. The everyday and here-a-lot groups correspond to the terms *core* and *regular* members, respectively.

There is a segmentary quality to these social groups. Few kids hang out all the time, but dozens of kids are available to the Fremont Hustlers should help be needed. Wendy captured this segmentary quality: "If somebody fucks wid us," she said sternly, "we can get all the help we need."

A subtle difference exists between what it means to "hang out on Fremont" and what it means to be "down with Fremont." To be "down with Fremont" is the expression closest to our use of the term *member*. But being down with Fremont doesn't mean a kid hangs out on Fremont every day.

A number of Fremont kids have been down with other KC gangs. Cara was down with the Southside 39th Street Crips, as well as the 31st Street Eastside Crips, before hooking up with Wendy. Steele Bill has been a 24th Street Crip.

There is a finer distinction as well. I've heard kids ask another kid, "Is he (or she) Fremont or Fremont Fremont?" This is an interesting distinction. Kids, including Cheri, Wendy, Angie, and Roger, who were reared in the Fremont neighborhood and whose family history now links them to the neighborhood are denoted with the label "Fremont Fremont." Afro, by contrast, is a down with Fremont member but is not Fremont Fremont; recall that Wendy said she had "brought him" to Fremont from the east side. Thus, a kid can be Fremont Fremont or Fremont, and either down with or hang out with Fremont. Generally speaking, boys and girls in the everyday and here-a-lot groups are Fremont Fremont and down with Fremont.

Cara, Wendy, Cheri, and I explored how they perceive Fremont social grouping.[7] This was a productive way to learn about social relations from a single-informant, or egocentric, perspective. Simple "social role" labels for gang members as defined by gang researchers, such as "core," "peripheral," "associate," "wannabe," are outsiders' categorizations and simplistic when compared with gang members' perceptions of their own social world.[8] Rather than imposing my labels on each girl's subgrouping, I asked them to give me labels.

Wendy's and Cheri's social groupings are mostly egocentric; that is, each subgrouping is defined with them at the center. The strength of the social ties is denoted with labels such as "my babies," "my real mothafuckas," "kind of cool with, but ain't seen for awhile," "my niggahs," "I'm cool with, but don't fuck with anymore," "people I don't care about," "still all right in my life," "boys I used to talk to" (former lovers), "true bitches" (or "people I hate"). Some labels denote Fremont kids' prior gang affiliation, such as Bloods, Southside (51st Street), Latin Count Brothers, and La Familia. Other labels referred to time spent on Fremont: "hardly come over," "never come over," and "used to come over." Interestingly, Fremont kids who were killed or committed suicide, as well as boys in prison, are still considered to be Fremont members. Imprisoned kids are either labeled "in prison" or are placed in some other group, such as "my mothafuckas." Tyler, the 14-year-old boy killed by Fremont TJ, is always placed in a group with kids who are alive.

Cara's view is much less egocentric than Wendy's and Cheri's, and it has a "fly-on-the-wall" quality. She divides the Fremont Hustlers into these groups: Bloods (friends of Chucky D's from the east side and former Latin Count Brothers); used to visit a lot (girls from the Seven-Miles rap group); grew up on Fremont; in prison; La Familia (members of the gang La Familia, but hang with Fremont anyway); hang together; hang out (these kids are tighter than those in hang together); hardly come around; and Southside.[9] Cara's subgroups, with kids' names and pertinent facts, are listed below.[10]

Bloods: J-Love, JC, and Joe Green.
Used to visit a lot: Kiki, Erica, Felisha, JoJo, Kizzy (all members of the Seven-Miles rap-group; Felisha and Kizzy are sisters). These girls hung out on Fremont in the early days of the Fremont Hustlers. I never met any one of them, although Wendy talked about them, and in the spring of 1997 she started to hang out with several of them, because she was interested in recording rap songs.
Grew up on Fremont: Anthony Contreras, Curly Contreras (these two are brothers; they have three more brothers—Sam, Eddie, and Sal—whom Cara puts in the "hardly come around" group).
In prison: Buck, Dwayne, Snapper, Fremont TJ, Little Man, Rick. Cara put Tyler (RIP) in this category and said it includes kids "who's never coming back." Rick was a crime partner with Anthony and Curly Contreras.
La Familia (also known as KCBs, Kansas City Barrios): Tre, Jacob, JD, John, Chill, Maria, Speedy, Duce. Chill, Maria, and Speedy are cousins. Speedy's sister used to be a member of La Familia.
Hang together (A): Chucky D, Tervis (also called Earl), Steele Bill, Cara, Cheri, Wendy, Joanne, Sequoia. Sequoia is the two-year-old daughter of Joanne and Charles B, Cheri's brother (he was in prison in March 1996 and released in the summer of 1997 but returned a month later on a parole violation). Joanne has another daughter, Charlene, whose father is Chucky D.

Hang together (B): Johnny Murillo, Steve Holly, Joe Murillo, House of Pain, Cain, Greenbean, Lucky, Wayne, Taz, Zipper. Taz and Zipper were brothers. Taz was 16 when he was killed by Afro in what the police called an accidental shooting. Zipper was 15, a member of La Familia, when a Northeast member shot him in the chest, leaving a scar that looks like a zipper. Zipper is tight with Fremont, despite his affiliation with La Familia. Cheri was once pregnant by a brother of Zipper and Taz; the baby was lost in a spontaneous abortion. One of Taz's brothers told me that Afro intentionally killed Taz, and was released by the police because he is a snitch. Johnny Murillo, Steve Holly, and Joe Murillo are cousins. House of Pain and Cain are brothers.

Hang out (tight): Angie, Chica Bitch, Netta, Donna, Roger, Christina, Melissa, Rosa, Afro. Netta and Donna are sisters (they have a third sister, Teresa). Melissa and Rosa are cousins. Melissa and Lucky are siblings; Christina is their stepsister. Melissa and Lucky's father married Christina's mother. Lucky and Christina had a child born in the spring of 1996. Rosa and Joe Murillo are cousins. Rosa and Afro were lovers and had a baby girl in the fall of 1996. When Rosa was 13 she was shot in the chest by a Northeast member wielding a .38. Afro is a cousin of Cheri and her siblings, Dante and Charles B. Roger and Angie are siblings.

Hardly come around: Dallas, Frosty, Milk, Joey, the Contreras brothers (Sam, Eddie, Sal). Joey is Frosty's little brother. Milk has the dubious distinction of being the only Fremont Hustler to be initiated with a beating.[11] Cara said, "The boys whipped his ass 'cause he's stupid." The Contreras brothers are Fremont's carjackers.

Southside: Bill Bill, Little E, Tony, Scandalous Herb. Bill Bill, Little E, and Tony are brothers; Tony and Bill Bill are twins.

These are perceptions of social groupings and aren't day-to-day operational subgroups within the Fremont Hustlers. Understanding daily social, emotional, and economic dynamics is a complex issue.[12] Recording and analyzing Fremont kids' speech can offer insights.

Two-person relationships and intra- and interclique relations are marked by emotions and behavior, including passivity, standoffishness, friendliness, dependency, anger, aggressiveness, violence, vindictiveness, fearfulness, and withdrawal. These emotions and behavior are captured in the complexity of kids' speech as it's played out in daily social life.

Fremont social life is rich in jokes and laughter, as well as anger, aggression, unresolved disputes, and inter- and intragang incidents of mild to serious violence. Hardly an hour passes without some kid claiming to be pissed off about something or at someone. When one kid gets angry he usually has a lot of companions willing to talk about violence, and some of them are willing to engage in it. Talk about violence is far more common than violent acts.

A number of vocabulary terms connote the quality or affective nature of social ties and, by extension, the likelihood of violence between kids. Three such terms are *niggah, dog,* and *mothafucka.* In nearly all instances *niggah* is used without regard to the color of the speaker or the addressee. Sometimes *niggah* is used as a synonym for *homey,* though the terms *home, homeboy, homegirl,* and *homey* are rarely used in natural conversations.

Rather than denoting racial affiliation, *niggah* is used symbolically for more complex issues. A black, white, or Mexican Fremont boy or girl can call a black, white, or Mexican boy or girl a niggah, as long as the speaker and addressee are "cool," said Wendy.

"Niggah, you ain't shit !" is a common aggressive statement, but it isn't a racial insult to the addressee, who may or may not be black. A common use of *niggah* comes in statements such as, "That niggah over there, he got some."

In natural conversations the term *niggah* is distinguished from *nigger.* *Nigger* is always an insult, but it's a raceless insult used in an already heated conversation. *Nigger* has triggered fights even between black Fremont kids.

The term *dog* has the synonyms *ace deuce* and *number one.* To say "Wha's up, dog?" is a friendly greeting; however, "You're a dog" can, in an already tense situation, trigger a fight.

The term *mothafucka* is used commonly in natural conversations and has a range of connotations as wide as the word *fuck* in colloquial English. In friendly expressions, it is used this way: "You my mothafucka." However, the term *mothafucker*—that is, the form with the *-er* ending, like *nigger* as opposed to *niggah*—can be an insult and can be directed toward someone during an already tense verbal interaction.

Fremont girls and boys form cliques; however, girls' cliques, more so than boys', act as social units. Wendy and other girls too use the girl's term *my mothafuckas* to denote cliques; boys don't use such terms to label cliques. The term *together* is a synonym for *my mothafuckas.* Cara, Wendy, and Cheri are together, at least most of the time. This means if someone angers Wendy, Cara and Cheri will act with Wendy to support her and oppose her enemy. This works best if the girl who seeks support also controls resources the other girls need. Wendy, for example, had absolute control over her room on Fremont, and Cheri and Cara needed it as a safe spot. Whenever Wendy got pissed off at someone, as she did at Janet for stealing Steele Bill, Cheri and Cara supported Wendy against Janet; however, as you'll see, when Wendy's resource disappeared so did her support from Cheri and Cara, and from everyone else on Fremont.

"Sticks and stones can break your bones but words will never hurt you" doesn't apply to Fremont social life. Social life rests on words and how they are uttered and on stylized forms of verbal interaction. Friendly words, angry words, misspoken words, misinterpreted words, filthy words, clean words, all sorts of words are elements in complex social and verbal scenes called verbal duels.

Verbal duels are organized by rules that allow "players" to insult one another, within limits. Verbal duels (structured verbal forms of teasing) publicly verify informal social hierarchies and release tension without violence.

A Fremont insider (a so-called member) may verbally challenge and insult an outsider, as Wendy did the teenage girl walking across Truman by the Quick Trip, but that girl remained silent and didn't exchange insults with Wendy. To do that would have instigated a verbal duel with Wendy's partners in my car, and that might have escalated into a brawl. Fremont Hustlers' membership means that only insiders verbally duel (insult, challenge) one another with impunity. Stylized verbal dueling is a privilege of membership.

Cara and Wendy tease Cheri. Cheri teases boys, and because of her reputation as an impulsive and violent girl, boys take it and leave her alone. Girls tease Angie about her hair and aggressiveness; she accepts such teasing as a sign of companionship, rarely ever retaliating with words motivated by angry emotions. In this way, friendships are denoted with teasing.

Fremont kids don't often say things to one another that outsiders would interpret as friendly and affectionate things to say. *Mothafucka, bitch, stank pussy, niggah, dog,* and other terms are signs of companionship if they are spoken correctly between kids whose relationship has already been established and allows for such talk.

Boy-girl, girl-girl, and boy-boy relationships are built on verbal duels. Boys duel by calling each other bitch; girls call each other bitch; boys call girls stank pussy; girls call each other stank pussy; girls accuse each other of sleeping around; and both toss allegations of disloyalty at partners in previous relationships. A girl who wants a boy's attention, or one who is sleeping with a boy, smiles and tolerates his teasing, insults, and accusations.[13]

Boys don't engage in verbal duels as often or as intensely as girls. Boys tease each other momentarily, calling each other bitch or pussy, but verbal dueling, even among boys in the same clique, isn't as elaborate and stylized as it is among girls.

Verbal dueling partnerships exist in pairs, triads, and cliques (four or more) of girls. Wendy, Cara, Cheri, and Angie challenge and insult one another, and emergent among them is an informal pattern of verbal-dueling partners. Wendy challenges Cara more often than she does Cheri and Angie. Wendy and Cara tease and challenge Cheri more often than they do Angie. Angie and Wendy tease Cheri more often than they do Cara. Cheri is known for bursts of anger and violent behavior (see chapter 4, "Families"), and girls, as well as boys, tend not to push her.

Verbal duels are stereotyped. When a duel is happening between boys, it's never imbued with the same ferocity as a boy-girl or a girl-girl verbal duel. Nearly always, a boy-boy duel is a brief challenge of a boy's ability or willingness to fight: "You ain't shit," asserts one boy. "Fuck you, niggah. I'll kick your mothafuckin' ass" is a common retort. The "loser" (the second speaker) defers and walks away. The duel ends. A less aggressive boy wouldn't say "You ain't shit" to a more aggressive boy, who might then punch him. No one ever verbally challenges Chucky D and Afro.

Girl-boy duels happen regularly. Some girls don't duel with boys or other girls and aren't chided or judged to be cowardly for not doing it. Most girls are thrilled to insult boys with terms for male and female genitalia, for excrement, and for challenging a boy's sexual prowess and fighting ability.

Verbal duels are street theater. Verbal duels always occur in public settings, in earshot of others. Public duels allow girls to display bravery against boys, adjust social network alliances among themselves, and shift their romantic pairings. During a particularly loud and boisterous performance, kids circle the performers, shouting support for stylistic insults, and laughter reigns. Verbal duels sow the seeds of "domestic" and "dating" violence when such duels run amok. The rules of the verbal duel help to control kids' tendencies to carry aggressive talk too far. When a kid bends verbal dueling rules too far and breaks the unwritten code of conduct, an expected outcome is violence. Controlling their speech helps these kids control their emotions. Once speech rules have been violated, anger pours out of these kids like water gushing from a drainage pipe after a thunderstorm.

Girls always instigate duels with boys. Girl-boy duels are more theatrical than girl-girl duels. Obscenities punctuate the discourse between dueling partners. Boys call girls by the standard list of insulting terms, including *bitch, rotten bitch, stank bitch, pussy, cunt,* and *slut,* among others. Girls retaliate with a vengeance, shouting, "bastard," "prick," "pussy," "bitch," "little dick," and "cocksucker," among others. Girls call one another by the standard list of insults.

Boys and girls toy with the pronunciation of the terms *bitch* and *bastard*. As we've seen, they exaggerate *bitch* until it sounds like "biy-yitch." Girls exaggerate *bastard* until it sounds like "baas-TURD" (emphasis on the second syllable). These stylized pronunciations signal the end of a duel.

Verbal duels can turn violent. *Niggah* signals a challenge by a girl who wants to play-fight with a boy. Sometimes, this playful fighting escalates. One Sunday afternoon, I was interviewing Angie at the picnic table next to Wendy's. Other kids were nearby. House of Pain walked over to listen.

"Get outta here, niggah," Angie said to House of Pain. He looked at her but said nothing. She growled at him a bit more.

He responded, "Fuck you. I'll stand where I want."

She stood up. "I calling you out, NIGGAH. Wha's up?"

Words were tossed back and forth. House of Pain ended with "You ain't shit, you stank bitch."

That should have ended the duel. He turned and slowly walked away. She kept insulting him and walked after him. House of Pain told her to stop: "Fuck you, bitch. Shut up or I'll kick your ass." That should have been Angie's cue to end it.

She continued to berate him. Wearing a very angry face, he walked up to her, grabbed her by the arm, held her close to him, curled his right hand into a fist, and repeatedly punched her thighs and shoulders. To her cries of pain, an onlooking boy said, "Fuck you, you stank bitch, whatcha do that [push him] for?" Girls paid no attention once the punching ended. They walked away and let Angie rub her wounds by herself.

This scene was awful to watch. I wondered what motivated Angie to persist to the point where words turned to punches. After all, I thought, Angie isn't new to the street, and House of Pain's short fuse is well known. Angie knew that no one would intervene if he beat her.

"Violence doesn't scare me. I'm used to it, it's normal," said Poodle Bitch in a matter-of-fact voice. "I seen shootings and drive-bys." Poodle said she had been arrested for assault in a courtroom. She had punched her mother in the face and "knocked that bitch on her fuckin' ass." Roger, Angie's brother, said "It's true," adding, "We used to get into fistfights at home too."

Fremont girls are used as punching bags by the boys. Many girls have experienced similar violence inflicted by a parent. One afternoon in the summer of 1994, Angie told me, her father drove to Fremont. Her mother had told him that Angie was dating a black fellow. Angie's father beat her and drove away. Her eyes swollen shut, the teenager was black-and-blue from head to toe.

Violence at home and on the street isn't new to these kids. I sat with Cheri, Wendy, Cara, Angie, and Chucky D in Wendy's room and asked them to list the Fremont Hustlers who'd been killed since August 1992:

- A 15-year-old boy and a 25-year-old man were shot in the chest four to six times and murdered by unknown killers.
- A 23-year-old Fremont man was murdered by Northeast on the same date that his brother had been killed by Bloods two years earlier.
- A 16-year-old was shot accidentally, and his 15-year-old brother was shot by a rival. Both survived.
- A 17-year-old boy was shot in the head by a rival and now sits permanently in a wheelchair.
- A 14-year-old boy was accidentally shot in the head by his best friend while they handled a .45 handgun.
- A 13-year-old girl survived being shot in the chest with a .38 handgun by a Northeast member.
- A 16-year-old was shot in the arm with a 12-gauge shotgun at close range by a member of Northeast in a drive-by shooting on Fremont.
- Two 17-year-old boys survived being shot by rivals.
- A 16- and a 17-year-old boy were shot and killed with a 12-gauge shotgun when they kicked in the front door of a house where Northeast members resided.
- An 18-year-old boy survived being shot by a female member of Northeast.
- A 21-year-old woman who was the sister of a Fremont kid and a member of La Familia was killed by Northeast.

Suicide occurs too. One Fremont boy committed suicide; no one talks about him or knows anything about the details. Two Northeast boys, said Bernard and Cara, killed themselves between mid-1996 and early 1997. "Cuban Louie blew his brains out," said Cara. "He was fucked up."

The suicide of 18-year-old Larry Cruz bothers everyone. "He was getting strange, talking weird shit, you know," said Bernard. "He got his baby and his baby's mother and told her to drive out in the country no slower than 75 miles an hour. He said if she slowed down he'd kill her. They were flying, and he started shooting [a handgun] all around the car and then blew his head off. Man, he was smoking crystal and doing acid all the time. He was fucked up."

No Fremont kids committed suicide between June 1995 and February 1997.

Violence has led Fremont boys to prison. As of July 1995: Jack, Cara's fantasy boyfriend, whom we'll meet later, was serving a 12-year sentence for beating someone to death. Another was serving two life terms, two

55-year terms, and three 15-year terms for involvement in a murder. Little Man, whom we'll meet later after his release, was serving a 15-year sentence for possession of drugs. Another was serving 15 to 20 years for murder. Snapper had been in prison five years for murder. Dwayne's sentence was 255 years for the possession of a gun that "had bodies on it," said Cara.

"My biggest fear," Cara told me, "is watching all my friends die. I don't want to fear dying. I don't want to die violently. It'll all get better someday. I wish it would all stop."

Bernard, one of the hardcore members of the Northeast Gangstas, said, "I got 20, maybe more, boys locked up or dead. Why? Bullshit, man, over kid's stuff. You call me dis, I call you dat. It's all bullshit but, hey, when you out dere alone and scared, hate and jealousy is what it's about. Know what I'm sayin'?"

Violence is difficult to explain in the context of daily Fremont social life.[14] Generally speaking, there is gang violence, or violence perpetrated by the Fremont Hustlers to protect their collective resources (marijuana and cocaine sales), and nongang violence, or violence perpetrated by individual Fremont kids, each acting on his or her own behalf.

While I was physically on Fremont and 13th and closely associated with Fremont kids (June 1995 to July 1997), Fremont Hustlers did not perpetrate any acts of offensive or defensive gang violence against any KC gang or gang members.

Nongang Fremont violence is personal violence. Personal violence includes incidents among Fremont members and between Fremont and members of different KC gangs. Personal violence originates in verbal insults and challenges, envy, public humiliation, and most often in fights over suitors.

Fremont girls, more so than boys, are troublemakers. Girls argue about boys and compete for the few of them who have cash and drugs. That's why Chucky D and Afro are in hot demand; however, boys don't need to compete for girls.

When girls fight over boys, it is physical and always intensely emotional. Earl's sister pistol-whipped Wendy in front of her house on a Saturday afternoon, with dozens of kids watching. Why? Earl's sister thought Wendy had eyes for her boyfriend. Angie was stabbed in the thigh by another girl who was jealous over Angie's attention to that girl's boyfriend. Such encounters never occurred among Fremont boys contesting for the attention of a girl. There are a lot of Fremont girls; thus, Fremont boys can have sex with someone without much fuss.

Intergang violence is a different matter. Violence between a boy in the Fremont Hustlers and a boy in the Northeast Gangstas, La Familia, or Southside is caused most often by Fremont girls (or a girl from one of these other gangs) hanging out with a competing gang. While there, she gossips about something a Fremont boy might have said about a Northeast or a Southside boy, and before long, a drugged boy wields a handgun or rifle and a drive-by shooting occurs. Several Northeast boys perpetrated a drive-by shooting in early 1996, Bernard said, on one of their own members, over something a non-Northeast girl had told the shooter the victim had said about him.

Girls who have a strong social tie to Chucky D have power. Cara is one of these girls. Chucky D has rescued her honor more than once by threatening to the "kick the ass" of someone (boy or girl) who has insulted or slapped her. When it's publicly announced that Chucky D is after someone, the potential victim hides.

Serious public violence, such as the 1996 Northeast Gangstas' drive-by mentioned above, attracts the attention of the police; however, intra-gang violence—boys beating girls, girls beating girls—is far more common.

The violent incidents listed above are difficult to interpret. Whether these are examples of gang or personal violence is unclear. The motivations soon fade, but my sense is that each of these incidents was personal violence, despite a gang affiliation of the victim and the perpetrator.

Fremont and Northeast kids talked to me at length about violence, fistfights, street robberies, drive-bys. They had a hard time identifying motives which spurred violent incidents. It's easy for gang kids to say, "It's over jealousy, money," but, when I asked for detailed explanations of the dynamics of intergang violence, the details were unknown.

To an outsider, the shooting of a Fremont kid by a Northeast kid may look like gang violence, but that's deceptive. Recall that, when kids shoot at kids, the shooters and the victims are most likely high, and being high doesn't lend itself to clear thinking, rational decisions, good recall of an event's details, and the ability to explain an incident a day, a week, or a month later. When an incident's details are fuzzy and kids are pushed for answers, they offer violence folklore, which sounds realistic and rational: He hurt me, I hurt him. But whether such simple social logic makes sense within the socioeconomic complexities of gang life is another issue, especially important to the notion of retaliation.

Kids talk about violence much more often than it occurs.[15] I heard a number of tales about violence that had occurred before I went to Fremont; then in the summer of 1995, my experience with gang violence became more personal.

Wendy and Janet are the only Fremont kids who openly admitted to the use of firearms in a shooting. "We'd walk up to a house and unload and then run." They said they did this four, maybe five, times using 12-gauge shotguns, but wouldn't tell me when, where, or why they did it.

On August 16, 1994, at about 7:45 in the evening, Wendy and Cara were the victims of a walk-by shooting. I have many versions of this tale told to me by Cara, Wendy, Bernard, Cara and Wendy, Cara and Bernard, and Jerry, Wendy's uncle; each version is different, even in the number of shooters. Cara and Bernard, sitting together in Cathy's living room in March 1997, told me the tale. Bernard says he was an eyewitness.

"I was up dere chillin'," Bernard began, with Cara smiling at him, "jus' hangin' out. Wendy and Cara pulled up . . ."

"It was Wendy's birthday," Cara interrupted. "We was all at her house partying. Then we wen' driving and saw B, Lucky, Greenbean, Roger, and the guy who did it . . ."

"Thomas Cook," Bernard interrupted Cara.

(In August 1995, Wendy had told me that Harold, Jamie, Lucky, and Greenbean were the only boys at the scene; she omitted Bernard.)

"Lucky and Cook, they had some words. Lucky grabbed his balls," Bernard laughed, "and said, 'You wanna box?' He wanted to fight 'im. Cook grabbed his shit [crotch], and he say, 'Box dese nuts, motherfucker,' and pulled out an AK and, blam, we all ran, goin' over shit, gettin' da fuck outta dere." Neither Bernard nor Cara know why the shooter did this, although both of them agree that he had been acting "crazy." In August 1995, Wendy had said the motive was jealousy. Fremont had been making a lot of money selling rock cocaine, and members owned cars. Northeast was envious, she said.

Cara and Wendy said there was a second shooter, but neither they nor Bernard knew his name. The girls were sitting inside Wendy's Honda, according to them, the shooter circled the car, firing through metal and glass and into them. Cara's ankle was shattered with shots through the door; broken glass cut Wendy's face, but otherwise she wasn't hurt. Someone on the block called 911.

On August 17, 1994, the evening after the shooting, Wendy's uncle Jerry called my 800 number to tell me about it. By this time I had already met Wendy. His tale is different from the one told by Cara and Bernard and has a folkloric flavor:

Wendy and Cara (Jerry calls her Carrie) were sitting in Wendy's car at 9:30 P.M. on the corner of 12th and White. They had been celebrating Wendy's birthday at her house. Two Fremont boys, whose names are unknown, had asked Wendy for a ride the few blocks to 12th and White, knowing that Wendy was to be the target of a prearranged gang hit.

When Wendy and "Carrie" stopped the car, their homeboys got out and walked down the sidewalk past three boys standing on the corner.

The boys wore long jackets, the variety that outlaws in western movies wear. When the Fremont traitors passed them, the shooters withdrew from under their coats an AK-47 and another high-powered assault-type rifle and shot into the car as they circled it.

Wendy was shot in the face; Carrie in the foot and legs. The firing over, Wendy opened her door, walked around the car, pulled out Carrie, and carried her to a friend's house several blocks away. There, Wendy called Jackie.

Jackie and Mike, Wendy's father, visited Wendy in the hospital. "Well, Wendy, have you had enough?" asked Jackie.

"They got theirs coming," replied Wendy in anger.

Mike threatened to kill the shooters.

Within days the KCPD arrested several gang members, and Fremont was planning a retaliation hit. The gang owns a Tech-9. Local rumor had it that the hit on Wendy had been arranged by Fremont kids who were angry at Wendy because she'd been hanging around Northeast boys.

KCPD investigated the shooting and, at the same time, arrested Afro, who was then Wendy's boyfriend of several years (she had conceived a child with him), on two counts of aggravated assault for several walk-by shootings and armed criminal assault. He had a $55,000 bond on each count. He rolled over (snitched) on everybody on Fremont and other gangs too in order to be released.

A week later on August 24, 1994, Wendy called my 800 number at 2:30 P.M. and left a message on my home answering machine. I returned her call, but she wasn't there. Jerry called me again a week after that.

He told me that Wendy was then staying with a nongang companion who rented an apartment well north of Fremont, outside KC. Wendy would stay with this girl again after the 1995 bust. KCPD arrested three boys—one 17-year-old, two minors—whom they certified as adults. The boys are members of Northeast, otherwise known as Norweak by Fremont. Three weapons had been used in the walk-by: a Tech-9, a shotgun, and an AK-47. The shooters were charged with two counts of attempted murder and armed criminal action.

Thomas Cook, 14 years old, was arrested, prosecuted, and convicted of armed criminal assault and began serving a three- to seven-year term in a Missouri state prison. No one knows why he shot Cara and Wendy.

Once in July 1995, La Familia and Southside appeared on Fremont early on the same Sunday morning and fired weapons. No Fremont kid knew why they were fired on.

On that Sunday, July 22, at 1:00 in the morning I drove away from Wendy's. Later in the day, at about noon, I returned and hung out until the kids woke up and trickled outside. Before long, Roger and a few others were smoking weed in Steele Bill's room, retelling and laughing about what happened around 90 minutes after I had left Fremont 12 hours earlier.

"We'd just smoked two dank sticks[16] and got back, and some dudes from 24th Street [Southside] were parked down the street. They tried to jump Lucky and Greenbean. We loaded a 12-gauge and a 30-30 and went down the street. They had a pistol but didn't shoot. They bitches. They scared."

Fremont's arsenal includes three .22s, one 20-gauge and two 12-gauge shotguns, a 30-30 rifle, and an SKS (Chinese assault rifle similar to an AK-47).[17] At one time these firearms were stashed along with ammunition in what was the empty house on the downhill side of Afro's. Each rifle and shotgun is owned individually by a Fremont boy. Boys own these firearms as well as handguns, which weren't kept in the abandoned house.

All these weapons were stolen in residential and commercial burglaries, said the owners. Some gang kids regularly burglarize houses and steal whatever is valuable. Guns are valuable and easily sold on the street. Fremont shotguns and rifles were stolen north of the city. There are other street kids who make a living selling stolen guns to gang members. These kids do burglaries to get firearms, or they broker firearms stolen by other young burglars. Cars and vans, to be used once or twice in a shooting or some other crime, are stolen by kids who hang around Fremont and other gangs and are sold in the same way as firearms.

Not too long after Southside drove off, said Roger, a carload of La Familia members showed up. "Them motherfuckers rolled down the street twice and busted on us," said Roger, his eyes bleary from too many dank sticks. "We opened fire and shot so many shells, it was pathetic."

While Roger told his tale about the night before, kids smoked weed and then piled outside to hang around out front. Roger and a partner of his walked down 13th Street heading west, just a casual walk on a hot and humid Sunday afternoon.

I was standing between Wendy's and Afro's chatting with a few kids, a boombox thumping in the background, when Roger ran up and shouted, "Northeast is coming."

A van carrying Northeast's Cruz brothers, young men in their early twenties, who are notorious among youth gangs for violent behavior, were cruising the neighborhood, just a casual ride. The Cruz brothers had a relative in the neighborhood. Words were exchanged, one boy threw the finger at another, someone called someone else a punk motherfucker, more heated words flew, and one of the Cruz brothers said that he'd been punched by House of Pain and pointed his finger toward his house at the corner of Fremont and 13th.

Roger's cry, "Northeast is coming," and the van's pass-through set in motion events that were terrifying: boys going to war. Fremont prepared for battle.

Roger said the Cruz boys and other Northeast kids as well were coming to shoot and fight, and a contingent of them would meet Fremont boys a few blocks west on 13th. Afro and Chucky D and House of Pain ran west on 13th to meet the Cruz brothers and anyone else they'd brought. Chucky D and Afro, former Northeast boys themselves, didn't like the Cruz brothers. Fremont fistfighters took brown, cloth, gardening gloves out of their back pockets and put them on their hands to protect them. (Fremont boys who enjoy fistfighting carry these gloves in a back pocket of their pants; in other KC neighborhoods too, I saw boys carrying similar gloves in their jeans.)

Roger and a few others ran to the abandoned house where they kept their arsenal. One boy stood inside and tossed out the weapons one by one through the window. A boy standing outside took them and handed them to a third and fourth kid, who loaded each one and handed it to its owner. Shawn reached for his 12-gauge, Wayne for his, and so it went.

At the same time boys came running from houses up and down Fremont carrying handguns; some concealed 9-millimeter handguns in their shorts. The excitement, the anticipation of the impending firefight electrified the air. Kids buzzed excitedly and talked about other shootings they'd been in and bragged in anticipation of this one. A few boys climbed onto the roof over Wendy's front porch and stood holding rifles and handguns. Fremont shooters were higher than the roadway, and they had a good shot at anyone coming down the street.

Armed boys darted back and forth along the ridge between Wendy's and Afro's. I stood there with my tape recorder running and notebook in hand. Across the street a preschool boy looked through the screen door. His father walked up behind him, put a hand on each of his shoulders, pulled him away gently, and closed the front door.

Girls went inside Wendy's. Boys didn't hide behind trees or other objects that might stop a bullet. They stood unprotected on high ground. Standing among them, I felt vulnerable; I was the only one without a weapon. My tape recorder wouldn't help me defend myself.

I felt exposed, I *was* exposed, but the Fremont boys didn't seem to sense real danger. Maybe they're still hungover, I thought, or just stupid.

"It's some funny shit, man," said a young warrior. "I'm gonna jump right out in the middle of the street. It's the Fourth of July!"

"I'm ready to rock 'n roll, ready to ride," exclaimed another. A boy holding a weapon announced, "I'm rollin' on everybody that I fuckin' feel like shootin'."

Still standing among these armed kids, holding my notebook and tape recorder and feeling like an idiot, I had to decide if I would stand there and watch, unarmed, or hide. I decided to stand my ground. I wanted to watch the shooting and told myself right then and there that I would die one day anyway; it may as well be in a gang fight.

We waited—5 minutes, 10, 15. The Cruz brothers didn't show up. Afro, Chucky D, and House of Pain walked into Fremont's armed camp and said, "Da motherfuckers ain't around. Pussies." There was no shooting. The value of watching and listening to Fremont boys and girls rehearse for a drive-by shooting was, well, the best way to learn about such an event, without death or injuries.

What frightened me next was the thought that someone on the block, perhaps the man across the street, had dialed 911, and the KCPD were speeding to Fremont. And there I was, standing on a hill holding a tape recording of Fremont boys talking about prior shootings, who had shot whom, when the shootings had happened, and why. That really frightened me. I ran across the street and hid my tape recorder and tapes and notes about these shootings and the ones from earlier that day in the spare-tire compartment of my Acura. Then I waited for the police. They, like the Cruz brothers, didn't show up. I burned those tapes and destroyed the notes.

The excitement ended; kids put their weapons away. The girls walked out.

"That's some heavy shit, huh, Mark?" said Cara in a matter-of-fact way.

"Yeah, heavy dangerous shit, Caramel."

"Hey, biytch," said Cara to Cheri, "go up in there 'n roll us a big ol' fat ass joint."

Cheri smiled.

The rest of the day was quiet, though kids turned quickly to look uphill at the sound of any car driving down Fremont or across 13th Street.

Violence has an opportunity cost, especially in cases of retaliation. Fremont's major drug sellers—Afro, Chucky D, Wendy, House of Pain—are the kids most likely to be violent, yet they ask themselves an economic question: What will the violence cost me? Dramatic incidents of violence, drive-by shootings, for instance, the stuff that brings the cops, oppose Fremont Hustlers' economic interests in selling drugs and making money. Simply put, outrageous and unnecessary violence is bad for business, and everyone knows it. Chucky D and Afro have vested interests in the drug business, and they protect their interest. For example, Afro and Jackie got into a screaming match in the middle of Fremont one Sunday afternoon because the cops had arrested Robert and his partner, Ryan, for burglary. Afro was furious at Jackie for paying so little attention to the kinds of crimes her son committed. Afro didn't care one bit if Robert was a criminal; his concern was that the cops showed up to pick up the boy burglars, and that ruined business.

These gang businessmen have a great deal to lose by having a thin skin. If they take offense at every word, glance, or mutter that offends them and then act out in a dramatic way and beat or kill someone, they'll lose business. Honor and revenge are topics of violence folklore, but money affects behavior.[18]

Retaliation is an easy idea for citizens and researchers to grasp as a cause of violence. In fact, when a Northeast Gangsta shoots a Fremont Hustler, no one on Fremont really cares about the victim anyway. No one on Fremont took revenge against Northeast for shooting Cara and Wendy. Why should they? Had Wendy been killed, Chucky D, Afro, House of Pain, and others too would have taken her drug customers. Wendy was worth more dead than alive.

Common sense also dictates to street kids that there's no benefit in violent retaliation. Amassing a carload of kids willing to face death or years in prison to avenge the so-called honor of an injured or killed comrade or the honor of "The Gang" makes no economic or practical sense. Except for Afro, Chucky D, and House of Pain, they're cowards who wouldn't under ordinary circumstances willingly face death to avenge someone else's honor. They never talk about doing such a thing. No one has ever said, "I'd be willing to give my life for Chucky's." No kids get rewarded immediately, with either property or elevated status, for being braver than someone else or offering to get hurt or killed for the honor of the group.

Fremont Hustlers aren't Marines. These kids don't invest in their own future; why would they invest in someone else's well-being? Honor is in short supply on the street and, unless it has some economic value, it isn't meaningful enough to cause violent behavior. Tinker with the material security of kids on the edge of starvation and you tinker, at the same time, with their emotional insecurity, and that is likely to cause a problem, especially with kids like Wendy, Chucky D, and Afro, who are prone to flying into angry outbursts.

Fremont kids are frightened adolescents easily stirred into paranoia and anger at just the thought of a threat made by an aggressive insider or outsider. When violence happens to them or around them, they strike out, but out of fear, not for the sake of honor, despite the violence folklore. Fear is a personal, private feeling. Fear isn't an acceptable emotion on Fremont, and it's cleverly transformed into the talk of retaliation.

Chucky D uses the opportunity of violence to play on elements of street culture and enhance his own street image by claiming to defend Fremont. A strong theme in gang violence folklore is, "What I do, I do for you." Of course, the subtext is, "Now, what are you going to do for me?" This form of defense is, in fact, entirely selfish and economically motivated, because the violent defender is protecting his stake on the territory where he makes cash. Should other kids, inside his gang or outside, think he's a pushover, they're likely to move in and take his drug customers. A gang member's street image is best molded and modified by his or her willingness to be aggressive and violent, at least within his or her account of violence folklore.

Except for Chucky D, Afro, and House of Pain, Fremont boys are cowards. Recall when the Cruz brothers threatened Fremont. Only House of Pain, Chucky D, and Afro pulled on their brown, cloth, fistfighting gloves and ran off down 13th Street, because these boys like to fistfight. The other boys pulled out handguns and rifles and shotguns. These are the weapons of cowards.

Street violence scares me. It can easily slip into something fierce and uncontrollable. Cowardly boys need fierce warriors like Chucky D, Afro, and House of Pain to protect them. For that service, cowards pay a toll by letting Chucky D, Afro, and House of Pain do business as they please. Protecting the neighborhood means protecting one's bank account. That's something we all understand. On Fremont, violence is never committed for any altruistic reason, never committed for the "good of the gang." There's always a price.

Fremont kids love guns. When they talk about their weapons, these youngsters' faces glisten and brighten and their bodies inflate like a gas balloon. Their backs straighten and limbs stiffen; excitement and passion overcome them. I saw boys sit on Wendy's porch in groups of two, three, and four and pour over magazines like *Ammo*. These kids talk about guns like a fat man talks about double-rich chocolate brownies.

Fremont kids play with guns like school kids fiddle with the World Wide Web. It's a favorite pastime, engaged in most often at night, when the kids are high on weed and dank and alcohol. Then shotguns and rifles come out of hiding and are shot into the air or at the street light across the street from Wendy's—the one I so naively thought they'd smashed with rocks.

Whenever I could I stopped high shooters when they blasted weapons into the night sky, and I took away the weapons. That made me nervous only because my fingerprints were then on shotguns, assault rifles, and hunting rifles. As a former employee of the U.S. Department of Justice, my fingerprints are on file with the FBI. What if the cops pick me up for a shooting? I'd ask myself.

"Let me tell ya, when you shoot into the air, rounds come down, you know. Do you know where bullets come down? You know you could hurt someone?" I said more than once. One time a young shooter looked at me with glassy eyes and said, "Fuck it, who cares?"

4
Families

Train up a child in the way he should go: and when he is old, he will not depart from it.

—Proverbs 22:6[1]

On the first Sunday in July 1995, I met Cathy, Cara's mom, at about 3:00 in the afternoon as she lay curled up under a comforter on a double bed watching a black-and-white movie on a color television. Heavy, dark wood furniture lined the walls; a shaded window dimmed the room.

Cara and I walked into Cathy's room, "Mom, this is Mark. He's a professor doing a story about us kids on Fremont. Know what he said? He said we can sue that asshole who shot me, get him to pay the hospital bills."

She sat up in bed, pulled a pillow onto her lap, and smiled at me. "Car-rah," she said with emphasis, "I look terrible." She lowered her head and turned away from us. I knew she was embarrassed, and I felt it too, walking unannounced into an unfamiliar woman's bedroom.

"Cara said you owe a lot of money because of the shooting," I said, wanting to be helpful. Cathy looked back at us.

"Yeah, about $8,000 in hospital bills. You think we can sue him?" she asked.

"In a civil case, I don't see why not. I'll talk to some of my lawyer friends in town and let you know."

"I'd appreciate that," she said to me.

"Next time you bring him here, Cara, let me know first so I can comb my hair and get out of bed."

"Ah Ma, he's a nice guy. Don' worry about that," Cara said pleasantly.

"And Cara," Cathy said, in a mother's voice, "watch your language, you know I don't like it when you cuss."

Cathy's Gladstone duplex was tidy, had polished hardwood floors and nice furniture, and a Krups espresso machine was perched on the kitchen counter. This place didn't match my expectation of the family setting that had spawned Cara, a teenager I had found sleeping in a gang-operated drug house. How did Cara end up there? I asked myself.

Cathy and Cara being stuck with thousands of dollars in hospital bills seemed outrageous to me. Cathy's debt to Truman Medical Center was a third of her gross annual income. I asked two lawyers in KC about filing a civil suit against Cara and Wendy's Northeast shooter. Even though Cathy was working two jobs at the time of the shooting, the additional medical insurance premium for Cara, who was then staying outside the house most of the time, was simply too expensive to pay on low wages. Cara has chronic ankle pain and arthritis as a consequence of being shot by an AK-47, and neither Cathy nor Cara could afford the medication Cara needs to ease the pain.

My lawyer friends listened and asked me one question: "Does Cara or her family have money?" I said, "No, but if you work on a percentage, why does she need money?" They responded, "Does the shooter have money, or his family—maybe valuable property, a house, cars, something worth enough to pay the hospital bills?" I told them the shooter was dirt poor, estranged from his mother, and no one knew the location of the shooter's father, not even kids in Northeast.

The lawyers didn't like the case, because no one, neither the victim nor the perpetrator, had money. If the case went to trial, the lawyers said, Cara's character would be impugned and that would weaken the lawsuit. "Why would Cara's character be called into question?" I asked. After all, she was the victim. The lawyers said she's a gang member who was hanging out in a dangerous neighborhood. They said she is partly responsible for being shot. Odd logic, I thought. The lawyers also said they'd need at least $1,000 up front. Should they lose the case, someone—in this case, the victim—would have to pay the bill. This taught me a cold lesson: poor people suing poor people is bad business.

I told this saga to Cara. "Mark, that's fuckin' unfair," she screamed. "That motherfucker shoots me, goes to prison for a few years, and has mothafuckers up in there takin' care o' him, given him free medicine when he's sick. He'll get out and be on the streets. We got all them fucking biylls, my ankle aches when the weather's cold, I cayn't stand on it for eight hours at work, I cayn't afford no medicine, and he'll walk on the streets like nothin' ever fuckin' happened. Fuck dem all. When he get out, I'm gonna kill that motherfucker. And if I don', Chucky said he beat the motherfucker's ass to death."

Years of street research should have numbed me to dipping into other people's lives. Unfortunately, it hasn't. The more deeply I became involved in the lives of Fremont kids and their relatives, the more intrusive I felt. Maybe, I thought, this is a sign of my mental health.

It wasn't until the summer of 1996 that I felt comfortable enough to interview Fremont kids' parents. No doubt I could have interviewed them sooner, but I wasn't ready. Seeing drug-numbed kids, pregnant 15-year-olds, boys in jail, and babies whose lives depend on drug-addicted mothers made me weary and angry at KC for doing nothing but arresting these kids.

I didn't feel comfortable probing into Cathy's family life. I didn't want Cathy to think that I was casting blame onto her for Cara's behavior. I had to remind myself that Cathy's life and her relationship with Cara in 1995, 1996, 1997 wasn't of primary interest. Rather my interest focused on Cathy's life at the time when she was a teenager and was rearing her daughters.

When I listened to Cara talk about Cathy, I heard an account different from the one I heard from Cathy. If I listened only to one side, the tale seemed cut-and-dried. Cara blamed her father and step-father for her life-long delinquent behavior. Cathy said she had done the best she could, but she never mentioned her husbands and lovers as a possible source of Cara's turmoil. Cathy's account doesn't look for someone to blame; rather, it finds an anonymous source, the "bad seed" of poor mental health influenced by genetics.

Cara's autobiography and Cathy's autobiographical account of her own family and of her life with Cara are a complex weave of domestic abuse; however, their story isn't unique. Four autobiographical sketches given by my principal Fremont girl informants—Cara, Wendy, Cheri, Angie—each deeply involved in Fremont street life, are riddled with facts about family violence, parental neglect, and parental drug and alcohol abuse.

"My mom was 21 when I was born," Cara said, "and my dad was 15. Dad was in prison for murder when I was born. Dad was bad off into drugs. He was deranged too."

Cathy divorced Cara's father when Cara was two and married the man who reared Cara from age three to nine.

"He was a real bad alcoholic. He used to beat us real bad. He put knives at Mom's throat, threw things at us kids, hit us in the face. Mom put locks all around my bedroom door, but he kicked down the door. He was always drunk all the time. He was just mean."

At age nine, Cara said Cathy tried unsuccessfully to relinquish her parental rights and place her permanently with the state of Missouri. Cara wasn't clear on the details and Cathy didn't mention it, but Cara said that between ages 9 and 11 she stayed with a woman named Robin.

I met Robin on March 1, 1996. She was in her late thirties then and had a 16-year-old daughter, Amy, who had been a member of La Familia. Amy was the mother of a four-month-old son. The baby boy's father is two years older than Amy, a member of La Familia, and worked at the local Ford plant.

Cara and Amy chatted. Amy talked proudly about the new carpet and furniture in their apartment, described Tom's job on the assembly line, and beamed about owning an almost-new Ford. Cara listened, nodded, and remained uninvolved in Amy's happiness.

Cara paid attention to how Amy spoke to her son. Cara chided Amy about using only high-pitched baby talk. "Biytch," said Cara, "if you talk to da kid like dat, he gonna talk like dat. You want dat?" Amy didn't listen; Cara gave up offering unwanted advice. Cara and Robin talked indirectly about Robin's having cared for Cara many years earlier.

Robin was now caring for an infant and a two-year-old who are the children of a stripper who works for an escort service and rents an apartment in Robin's government-supported housing project. The stripper, in her middle twenties, accompanies local businessmen on junkets around the United States and overseas. The last time the stripper dropped off the two-year-old, Robin said, she asked Robin to care for him that night. More than a year later, the toddler was still with Robin. The stripper later pulled the same routine with the infant. I asked about child-care costs. Robin said that children's mother offers her no support.

After her stay with Robin, Cara was hospitalized and imprisoned seven times between ages 11 and 17. "Doctors said I had an anger problem and a chemical imbalance."

At 11, she was in a KC treatment center at Christmas and was allowed to go home for the day. Cathy said, "I picked her up out front. She was still wearing her PJs." Cara said her sisters had refused to open gifts until Cara joined them.

At age 13, Cara was hospitalized for nearly a year. Inside a state hospital Cara met Wendy.

Jackie said she had married Wendy's father, Mike, inside a county jail before he was transferred to a state penitentiary to serve a sentence for murder. Jackie's brother, Jerry, said Mike was a violent alcoholic and an outlaw biker. Jackie's second husband, whom she married when Wendy was nine, was, like Mike, a violent drunk, Wendy said. Jackie told me her husbands "had some trouble."

At age eight, Wendy smoked her first joint. By age 12 she drank and smoked bud every day, gambled, enjoyed street fights, and stole cars. A juvenile court recommended a 30-day psychiatric evaluation of 12-year-old Wendy. She rebelled, and a month's evaluation turned into years inside a secure detention center in Beloit, Kansas.

"I hated the matrons," she said with a scowl across her face. "I fought 'em, jumped 'em, beat 'em whenever I could, and I ran away. But they kept bringing me back."

Wendy adjusted slowly and learned to live with counseling, planned recreation, good food, and a clean bed. She was released and returned to Fremont.

Rosa, Taz, Wayne, Northeast TJ (Bernard's brother), Poodle/Angie and Roger, Christina, Harold, and others were residents in the same residential treatment facility during their early adolescence. Each escaped more than once.

Poodle said she had been locked up in juvenile facilities almost continuously from age 12 to 17. When Poodle was five, her dad, a local armed robber, went to prison for seven years. Poodle said she recalls clearly her first arrest for car theft and possession of a weapon at age 12. "From then on out, I never went to school, I never went home."

Poodle's mother divorced her father after he was imprisoned and, according to Poodle, began relationships with a series of boyfriends. The man she remembers best is the one who beat her mom and put a knife to her throat and threatened to kill her.

"He was always mean. He kicked our dog's teeth out. He was a hateful person."

At about the time Poodle's mom was suffering at the hands of her boyfriend, Poodle's dad was released from prison and was committed to an honor center, a minimum-security halfway house. He absconded and returned to his former wife's residence. There he found her boyfriend. Poodle's dad stabbed him, and was returned to prison.

"When I was 12, I used coke, but I didn't make a habit of it. I almost ODed. But I started smoking weed and drinking and getting high every day." And at about the same time, Roger, a year younger than Poodle, "started getting in trouble, robbing houses." Roger's crime partner then was Northeast Bernard. Roger was known for his love of dank (see n. 16 of Chapter 3 for a description).

Angie said she was arrested the first time for possession of a gun, and was arrested at least 50 times for absconding from group homes and treatment centers between ages 12 and 17. Periods of confinement lasted from weeks to months.

"I was in and out of group homes for four years," Poodle said. "Finally they committed me to state [Department of Youth Services]. I just got released from that May 17, 1994. I spent every holiday in custody," Angie said nonchalantly.

Like Cara's, Wendy's, and Poodle's fathers, Cheri's is a penitentiary inmate. He is serving a life sentence for murder at the Angola State Penitentiary, the infamous state prison in Louisiana. He's been inside since Cheri's infancy. Cheri said she gets a letter from him every day. I asked to read those letters, but Cheri always "left them somewhere."[2] "It's not his fault that he's locked up. He did what he had to."

Cheri's anger scares Fremont kids, including the boys. "When she gets pissed," said Wendy, "and heads for the kitchen to get a knife, we all leave."

Two personalities dominate her world, Cheri said. The kind one is called Cheri, the angry one is Penelope. "Cheri loves to have fun, talk about people's problems, help people with their problems. She, well, she like to do [things] for people. Know what I'm sayin'? When I get older I want to help kids, tell them what I been through in my childhood, that I don't want them to go through, and I also want to be a doctor.

"Penelope comes when I'm real stressed out. She will never hurt my mother, but she does not like my sister at all. She hates my sister. She'll throw something at her like a knife or something. She loves my brother though. She's cool with him. She won't never do nothing to him. You'll know when Penelope's comin'. I'll sit there. My eyes'll get real big, I'll black out for a minute, and when I look up, I'm not Cheri. I have more control over Penelope than when I was little. When I was little, she had control over me."

When we met, Cheri was 15. She had already been pregnant twice and hadn't attended school in a year. She had been stabbed three times in school fights and said she'd quit; more likely she had been expelled. She smokes weed every day and dank whenever she can get it. Cheri's mother is a dank and speed addict.

"If it weren't for my homeys," said Cheri, "I'd have nothing. At Fremont I can do whatever I want."

Cathy and I saw each other dozens of times between our first chat in July 1995 and the summer of 1996. I called her regularly. We talked about April and Melanie and about her job. In June 1996, I decided the time had come to sit down and open my notebook, turn on my tape recorder, and ask her tough questions about Cara's behavior. How would she explain Cara's involvement with Fremont, I wondered, as well as Cara's dropping out of school and drug use?

On a late Saturday afternoon, Cathy and I sat together. I had a notebook out and the tape recorder balanced on the arm of my chair. Little afternoon light penetrated the front window's venetian blinds. They'd been pulled flat, dimming the living room. The television was showing an old movie. The air conditioner kept the apartment cool in KC's humid weather. Virginia Slims and Newports filled the air with smoke and created a haze in the dim light that filtered through the closed blinds.

"I used to cry and say to myself, 'I have other children,' " mourned Cathy, with deep sadness in her eyes, almost guilt, for saying these words out loud. "When Cara was in day care she took a plastic knife and stabbed it into a teacher's thigh, and she set the teacher's dress on fire with a cigarette lighter. Once she took a boy about a year and a half old and put the kid in the middle of a busy road and told him to stand there. Lucky I saw it, and I ran out and pulled the kid in.

"Cara never fit in a family, and we could tell she was different. A psychiatrist at North Hills [treatment center] said, 'Some kids are born this way.' He said she had a personality disorder, a schizoaffective conduct disorder. Our nickname for her was 'Terror Terror.' You know once Cara pulled down April's panties on a school bus and then called her 'lesbian.' "

Cara is the third of four girls. April is two years younger than Cara, Melanie is three years older, Mary is five years older. Cathy said Cara has mannerisms similar to her father's and shows a temper, anger, and violent behavior like his, too.

For eight and a half years while Cathy's girls were young, she worked two full-time jobs and spent time with her daughters only on Sunday night. She worked as an assistant manager at an IGA grocery store and an office worker at a paper goods company. At age 32 she had a heart attack.

Hard work has emancipated her from a man's grasp. Cathy had many years of bad relationships. Her four daughters have three fathers, two of whom have been violent alcoholics and criminals.

At age 11, Cathy had Cara under treatment in North Hills. There she attacked a staff member with a nail; he needed surgery to repair the damage. Then Cara was committed to the Western Missouri State Hospital for eight months of treatment (this was where she met Wendy). Cara showed dramatic mood swings and often pounded her head on the concrete floor of her unit.

"Doctors said she had a bipolar disorder. One of her psychiatrists said she has no core personality, which means there's no home for Cara. The only times these people connect to the human race is during the act of sex and when they're pregnant." Cathy took a Virginia Slim, paused a moment, took a deep breath, and continued.

"Cara blends into whatever environment she's in. Part of Cara is kind, part of her will shake a baby. She gets swept up in the tide of things and people. And blacks are accepting of odd behavior, so they let her hang around."

Cathy returned to the subject of Cara's effect on the family. "April locked herself in the bedroom, and Cara stabbed at the door with a knife over and over. Mary called the police and me, and I called the psychiatrist. Oh poor April. She felt so guilty afterward when she cried, 'I just can't love Cara now.' "

"April wouldn't play outside because Cara would be out there, and she abused and embarrassed her in public. Cara once got April on the couch, bent her backwards over the arm and choked her, choked her. Mary pulled Cara off and punched Cara."

Cathy's eyes filled with tears. "She embarrassed me too, because I had to leave work so often. She's very manipulative and says, 'You never did anything for me.' My only regret with Cara is, when she was in Western, she took on every disorder of each group she was in. She'd hear voices and she'd say she was sexually molested by her father. I didn't believe her then, and should have."

I didn't have the courage to pursue Cathy's innuendo about sexual abuse of Cara.

"She has the need to be the center of attention and everybody's best friend. I worry about her choice of friends. I've always expected Cara to die young. I have often wondered how I couldn't have killed Cara."

In talking to parents of Fremont kids, I felt much less empathetic when I sensed that parents didn't care about their kids' well-being and how they would fare in life, even though these parents uttered politically correct rationalizations to answer my questions. Cathy is different from other Fremont parents. She suffers and for a long time has tried to tie the pieces of her life together into a coherent fabric that makes sense and is beneficial to her and her kids.

Had I listened only to Cara's tales about her mother, I'd have thought Cathy was a tyrant, a screaming, careless woman who doesn't give a damn about her girls. But that's not how I saw Cathy, and that's not how Cathy perceives her interactions with Cara. Cara is a tough kid, I thought. How would I have handled her had she been my daughter?

I became an appendage of Cathy's family and watched and listened and tape-recorded conversations. Truth is, interviews with her felt more like interrogations. I felt meddlesome, as if I had pushed my way into someone else's nightmare.[3]

These interviews had to continue if I were to understand at least in part the forces at work which created Cara. After all, the dynamics of Cathy's family between July 1995 and February 1997 hadn't had the greatest impact on Cara's behavior. I needed to know about Cathy's life when she was Cara's age and then about Cathy's life while her girls were young children. As you'll see, Cara and Cathy share similarities in their life stories, although neither of them, I thought, recognize it.

Hours of conversations with Cathy didn't reveal anything about her four daughters' three fathers. Melanie and Mary had one father, Cara another, April a third. Cara's father and April's, too, were prison inmates. Cara said her "official" father, the man noted on her birth certificate, is really Melanie and Mary's father. It was as if Cathy's four daughters sprang to life from the earth, three healthy, one disturbed. The truth is, I felt like a family friend and was embarrassed to ask Cathy about lovers and husbands.

I don't need to know about those men, I told myself, to understand Cara and tell the story of the Fremont Hustlers. Had I asked Cathy about husbands and lovers and had I gotten answers, I wouldn't publish that information anyway. By this time, I had reached an overload of prying into others' lives.

Until I heard Cathy's account about Cara terrorizing the younger April, I thought the grousing and the loud and often angry voices connecting these girls were the typical, albeit more exaggerated, bickering of adolescent siblings.

"April, would you mind talking to me about your relationship to Cara?" I asked quietly on Sunday morning while she was fixing a cup of coffee.

She stopped dead in her tracks and stood still for what seemed minutes, not moving, just staring. She turned toward me, saying, "It's a long story."

"That's OK, I have time," I said.

"Sure," she said.

I thought further about prying into April's hidden world and decided that her feelings and memories of Cara would best be told to someone who could help her repair the damage Cara had caused. I was afraid that opening April's hidden world, even if I didn't record a word, would hurt her. I'd have no part of hurting this kind child.

I watched April slowly pull herself out of school over the 1995–96 academic year. She said she got into too much trouble and didn't like the "black girls" because they picked on her, and in turn, she had to fight to protect herself. Cara encouraged April's return to school, at least when I was in earshot, offering to buy her a pair of $100 Nikes as a reward for staying in or returning to school, as the case may be. April didn't want Cara's gift.

April stopped going to school at age 16 and hid from the aggression there, as she did from Cara's bullying. April worked as a waitress at Pizza

Hut and then took a second job as an evening janitor; Cara worked with April as a janitor for a few weeks, then quit.

April stuck it out for months, but was displeased with the unrewarding work. She then got a job as a cook in a Mexican restaurant in North Kansas City, about 10 miles north of her home on Van Brunt. She rode the bus to work, and on weekends Cathy drove her. When she ended work at midnight and later on weekends, Cathy picked her up, or April got a ride with someone she knew.

April saved her earnings and returned to school. She paid tuition at a local community college, where she completed a GED. In the fall of 1996 and spring of 1997 she was earning college credits. April dreams of being a marine biologist and plans to join the Marine Corps to get college funds. One Saturday afternoon while April was working, Cara and I were chatting in Cathy's living room and the phone rang. It was a Marine recruiter responding to April's request for information. April has a path to the future. I have no doubt that she will do whatever she must to get as far from Cara as possible.

Cathy grew up in Greenlake, Washington. "I came from a huge, dysfunctional, Irish family," she said as I was walking out the door one afternoon with Cara. We were on our way up to Fremont to hang out.

"Would you mind telling me about your family?" I asked.

"I'll talk about it," she said. We did, a few weeks later, after we finished talking about Cara.

"My dream was to grow up in an Ozzie and Harriet family," she said clinically, leaning forward to reach for a king-sized Virginia Slim cigarette. The Ozzie and Harriet family of 1950s television, with two children, a working father, and a happy stay-at-home mother, was as dissimilar to Cathy's early-life family as Fremont is to Overland Park.

Fourth youngest in a family of 13 children, Cathy escaped home at age 16 by telling her mother she was pregnant and had to get married. She married a 21-year-old fellow named Michael.

"In third grade I started doing all the cooking and cleaning, because my mother was sick and my older sister, well, she was a drunk and didn't help."

Cathy told me her mother became abusive when Cathy was a young teenager. She claimed that her mother broke both her arms and legs just before she left home. "She beat me with a broom handle and punched and kicked me, and she'd get angry and throw [kitchen] glasses at me. I refused to let her know she got to me. She was just horrible to me."

Cathy's half-brother, an offspring from another of Cathy's mother's three husbands, also treated her badly. "Johnnie molested me when I was eight. He was 26. He'd sneak into my room at night when I was asleep, and he molested my sisters April and Robin. Then one day Michael beat the hell out of him. I didn't enjoy sex till I was 23 years old and had a hard time separating myself from what happened. I still don't like being touched and closed in."

Cathy said she was aggressive, too. "I'm not afraid of a single soul. I don't get afraid of people. When Cara was two we lived in the projects; a black woman was beating her," Cathy said, pausing. "Well, I sent her and another woman who butted in to the hospital."

Cathy has six brothers, one is gay and dying of AIDS, and the other five were convicts at the Washington State Penitentiary, at the Arizona State Prison in Florence, and in a state prison in Alaska, in the late 1960s. One brother, the fellow who did time in Alaska, was stabbed to death in prison.

"Alan [Cathy's gay brother] threw a pie in Goldwater's face and was involved in the bombing of the Library of Congress. He was the political activist," she said proudly.

Sitting at Cathy's one Saturday afternoon, we looked through the five-inch-thick family photo album. There was a photo of Cathy's mother, the eldest of 15 children. She had her first child at age 14. "She didn't enjoy sex, she just had to endure it," said Cathy clinically.

I spotted photos of men dressed in Prohibition era clothing. "Who are these guys?"

"The Barrow boys," Cathy said.

"The Barrows? Like Bonnie and Clyde, those Barrows?" I asked.

"The same. The Barrows, all of them are fruitcakes. There was violence and alcohol and incest in that family." Cathy said her mother's first husband was a Barrow, first cousin to Clyde Barrow. She stopped talking, paused, apparently caught by a memory.

"There was violence in my family. That's just the way it was. Cara gets her craziness from my mother's family and the Barrows," quipped Cathy with a graceful smile.

Cathy tired, and I did to. Listening to this account drained me, it drained her. It's exhausting to listen to a life story that has no hope, little joy, and dim prospects for a happy ending. Cathy's life is not like the black-and-white movies she enjoys. While Cathy talked, she stopped now and then and grabbed a tissue off the wooden coffee table and wiped the tears from her cheeks.

Later, when Cara became anxious to run off somewhere, I packed up my tapes and tape recorder and notebook, stuck them into my black canvas bag, stood up, and looked at Cathy. I didn't know what to say.

"Thanks. Thanks for talking to me."

Cathy nodded and smiled.

"Come on, Mark, let's get the fuck out of here."

"Car-rah," Cathy drawled, "you know I don't want cursing in my house."

"Sooorry, Mom." Cara lowered her head.

Cathy looked at me. "Don't spoil her."

"Nah, I won't. I'm just trying to keep her out of jail."

"Yeah, good luck," Cathy said. We all uttered a nervous chuckle.

By then I felt that keeping Cara out of jail might be the hardest thing I've ever tried to do.

5
Dark Side

Fremont's drug business operated 24 hours a day, 7 days a week during the first part of my Fremont research. Business was brisk every day, but on Friday and Saturday at dusk and throughout the evening, business was especially good. Young drug sellers were protected somewhat by the darkness cast since Fremont boys had used their 12-gauge shotguns to blast out the street light across from where Wendy's drug house stood.

Wendy's front porch was a good perch for me to watch the drug scene. Regular "Joes" as well as ex-cons in their thirties and forties walked up the grassy, broken-concrete driveway that led to the garage, went in, then came out and went back down again in a few minutes. Some customers parked around the corner on 13th; others stopped on Fremont in front of Wendy's, parking against traffic. Being on the wrong side of the street is a striking metaphor, I thought, for the kids who sold drugs from Wendy's and the folks who trekked there to buy them.

Ex-cons always looked suspicious of me sitting on the porch. Who wouldn't be suspicious of a guy with a notebook and tape recorder sitting on the front porch of a busy drug house? If drug customers hadn't been suspicious of me, I'd have been suspicious of them.

Ex-cons' prison tattoos give them away. Ink is engraved into their arms, sides of the neck, and, on hot days with their shirts off, the ink adorning their back is visible. Now and then, customers had full back tattoos showing maidens and knights riding horses. These customers were KC's Aryans, the white racists who hate everyone but each other. Working cellhouses at USP Lompoc had taught me about them. They exude evil; it drips from them like sweat, and they don't hide it.

Bobo is black, but the Aryans showed him respect. When Bobo barked, Jackie was alerted to customers. She dropped her rock pipe and walked out the kitchen door into the garage, grabbed Bobo, who was by then baring his canines, moved him one house uphill, and tied him at Plumber Mike's. Bobo protected Jackie's drug action, but his long canines and bad temperament were bad for business. There may be nothing worse to a druggie, I thought, than a vicious dog standing between him or her and a rock.

After a few weeks the rock and weed customers were used to seeing me. We'd nod, and I'd mutter, "Wha's up?" under my breath but never out loud. I didn't want to scare away Jackie and Wendy's customers, but then again I needed to show them some respect by acknowledging them. This isn't to say that I didn't feel guilty and irresponsible when I saw women with concave cheeks walk up the driveway with preschoolers dragging behind in tattered clothes.

In the best days of Fremont's drug operation, Wendy served customers all over the KC metropolitan area, east to Independence and Raytown, and southwest to the high-income homes in Johnson County, and west to KC's downtown businesses. Wendy's local drug territory extended from Fremont and 13th Street north to 16th Terrace, south to 10th Street, west to White, and east to Ewing.[1]

The Fremont area is a relatively safe drug spot. Fremont is well off the beaten path, and unless members of the KCPD have a reason to be there, police cruisers don't drive through in their pursuit to end street crime.

Wendy's customers drove up in front of the house, stopped and yelled, "Hey, heard this is the spot." One of Wendy's workers would run down the broken concrete steps that led from the porch to the street and hand the driver his or her order. Wendy claimed that she and her helpers also delivered around the Kansas City metropolitan area. If you're a smoker, this was the ideal place to reside. How much better could it be than to have a youth gang nearby and a friendly drug seller who'll deliver to your door? This was the dark side of Fremont life, the devil's paradise.

Home drug delivery is less risky to a smoker than driving roundtrip to a drug spot or a drug house miles away in some other neighborhood. With Fremont's service, smokers didn't care if the Fremont kids blasted shotguns in the middle of night, hung out on the corners, raised a little hell now and then. Even an occasional drive-by shooting was overlooked. No one called 911. Nonsmokers just kept quiet. It was safer that way.

A roll of twenties and fifties in grip changes social and material life on the street. Folding money changes everything. Ten- and 20-dollar bills were the fuel of Fremont social life. Cash pays rent and buys cars, food, clothes, girls, and parties. A pocketful of bills folded over once and tucked into a back or side pocket of jeans slung at hip level was the financial goal of Fremont's drug business.

A number of kids on Fremont sold drugs, but only Wendy's business was a gang-protected drug operation.[2] A continuous source of rocks and marijuana created a social hierarchy whose purpose was to redistribute the drugs systematically from Wendy to other Fremont kids, who resold the drugs in personal small-scale businesses.[3]

Afro called Wendy's room the weight room or the drug room; in street jargon, *weight* refers to sizable quantities of illegal drugs. Wendy bought rocks from Steele Bill, who was available full time because he rented a room across the hall from Wendy's. He bought rocked up cocaine from a supplier called the Million Dollar Man, who, folklore says, resides somewhere in the bowels of Kansas City.

Wendy said she was a "dealer," or redistributor of drugs, as well as a supervisor who handed drugs to street sellers and collected cash from them. She also was an occasional salesperson who handed drugs to customers and collected cash. As a dealer, Wendy sold quantities of rocks to two groups of Fremont boys. One group was Gordy (Rosa's brother) and Roger, and the other was Shawn, Lucky, Frank, Greenbean, and Afro. With the exception of her former lover, Afro, whom she held a grudge against, Wendy allowed these boys to sell drugs out of her house. Selling drugs out of Wendy's was safer than standing on street corners, where they would have been exposed to KCPD cruisers. Wendy took 35 percent of the boys' sales as a fee for the use of the house.

Wendy sold rocks to Chucky D too, but his main business was weed, and his weed supplier stayed off Fremont. He had a separate supplier for rocks as well.

Wendy also let Jackie into her business. Wendy joked about it and missed the irony: "A family that sells drugs together stays together." Wendy "fronted," or loaned, Jackie rocks, which she used in two ways. Jackie was a rock addict who smoked some pieces and sold others, using the cash to repay Wendy for the fronted rocks and to buy more rocks for personal use.

As a supervisor, Wendy let Fremont girls, like Cara and Janet, sell rocks and get paid. Before the rift between Wendy and Janet over their competition for Steele Bill's affection, Janet stayed at Wendy's full time and sold weed and dank.

Wendy claimed that, as a salesperson, she drove all over her wider territory (described above). Wendy's pager beeped and beeped and beeped. There was no shortage of drug customers, and there was no competition in the local Fremont area. The violent reputation of the Fremont Hustlers protected them.

On one weekend in the summer of 1995, House of Pain and Cain, along with their business partners, transformed their parents' house into a "smoke house" while their parents were out of town. The boys pulled down the window shades, and folks I'd never seen walked up, knocked, entered, and smoked whatever they wished. Late Sunday afternoon, the young entrepreneurs opened the windows and doors and aired out the house before their parents returned home.

Out of Wendy's house, weed, rocks, and dank were sold. Wendy and Chucky D told me the going prices for weed in the summer of 1995: a pound cost between $800 and $1,000; a half pound was $470; a quarter pound was $240; an ounce cost $85; a half ounce was $50; a quarter ounce was $35. Wendy and Chucky D repackaged the weed for sale. Chucky D sold ounces in two-gram lots at $10, in a so-called a dime sack (an ounce yields 14 two-gram lots). Each dime sack was a wrapped plastic bag of weed, tied off with a metal twist; it would yield four joints. He claimed that he collected $150 on an ounce, or $65 above his cost, nearly doubling his investment. If he was forced to buy, say, a half ounce, his return on investment was slightly lower, $45 to $50, depending on the quality of the weed. Rock profits were higher. Chucky D bought rocks in 8-balls (3.5 grams). Each 8-ball cost him $150, which he said he could resell for $300 to $400.

On his weed business alone, Chucky D said he could earn at least $100 a day, or $3,000 a month, and not work too hard. Wendy said she easily earned $300 an hour. Of course, they didn't pay state and federal taxes. To Chucky D and Wendy the drug business wasn't an eight-hour-a-day job.

Wendy said her best customers were the parents of the Fremont Hustlers, many of whom resided in the neighborhood. Chucky D said, "There's a plenty o' addicts for everybody to keep working." Chucky D worked only when his roll of twenties got thin. He had regular customers to serve, but that took him only a few hours a day. Chucky D said he had started selling weed at age eight and now had a good sense of what his customers wanted. He gave customers a "fat" sack, good-quality weed with few seeds and stems, and high-quality rocks, and they rewarded him with their return business. Many customers, he said, resided in public housing projects off The Paseo, so he spent time there at night, especially at the beginning of the month, when government checks arrived.

Weed and rock are profitable, but dank profits are astronomical. Formaldehyde is harder to obtain than rocks and weed. Kids who sell dank are continuously on the hunt for this chemical. Drugstore and beautician school burglaries are its best sources. Dank sellers say they sometimes find someone who attends a mortuary program at a local community college. With an adequate bribe, the student will steal embalming fluid. House of Pain told me in January 1997 that he was interested in a mortuary program at a local community college.

Dank is sold by the "dip." A cigarette is dipped into dank and smoked in 5 to 10 minutes, while the cigarette is still wet but not soggy. So-called dank sticks are sold in plastic sandwich bags. A "full dip" cigarette, from its tip to its filter, sells for $20; a half dip, for $10; a quarter dip, for $5. An ounce of formaldehyde can be purchased for $200–$300, so theoretically one ounce yields a profit of $1,000.

Dank smokers are said to be wet or danked up. Dank keeps kids high for as long as 20 hours, they say, and when they come down, a drink of water refreshes the high. Milk, kids say, brings them down. Roger and Gordy were Fremont's most avid dank smokers. Most kids said they got "too fucked up" on it. One hit off a dank stick and kids' legs weaken and bend, and they need help walking. Danked-up kids are lifeless lumps.

Remarkably, these adolescents worked well together in the drug business during its heyday on Fremont. It was more or less an egalitarian operation, in which everyone shared the common goal of making money, and they knew that fighting and especially serious violence would only cost each one of them the loss of cash. However, in some limited way, the threat of violence lurked in the background. Wendy was strong and had a reputation for violence, as Jackie did. Folklore had it that Wendy would shoot someone if that person really pissed her off, and no one wanted to anger Jackie.

During the period of my research when Wendy controlled the drug trade, Fremont's gang hierarchy, the segment of Fremont social organization devoted to the systematic control and sale of illegal substances, was raceless and genderless. Race and gender didn't influence who had the most drug customers or who earned the most money. Wendy worked well with Fremont's strongest and most violent boys, Chucky D and Afro. The fact is, when it came to earning money, the Fremont Hustlers appeared to be unselfconscious about gender or race. I told Wendy, Cara, Afro, and Chucky D on many occasions that they were raceless and genderless when it came to earning money. "Shit," said Afro, "the only mothafucka dat matters around here is money, cash."

Race had no influence over Fremont kids' casual and intimate social behavior, either. Kids hung out with the kids they liked, independent of color. Fremont boys of any color dated and slept with girls of any color. Girls or boys never told me, nor did I ever overhear, that a boy or girl had refused to date someone because of color. Race also had no obvious influence over crime partnerships. Kids who enjoyed particular kinds of crime, such as burglary and carjacking, hung out together.

In Fremont's surplus economy there were plenty of drugs and drug customers and thus lots of cash. That made life enjoyable, lowered tension, and reduced the arguments over money. As long as the cash flow was unimpeded, life was good. However, when cash diminished or resources, such as places to sleep, were in short supply, kids argued and haggled, and fights were more likely to occur. In times of shortage or group emergencies, such as the drug bust of August 1995, social cleavages opened in the blink of an eye and hostilities flared.

Where did the drug money go? I asked every kid who sold drugs how much he or she earned and what he or she did with the money. I also asked kids about their acquaintances who sold drugs, how much money those kids earned, and what they did with the money. Wendy, Cara, Angie, Chucky D, and the others said Fremont's most profitable days were the "ol' days" in the summer of 1994.

"Man," said Wendy, "we had so much mo-ney," she exaggerated the word *money* so that it oozed from her lips. "Shit, I bought stuff—clothes and forties [40-ounce bottles of malt liquor]. We all the time had forties and hotel parties. We had hotel parties with room service. We had one downtown, and I ordered room service—big platters of meat, fruit, cheese, and cakes. We had plenty of weed too," she grinned.

Talk of earning big money is simply talk as far as I could tell. No one could tell me exactly how much he or she earned, although they talked about earning a lot. In the months on Fremont over the summer of 1995, I didn't see evidence of big drug earnings. No boys or girls had new clothes; there were no new stereos; there were no new cars or even late-model used cars; there were no kids in $100 Nikes; there were no kids going to expensive restaurants; I never heard a kid say he or she gave money to a parent; and few of the young Fremont drug sellers wore gold jewelry.

Let's assume these young drug sellers did make big money. Even if each one had made $100 a day, which is a tiny amount of cash to earn for selling weed and rocks, that's about $3,000 a month. One thing's for sure: they didn't save any of it. Had Wendy saved, she could have rented an apartment after the bust, and she could have bought a car while she was earning cash. However, in the summer of 1994 when I met Wendy, which she said was the time of her biggest drug profits, she had no car and no cash to buy one. Were there big profits? If so, where did the cash go? What's the truth?[4]

In the time that I watched Fremont kids earn and spend drug money preceding the bust, I saw them engage in a subsistence drug economy, meaning that they earned just enough to meet their daily needs but little more than that. Earning more would have meant they'd have to spend more time working and less time hanging out. The balance of work and hanging time was weighted heavily toward hanging out. They sold enough drugs for food, a new tattoo, an occasional trip to a drive-in movie, sodas and candy at the QT on Truman, and that's all, with the exception of Chucky D, who also managed a monthly car payment.

Chucky D said he had a circle of drug customers just large enough to meet his daily needs. What's more, these drug sellers knew and talked about the consequences of "gettin' greedy." That meant too much drug selling to too many customers around the city would attract the KCPD. And given the attention Fremont had been getting for more than a year before my arrival, these young entrepreneurs balanced their needs against the risks of arrest and imprisonment.

Fremont's drug business, Wendy said, reached it peak over the summer of 1994, slacked off over the fall and winter, and climbed again in the spring and summer of 1995. But on August 24, 1995, the reality of the outside world crashed in when the KCPD brought helicopters and a battering ram to Fremont.

"Cops kicked in my house," Wendy said, "tore it up, ripped up our shit, tore apart the walls, and took my mom off to jail. They put Robert in a foster home. I lost everything. I lost my clothes, stereo, all my shit, my mother, and my brother. This shit ain't worth it."

The KCPD busted Wendy's drug house and arrested Jackie and Chucky D for the distribution and possession of rock cocaine and Wendy for possession of a small quantity of marijuana; in my months on the street, every kid I met had at one time or another been arrested and put on probation for marijuana possession.

When the bust came, Chucky D was staying now and then at Taffy's. He also had an apartment in Independence, but that was a long way from the action on Fremont and his customers. However, getting away from Fremont is safer for a drug dealer than staying there with all the police scrutiny.

The cops tossed everyone out of Taffy's house, shook it down, and boarded it up. Everyone who lived and stayed there, including her children, was temporarily homeless.

Afro's shanty, where he and Rosa squatted in the basement, was busted up too, because Afro had jerryrigged electricity to it. When the cops finished, Jackie's and Taffy's and Afro's looked like the set of a Tarantino film. Plywood sheets filled the windows and doors, and encircling Jackie's and Afro's residences was an eight-foot-high anchor fence. The neighborhood looked like a makeshift prison.

When the search of Taffy's turned up no drugs, her family reclaimed the house. She "really wasn't into anything," said Wendy. But Jackie owed so much money in back taxes on her house and property, the city took it. Then one night out of the blue, it burned down. She told me, "Those bastards [the KC police] sat out front of my house and laughed when my house burned down. And I know they set the fire too."

After the fire, someone used green spray paint to write the words NO TRESSPASSING [sic] on the edge of the front porch.

My initial thought was that the bust had ruined my research. As it turned out, however, the bust opened new research vistas that wouldn't have appeared without it. First, it showed what happens to a gang-protected drug-distribution hierarchy when a stable resource base (marijuana, cocaine) rapidly ends. Second, it showed the resilience of some of the social ties between kids, such as Wendy, Cara, and Cheri, and the brittleness of other ties. Third, it showed how a gang-protected drug business devolves into cliques of delinquent kids and how those cliques act as economic and social survival units.[5] Fourth, it showed that the Fremont Hustlers formed an opportunistic network of instrumental (purposeful) relations and were surely not a surrogate "family" within which marginal kids "loved" one another.[6]

The Fremont bust stopped wide-scale gang-oriented drug distribution. The drug bust didn't stop drug selling on Fremont Avenue, it didn't stop Fremont kids' drug use, nor did it stop Chucky D, now arrested and imprisoned, from involving Fremont girls in behind-the-walls drug distribution. In the end, the Fremont bust altered the nature of the social group selling the drugs, splintering the gang hierarchy into small cliques and driving these cliques farther away from street view.

The August 1995 bust had a prelude. The KCPD had long sought to end Fremont's drug operation and tried to no avail to do it in the summer of 1994, when Fremont's drug action was booming and the cops knew it. Wendy and Cara enjoyed telling me how they had outsmarted the KCPD. To be clever, the drug-crime unit had sent a "married couple" to Fremont Avenue. They rented the house two houses downhill from Wendy's, the place the Fremont boys' later used as their armory. In the house's front window, the undercover cops set up a videocamera to record the drug action on the street. Every Fremont kid knew the neighbors were undercover cops. "Shit, who those motherfuckers think they be foolin'? We just chilled." The boys, Wendy said, just moved their drug action around the corner. But Wendy had to close down for a while. With no source of income, she and Janet got straight jobs selling concessions at the Kansas City Royals' Kauffman Stadium. Wendy laughed, "I went from rocks and weed to selling cotton candy." With no action to record, the police left. Wendy's drug house then opened again.

An illegal drug business faces two strategic issues. First, it must attract customers and offer them a good product at a reasonable cost. It's a buyers' market in illegal drugs, and inferior quality weed and small rocks force buyers to search elsewhere, because there's no shortage of drug sellers. Second, the business must protect itself. That's simple, too, when boys and girls are armed with shotguns, assault rifles, and 9-millimeter handguns.

Despite good products and service and a large customer base, Fremont's gang-oriented drug business was operated by adolescents and was self-destructive. Kids are jealous of other kids' possessions. Anyone who has children knows this: if one kid gets an ice cream cone, every other kid who gets one must have exactly the same amount. The same principle operated on Fremont, but the consequences were more serious than kids bickering over the size of ice cream scoops.

Fremont's gang-oriented drug business didn't decay on jealousy alone. "After the boys started smoking rock," Wendy said, "it all got crazy and out of control." Wendy and Cara said that jealousy and irrational thinking that comes with smoking rocks led to the bust.

Between the summers of 1994 and 1995, Fremont drug sellers made a lot of money. I don't know how much they made; I wasn't there to see it. Wendy, Janet, Cara, Chucky D, and the others said they simply don't know how much they earned because they spent it so fast. In any case, money wasn't distributed equally among drug sellers; some earned more than others. And kids who weren't in the drug business were resentful of those who were. "Wantin' too much is the problem," proclaims Wendy. "People wantin' what everybody has. These mothafuckas fight over customers and the percentage of money they put in to buy drugs. It's all fucked up."

Wendy, Cara, Afro, Joanne, and others too are convinced that a Fremont boy cut a deal with the KCPD to bust Wendy's drug house and Chucky D, Fremont's most successful drug sellers. Wendy talked about the snitch: "He was fucking jealous of all the money we was makin'. Bitch [snitch] couldn't make no money, so he fucked the rest of us. Man, wait'll Chucky gets out."

"When the cops came in," Cara said, "Chucky knew the dude was undercover. He felt it but sold to him anyways, 'cause he wanted the money. When you gots money you don' wanna lose it. When you poor you don' give a fuck."

However it happened, the snitch—some say it was Angie's boyfriend, Wayne—walked an undercover drug detective into Fremont and vouched for him. The cop made repeated drug buys at Wendy's and from Chucky D. In return, said Wendy, the gang and drug detectives didn't pester the drug-selling snitch on the street. With Wendy's drug house closed and Chucky D out of the way, the snitch thought that he would get all Wendy's and Chucky D's customers, according to Cara and Wendy.

Wendy said she remembers seeing the undercover cop, and she said she cautioned others. "I told 'em, 'We don' know him. What's he doin' up here? Stay away,' but they wouldn't listen."

The detective bought rocks from Jackie and Chucky D. Wendy said she was lucky. She got busted for the possession of marijuana. She received probation and 100 hours of community service.

"Chucky's a dumb mothafucka," said Cara, annoyed at him. "He don't give a shit. He thinks he never be caught. Now look at 'im."

The bust changed the direction of kids' lives. Chucky D was sent to Cherry. Cara, Wendy, and Cheri told me they worked for nearly a week full-time to sell all his and their own possessions, including radios, Walkmans, stereos, and Chucky D's gold jewelry—which serve as a drug seller's bank account—to get the $2,000 bail. Chucky D was released and stayed on the street until his November 1995 court date, at which time he was imprisoned on a parole violation as well as convicted of a new criminal charge, possession and distribution of cocaine.

Cara returned to Cathy's apartment on Gladstone, off The Ave. Wendy disappeared. Cara and Cheri didn't know where she was staying most of the time. Immediately after the bust, Wendy stayed for two weeks with Smoker Mary, whose house was around the corner from Wendy's. Then she spent four months with a woman in the neighborhood, to whom she paid $100 a month rent. That was too expensive and she needed a cheaper place. From January to May 1996 Wendy roomed with Angie Lang, who Wendy said was "one o' Chucky's 'ho'es" and a shoplifter.

After the bust Jackie and her son, Robert, were homeless and off in different directions. Robert went into foster care. Jackie went to Cherry for two weeks and was placed on probation and ordered to attend a year-long substance abuse and counseling program. On the street again, Jackie stayed with some folks near Fremont. Soon afterward, Wendy said, Jackie "got fucked up" (used drugs), failed a compulsory urinalysis, and went back to jail for a few days. Released again, she moved in with a companion in downtown KC and worked a series of hourly wage jobs. Jackie's probation and substance abuse program lasted about a year. I didn't see her between August 1995 and the summer of 1996.

Kids who had parents on Fremont, such as House of Pain and Cain and a few others near Taffy's, stayed on Fremont and sold drugs in a small way. Afro and Rosa, pregnant with her first child by now, rented a spot on the floor from Joanne. Joanne rented a house across the street from Taffy's.

Other kids who were estranged from parents and had nowhere to stay except Wendy's were compelled to find somewhere else after the bust. Many hardcore kids were siblings and cousins, and they retreated to the home of an aunt or a grandmother. Some girls, Poodle/Angie, for one, was absolutely alone. Poodle and her mother hated each other, said Poodle, and she couldn't go home.

Poodle and Wayne lived together; over the months preceding the bust, Poodle didn't give him even a glance. They had dated for a while years earlier, but that relationship had ended. Now Wayne was convenient, but within six months, he was beating Poodle. Cara said she heard from Taffy that Wayne had beaten Poodle's legs with a two-by-four because he thought she was seeing another boy.

I saw Poodle the last time in March 1996. She was hooking and selling dope. Wayne had a job with the highway department, according to the Fremont kids who saw Poodle or heard about her through the grapevine that ends at Taffy's. Cara told me, by mid-1996, Poodle was pregnant, had an eight-dollar-a-month apartment in HUD housing in Independence, was unemployed and collecting government checks, and was staying alone.

While I don't have police statistics to prove it, crime on Fremont diminished after the bust, at least to my eye. Northeast, La Familia, and Southside didn't drive down Fremont challenging the boys, because Fremont kids had dispersed and weren't concentrated at Fremont and 13th. There were occasional shootings, but those weren't over gang business; they were motivated by personal drug "rip-offs."

Rip-off violence happens when someone rips off a supplier by shorting him on cash payments for drugs or by not paying him at all. In such a case, a supplier takes a pound of flesh. House of Pain and Cain allegedly ripped off Duck, Afro's brother, over dank. Duck said he would kill them; it was an idle threat.

House of Pain's house was shot up by La Familia in the fall of 1996, after a drug rip-off. Apparently, House of Pain's brother Cain hadn't paid the debt on drugs he'd been fronted. Angry La Familia members came to collect.

Afro and Duck ripped off a notoriously violent trio of brothers from southside KC. They hunted Afro and Duck to kill them, but Afro and Duck wisely hid away. The southside brothers grabbed Afro and Duck's younger brother and nearly beat him to death on Fremont.

The sight of Wendy's burned-out house signaled the end of the social life there. I was troubled about the increased uncertainty of basic survival that the bust had suddenly infused into these kids' lives. Wendy's drug house had been a stable social, as well as a relatively safe, venue for a lot of kids. That spot had also provided these kids with a regular source of income. The illegality of the Fremont kids' drug trade didn't bother me. I didn't see any other realistic opportunities for these kids to obtain constant income and social stability. No federal, state, or local government officials ever walked down Fremont and asked these kids if they wanted jobs or needed help of any kind. These kids' lives after the bust show just how difficult it has been for them to earn money and remain stable. I asked myself, Where would these kids go now? With whom would this kid and that kid stay? How would these kids earn enough income to survive?

KC cops acted as law enforcement officers. But over the years of pursuing Fremont kids, the KCPD could have played a softer, more proactive role and could have seen to it that social service agents were brought there to help these teenagers, who were legally minors living in a dangerous environment.

The KCPD busted the drug house and locked up Chucky D. Doing those things intervened in some gang crime and prevented some. Locking up Chucky D, a ticking bomb of social destruction, saved the lives of some of the people who now walk the streets only because Chucky D is behind prison walls. But busting and closing the Fremont drug house did more than end the wide-scale, gang-oriented drug distribution. Wendy's was more than a place to buy drugs. It was Fremont kids' safe place. Everyone who stays on the street needs a safe place protected by people they know. It may seem unsound to say that a drug house can be a safe place; however, compared with the other options these kids had at that time, Wendy's drug house was as safe as life could be for them.

The bust showed the Fremont kids and me the point-blank reality of street-level drug selling, and the effect of the bust lingered for a while. Kids hanging on Fremont cooled the drug action over the 1995–96 winter, and police attention to Fremont waned too. In the spring of 1996 Fremont was relaxed, kids were less paranoid, and slowly during that season Afro's drug business grew. By the summer of 1996, there was drug action again on Fremont. The street has a very short memory.

Over the summer of 1996, I visited Fremont regularly and chatted with whomever was around. On one warm and sunny Saturday afternoon in June, I stopped by Joanne's. Rosa sat on the three-cushioned cloth couch on one side of the living room; an old overstuffed chair sat in a corner of the room. A 21-inch color television was the room's center of attention. What should have been used as a dining room was empty, except for a few toys scattered on the floor. Charlene, Joanne and Chucky D's daughter, now nearly two, was wandering from room to room. She stayed inside; inside is safer when drug selling is outside.

Afro sat on the floor in front of the television watching the A&E (Arts and Entertainment) channel's program on gangs, drugs, and violence. I walked in just as urban cops were arresting gang kids.

"Hey, 'Fro, look familiar?" I joked.

"Mark, try some o' dis."

A pile of fine white powder lay on the front cover of a *Romance* magazine. This issue had stories on love and sex and child abuse. A balloon with the top cut off, a pair of nail clippers, and a soda straw were next to the powder.

"What's this, coke?" I asked.

"Nah, somefin' new."

"Called what?"

"Ghost rider, mothafucka, ghost rider."

"What is it? Do you inject it, snort it, what?" I asked.

"I don' know, jus' got it."

"From where?" I asked.

"They been sellin' it at strip joints. Cheap but goood," he said, smiling. "Do some, man, do some," he urged.

"Nah, not me, 'Fro. I don't do drugs."

"Bullshit, I seen ya smoking blunts and dank last summer."

"Well, you saw wrong, 'Fro."

"Hey, bitch." Afro called Joanne.

"Fuck you, 'Fro, don't call me bitch in front of da kid."

"Fuck you, get yo' ass over here 'fore I smack ya," he insisted. "Try dis shit."

Joanne dipped her finger into the white powder and sucked on it. She paused. "Damn, my lips are numb, my tongue's numb, and I cayn't feel the top of my mouth." She walked away.

"You goin' down ta Cherry?" Afro asked.

Joanne turned and nodded. Chucky D had been transferred to Cherry to attend a sentencing hearing. When I walked into Joanne's, she had been on the phone with Chucky D, who was trying to coax her into smuggling weed to him that day during a contact visit. Joanne listened to Chucky D, nodded, spoke in one- and two-word responses, and walked out of the house, leaving Charlene with Rosa and Afro.

"Is she gonna do it?" I asked Afro.

"Gotta do whatcha gotta do," he said.

"How's the rock bidness, 'Fro?" I asked.

He reached for Rosa's purse, opened it, stuck his hand inside, pulled out a folded piece of lined notebook paper, and opened the folds. He showed me rocks of all prices, fifties, thirties, twenties, and tens.

"Hey, come wid me. I wanna show ya somefin'," said Afro.

We walked down the center of Fremont toward the corner of 13th and turned left toward Plumber Mike's house, on the northwest corner. Afro had been tending a marijuana field, a small and manageable one next to Plumber Mike's. Afro had a nice operation. He germinated seeds in a makeshift minigreenhouse made of a plastic-domed cake container, the kind used to protect a two-layer cake lathered with gooey icing. Afro moistened paper towels, lined the bottom tray, laid seeds there, covered it with the plastic dome, and tucked the greenhouse away in a warm spot till he could plant the germinated seeds.[7]

"Hey, 'Fro, you got a green thumb, man," I teased. He smiled. "Careful," I warned, "the cops come by here and your ass is in jail."

"Hey, I don' know who did dis. Ain' *my* shit." Afro tried to be clever.

Afro's marijuana plants were mixed in among high weeds well back from Fremont. They weren't visible from the street, and even if they had been, no one on Fremont would have messed with Afro's plants. By this time, few kids in other neighborhoods even bothered driving down Fremont looking for some action. Afro's plants were safe. Anyway, his reputation, along with an anchor fence, protected the garden. What's more, there's so much marijuana available that getting killed over a plant or two is seen by kids like Cara as "jus' fuckin' dumb."

Afro parked an old car on the east side of Plumber Mike's house. House of Pain kept his junker up there too. Afro covered his car with a heavy tarpolin, protecting it as if it were a new Beemer. I had no idea if the car would start; neither did Afro. Owning it was the point.

Before he started work in the garden on this hot summer day, he pulled back the tarp and opened the driver's side door and blasted music for the entire neighborhood's enjoyment. Kids congregated. On days when Cara joined me and Afro toiled in his patch of increasingly tall and wide plants, the music played and Cara would smile and sing along, dance in the dirt, and take long drags on a joint.

Afro often invited me to buy into his drug business. I was beginning to think Wendy and Cara were right: maybe he was a snitch, too.

"Got a grand?" he asked with a glint in his eye.

"Hey, 'Fro, I'm a college professor, who don't have that kinda money. You guys got that kinda money. What would ya do with my money if ya had it?"

"Turn it over in two, three days into three grand. A grand into three." He paused a moment. "See, if ya had some real money, we buy a kilo, triple it in fi' days. Thirty-five [thousand] getcha 100 [thousand] by da en' o' da week." He smiled.

It's illegal to sell rock cocaine. But you'd never know it on Fremont. Afro's offer was tempting. By one year after the bust, rocks on Fremont were again as easily available as McDonald's french fries. No one on Fremont gives rock, weed, or dank a second thought. Illegal drugs are sold in the middle of the street, in the middle of the day, every day of every week. On the street the line between what's safe and legal and what's dangerous and illegal gets fuzzy. And if the line between legal and illegal behavior is fuzzy to me, it must be invisible to Fremont kids.

When the Fremont drug house was busted and arrests were made, no drug customers hidden behind closed doors in the Fremont area, Overland Park, Independence, Raytown, and downtown KC businesses were handcuffed. Only Jackie and Chucky D went to jail. Only Jackie's, Taffy's, and Afro's houses were rammed and ransacked. These are the poorest KC citizens, the least capable of defending themselves, and the most likely to face the severest penalties for making a buck.

Is there something wrong with the scene? I thought. The folks with money who buy Afro's, Chucky D's, Wendy's, and Jackie's rocks walk away untouched, perhaps only to get a speeding ticket by KC's finest. Busting Wendy's drug operation cost taxpayers a bundle of cash, and taxpayers got little for their money. Rocks are still sold, citizens still buy them, and now Missouri taxpayers invest in the imprisonment of Chucky D, an investment that generally brings relatively little return.

Early one afternoon at Joanne's, I spoke to him on the phone. He told me he had finished his GED. In the jaded mood I was in by then, I thought, Great, now Fremont will have a better-educated drug seller. Maybe I should have taken that thought as a sign to go home. I didn't; instead, I had already become involved with the household that had replaced Wendy's as Fremont's main chill spot and drug house.

6
Misery

By the time social life stabilized after the bust, the humid summer of 1995 had been replaced by the crisp air of the 1995–96 football season. Kansas City loves Chiefs football, and the town was alive and bubbling with the excitement. On Fremont, leafy trees towered over small, two-story, wood frame houses and endowed the street with a feeling of calmness and serenity. It was a facade.

Over the early fall of 1995, the owner of the QT on Truman, the place where Wendy had harangued a young girl walking across the street, purchased and tidied the abandoned shack two houses downhill from Wendy's. It was the house the Fremont boys had used as an arsenal. Teresa and two of her three children moved into the shanty in December 1995 and stayed there through July 1996.

Teresa's house replaced Wendy's as Fremont's main chill spot, although her house didn't have the intense drug and social action Wendy's had had. Cara and Wendy drifted off after the bust, but most of Fremont's hardcore stayed on Fremont and hung out at Teresa's. House of Pain, Cain, Lucky, Wayne, Taco, Steele Bill, Afro, Poodle Bitch, Netta (one of Teresa's younger sisters), Chica Bitch, Christina, Rosa, and others came and went with more freedom than they had had at Wendy's with Jackie controlling the front door. At Teresa's there were no responsible adults to be found anywhere.

Cara's temporary residence at Wendy's had been lost with the bust, and she moved back into Cathy's duplex on Gladstone. She stayed there until January 1996, when she rented an apartment at 5403 Smart, in Northeast Gangsta territory, just a few blocks north of The Ave. When Cara wanted to join me, I'd pick her up and we'd drive to Fremont.

Cara and I walked up the dozen broken-concrete steps leading to Teresa's front door. As we walked she turned her head slightly to the left, gazing uphill, the direction from which Northeast, La Familia, and Southside

86

came to harass Fremont. Cara's head twist and slight paranoia were old habits.

Cara banged at the door with the back of her hand. The painted-over doorbell was dead.

"Who's it?" shouted someone from behind the locked, thin, and unpainted wooden door. This is the customary greeting. Only a fool opens a front door without verifying who's standing on the outside. Bust paranoia was still high.

"Cara . . . and Mark."

"Who?"

"Mark . . . ya know, the writer."

An arm pushed back the heavy wool blanket covering the two sash windows on the left of the front door. Hair, a forehead, and eyes appeared in the space between the blanket and the window. I heard the door unlock. We walked in.

In the summer of 1995 I had prowled around this house. It was then piled high with filthy broken furniture and rusted metal chairs. In the spot I stood now, a box of hollow-point .22 bullets with five missing had sat on top of a torn, stained mattress. Since then the owner had cleaned out the garbage and installed a gray-striped industrial carpet.

The scene I walked into this day was distorted and odd and had a surreal quality to it. What my eyes saw I wanted to be a staged drama, not real life being played out in front me.

In the middle of the floor was Kevin, thin and shirtless, wearing unbuttoned and unzipped jeans; his legs were splayed into a V-shape, his feet covered by off-white cotton socks with soiled bottoms. Standing above him was Teresa, 100 pounds overweight, with hair unwashed, uncombed, and matted. Her pouching stomach sagged toward the floor and was exaggerated by tight jeans slicing through her midriff, dividing her obesity into upper and lower waves of blubber.

"Fuck *that*," Teresa hurled insults into the black receiver of the telephone as if to intimidate a phone company representative with her verbal ferocity and skills at hurling insults.

Teresa shouted insults into the phone as Kevin shouted insults to her, which she was supposed to shout into the phone. Teresa also shouted insults at Kevin, he shouted some at her, and in an irrational chorus of anger and obscenity they both shouted threats of law suits into the telephone receiver for the benefit of some unknown, underpaid telephone worker.

"Fuck that, fuck YOU." Teresa threw the receiver to the floor and cursed at Kevin.

"Will somebody gim me a fuckin' cigarette? My nerves are shot. I need a fuckin' cigarette," she barked. A mouth like that, I thought, doesn't need a phone.

The argument with the phone company was about who had turned on their phone. Teresa claimed someone had turned on the phone in the house and used Kevin's name to do it, then made lots of long-distance calls they now couldn't pay for. Instead of working out a payment plan, Kevin and Teresa used the "let's deny it and threaten them" manipulation, a common technique on Fremont, without the slightest idea that the phone company simply flips a switch and zaps their phone service.

"Hi, Amy," Cara greeted Teresa's four-year-old.

Amy was adorable. The top of her head hit me about midthigh; I'm five-seven. Her shoulder-length light brown hair felt like angel hair. During the telephone war, Amy and Victoria, known as RoniRo, two years Amy's junior, wandered about the living room, stopping now and then, looking up to listen. The few old dirty plastic toys in the corner of the room didn't interest them.

There were no children's books anywhere, no drawing pads, no crayons. A small TV sat atop a round table near the front door. It showed fuzzy images. No "Sesame Street" in this house; for that matter, not even any TV violence. But who needs TV violence and actors pretending to be criminals and drug dealers? Amy and RoniRo had the real deal; the living room was full of them. Their house, I thought, should carry the ratings V (violence), AL (adult language), and S (sex).

Amy held a ragged doll close to her chest. "I haven't seen you in a long time. You're getting soooo biiiig," said Cara. "You remember me, don'chu?" Cara asked, crouching to be face to face with Amy.

"Cara-mel," murmured Amy.

Kneeling on her right knee, Cara looked upset and reached toward Amy. "Who did this to you, Sweetie?" Cara took her finger and pointed to Amy's blackened eye and forehead but didn't touch her bruises.

Teresa and Kevin were still screaming obscenities at one another, Teresa blaming Kevin for the phone bill, Kevin howling back at her and deflecting blame onto the phone company.

The fight shifted in focus. Teresa harangued Kevin for being with other women and claimed that it was one of his "bitch 'ho'es" who had set up the phone service she now had to pay for.

Amy pulled away from Cara, squeezing her doll as if it could protect her from the question Cara asked over and over.

"Which motherfucker did this to you?" Cara asked quietly. Amy stood still, staring at Cara's face. "You can tell Cara-mel," Cara said in a kind mother's voice.

Amy's head dropped, her chin pulled back toward her chest. Standing up and turning toward me, Cara exclaimed, "Some one of these sick mothafuckers up in here beat her young ass."

She turned back toward Amy and knelt again. "That's a nice dolly, Amy. What's the dolly's name?" Amy gave no response.

Teresa's screaming paused, the house quieted down. She looked at Cara and me. Self-consciousness crossed her face. "She fell down some steps in the house," Teresa said.

I didn't know Teresa had overheard Cara's questioning of Amy. I looked around. There were no steps in the house, no basement, no upstairs.

Teresa quickly turned back to Kevin and pursued her verbal assault on him and his unnamed whores and anyone else close by.

"Fell, my fuckin' ass," Cara noted. She shook her head in disgust. "Let's get the fuck outta here. These motherfuckers is sick bitches," she said, speaking into my ear. We walked out.

As we descended the concrete steps to the street, we could still hear Teresa continuing her harangue about the telephone company, Kevin's 'ho'es, and her unrequited love for him. It would be easier to love a poison ivy plant, I thought, than show Teresa affection.

A few days later in the midafternoon, I returned by myself to Fremont and drove slowly downhill. Cara didn't like the chaos of Teresa's; at the time, I was drawn to it like a moth to a light. Coasting along, I remembered the places and the people on Fremont in the summer 1995. No matter how dirty and chaotic it was then, I thought, it was saner than Teresa's.

Despite the cold rain, I had the driver's-side window open with my head sticking out. I spotted Afro standing on Teresa's front porch, talking to Duck, whose four-door black car sat parked at the curb. Afro yelled, "Whas' up?" and lifted his arm, motioning for me to come in. This was the first time Afro had ever made a gesture to bring me closer to him. He usually tolerated me and didn't say much when I was around him.

I parked on the other side of the street, walked through the drizzle, and greeted Afro and Duck, standing under the roof of the front porch. They were gazing over the street and talking about drugs.

"Yo, 'Fro. Wha's up, Duck?" I said.

"Wha's up?" Duck responded.

Inside the house I greeted Teresa and Kevin, Amy and RoniRo, and Rosa. Lucky, Cain, House of Pain, and Taco were there too. We chatted, I blended in, and folks resumed what they had been doing.

I walked into the kitchen. Heavy black garbage bags were tacked up over the windows in the filthy kitchen. The refrigerator was empty; the stove top was littered with a grease-encrusted cast-iron frying pan and an aluminum pot. The sink was filled halfway with plastic dishes covered with dried food and take-out food containers. Cockroaches crawled everywhere.

It was as disgusting as it had been when I was there earlier with Cara. Why would it be any different? I asked myself.

Afro and Rosa were staying at Teresa's. Afro paid her $20 a week to rent a bedroom. Rosa was pregnant with her first child. One bedroom was rented to Afro and Rosa; the second was used by Teresa and Kevin; Amy and RoniRo slept in the dining room on two thin and bowed single mattresses covered by dirty thin blankets.

Rosa was showing her pregnancy. It scared me to think of Afro as the father of anything human. We've already seen that Afro shot and killed another Fremont Hustler, Taz, which the police ruled accidental. Some Fremont kids said that Afro also killed one of Rosa's brothers; others said he was implicated in the killing. In either case, this killing had earned Afro a spot on KC's Most Wanted List. Teresa and Rosa's family had turned in Afro for a $1,000 reward, but there wasn't enough evidence to prosecute. Taz's brother told me that Afro "straight out" killed Taz, shot him in the head with a handgun, then said it was an accidental shooting. The KC police investigated and ruled it accidental. Afro remained on the street. Many hardcore Fremont kids say Afro was released because he is a snitch, but they don't say it loudly. "Why else would the cops let him stay out here, selling dope? Shiyt," said Wendy. "Don' trust 'im."

Teresa was 28 when I met her on Fremont. She said she'd been "married" once, to a man who now lived with another woman. Married can mean a lot of things on the street.

Teresa and her two sisters, Donna and Netta, had been reared in the Fremont neighborhood. They have a brother, the youngest sibling, who, in his late teenage years, was involved in a drug and murder case and was prosecuted in federal court on drug charges.

Amy and RoniRo have an elder brother, Jeffrey. He's a nice little fellow if you like foul-mouthed, cigarette-smoking, highly aggressive 11-year-olds. He wore his hat brim turned to one side, sagged his pants, and tried to be cool. The youngster looked odd and awkward trying to blend in with real-life young gangsters who didn't wear hats and saggy pants. Jeffrey didn't talk to his mother, Teresa didn't talk to him, except to tell him to watch his mouth after he spoke the word *mothafucka*.

Over the summer of 1995, I had seen him hanging around Wendy's, but I didn't know much about him. Kids said he was Netta's brother, but that's all. Jeffrey picked on Robert and bragged about "kickin' that little fucker's ass."

Jeffrey stayed with Donna. Teresa said she doesn't want him around "the shit" on Fremont. Donna is a heroin addict, sucks on the rock pipe, and has an explosive temper. In early 1996, the last time I saw her, she was pregnant. The thought of Donna being a mother seemed as horrifying to me as Ted Bundy being the maintenance man in a college sorority house.

Netta, the youngest sister, was Poodle Bitch's closest companion at the time of my Fremont research. She and Poodle dressed up, used lots of make-up, and wore provocative clothing. On weekends they'd stop by Teresa's, chat, and smoke a joint before joining a party somewhere in the city. In carefully arranged, though oddly stiff, hairdos, tight and short clothing, and sufficient facial makeup to coat a two-story house, these girls thought they were glamorous. Amy and RoniRo's granddad, the father of Teresa, Donna, and Netta, is an alcoholic. One Saturday afternoon in February 1996, Donna walked in with an old withered man tagging behind. I thought at first that Donna was bringing a drug customer, but this man's face gave him away as a heavy drinker and smoker. No one in the room reacted to him. Their lack of response to him told me everyone knew him. He leaned against the wall by the front door and was silent. Amy and RoniRo kept their distance from him.

"Who's the old guy?" I asked Jeffrey, who sat near me.

"That's my granddad," he said.

Donna was irascible and blasted into angry tirades at the drop of a hat. One day she was furious at Teresa for letting Afro slide with $20 rent.

"You let that mothafucker stay in here for $20 a week. He's fuckin' you. He earns money; take what's coming to ya. Where can he get a room for $20 a week?" she screamed at Teresa. Then she yelled at Afro, "You motherfucker, pay her more money. She's pregnant, you bastard. You're fucking her."

"Hey, bitch, I pay what she ask for. Rosa suppose to pay too, but she ain't. Get money from her," said Afro, defending himself.

Once Donna harangued Teresa for letting me hang out; she told Teresa that I'd report her to child welfare, and Teresa would have her children taken away. That was a thought I had many times.

Over the summer of 1995, I saw Donna a few times, but she didn't say much. I didn't approach her. Her face usually read, "Stay the fuck away from me, you bastard." It's hard to create rapport with an angry, drug-addicted person, and it wasn't worth the trouble.

Kevin is the son of a rock cocaine addict who relinquished her parental rights to him when he was a boy. Placed in dozens of foster homes, Kevin kept running. "Man, I couldn' do that, live in those place, so I kept runnin' away. Social services got so tired of me, they gave up too."

When I met Kevin the first time he was living with a man in his midtwenties in a small house in Kansas, a few miles across the Missouri state line. I visited the house and saw Kevin's chubby male lover.

Kevin busied himself with female lovers and male lovers too, and he sold his sexual services as a gigolo to middle-aged women. His love affairs drove Teresa nuts. He once had a lover Teresa called "the fat bitch." How ironic, I thought. Kevin explained his relationship to the fat bitch in front of Amy and RoniRo and the rest of us in the room. "All I did was take out my dick, and she sucked it. It was nothing." Teresa swelled with anger.

Teresa's relationship with Kevin was like an addiction. Nothing he did and said was ever sufficient to satisfy her thirst for love and security. She questioned every word he said, wanted to know where he was and with whom whenever he was out of her line of sight.

Kevin used Teresa's house as a place to stay if he had no other place better, and he used her to have sex. In Teresa's endless quest to satisfy Kevin, she let him do anything to her, anywhere he wanted to do it.

One afternoon with the house full of Fremont kids and with Amy and RoniRo wandering about the place bored, Kevin pushed Teresa onto her back on the couch, climbed on top of her, sucked her neck until a hickey appeared, and "dry humped" her. Amy and RoniRo watched Kevin lie between their mommie's bulging thighs, kiss her mouth and neck, and tell her that she's a "good fuck."

We all watched Kevin dry hump Teresa, who laughed and giggled as a teenage girl might on her first date. Afro screamed, "Who got the best pussy on Fremont?"

"Don' talk about my body in public, niggah," quipped Teresa.

Kevin once threatened to leave Teresa unless she bought him something. In this case, the "something" he wanted was a car. Teresa paid for it with WIC (special supplemental Food Program for Women, Infants and Children) and disability checks she received for what appeared to be some trumped-up medical problems she said kept her from working.

Even Steele Bill was outraged by her behavior. "She used her kids' welfare checks to buy him a car, fucking crazy bitch. They don't have no food up in there for those kids, neither. They live dirty, real dirty."

Kevin is a thief, and neighborhoods like Fremont need thieves.

"I steal stuff," he told me.

"What kind of stuff?"

"Anything I can sell."

"Like what?"

"Anything you can get out of a house. TV, stereos, jewelry, drugs."

"Anything else?"

"What do you mean?"

"I mean what else do you steal? Do you break into businesses too? Steal cars?"

Kevin paused.

"Sure you not the cops?"

"Look around, Kevin. Ask anyone in the room." Afro, Rosa, House of Pain, Lucky, and others were there. "He's cool," nodded House of Pain. Kevin continued his tale.

"All over Kansas City there's these rings of guys who steal shit and sell to the gangs. You know, gangs need guns for a drive-by; they buy them guns from me. They need a van for something—a drive-by or some shit like that—I steal it, sell it to 'em."

"Ever been busted?" I asked.

"No, not yet. Ain't gonna get busted now, am I?"

In early 1996 Teresa was pregnant with her fourth child. Kevin was the father and 18 at the time. Expecting a baby Kevin had fathered made Teresa even crazier than usual, because, she said, she knew in her heart that Kevin would leave her. Some loss, I thought.

Teresa's pregnancy bothered me a lot. Kevin, like Afro, shouldn't be the father of anything human. Even Fremont kids know Kevin is, as Steele Bill said, "a fucking freak." Bringing an infant into the mess of Teresa's life would be awful.

Teresa's child care is equivalent to a lawn care service that sends a stranger to your house to feed the grass and drive off. That's what Teresa does: she pays attention to Amy and RoniRo only when they're screaming or when a Fremont kid says the girls are in dire need of something.

There's no food in the house, ever, so when the kids eat, it's always junk food from the QT on Truman, Hardee's, McDonald's, or Texas Tom's on The Ave. Texas Tom's is a favorite among Fremont and Northeast kids. I've spent a small fortune there buying cheeseburgers, Italian sandwiches, soda, ice cream. This place is always filthy; the food is low quality and always full of grease. Eating at Tom's is like eating in a low-quality prison dining hall. Smoke fills the place and creates a haze, and no one ever cleans the tables. Oh, and there are flies, lots of flies. It's here where Teresa buys food for Amy and RoniRo.

When Amy and her sister get rowdy, as preschoolers do, Teresa smacks them or asks someone else to hit them, or she tells them, "The cops'll getcha. They'll come in here and arrest ya and take ya to jail, and you'll never see me again. So shut the fuck up."

Feeding Amy and RoniRo was always the priority item on my "must do" list. I couldn't sit and watch Amy and RoniRo eat a breakfast of yesterday's leftover french fries or a McDonald's cheeseburger. I bought food in clean restaurants and offered to take Teresa grocery shopping, but she resisted. Instead of food, she wanted me to give her cash for groceries, and she even wanted the cash I was about to spend on restaurant food for Amy and RoniRo. The cash would have become drugs and gifts for Kevin. I never gave her cash.

I also lectured Teresa about prenatal care, but she never listened, nor did she seek any.

One cold, dark, rainy winter afternoon in late February 1996, I walked outside Teresa's house to escape the cigarette and joint smoke and to clear my ears of the screaming and irrationality all around. I felt horrible. I stood outside, urinating against the side of Teresa's house. The toilet in the house was filthy, filled with feces and urine that no one ever flushed away; it reminded me of public toilets in markets in central Mexico. How can a mother let her children near such filth? I have no idea where or if Teresa bathed the girls.

These sights and sounds were transformed into physical and emotional pain inside me. My chest ached. I couldn't sleep. I'd lie down and close my eyes, and my brain would replay scenes in which Amy and RoniRo were surrounded by teenagers yelling, "fuck you, bitch," "motherfuckin' cocksucker," "stank bitch, fuck you," "gimme a hit off dat, bitch." Many times I wanted to call child welfare. I debated with myself for months about making such a call, but in the end I knew child welfare would do nothing good for those girls. Given the irrationality in Teresa, she might blame the girls and hurt them.

At the end of the winter of 1995–96, Teresa said she and the girls and Kevin were moving in with her mother. They couldn't pay the rent. That's no surprise, with all Teresa's checks and cash going to buy Kevin gifts. Moving into an apartment, staying as long as possible before being evicted, and then moving out is why Teresa has had so many addresses.

I visited her mother's house once. She, Kevin, the girls, and I drove five miles east of Fremont on The Ave and wove our way through tiny wood houses, trailers, and junk yards to find her mother's house empty.

We had left Teresa's house at dinner time, and by the time we had driven around and found Teresa's mother's house, the girls were hungry, whiny, and irritable. As the girls grew agitated, so did Kevin, and he expressed his discontent with silence. The quieter he grew, the more irritated Teresa became with the children.

"Cops are gonna get you, you little shit," Teresa barked at Amy. "Now sit still or I'll tell Mark to drop you off out here, and then someone'll pick you up, and you'll never see me again. Now sit still," she screamed. My head ached.

"Are you OK, Kevin, you feeling OK?" she muttered in a quiet voice. Her mood quickly changed. "I know, I bet you're thinking about that fuckin' whore you were with. That's it, that fuckin' whore. Are you thinking about that fuckin' whore? I'll kick her fuckin' ass. I'll beat that bitch if you ever see her again. Do you love me, Kevin, do you love me, not that fuckin' bitch?"

"Yeah, I love you," he said with the passion of a fisherman buying worms at a bait shop.

"You sure you love me? I know you fucked that whore, and you know I know you fucked her."

Amy and RoniRo sat quietly and listened.

"I didn't fuck her, I told you," Kevin insisted.

"Why you lying to me, Kevin? I know you fucked her. She called me and told me you fucked her, and you fucked her more than once, didn't you? Do you love me, Kevin?"

To tell the truth, I couldn't stand much more of this bizarre psychodrama. I especially disliked Teresa's terrifying the girls and including me in her unconscionable plot against her children. As she was drawn into her own anger about Kevin, she screamed more and more at the girls, threatening them again and slapping RoniRo. The little girl sobbed.

No one, I thought to myself, would believe the horror of this scene. Why do we allow women like Teresa to have children? Why do we arrest teenagers for selling rocks and weed and allow Teresa to terrorize her daughters? There's a sickness in our land, and I had no direct way of resolving it.[1]

"Look," I said, "it's past their dinner time. Let's get some food." I knew the girls were hungry and, if they ate, they'd calm down.

"Food? I don't have no money," said Teresa.

"I have money. Where do you want to eat?"

Teresa and Kevin remained silent. I asked the girls if they were hungry and what kind of food they liked. Amy said she liked chicken. Teresa suggested a Popeye's Chicken on The Ave, which wasn't too far from where Cara was now staying on Smart.

I pulled into the parking lot, went inside, and bought dozens of pieces of chicken. I got a special deal. It was near closing time and a nice counter girl gave me all the chicken they had for sale, because they'd just throw it away anyway. Amy made a special request for mashed potatoes and gravy. I bought her a quart container full of it.

We drove to Fremont with bags full of food. Inside Teresa's house, the girls took small bites of food, which engendered more screaming from Teresa and threats of beatings from Kevin. "You're not eating all your food. You wasted McDonald's at lunch, now you're going to waste this," growled Kevin.

Rosa and Afro helped themselves to chicken and biscuits. Rosa listened, her belly swollen with Afro's child. This young mother-to-be had an attitude about child rearing which gave me a headache. When Amy or RoniRo were close to me and playing and crawling on my lap, Rosa would admonish me in front of the preschoolers, "Don't spoil them kids. I hate them kids. They waste food. They can starve. They just spoiled little bitches."

I once asked Teresa about birth control. "Why" I asked, "don't you use the pill?" She said, "I can't swallow pills." I asked Kevin about condoms. "I ain't never gonna use a rubber 'cause you don't use 'em with the one you love." He smiled at Teresa. Kevin needs to be castrated, I thought.

In the midsummer of 1996, Teresa and her girls moved off Fremont, and in late 1996 moved back to the neighborhood to an apartment on Bennington. I wouldn't go there. I couldn't stomach Teresa and Kevin anymore. I dislike them so much that I talked to Cara about urging Chucky D to do to Teresa and Kevin what they had done to the little girls—terrorize and beat them.

In early 1997 Teresa gave birth to baby Kevin. "That place is dank, man," commented Steele Bill about the Bennington apartment. "It's dirty up in there, you know. The baby was sick too. Teresa didn't do nothing for the kid for weeks. It was sick with the flu, wasn't eating or nothing. Man, we made her take it to the hospital.

"Kevin, he be one sick mothafucker. He turns tricks right up in there with the kids around. Guys come to the door, he does 'em right in there."

The days spent hanging around at Teresa's were the most emotionally draining and dreadful of my time on Fremont. There were other difficult times too, and it seemed as if the longer I hung out the wearier I became. Even my teenage daughter, Emily, saw the effects the Fremont environment had on me. "Dad, don't get paranoid. I'm not one of your gang girls," she'd argue when I insisted on knowing her whereabouts at all times and the names of all her friends. Imagine, I thought, the effect families like Teresa's had on youngsters like Amy and RoniRo. This was a real-life nightmare.

The radio played 103.3 JAMS even when Fremont and Northeast kids weren't in my car. Their music reminded me about why I was in KC. I'm an avid national public radio fan, but I'm annoyed by reports about expensive, ineffective crime policies broadcast from offices in Washington,

D.C., and discussed by college professors whose only knowledge of crime has come from the reference library and by U.S. congressmen pandering for votes by scaring and then placating naive voters with another "get tough" policy. I didn't listen to NPR until I decompressed from the KC streets.

It always took me a week to 10 days before I stopped recalling in my mind's eye the sight of Amy and RoniRo sequestered with Teresa and Kevin. In the first six years of a child's life, a youngster spends 24 hours a day, 7 days a week with some caretakers. That's 8,736 hours a year. Over six years that's 52,416 hours at home or at day care and home. Amy and RoniRo stayed home. This number of hours is the equivalent of 6,552 workdays, or 1,310.4 work weeks, or 25.2 years in the workplace (at 40 hours a week). In other words, in the first six crucial years of Amy's and RoniRo's life, they spent the equivalent of a quarter of a century of work years with Psychoqueen Teresa and Demonic Kevin. The citizens of America let it happen as though they didn't know about horrific households like that one. Now they know.

7

5403 Smart
The Northeast Gangstas

Fremont girls don't welcome a move home. Unless they have no other choices, they resist it. Fremont boys are even less willing than girls to retreat home, and I don't know a boy who did it. Fremont kids said a return home is a retreat, a sign of weakness, an inability to make it on their own. But that's just what I'd expect these kids to say. The truth is, these kids don't want to face the problems at home that forced them leave in the first place. When I waited long enough and listened to them, they said it in their own way.

When I met Cara she said she hated being at home. She fought the rules that Cathy imposed: no phone calls after 11:00 at night; no boys knocking on the door in the middle of the night; no drugs in the house; no bad language; no gang stuff in her house. Cathy wanted a calm, safe household. Calmness and Cara are mismatched.

If Cara didn't want to sleep on the street after the bust, she had to play her mother's game, for a while anyway. Cara stayed with her mother from August until she accumulated enough cash to move out. Just deciding to work was difficult for Cara, because in the heyday of the Fremont Hustlers, Cara said more than once, "If I had to choose between smoking a blunt or going to work, shiyt." That means drugs and partying come first.

With her financial back against the wall, Cara had no other choice than to accommodate to her mother's rules. Cara had no job and at first no willingness to get one, no cash, no one to sponge off. Her Fremont companions had drifted away; no one reached out to Cara. Cheri went home, back to her drug-addicted mother. Angie grabbed Wayne. Wendy disappeared. Janet still wanted Steele Bill, but now so did Cara, and that caused Janet and Cara to split forever. A fundamental rule of street life: Help yourself first.

Cara's attitude toward work had to change if she wanted to live on her own. Fremont kids talk a lot about renting an apartment, owning a car, partying. Independent living is freedom from parents' rules, they say, and at the same time a measure of economic success and adulthood. "If I can pay my own biylls," Cara said, "I know I'm doing good. You gotta grow up sometime."

The only way Cara, who would turn 19 on March 5, 1996, could live her fantasy was to find and keep a job. It took her a while to adjust to this idea; in fact, it took months, but she got a job and worked hard.

The fantasy of independent living is accompanied by Fremont girls' love-escape fantasy, in which a boy who's now in prison will rescue the girl and together they'll ride off into the sunset and live happily ever after. These fantasies are by far the best relationships with boys Fremont girls ever have. Real lovers beat and exploit them and leave them alone, penniless, and pregnant.

Cara knew a boy, Jack, who was imprisoned long before I showed up. She said of him, "He's my heart, he's my heart." She told me Jack was a murderer, but he was her guardian angel. Cara called him "my boy" and posted on her bedroom wall a photograph of him taken in a Missouri prison yard.

Cara talked about him as if they had known each other for years and had been intimate companions before his imprisonment. Cathy said that Cara and Jack barely knew each other from junior high school and that Cara had created a love relationship with Jack after his imprisonment.

We've already seen Wendy's similar fantasy involving a convict who, when released, never bothered to contact her during the brief time before he was rearrested and imprisoned again. Angie shared the same fantasy. Her "boy" was imprisoned too, and once released, they'd move away from KC and live a wonderful life. Cheri also had a fantasy boy. After Chucky D's imprisonment, Cara created a love fantasy about him, and it blossomed on Smart Street.

When Cara got a job and an apartment, I saw the economic function of Fremont kids' personal social ties. Although I was not on Fremont during 1992–94 and didn't watch the emergence of Wendy's drug house, Cara's life on Smart, from January to March 1996, shows the evolution of a social and economic unit similar to, albeit smaller than, Wendy's drug house. Here's how it works.

A youth gang is a ready set of social ties with varying degrees of economic value; gang members protect most valuable resources with violence, if necessary. A kid's link to someone with resources is necessary for his or her survival; thus, that link is nurtured and protected, not for altruistic reasons (for the good of the gang) or affective reasons (friendships, love), but for instrumental (economic and material) survival. Kids' talk about friendship, homeboys and homegirls, the "gang as family" is homeboy folklore, analogous to violence folklore. Homeboy folklore protects social ties of economic significance. Kids stay attached to one another only because a particular kid has something another kid needs.

What happened at Cara's, and at Wendy's, is what happens when a piece of cake drops to the kitchen floor in the summer. Ants from everywhere run in and swarm the cake, and as long as there is cake, the ants are there. If cake were illegal for ants to possess, and if the ants could find for themselves a regular supply of cake, a social arrangement would be formed to provide, protect, and distribute the illegal cake for a price. These young ants would then be analogous to a "youth gang." Without a regular supply of illegal cake, the ants wouldn't need to have a social arrangement to provide, protect, and distribute it. Instead, individual ants or small groups of them would search out illegal cake whenever and wherever they could get it. In this case, these ants would be a "delinquent group."

Cara interpreted her job and an apartment as measures of success, freedom, and adulthood. But to kids who didn't work and had no place to stay, Cara's apartment and job were "legal cake" and a stable economic source. With this resource in hand, they could do whatever they wished. In this case, the "ants" were members of the Northeast Gangstas.

I thought Cara could resist the pressure of their invasion and stay straight. Cara was dissimilar to other kids on Fremont. From the first day we met, I had the sense that she blended with kids around her in order to do whatever was necessary to survive alone on the street. She was too stubborn and angry to let her mother rein her in; thus, Cara's legal economic alternatives to independent life were few, so she found income on the street. When kids are young, alone, and frightened, it doesn't matter if the cake is legal or illegal.

Whatever has contributed to Cara's anger, drug use, and sexual promiscuity, it was well beyond the field of vision. I saw a teenager who had a soft and tender core and a loud and angry verbal defense system. I never saw her hurt anyone, although she talked a lot about "beating the shit out of" so-and-so, which thus far had been only street talk.

Cathy said Cara felt a need to conform. Cathy is right. Cara is unaware of her strong desire to be liked, to be part of the group. Cara carries that desire to an extreme and, for whatever reasons, lets that desire propel her into dangerous situations. In the right environment, however, I thought Cara's willingness to conform might propel her toward a productive end, just as in the wrong environment her willingness to conform hurts her.

Economic, but more often legal, pressure forced some Fremont and Northeast kids to alter behavior. Even Chucky D had a legitimate job once. He worked in a fast-food joint. He was on parole after his first release from prison and had to work or face a parole revocation (recall that I met Chucky D after his second release, at age 17). He worked for two weeks. Cara told me that one afternoon he had called her from work and asked, "Wha's up?" Cara was hanging out at a kid's apartment, and a bunch of Fremont kids were listening to music and smoking weed. Cara invited Chucky D to join them, but he said he had to work. A few hours later, Cara said, there was a knock on the door. Chucky D had quit and come to party. Because parole supervision was weak, Chucky D stayed on the street and sold drugs.

By January 1996, Cara had put some distance between herself and most Fremont cronies, except for Cheri, Steele Bill, and Chucky D, who had then been in prison for two months.

Whenever I arrived in KC, I visited Cara first, checking on her to make sure she was well, and then headed up to Fremont. I always invited her to join me. Many times she refused to accompany me, because she was angry over feeling abandoned after the bust.

"Fuck dem Fremont mothafuckas. They ain't shit. They never did nothin' for me, so fuck dem niggahs. I ain't goin' up dere."

More often than not, she'd give in and we'd drive up there together, hang out at Teresa's or Joanne's, and in warm weather, stand around at Fremont and 13th and talk about the old days. Others would join us to hang out, smoke, talk, joke, laugh.

Cara thought that putting physical distance between herself and Fremont would separate her from her social ties on the street. Cara said repeatedly that moving away was the only way she could stay "out of the shit." Cara, like Wendy, didn't realize that she brought trouble with her by continuing to stay in contact with Steele Bill, Chucky D, and the boys who were the Northeast Gangstas. Cara also didn't realize that social life inside her apartment at 5403 Smart was a re-creation, a miniversion of the social life that had typified Wendy's drug house.

As I hung out with Cara over the next 90 days and watched her develop a relationship with Northeast boys and further sever ties to Fremont, I realized that it wasn't Cara's need, or perhaps the need of any of these kids, to be the center of attention that influenced her decisions to stay aligned with Fremont and Northeast. Rather Cara's decisions were motivated by a need to avoid social, thus economic, isolation. These kids aren't pulled together by so-called peer pressure. No one forces Chucky D, Afro, and House of Pain to do anything they don't care to do; nor do kids go along with the crowd only to please other kids or avoid social isolation; there are plenty of kids to go around. Rather, Fremont and Northeast kids link themselves to kids who control access to something of economic value. This alone determines so-called homeboy relationships.

I watched kids choose one social tie over another. It's always the social tie with economic value that gets attention, because kids need the material benefits that come with that social tie. While Wendy's drug house was a hot money-making enterprise, Wendy was the center of attention. A moment after the bust, Wendy was abandoned and no one cared what happened to her.

The street is a lonely place; the fear of being penniless pulls kids into trouble. A youth gang is a kind of "trading partnership," a shifting network of social ties driven by economic need and a quest for material goods; however, such a network ultimately creates and then worsens social isolation. Its effect is to threaten a kid's long-term economic viability on the street and virtually kill that kid's economic prospects in the mainstream community.

When a kid chooses one gang over another, he or she selects a set of social affiliations, thus isolating himself or herself from other social ties. If a kid's newly found social ties are lousy street entrepreneurs, the new youth-gang member will have made a bad economic decision. Boys have less negotiability than girls—that is, childless girls—and seem to be trapped; however, if such a kid has ties to kids in other neighborhoods or cousins in other gangs, the trapped kid may be able to shift gangs and improve his economic viability. Such socioeconomic negotiability may underlie the pattern of gang-shifting practiced by Fremont's hardcore boys.

Girls like Cara, who are attractive and entertaining, have practiced social skills and move between youth gangs; then too, let's not forget that teenage girls have "something" all boys want, irrespective of gang membership. Joining a youth gang with hard-and-fast social boundaries is a poor social adjustment to a viable economic strategy for street survival. Youth gangs with such hard-and-fast boundaries aren't typical among KC gangs.

Cara saved enough cash to rent an apartment in a ramshackle building at 5403 Smart, apartment number 4. The apartment was a 2-minute drive, a 10-minute walk, and a 5-minute run from "the spot." A common street expression, the term *The Spot* designates a place where drugs are sold. In this case, The Spot is the intersection of Roberts and Bales, narrow tree-covered streets lined with unpainted, untended wood houses and rusty, dented cars dating to the 1970s. The Spot is where the Northeast Gangstas hung out. Northeast's core members, many of whom hung out at Cara's new apartment, were marauders who found more excitement and pleasure in hurting people than in making money. Pushing at Northeast kids was like poking at sunburned skin with a sharp stick.

Cara's northeast neighborhood was dangerous, because the Northeast Gangstas are more violent than Fremont. I didn't have "hard" data to prove it, because such gang data are unavailable from the KCPD. By January 1996, the gang cops said publicly that there are no gangs in KC. They also said they no longer police gangs; instead, they seek street criminals, and if a criminal has a gang affiliation, that will be another fact in the case.

A chat with three KC gang cops one day explained why the KCPD claimed that KC has no gangs. In an attempt to stop gang crime, the state of Missouri enhanced, or lengthened, the prison sentences of alleged gang offenders. Afterward, these offenders filed appeals which forced prosecutors to prove in court that offenders had a gang affiliation. Given the free-flowing nature of KC's gangs, I'm not surprised that prosecutors have a difficult time convincing a jury that young adults like Cara and Chucky D are gang members.

Fremont and Northeast kids aren't fussy about meeting law enforcement's overt criteria for a street gang, such as graffiti, gang clothes, gang hand-signs, gang walk and talk, hats turned left or right, shoe laces tied or untied. And of course, no member of the Fremont Hustlers and Northeast Gangstas would ever self-admit gang membership.

Chucky D said, "If yo serious about money, makin' real money, why would you wanna look like a *fffooool* and wear all that kid stuff?" Fremont kids and Northeast kids don't go to school and don't have to impress schoolyard companions with a gang membership. Chucky D and the others don't waste their money on Chicago Bulls, Charlotte Hornets, and Los Angeles Raiders hats, shirts, and coats. If Northeast kids want athletic clothes, they rip them off someone's back.

The KCPD scared me. I hung around in the middle of a drug gang and was now hanging out with Northeast kids. That angered the detectives. How do I know this? I have well-respected colleagues who are gang researchers. These friends heard a KCPD official "bad mouth" me at a national gang conference sponsored by the U.S. Department of Justice. In fact, a colleague said to me, "What did you do to piss off the Kansas City cops?"

With the KCPD angry at me, I felt like a Fremont or Northeast kid. I was frightened enough to have conversations with the chairman of my department about the role my university would play if I were arrested and prosecuted for drug conspiracy or other street crimes. I also had conversations with attorneys about what I should do if I were subpoenaed to testify in a Fremont or Northeast criminal case.

If one goal of the ethnographic enterprise is to experience life as the "natives" do, I think my fear and paranoia about being arrested gave me those experiences. I got even more nervous when Cara, Snoop (Steele Bill's cousin), Northeast TJ, and other Northeast Gangstas were arrested and jailed on March 6, 1996. Bernard missed being arrested this time only because he was already in jail on charges of assault and carrying a concealed weapon.

Like the Fremont Hustlers, Northeast is a new youth gang, formed gradually between the summers of 1991 and 1992, according to Bernard. But Northeast Gangsta folklore says that Edward Walker, now an inmate at the United States Penitentiary at Leavenworth, founded the gang when he was a boy on KC's northeast side. Walker's two sons are Northeast members. Even though Fremont and Northeast have shot at each other for years and their respective boys and girls fistfight, these kids have known one another, in some cases, half their lives. Recall that a number of Fremont Hustlers and Northeast Gangstas were members of the Latin Count Brothers prior to 1992.

Cara knows Northeast boys from years on the street. Cara met Bernard at The Spot when he was 14 and she was 13. Cara was hanging out with a Northeast girl, Michelle, who was dating a Southside boy named Brian.

Cara said, "B[ernard] wanted to get close to me and thought he could just step up and fuck me." She and Bernard both laughed. Bernard, known as B, and Roger, Angie's brother, were burglary partners, stealing and selling what had street value, before Northeast and Fremont animosity grew. The talk of fistfights and Wild West shooting between Fremont and Northwest, initially motivated by rivalry over drug-selling proceeds according to Cara and Bernard, has been inflated and glamorized by Cara, B, Wendy, Cheri, and Northeast TJ.

One Saturday afternoon, Cara, TJ, Chris, and Dusty packed into my Acura and drove around Northeast territory looking at so-and-so's former house, recalling a fight at such-and-such a spot and a shooting at another. Cara laughed and told the Northeast boys that, in the heyday of the Fremont Hustlers, she and Wendy had gotten high and driven through Northeast territory looking for someone to shoot with a .45-caliber handgun hidden in the dashboard vent of Wendy's 1995 Honda Accord, the same car Wendy and Cara had sat in when Northeast's Thomas Cook shot them. The Northeast boys laughed. "Yeah," TJ said, "we seen yaz too and pulled our shit [guns] and shot at cha as yaz drove by. Didn' we hit ya car?"

The veracity of such violent folktales is questionable, but these tales bind kids together when such cohesion is necessary. In this case, the Fremont-Northeast shooting tale drew Cara and the Northeast boys closer. Maybe some elements in violence tales are factual, but consider how sad it is that teenagers frolic over tales about shooting handguns at one another. There was nothing funny about the drive-by shooting that would put Cara in jail on Cherry and nearly land her in state prison.

By January 1996, I hadn't seen Cara for six weeks. The frequency of my trips to KC dropped over the winter. In November and December 1995 on many weekends when I wanted to drive the seven hours to KC for a four-day field trip, the weather was icy and snowy. One Thursday I drove to St. Louis and couldn't go beyond. Westbound I-70 was an icy ribbon for 250 miles. In winter, I increased the phone calls to stay in touch with Cara and listen to the news of the street, always asking if anyone had heard from Wendy.

Cara and I talked three or more times a week. When I talked to her and other kids were around, I chatted with them too. Cara knew the news of the street, and she'd give me a rundown on shifts in boy-girl relationships, who got arrested and who got released, who got shot or stabbed or beaten up, who's pregnant and who lost a baby. Even at a distance I didn't feel too out of touch, nor did they. If I wanted to reach someone else, Cara would almost always know the phone and pager number. Because addresses and phone and pager numbers change as often as tennis match scores, it's essential to know someone who has the new information. If Cara didn't know the score, no one did. Her desperate need to be at the center of the action led her into trouble and also made her a wonderful informant.

I visited Cara once more in January and on every other weekend in February. We talked, ate out, visited Cathy on Gladstone and then Van Brunt, hung out at Fremont chill spots, and spent time talking and getting to know each other better than we had over the summer of 1995. The hustle of Fremont in those days made it difficult to get close to individual kids. They were high or "had to do" one thing or another. But now their lives were slower paced, and that gave me a chance to listen to them.

The next series of events occurred from March 1 through March 6, 1996. These events forever altered the direction of Cara's and many Northeast boys' lives.

March 1. I slowed down in front of 5403 Smart on a cold, windy day at about noon. Four blocks south was The Ave, with McDonald's and Pizza Hut to the west on the south side and Cara's Taco Bell on the north side.

The Ave still shows traces of historic elegance, with its two- and three-story, ornate, stone apartment buildings. Many are still used, many are now boarded up, some are drug houses. Eddie Solo, one of Northeast's most violent 20-year-olds, dished cocaine out of a formerly elegant building on The Ave.

Eddie's violent behavior is notorious; so is his love of high-powered handguns. Chucky D and Eddie grew up together on the east side and were Latin Count Brothers. Eddie, like Chucky D, is a young predator. In 1995, Eddie and a Northeast partner, who dished weed out of his house north of The Ave, were arrested and interrogated for the slaughter of an aging man and the robbery of his $2,000 gambling winnings. As the street story goes, Eddie and his partner allegedly shot the 60-something-year-old man in the stomach in his garage after following him home from a KC casino. Casino videotape shows Eddie and his partner stalking the man inside the casino. He was killed by a bullet from a high-powered handgun. There was no hard evidence, no prosecution. The street says Eddie did it.

I parked my car in front of 5403 Smart and looked up through the passenger-side window. Cara and Cheri were descending from the second floor, slowly stepping down a rickety unpainted wooden staircase. I got out and called, "Cara-mel." She smiled, and we embraced on the grassy strip between the road and sidewalk. She pulled me close, as my kids do when we haven't seen each other for a few days.

"Hi, Maaark," she murmured.

"You' looking good, Caramel, looking good. Cheri, give me a hug." Timidly Cheri walked over and hugged me. No one hugs these kids. I was truly happy to see them safe.

"Girl, you look whipped. Did you work all night or party?" I asked Cara. Standing on the sidewalk in the cold wind, she told me what had happened the day before.

Beginning on February 29, Cara said, one black and one white homicide detective detained her at 11:00 A.M., and she remained in custody until 8:00 A.M. on March 1. Police were interrogating her in the investigation of the July 1994 murder of a teenager named T-Man.

On the night of T-Man's murder, Fremont had had a hotel party at a midtown KC hotel; Wendy paid the bills with coke money. The party lasted all night. In the wee hours of the morning, three boys drove from the midtown hotel to Fremont, hung out for a while, and drove off together. The next day T-Man was dead, shot to death at 16th and Lister, the hangout area of La Familia.

Cara and other Fremont kids said the August 1995 Fremont drug bust wasn't simply a drug bust. It was really about T-Man's murder. Kids say it's easy to arrest them on drug charges, but once they are in custody, the interrogation of one case blends with other cases. Cara said the detectives allege that Chucky D, Afro, or Shawn killed T-Man, and squeezed her to name one of them as the shooter.

Cheri, Cara, and I walked upstairs together. Cara's apartment was down a narrow hallway covered with a threadbare, filthy, industrial gray carpet, which looked like it had been laid before the Vietnam War. No one vacuumed it or painted the walls.

Cara unlocked the apartment door. The door always stayed locked and was never opened until the person who knocked was clearly identified. There was no peep hole. We walked inside.

Whenever Cara stayed with Cathy, they argued over Cara's refusal to help clean the apartment. April cleaned, Melanie cleaned, Cara refused, and her uncooperative attitude was a continuing irritation to Cathy and to Cara's sisters.

Cara's Smart one-bedroom apartment was neat and clean, a whole lot tidier than my daughter's room. Cara was always cleaning something and howling at kids who knocked cigarette ashes onto the floor, put their feet on her rickety wooden coffee table, and laid dirty Nikes on her wornout, yellowish-orange couch cushions.

"When they disrespect my shit, they disrespect me, and they can get the fuck out," she'd scream, emphasizing *fuck*. She had posted on the living room wall a proclamation, handwritten on a piece of lined paper torn off a legal pad. It read,

---

MOTHAFUCKAS
If you can't shut the fuck up,
get the fuck out.

The living room had a three-cushioned couch, a two-cushioned love seat, as Cara called it, an overstuffed chair, a coffee table with a huge ashtray and a phone with a built-in caller ID, a stereo, a small color TV, and black-and-white photographs stapled to the walls.

Her bedroom was at the front of the apartment. She slept on a thin mattress on the floor; a few wool blankets had been tossed onto it and lay in a heap. A few pairs of jeans and sweatshirts had been thrown onto the floor in front the closet door.

Cara always constructs a wall of memories, a shrine to the past and to the kids she's known, wherever she stays. She had had one shrine at

Cathy's duplex on Gladstone, now had one on Smart, and would later have one in Cathy's apartment on Van Brunt. This shrine had more than a dozen photographs of inmates she called her boys. These young men posed in typical convict postures. Some kneeled in front, with others standing behind them; some held cigarettes as if these were the Holy Grail; some threw gang signs with their fingers; others flexed muscles and showed off arm and shoulder tattoos. There was a photo of Amy, the daughter of Robin, with whom Cara had lived between ages 9 and 11. And there was a color photograph of Cara and me standing in front of Wendy's burned-out drug house. The photo had been taken by the sister of House of Pain. There were a half dozen empty beer bottles too, each one commemorating a party.

In a central spot was the program from Tyler's funeral. Earlier, in the fall of 1995, "Tyler RIP" (rest in peace) had been inscribed in a new section of concrete sidewalk laid in front of where Wendy's house once stood, after demolition workers had removed the charred building.

The kitchen had a refrigerator with a long list of phone numbers taped to the door, an old formica-top table that rocked on the floor with tiles loose and missing, and empty cupboards.

The bathroom had a tub-and-shower and a toilet. Ceramic tiles had fallen off the wall above the tub, leaving bare patches and remnants of tile mastic.

In the rear, off the kitchen, was a mudroom, which would have served as a laundry room had Cara owned a washer and dryer. A door in the mudroom opened to a back porch and an S-shaped heavy wooden staircase leading into a wooded backyard.

"Mark, this is Carmen." Cara spoke as if she were introducing a teacher to a child on the first day of school. Carmen was huddled under a few old blankets, lying curled up on her right side on the love seat. She didn't lift her head off the old large throw pillow sandwiched between her and the arm of the couch.

"Hi," she muttered softly.

"He's my friend. He's a writer. He's doing a story on us Fremont kiyds," Cara explained. Carmen lay there expressionless.

Cara just moved in here, I thought, and already there's something going on. Who is Carmen? Where did she come from? Why is she here? Cara can barely take care of herself; why is she babysitting a 15-year-old girl?

"Cheri and Carmen are stayin' wid me," Cara explained.

I nodded and said, "Hi, Carmen," reaching out to shake her hand.

I understood why Cheri was there. She seeks the path of least resistance. After the Fremont bust, she had returned to her mother's house on

Van Brunt, across the street and south of where Cathy would soon move, and stayed there until something better—and free—turned up.

Over the next year, Cara had tried to get Cheri a job at whichever Taco Bell Cara then worked. At first it was the Taco Bell on The Ave. Cheri resisted by not showing up to meet the boss when Cara asked her to. When she was hired, her tardiness, reluctance to take orders, and impoliteness with customers got her fired.

Cara's 18-year-old supervisor at Taco Bell, the mother of an infant and former group-home resident, is Carmen's sister. Carmen was five-one, maybe 105 pounds. She had a beautiful smile and the face of a girl I'd expect to see on the cover of a teenage fashion magazine. This beautiful child had come from a nightmarish young life.

Carmen had been alone on KC streets; Cara brought her home. Carmen's mother is a drug addict and the mother of six. "She does crystal, shoots up, and smokes weed, a lot of weed," Carmen said. Carmen has grandparents in KC but doesn't have contact with them, and they don't care where she is.

Carmen said she was sexually molested at age three by her paternal grandfather, who years later offered to pay $100 for the sexual services of Carmen's younger sister (then 13). The girls' mother was the pimp. The youngster fled.

My questions about her mother transformed Carmen's face into stone and her torso stiffened. She reacted to the thought of her mother as you might react to the sight of a diamondback rattlesnake coiled at the side of your bed in the morning.

"My mom hit us a lot, hit us on our head, choked us a lot, and tried to kill us. She used to beat us up. She threw water glasses at me. We had to steal food from grocery stores to eat. I used to get so angry I'd bite the window ledge. I was ready to die. My mom choked my dog and stabbed my sister with scissors and forks." Flatly and coldly Carmen said, "I'd rather go to jail than go back to her home."

In elementary school, Carmen was diagnosed as "learning disabled," she said, and labeled with attention deficit disorder. School officials didn't look beyond the labels. Carmen didn't get the help she needed to compensate for her neurological problems. Instead, doctors prescribed lithium for her "anger problem."

During age 12 and 13, she lived in a group home in KC and attended a junior high school in Independence. At age 13 she got into a knife fight and was arrested and charged with assault with a deadly weapon. She was then arrested for auto theft and sent to a juvenile detention facility in St. Louis for a sentence of one to six years. She remained there from September 1994 to September 1995. Even though St. Louis and KC are only 250 miles apart and connected by I-70, Carmen's mother was too busy to visit her.

In her last month in detention, Carmen "acted out," set off a fire extinguisher, got into fights with other kids, and assaulted staff members and stole their keys. "I didn't want to go home, and now none of my [case] workers want nothing to do to with me."

Cara protected Carmen with the deliberate energy she used at Taco Bell. Carmen had a cold one weekend; Cara had no aspirin or other symptom-relieving pills. Marijuana, I told them, wouldn't help sneezing and coughs and a headache. They listened. We went to buy cold medication.

Cara made sure Carmen put on a warm coat before we walked out into March's biting wind. We jumped into the Acura, drove down The Ave, and stopped at a drug mart west of Eddie Solo's drug house and across the street from Texas Tom's, the greasy joint the kids love so much. I parked in the lot, gave Cara five dollars, and watched.

Cara and Carmen stood on the sidewalk and, before they stepped onto The Ave, Cara reached down and took Carmen's hand and guided her across the street. They talked and laughed like the teenage girls my daughter has brought home. It was a nice sight, refreshing and light, and it relieved the tension that always hovered around Cara's apartment. There were drive-by shootings near Smart, drug addicts across the hall, hollering from an apartment on the first floor, cockroaches, no food in the cabinets, joint papers on the coffee table, and Northeast boys continually knocking at the door. But for a moment, when these girls crossed the street, I felt good about their future, at least over the next hour.

Cara made sure Carmen ate and brought her burritos from Taco Bell. She wouldn't let Carmen smoke cigarettes. And because Cara mothered Carmen, she objected when boys used words like *mothafucka* within Carmen's earshot. Most important, Cara protected Carmen from the endless line of walking erections, otherwise known as the Northeast boys, who wanted to have sex with this beautiful teenager with light blonde hair.

Cara told the boys that, if they wanted to hang out in her apartment, they'd have to "respect" Carmen. She lectured at them. "Keep yo' fuckin' hands off my baby, mothafuckas," emphasizing *my baby*. The boys smiled at one another but respected Cara's request; she had control over the apartment the boys needed.

"They be pussy out there," she'd point toward the street. "Yo' don't be needin' the pussy in here. Stay away, niggahs."

This was Cara's dream, living on her own, paying her own bills with money earned at Taco Bell. Now vested in independent living, she thought about Fremont and staying at Wendy's drug house and realized that that situation had been fraught with danger. Back then, getting high masked the danger.

Cara smoked weed, but she had to cut back. Her work hours were brutal. At least five but sometimes seven nights a week, she began work at 7:00 or 8:00 and ended 8, 9, or 10 hours later. In the cold winter months, long hours on her feet caused her ankle, the one shot with the AK-47, to ache so badly that she often called me in tears.

"Mark, I cayn't do it no mo'. My ankle's fuckin' killin' me, and I ain't got no money for the prescription they tol' me ta buy."

"Ask your mother to call a social service agency and find out if there's a way to get the drugs free?"

"That's Medicaid and my mom makes too much money."

"You don't. Go downtown and sign up for it."

"Where do I go?"

"I don't know, ask your mom to find out. Open a phone book and call the mayor's office and ask the person who answers the phone."

"Then I have to drag downtown, and I don't have a car, and I ain't ridin' them buses. It takes too long."

"Look, I'll send ya some money to get the prescription, and we'll find out about all this when I come over next time."

We had this conversation many times. She cashed the money orders I'd send her to buy her prescription medication, but whenever it came time to search out the proper government office, she was always too busy or her ankle didn't ache. "No need, no action" is the rule of the street.

Cara devoted herself to Taco Bell with the same relentless energy she had devoted to hanging out and smoking weed on Fremont. I was amazed at her hard work and dedication. If only, I thought, Cara's energy could be channeled in the direction of long-range goals, she could be off the street forever.

March 2. About 11:00 in the morning I drove to Cara's apartment. I got out of my Acura, and the cold crisp winter air bit my skin as if to alert me that I was moving into something dangerous and I'd better pay attention.

I climbed the dozen unpainted steps and walked down the hallway. It was always a relief not to find a body penetrated by a bullet lying there. With Cara and the Northeast boys on the left side of the hall, and Carol and Joe on the right, it wasn't an altogether crazy thing to anticipate.

Cara usually worked from Friday night at 8:00 until Saturday morning and returned to her place about 5:00 A.M. She slept until someone banged at her door or phoned her. She told me to come over anytime, but I didn't; I always waited until late morning. Even if she didn't work the night before, she and the others would still stay up all night, so I let her sleep.

I knocked quietly on the unpainted door. "Yeah, who is it?" asked a male voice.

"Mark," I responded. I didn't recognize the voice and didn't antici- pate a friendly greeting.

"Who?" the voice asked again, a bit more aggressively.

"Mark. I'm a friend of Cara's."

I heard noise inside, shuffling around, and then the door slowly opened. A boy I'd never seen stood there wrapped in a blanket. He looked at me, I at him. He stepped back to his chair, dropped into it, and curled into a fetal position, wrapping himself in his yellow wool blanket and pulling it over his head. Prisoners do that to give themselves some privacy. This is, I thought, a gang researcher's paradise.

The apartment was quiet. Cigarette butts filled the large plastic ashtray on the coffee table. The phone was on the floor under the table. Kids all around had blankets over their heads.

"Mark," Cara called to me. "Come in here." I walked into her bedroom and found her curled up on the paper-thin mattress and covered by a few blankets. We chatted, she stood up with a blanket wrapped around herself, turned her back toward me and bent over and pulled on her jeans and a sweatshirt. When I had hung around Wendy's drug room with Angie, Cheri, Wendy, and Cara, they had had no qualms about getting dressed with me in the room. They were always discreet, turning their back and covering themselves, but it made me feel uneasy.

Together we walked into the living room and Cara roused Northeast TJ, Chris, Snoop, and Dusty from their sleeping perches. Snoop slept at one end of the couch, Chris at the other; TJ, the boy who had opened the door, was folded up in the overstuffed chair, closest to the door. Carmen had one end of the love seat, Dusty the other. Cheri was tucked away in a corner of Cara's bedroom.

TJ stood up and, with one hand holding his blanket, used the other to rub his eyes. "Cigarette, Cara, got a cigarette?" "On the table, moth- afucka, you blind?" she responded. He grunted quietly and lifted the Newports I had bought Cara.

"Cheri, get yo' fuckin' ass up, biytch," growled Cara in a half-joking way. Cara was annoyed that Cheri still hadn't come to Taco Bell in search of a job. TJ and the others weren't interested in jobs and sneered at the idea of going to work.

Over the next hour, the kids lifted blankets off their heads, smoked cigarettes, wandered into the bathroom, chatted quietly. Except for Cara, everyone slept with his or her clothes on. About 1:00 in the afternoon, the phone started ringing, as it does everyday. Chucky D called collect from a state prison in central Missouri.

To get some privacy, Cara took the phone, walked into the kitchen, and sat at the kitchen table. She spoke in low tones, but I overheard her tell him who was at the apartment.

"Maaark," she exaggerated my name. "Chucky says hi," she yelled to me. "Yo, Chucky," I yelled back, "what's a nice guy like you doing in a shithole prison like that?" Cara repeated my words to him. He responded to me, "Time, mothafucka, time." Everyone chuckled.

The boys' faces wrinkled when Cara yelled Chucky's greeting to me, as if to say, "Who is this old guy? How's he know Chucky?" Recall that Chucky D is eastside and grew up with Northeast TJ, Bernard, Snoop, and the other Northeast boys. My link to Chucky helped me open the door to them.

Cara was now madly in love with Chucky D. She accepted his collect calls and regularly spent $250 a month on his calls alone. Jack also called collect. When Cara began feeling closer to Chucky D, she became slowly annoyed at Tamara, who was Chucky D's former girlfriend, Cara's running partner during the fall of 1995, and the girl she shared a pager with. Cara heard that Chucky D had sent Tamara an inmate visitor's request form, but he hadn't yet sent one to her. This form must be filed with prison officials in order to grant an outsider visiting privileges. Of course, Tamara hadn't told Cara about the visitor's request form, because she knew Cara would be upset. Joanne, the mother of Chucky D's daughter, Charlene, had told Taffy. Taffy told Cara. Such intrigue devastates these girls and shatters their fantasies.

There was no food, no coffee, no soda, nothing that could be eaten or drunk in Cara's apartment, except water. There was weed, though. I suggested that we get some food. Food opens mouths, and I wanted TJ, Snoop, and the other boys to like me and talk to me. I also felt a need to feed these kids. Cara brings home burritos and tacos from Taco Bell, and the kids eat them, but otherwise they don't eat. If they have money, they don't spend it on healthy food; they buy sodas and junk food and weed.

TJ and the boys were taken aback by my invitation and didn't want to go. "Nah, we ain't hungry," TJ replied.

"Fuck you," Cheri said, "I'm hungry. Let's eat." Cheri and the Fremont kids knew my routine and enjoyed it.

"TJ, he's cool," said Cara in an instructional voice. "Don' worry about him, he's been around a long ass mothafuckin' time. Chucky likes him." TJ's face relaxed. Out the door we went and off to McDonald's on The Ave.

I enjoyed taking these kids to eat. Beyond the pleasure I got from feeding hungry teenagers, I loved to watch their behavior in public places like McDonald's.

The counter servers at McDonald's and Pizza Hut looked at these kids when they walked in, and I could read their faces. "Oh, no, we're not serving them; they don't have money." I stood in front of the ragtag group and said, "Give 'em whatever they want. I'm payin'."

At McDonald's on The Ave, Northeast has inscribed its own long plastic booth with Northeast graffiti. Watching these kids eat tells me they don't eat often. Teenage boys are always hungry, at least my son is. TJ, Snoop, Chris, and Dusty ate with the deliberate energy of a tree surgeon's wood chipper as it devours limbs and branches, efficiently and with purpose.

Many times I saw that, once stomachs fill up, the laughter, joking, teasing, and name calling start. One kid's conversation feeds off another's. Soon everyone's talking at once and cursing and laughing. The "citizens" 20 feet away stare in wonder, afraid to walk over to tell these kids to stop yelling that so-and-so is a mothafucka, a niggah, or a bitch. Instead, citizens ease to their feet, with their fingers wrapped around trays of nuggets and fries and sodas, and sneak off to a spot well away from the street kids.

Now and again I'd feel embarrassed by all this raucousness. I wasn't personally ill at ease with it, but I felt awkward for the citizens who had to listen to it. I'd try to slow down the shouting and obscenities a bit. "Shh, they'll throw us out or call the cops," I'd say, using my father voice. Cara would stare at me, "Fuck dat, let 'em try to throw us out." They'd resume the commotion.

Lunch and laughter and story telling ended that day. The Northeast boys wandered west on The Ave, heading back to The Spot. The girls climbed into the Acura, lowered the windows a bit, and Cheri and Cara lit Newports. Carmen was forbidden to smoke.

After such lunches, we'd either go back to 5403 Smart or I'd make a quick run to Fremont to see who was out. In winter, Fremont is boring. No one hangs outside because it's too cold. After Cara had seen black-and-blue Amy, she no longer wanted to stop at Teresa's.

Driving through is fun anyway. We'd laugh and talk about the old days. I knew kids peeked out windows and saw us, and that's good for my rapport. In street ethnography with adolescents, absence doesn't make the heart grow fonder. Either I'm there regularly and stay involved in the lives of kids, or they'll drop me, close doors, fail to return calls. The research dies.

The cruise down Fremont led back to Smart and hanging around Cara's apartment. Cara unlocked the door, made a beeline to the caller ID, and began working the phone. It was her lifeline to the world.

Many times I watched her lie down on the couch, prop herself up against the arm, put her plastic lifeline on her stomach, light a Newport, and run her fingers over the telephone keys with the ease and precision of Michael Jordan floating above the lane, driving toward a twisting layup.

This time, she returned calls from Afro, Rosa, Joanne, Taffy, April, and others. I sat on the love seat and listened and recorded the names of the people she called and the topics of their conversations. Carmen thumbed through a teenage girl's magazine. Cheri sat bored and occasionally asked Cara if she could join in on a conversation.

The afternoon moved slowly. I felt the need to talk to the girls about a serious subject. Cheri was always quiet when I had group conversations about serious topics. I began this technique at Wendy's, because her room always had two or more people in it, and if I'd waited for one-on-one privacy I'd have never interviewed anyone. Asking someone for an interview in front of his or her companions and then going off somewhere with that kid, out of the neighborhood, made folks suspicious.

Yesterday Carmen and I talked about her mother and her earlier years. Today I asked them two tough questions: What's punishment? and How does parenting relate to your view of punishment?

"My mother throws me out of the house," Carmen said, "then calls the police to report I'm a runaway. I get arrested. That just ain't fair. If I'm going to get punished, the parents should get punished too. It ain't all the kid's fault. Look at my mama. Her kids are drug users, gangbangers, dope dealers, and runaways. Why would all her kids just walk off and do all that stuff. It has to be something wrong at home, but, nope, nobody even looks at that. They just look at the kids all the time. If parents ain't getting punished, I ain't getting punished."

"Everything," said Cara, "starts in the home, but people don't know that. I get my ass beat, stuck in a room, and she [Cathy] never let me know what's right. My mom used to hit me in the mouth, I ask, 'Why?' and she say, 'Cause I'm your mom.'"

"See, if you gots a mom like Carmen's and she beat the shit outta ya, how can you punish the kid for doing it? Your child will never understand you, and you'll never understand your child if you hit 'em." Cara lit a cigarette; the girls nodded in agreement.

At the end of our talk, Carmen looked at me and at Cara and said about Cara, "She's my mom for now." Cara smiled. Cheri sat silently. Carmen said she had to visit her nephew and sister, who stayed a few blocks away. Cheri walked with her.

Later that afternoon the phone rang. Cara listened, talked, became angry, listened some more, and then became livid and screamed into the phone. It was Joanne calling. She was asking Cara to watch Charlene the next day because she and Tamara were going to Jefferson City, Missouri, to visit Chucky D.

"Visit Chucky? That motherfucka hasn' sent me a visiting form, and he sent one to you and Tamara," she screamed. "Who else got one?"

Chucky D was managing his visits and lining up girlfriends by sending them visiting forms at different times, telling one girl one story, another girl a different story. He told Cara that he would soon send her a visiting form, but he didn't do it, probably because he didn't want Joanne, Tamara, and Cara to show up at the prison all at the same time and get into a war in the parking lot.

Over many years of hanging around penitentiaries, I've seen inmates arrange visits this way. I recall a Sunday in the early 1980s when I attended an inmate's wedding in the visiting room at the Washington State Penitentiary. The bride wore a white wedding gown, bride's maids wore pastel gowns, and ushers were adorned in black tuxedos. A multitier wedding cake had icing to match the color of the bride's maids' dresses. The next Sunday, seven days later, the new groom had a different woman on his knee in the visiting room. He alternated visits between his girlfriend and his new wife.

However, I knew there was more, much more, to Chucky D's behavior than a simple visit. Chucky D is a die-hard drug dealer. Drugs are far scarcer inside, thus of more value than on the street. Women visitors are the principal source of drug importation into every prison.

Cara screamed, yelled, and threatened Joanne. "I'll kick your fuckin' ass, bitch," she yelped, slammed down the phone, and then started screaming about it to me.

"Fuck all dem niggahs, fo' real. They all sorry ass niggahs and bitches." This went on and on and on, then she began to sob about Chucky D's disloyalty to her.

Within the hour, the phone rang again. It was Chucky D. Cara tore into him with both barrels blazing. She reminded him of all the wonderful things she's done for him, including bailing him out of jail after the August 1995 bust. Finally she told him she was leaving him. "Never call me again, niggah." A bold move, I thought.

Chucky D couldn't have got a word in edgewise; Cara didn't slow down for a second. If she couldn't shoot him with bullets, she would shoot him with words issued at high velocity from a high-powered automatic mouth. She slammed down the phone and sobbed.

Thirty to 45 minutes passed; the phone rang. Chucky D called again. This time it was his turn to blast. Cara listened quietly, said little, smoked Newport after Newport. Her tone changed. She became conciliatory and, before she hung up, sweet Cara had reemerged.

"What happened?" I asked. Chucky D had sweet-talked her, said she was the only girl for him, said Joanne and Tamara were "'ho'es," and that, when he got out, he and Cara would make a life together. Oh, one more thing: Chucky D threatened to have Cara killed if she left him; short of death, he would have one of his female cousins on the northeast side show up at her apartment and beat her. Cara took this as a positive sign. Chucky D, she said, must really love her if he would have her killed or beaten for leaving him.

I kept my mouth shut and didn't begin to explain to Cara that violence and love aren't appropriate bed partners. I did tell Cara not to get involved in a drug-smuggling deal Chucky D had devised. She said she wouldn't. I didn't believe her. She also said Chucky D would never ask her to do such a thing. Sure, I thought. I anticipated the worst.

What happened next came through the Fremont grapevine that always ends at Taffy's house. Tamara visited Chucky D. Joanne didn't go, but Cara called her and arranged to get Charlene for the evening anyway. In the visiting room, prison officials detained Tamara for the possession of drugs. She had two ounces of marijuana and an 8-ball stuffed into her bra. Tamara was arrested, jailed and booked, and transferred to Cherry. Chucky D was placed in segregation. In a later phone call to Cara, Chucky D said Tamara was caught because she tried to smuggle too much. Tamara faced serious felony charges that carried a 10-year prison sentence.

This pleased Cara. Now Tamara was out of her way and was punished, Cara thought, for interfering in her love affair with Chucky D. Cara was now worried that Chucky D would be prosecuted for attempting to smuggle drugs and would receive additional months or years on his sentence. Chucky D was released from segregation, and no charges were filed against him. Tamara remained on Cherry and eventually received probation.

Tamara's arrest frightened Cara. The next day, the day after the news of Tamara's arrest hit Fremont, Cara told me the truth: Chucky D had been pressing her to bring him marijuana and coke. He wanted Cara to bring him drugs, as Tamara had tried, and said the value of marijuana inside the prison was so high that she wouldn't have to work at Taco Bell. A "paper joint" (a very thin one), he said, sold for $50; a half gram of coke sold for $450 (on the street, a gram sold for $80 to $100). Chucky D had told Cara that, if she smuggled in the drugs, he would send her a share of the profits.

All the phone calls that day and the Fremont intrigue occupied the entire afternoon and early evening. It was about 7:00, dark and cold, when a knock came at Cara's mudroom door. It was TJ, Snoop, Chris, and Dusty.

8
The Arrest

When I met the Northeast boys, TJ was 16. He was five-eight, 150 pounds, well built. He and Bernard are handsome brothers. Both of them have a wonderful sense of humor, an ability to describe complicated social scenes with clarity, and they are colorful storytellers.

Snoop was taller than TJ, six feet and thin, maybe weighing 150 pounds. He too is handsome, and a quiet kid. Chris stood over six feet with the physique of a high school basketball player. Chris emits tension. Dusty was almost as tall as Chris, and he, among all the boys, broadcasts an aura of outrage.

I was hungry and hadn't eaten since McDonald's hours earlier, and I assumed all the kids were hungry too. I offered to take everyone to Pizza Hut on The Ave. TJ resisted, still unsure of me. The other boys and Cara were ready to roll. They twisted TJ's arm and off we went. Everyone piled into the Acura and sat on top of one another, laughed and smoked Newports; no one minded the four-block ride to The Ave.

Inside the restaurant I asked for a long table. For the moment, I sat alone. Some boys and Cara went outside to smoke a predinner joint; they always did this. Others drifted off to play video games with quarters I had given them. I felt like a Cub Scout master.

Cara came in from the chilly parking lot, her eyes glowing. She leaned over my left shoulder, laughed, and whispered in my ear: "TJ thinks you're the coolest white dude he's ever known."

The waitress came with menus and found me sitting at a long table alone. I called to Cara; she dragged all the boys to the table and made them sit down. Family folks at the restaurant didn't like the look of my "Cub Scout troop." I told them to watch their language because there were children nearby. Cara leaned forward over the table and whispered, "Listen, you crazy motherfuckas, no bad language or I'll kick your asses." They paused, then roared with laughter.

No one wanted to order until I said, "Order anything and everything you want." They did: breadsticks with pizza sauce, dessert pizza, and four large pizzas covered with meat and vegetables. The food arrived and these children ate and ate like they'd not eaten for days. No one spoke, they just ate. For once they seemed more interested in food than in marijuana.

Of course, Cara had to complain about the service because the waitress was slow bringing drink refills. She complained about service every time we ate out and used her behind-the-counter acumen to judge others. I told her it was OK that the waitress was slow with drink refills. "The place is crowded, Caramel, give her a break."

"Hey, Mark, you're paying for this. We should get good service. Fuck dat bitch." She stood up and walked to the counter, asked for the manager, and told him the service "ain't shit." I couldn't stop her.

Once stomachs were full, stories were told about violent incidents the boys had been in. They told these tales with humor and a nonchalant attitude you'd expect in tales about "what we did on summer vacation." TJ kept Cara enraptured with stories about early-morning drive-bys. Chris talked about sidewalk fistfights and how good it felt to punch boys in the face and watch blood splatter and bones break. Dusty told tales about how much he liked to use his knife as a stabbing and slashing instrument. Snoop kept quiet, but the boys talked about his exploits as a master fistfighter.

Everyone smoked Newports, and when they got bored and stopped talking, I paid the bill and walked into the cold parking lot.

My Acura faced the McDonald's next door, where we had had lunch. TJ and Dusty watched two boys, who looked to be 11 or 12 years old, ride up to McDonald's, lay down their bikes, and stand next to them, talking for a minute before walking inside.

"Bikes, I need a bike," said TJ.

"Fuck it, let's take 'em, and bust their faces if they say anything. TJ, I got the mountain bike," Dusty proclaimed.

"What!" I exclaimed. "You guys are going to rip off bikes from a couple of children?"

"Hey, the car's crowded, we need a ride back to Cara's," said Dusty.

"Fuck no, no way you guys are stealing those bikes. Those are kids. Leave them alone and get into my car," I said, using my penitentiary worker voice.

TJ and Dusty stopped in their tracks and stared blankly at me.

"Get in, get your asses in the car," I ordered.

"OK," said TJ.

We drove back to Cara's. Boys flopped down on the couch and love seat and overstuffed chair. TJ threw on gangsta rap CDs. Newport smoke filled the air. Boys drifted into the music, "So you wanna be a thug. . . ." It was a scene out of a Tarantino film.

Cara warned the boys about keeping the music low. She was afraid her downstairs neighborhoods would knock on the door and see the boys inside and complain to the landlord that too many people stayed at Cara's or, worse, call the KCPD. Each boy had at least one outstanding warrant, and all of them were on probation for offenses ranging from escape from a treatment center to assault.

A knock on the door, TJ lowered the music. "Who is it?" Cara asked. It was Taffy's daughter, a 16-year-old who was close to being morbidly obese, holding Charlene and a diaper bag. The fat girl handed Charlene to Cara and walked away; Cara would return Charlene to Taffy's the next day. Where Charlene was really didn't matter to Joanne; she was an addict and her life was easier if Charlene wasn't around. Chucky D said he'd kill Joanne if anything ever happened to Charlene. When Joanne passed Charlene along to folks who wanted to care for her, both Charlene and Joanne were safer.

Cara held the baby, who was now almost nine months old. She was a beautiful child with a round face and a pleasant disposition. The boys looked at Charlene and resumed their games.

TJ, Dusty, and Snoop played the hand-slap game and rotated opponents. Two boys stuck out their hands at waist height, first with palms together. Then one boy rotates his palms to face upward; his opponent places his hands on top, with palms facing downward. The bottom player tries to pull out his hands fast enough to slap the tops of his opponent's hands. These boys don't play friendly handslap. By the time it ended, the backs of Dusty's hands and lower forearms were fire engine red. They laughed as they pounded each other.

When Dusty stood up, I saw the outline of a knife in his right rear jean's pocket. "Hey, Dusty, got a knife in your pocket?" I asked, already knowing the answer. He reached into his pocket and took out a knife whose blade was six inches long. He opened the blade and looked at it like it was an old friend. He had already told us at dinner how much he likes to stab and slash people.

Snoop and Chris, in the meantime, shadowboxed, and when they weren't pulling up short on jabs and hooks and overhand rights, they challenged each other to do push-ups. Snoop and Chris looked at me as they boxed and did push-ups. Chris challenged me to do push-ups. These boys were lucky to do 15 to 20 of them. I ran 8 to 10 miles a day and knocked off 50 push-ups at a time. We hopped down onto the floor and did push-ups together, one by one. The boys quit at 20 or so; I quit at 50. They remained quiet and said nothing to me. Suddenly I felt apprehensive. Why, I said to myself, would I ever outdo a gang boy at push-ups? I wondered what would happen if either of them felt insulted. Nothing happened. I promised myself that the next time I wouldn't behave like a competitive adolescent.

All this was going on while Cara sat on the couch and held Charlene on her lap. Ten to 15 minutes later, Cara decided she had to clean the bathroom. She handed Charlene to TJ.

Shadowboxing and hand slap ended; the boys sat down. Cara gathered her cleaning buckets and sponge, stuck her hands into large yellow rubber gloves, and went off to scrub the toilet and the remaining tiles above the tub.

TJ held Charlene on one knee, sitting in the overstuffed chair. The other boys flopped on the couch and love seat. I sat at the kitchen end of the couch. Cara yelled from bathroom, "Don't you guys ever piss *into* the toilet?" The boys laughed. Cara finished the toilet and shower and then cleaned empty kitchen cabinets and killed cockroaches. Gangsta rap thumped and ricocheted off the walls.

I watched Cara clean; the boys smoked and bobbed their heads to the music. It shocked me to see TJ holding Charlene. It was so innocent, yet so dramatic. Here was a teenage boy who's father and mother had abandoned him, and he was now holding a baby whose father and mother often abandoned her.

These were typical days in Cara's life on Smart. TJ, Dusty, Snoop, Chris, and other boys too, like Sammy, would use Cara's place as their own. They'd meander in in the early evening or after she went to work, smoke weed, listen to music emitted by speakers four feet high, and eat leftover Taco Bell burritos and tacos Cara had put in the refrigerator for them. By the time she returned home from work at 4:00–5:00 in the morning, the boys would be asleep or ready to be.

Now and then, one or more Northeast boy would visit Cara at work and sit in the restaurant, watching and listening to Cara handle customers at the counter and drive-through window. One day, Cara told me, she and a Northeast girl got into an argument over an order. The girl was slow to make up her mind and changed her order several times. Cara was impatient and told the girl to hurry up. Cara said, "I mighta called her a dumb bitch." A hot argument ensued. Cara screamed at the girl, the girl screamed back. Threats were tossed back and forth, and the girl wanted to fight Cara then and there in the parking lot.

Sammy was Cara's guardian that day. When the girl threatened Cara, Sammy walked up, told the girl to "shut the fuck up" and get out. She insulted Sammy and Cara again, and Sammy ran out of patience, which he had in short supply anyway. He punched the girl in the face; she fell back into the counter and onto the floor. "Fuck da bitch," said Sammy. Cara agreed. "Oh, well," she said.

Another day Cara got into a raging screaming fight with a drive-through customer who was the cousin of someone Chucky D had shot. The customer recognized Cara as "Chucky's girl," and told her to tell Chucky D that he was going to kill him when he got out of prison. Cara, of course, had to defend Chucky D, but did it safely through thick glass and over a microphone.

March 3. I arrived at Cara's in the late morning. Carmen hadn't returned to Cara's the night before, Saturday night; neither had Cheri. Cara assumed they had spent the night with Carmen's sister. By early that afternoon the Northeast boys had wandered off toward The Spot. The phone rang. It was Wendy. That was a surprise.

Cara and Wendy had lost touch with each other after the bust. Cara hadn't seen her in months. Wendy had called Cathy and got Cara's phone number. What, I thought, did Wendy want? Cara told her that she and I would drive north of the river to visit her at the place she'd been staying for a few months. Before we drove away, I met Cara's neighbors across the hall.

Carol and Joe stayed in the apartment across from Cara's. Joe was an ex-con, in his middle thirties at the time, with a rock cocaine habit. Carol, a little younger than Joe, trips on rock and "meth" (speed). When I saw her she was always high or coming off a high and preparing to get high again.

Joe is short and round with dark short hair, and doesn't look like an ex-con. He has no tattoos on his neck or the backs of his hands and fingers. He has the look of someone who'd sell oranges door-to-door. In fact, he is a drug seller.

Carol calls herself the Gangsta Mamma. She is proud of her role as the protector of Northeast Gangsta kids. "Shit, I'm the gang mom. Just ask the cops, they'll tell ya. I let 'em hang out when they should be in school. They lay up, sleep all day, listen to music, and do their little things at night." Bernard said that when he was 14 and his brother Chris was 15 they stayed at Carol's on and off for more than a year. Drugs paid the rent. There's no free lunch on the street.[1]

Carol was once married to a KC fireman for 12 years and has several children by him and other men. Her 14-year-old daughter hangs out with Northeast boys and at this time was dating an 18-year-old fellow whom Cara knows from one of her commitments to a treatment center. Carol's daughter eventually became a teenage mother, as Carol once was.

Drug use has rotted Carol's teeth. Except for upper and lower incisors and canines, she is toothless. Nevertheless, Carol thinks she is a sexy woman, and she slunk around when I was at Cara's. That worried me. I didn't want Joe to think I was after his girlfriend, get jealous, and shoot me. I kept my distance whenever possible, but sometimes it was difficult. One afternoon Carol came into Cara's apartment. She said Joe bought her a black body stocking. I had never seen one before. Right there in front of Cara and me, Carol dropped her pants and took off her sweatshirt to show it, and herself, off. She made a point of yanking at the body stocking's crotch, to show me that she and Joe could make love even with it on. Cara was startled herself, but she laughed at the shock on my face. Cara told Carol to go home, because she and I had business to take care of.

A nearly naked, drug-addicted woman in a body stocking with an ex-con, drug-addicted boyfriend scared the hell out of me. "I saw her take off her clothes, Caramel, and I saw my life flash in front of my eyes as Joe chased me down The Ave, shooting at me with a 9-millimeter."

"Don't laugh, Mark. Joe's a silly ass, crazy, mothafuckin' doper. Don't trust him." Her words were prophetic.

Cara and I drove to find Wendy, who was staying 30 minutes north of Smart. She had moved several times after the bust and found a stable place with a former gang girl named Angie Lang, an 18-year-old with a 14-month-old son, fathered by a Southside gang boy. Wendy had met Angie three years earlier. When Angie was 14 and 15 years old, she hung out and had sex with LCBs, including Chucky D. Wendy met Angie through him. Angie had an apartment in an HUD housing complex. These were nice apartments for nearly no rent. Cara and I met Wendy and Angie in the parking lot when they were putting an infant seat in Angie's car.

Wendy and I hugged hello. We hadn't seen each other since the bust. We chatted and I caught up on news. Chubby-faced Robert was doing well with his foster family. He had been attending school and earning good grades, had stopped smoking weed, and hadn't been cursing as much, Wendy said. Jackie attended a court-ordered drug-treatment program, but Wendy didn't know where Jackie was staying then.

The point of Wendy's call to Cara was simple. Angie was driving Wendy crazy by offloading baby-care responsibilities onto her. Angie had a new boyfriend, and the baby was interfering with her love life. "I ain't no fuckin' day care center," Wendy howled as only she can do. "Dat bitch is not'in' but a 'ho'e."

Wendy needed a job. With income she could rent an apartment and escape from Angie and the baby-sitting chores. Wendy's need forecasted Cara's dim future.

Cara said she'd get Wendy an interview at Taco Bell on The Ave in the week of March 4. Wendy was thrilled.

Wendy, Cara, and I drove to Cara's. The girls smoked a few joints and just chilled. Wendy and Cara were hungry, and of course there was no food at Cara's. Cara said her income was too low to buy food, and "the boys" ate the Taco Bell burritos and tacos she had brought home. Instead of eating at Texas Tom's, I offered to take Cara and Wendy grocery shopping.

We went to Price Chopper, a proud sponsor of the Kansas City Chiefs. This is the store in whose parking lot chubby-faced Robert had lost the one-hitter his mother had given him on his ninth birthday.

Wendy and Cara, both in their late teens, didn't know how to shop and compare products and prices. Growing up inside treatment centers, detention centers, mental hospitals, and in a drug house had left a gaping hole in their knowledge about independent living.

As we walked down each aisle, I explained how to choose one product over another, how to compare the prices of products while keeping comparative quantities in mind, and how to select groceries on the basis of a menu plan. They enjoyed the lessons, and I did too, but the other shoppers, like the customers at McDonald's, were not thrilled.

Wendy and Cara carry street speech wherever they go and haven't learned how to switch vocabulary when social situations change. Cheerios were called "fucking Cheerios." "Hand me that package" became "Yo, mothafucka, gimme dat shit." In crowded aisles, customers must have thought I was a probation officer training young women on the basic life skills. Actually, if that's what customers thought, they weren't too far afield.

We left Price Chopper with $100 worth of groceries, and then stopped at the $1 Store in a strip mall on The Ave. The girls said they wanted to buy shampoo and conditioner and the other rubbing, smearing, and wiping products demanded by teenage girls. They wandered around, each with a plastic basket, looking at everything and comparing prices, talking about the inexpensive clothing for sale. I made sure they weren't shoplifting. I didn't want to go to jail.

Wendy and Cara stood in line. I stood next to them just in case they ran out of money, or in case Cara got angry at the checker for moving too slowly and started screaming, or in case Wendy picked a fight with another teenage girl. We waited for the customers ahead of us, and the line grew longer behind us. Companions of people in line milled about.

Cara looked into Wendy's basket and saw a box of champagne-flavored douche. Cara was taken aback. "You put that [champagne douche] up your shit?" she asked Wendy. She, of course, emphasized *shit* by shouting it.

"I always douche. I want my shit to be nice, biytch," Wendy responded.

"But you're not supposed to put flavor up yo' pussy," Cara said in the tone of an educator.

"Why not?" asked Wendy.

Cara explained that her mother had told her flavored douches aren't healthy. Wendy listened to Cara tell her to buy a vinegar and water douche.

"But biytch," Wendy proclaimed to everyone within earshot, "my boy like champagne."

A man, I thought, isn't supposed to be around teenage girls having this conversation. I was ready to crawl under the counter.

Customers, pretending they weren't hearing all this, stared at the ceiling, turned sideways, and, like me, tried to disappear.

Wendy asked Cara to hold her place in line. She walked back to the shelf and returned with vinegar and water.

"That'll keep yo shit nice, biytch, nice fo' yo boy, Glen." They smiled agreement at each other.

Glen is a marijuana dealer, about Wendy's age, whom Wendy had been dating for more than a year. Glen has a preschool-age son whom he rarely sees. He also offers the child's mother no social or financial support. Wendy had already been pregnant three times—once by Afro, once by Earl, and then by Glen. She lost these babies on January 13, 1994, in November 1994 (she didn't remember the date), and on August 2, 1995, respectively, because she didn't stop partying (drinking, smoking weed, staying up all night) and, like other pregnant Fremont girls, received little if any prenatal care. In this way, said Wendy and Cara, Fremont girls lose babies.

They paid for the shampoos, conditioners, and douches, and I thankfully fled that store and returned to Smart. We carried bags of groceries up the steps and into the kitchen and sent the legions of cockroaches scrambling when we piled the bags on the counters and wobbly kitchen table.

I watched Cara put away the groceries. Wendy made phone calls, one after another. She said Glen was driving over to pick her up. He arrived in about 30 minutes. On her way out the door, Wendy said to Cara, "Bitch, I'll let ya know if he like the taste of vinegar." They smiled.

Carmen had called earlier and said she was moving in with her sister. Cheri had wandered back to her mother's house. The Northeast boys hadn't yet shown up for the evening; it was still early, only 7:30. I told Cara I had to go home.

If I were to leave KC by 8:00, I'd be in my driveway at 2:30 in the morning and be on campus the next day. Driving long hours alone in the dark helped me withdraw. Days with Cara were long, 12 hours and longer, and by the time I'd spent 36 to 48 hours over three or four days with Cara or on Fremont at Teresa's, breathing secondhand marijuana smoke, which made me nauseous for hours, it took me from one to two weeks to see clearly all those things I'd heard and witnessed. I used time away from KC to write out the details of social scenes, listen to tapes recorded in those scenes, write up notes from the tapes, organize information in notebooks, outline each tape's content and assign each taped topic a counter number so I could find it again. And once that was done, I had to decide what I needed to do next.

Before I left, Cara and I hugged; she relaxed in my arms. I felt close to her. She had become one of my kids.

March 4. I called Cara in the evening and asked how she was doing, how work was going, and if TJ and his boys were there. Cara yelled to TJ that I was on the phone, and he asked to say hi to me. We chatted briefly; he's a laconic fellow on the phone. I promised to take him and his boys to Pizza Hut in two weeks. "Yeah, dat'd be good," he said with a pleasant calm tone in his voice. In the background I heard the Northeast boys joking as they listened to gangsta rap.

March 5. I called Cara; TJ answered the phone. We chatted. Cara was still at work. Our conversation was a bit longer than the night before. I asked what he'd done all day and teased him about staying at home while Cara worked and about being good.

"Hey, TJ, don' be gettin' in no trouble now, hear, mothafucka?" He laughed and thought it was funny that I used *mothafucka.*

"Yeah, I be good," he said.

"I gotta go, TJ," I said. "Stay away from the drug man."

He chuckled, "Shiyt."

I called Cara later that evening and spoke to her and to TJ again. The other boys were there too. Conversation wasn't serious, just chitchat and gossip. I told Cara I'd call later in the week or on the weekend. I reminded her that she could call me on my 800 number. She had memorized the number but kept forgetting the access code. I gave it to her again, and she said she'd add it to the long list of phone and pager numbers taped to the refrigerator door—her personal directory.

TJ tried to be good that night, but Dusty and a few other Northeast boys, Billy and Sammy, got involved in what the KCPD called armed criminal assault and robbery, and TJ was dragged into it, he said. He later gave me a partial version of all that happened that night after we had spoken.

Billy, Sammy, and Dusty were hanging out at Cara's in the early evening. The boys walked outdoors and stood outside the mudroom. They talked and stared down at the street. It was chilly but not too cold.

Four teenagers walked down the street, coming toward Cara's from The Ave. Two were wearing Kansas City Chiefs football jackets, one red, one black. Another wore a Notre Dame jacket; the fourth wore a gold jacket.

The three Northeast boys noticed the four boys and wanted their jackets. The Northeast boys ran down to the street to rob them. They pulled bandanas up over their faces, exposing only their eyes. Dusty, I was told, reached into his back pocket and said, "I'm coming back with blood on my knife." The Northeast boys met their victims and stood in their way, blocking the sidewalk.

TJ entered Cara's through the front door. Cara told him what was going on. He walked onto the back porch and saw his three boys robbing four boys, who were as big as and bigger than his companions. TJ ran down to the sidewalk and stood 20 to 30 feet behind the group, watching and waiting for a fight to break out, at which time he would help his companions.

The victims resisted at first. "If one o' you don't come outta that jacket, one o' you gonna get stabbed," Dusty said, pulling out his knife and opening it.

The boys gave up their jackets but apparently moved too slowly to please Dusty. He stabbed one, slashed another. The victims ran off. Northeast boys had four jackets, and they returned to Cara's. The jackets were stashed behind the couch. Cara washed blood off the blade and kept the knife.

March 6. At 11:00 in the morning my daughter, Emily, called me at my university office. "Dad, Cara just called and said to call her right away. It's very important, something about the police at her apartment."

I called. She answered on the first ring. "Mark, the cops are here. They surrounded my apartment house. There are cops and cop cars and vans all over this fucking place," she said in a panicked voice.

"Why are they there, Caramel? Were you inside the apartment?"

"They wanted to come into the apartment, and I wouldn't let them. I remembered what you said about making the cops get a warrant. I told them that, and the detective got very angry, and he said, 'If you don't let us in and make us get a warrant, I'll see to it you go to prison. But if you let us in to look around, I'll take care of you.' I told him to get a warrant, and he yelled at me. Should I make him get a warrant?"

"Absolutely, Cara, this is America, and police can't enter your apartment unless you let them or they have a warrant. Make them prove to a judge they have probable cause. By the way, what did you do? Why are the cops there? Everything was OK last night when we talked."

"Cops say I took guns the boys used in a drive-by last night across the hall into Carol and Joe's, and them motherfuckers say I did it. I didn't do shit, Mark. They just protecting their ass 'cause their place is full o' drugs."

"Where are you now, inside your apartment?"

"Nah, the cops made me stand in the hallway. TJ and them is inside."

The whole incident caught me so off guard and seemed so confusing that I still didn't realize Cara had already let the cops in. I went on reassuring her, "Don't panic, Caramel. Tell the detective to get a warrant, and whatever you do don't piss him off, don't tell him to go fuck himself, and don't call him a niggah mothafucker. You hear me?"

"I won't, I won't."

"Call me later. Tell me what happened?"

She hung up.

Then things took a turn for the worse after the mugging victims called the police. TJ was eventually arrested and picked out of a lineup. He hadn't worn a mask.

At 5:00 that afternoon the phone rang at my home. It was Cara.

"Mark, I'm in fucking jail. They arrested me."

"What charge?"

"Evidence tampering. Fucking Carol and Joe, them snitch mothafuckers, said all kinds o' bad shit about me, TJ, and the other boys too. They arrested a bunch of us. I don't have a lawyer, and the PDs are shit," Cara proclaimed.

"OK, here's a phone number for you." I gave her the phone number of the public juvenile defender's office. Early that day I had called a friend who's an attorney in a law enforcement agency in Kansas City; his wife has a general law practice and handles juvenile crime cases. Even at a discount to me, she wanted several thousand dollars up front. I knew Cathy couldn't afford it, and I didn't have that much cash. I talked to my lawyer about bailing out Cara or leaving her in jail. If Cara bailed out, she'd have to hire a private attorney; if she remained in jail, legal counsel would be provided.

I had cash to pay her $1,500 bail but decided to leave her inside. First, I didn't know the facts. I had no idea what her actual involvement was in the drive-by shooting; TJ and the other boys were allegedly involved in it, but that's all I knew. If Cara had been with them and if someone was injured or killed, Cara might certainly go to prison. I knew too little to bail her out. Second, if Cara had been on the street and involved in the drive-by, I was afraid that the victim's relatives would find some way to retaliate against her. Jail is uncomfortable, but there have been no drive-by shootings inside Cherry.

Jail was Cara's safest and healthiest temporary residence. Inside, I thought, she would sleep all night and during the day attend school and treatment programs. She'd eat, rest, and become more stable than she's been in a long time. I called Cathy. We discussed it. She agreed with me, for all the reasons noted, that the safest place for Cara was behind bars.

Her apartment at 5403 Smart was vacant but still held Cara's belongings. Her sister April was going to pack Cara's stuff and store it. Cara couldn't keep the apartment because she didn't know when, or if, she'd be released from custody. A week after the arrest, I called Cara's apartment on the afternoon that April had said she'd be there packing.

She told me that someone had broken into the apartment and stolen Cara's television, stereo, and CDs. April found three athletic jackets behind the couch, "neat ones," and packed them. A friend of Cathy's helped move the furniture.

Months later the Northeast and Fremont grapevine located Cara's property as well as the thieves who had broken down her front door and ripped off her stuff. Cara's television and stereo were now the property of Sammy's and Dusty's relatives.

Cara's dream ended in disaster. The disloyalty of the Northeast boys hurt her deeply. At first she refused to believe that kids who slept in her apartment and ate her food would be the ones to steal her possessions. Once the emotional pain and anger subsided, Cara said, "Oh well, they jus' be niggahs doin' what niggahs do."

The KCPD had arrested Cara and nearly two dozen Northeast Gangstas for a March 6 drive-by shooting. Cara's public defender told her that this event was KC's biggest-ever gang bust.

9
Borderline

Sitting on the seventh floor on Cherry, Cara knew she was in serious trouble. She was arraigned and held over for a grand jury hearing.

Cara tried to call me but couldn't, Cathy said, because the jail's phone system wouldn't allow inmates to use 800 numbers. What troubled me was that Cara couldn't call me collect either. Every two days I called Cathy's, and either Cathy or April shuttled information to me about Cara and her legal case. I asked Cathy to tell Cara to put me on her visitor's list.

I've worked in prisons and know why calling 800 numbers is disallowed prison and jail inmates: to prevent inmates from flirting with female operators, buying COD merchandise, and ordering catalogues about firearms and bomb manufacture. But why Cara couldn't call me collect made me suspicious and paranoid.

My name and 800 number had been posted on Cara's phone list taped to the refrigerator door. If detectives hadn't taken that list of phone and pager numbers, they'd have been stupid. That list was Cara's network of gang companions. I wasn't sure if the KCPD were lying in wait for me on my next trip to KC, or worse yet, if they had some scheme to file federal charges against me. Sounds paranoid, but it made sense to me at the time. I had been in the middle of two youth gangs, both known for drug distribution, both hotly pursued by the drug and gang detectives. I had imagined a trumped-up federal charge against me, maybe something to do with drugs, guns, and interstate flight to avoid prosecution, or maybe even interstate drug importation. After all, I live near Chicago, the home of America's big-time gangs.

Truth is, Cara's arrest and my active imagination scared the hell out of me, but not enough to keep me away from KC. I was more determined than ever to continue my research, but I knew I'd have to become sneakier. Cara's arrest and my paranoia altered the way I began to collect data. After March 6, I was frightened each time I entered KC. The KCPD aren't a friendly bunch of community-oriented police officers; to my mind, the only safe assumption about KC policing is that officers normally won't shoot you for speeding.

Before March 6, each KC trip had been motivated by a specific set of research questions, as well as a general agenda, which I considered to be the equivalent of a "fishing trip." I used my tape recorder to document interviews as well as natural conversations. I'd turn on the tape recorder in my car, Cara's apartment, Teresa's house, Joanne's house, Pizza Hut, Texas Tom's, McDonald's, Gate's, and while standing on the sidewalk on Fremont, and I let it document everything it heard. The kids trusted me and enjoyed listening to themselves on tape.

After March 6, I used the tape recorder to gather talk about murders, robberies, drug deals, carjackings, and assaults, but once I wrote up the information, I destroyed the tapes and notes and then "forgot" everything I'd seen and heard. And each time I visited Fremont and 13th and The Spot, I had both the office and the home phone numbers of my lawyer written in ballpoint pen on my upper calf. Should I get busted and have my property stolen, including my phone numbers, I wanted to be able to call my lawyer and get out of Cherry.

From June 1995 to March 6, 1996, I merely distrusted the police. After March 6, I feared the KCPD as much as the Fremont Hustlers and Northeast Gangstas did. My motto became: Hear no evil, see no evil, speak no evil.

Cara and I exchanged letters. She wrote regularly and used her letters to express emotions which were otherwise hidden from public view. The following letter was written a few days after her arrest:

Mark—
There's so much I must say. Everyday my body grows weaker, my mind slips away with it. I sit here and watch my life shatter piece by piece. The only things holding the little fragments together is my thoughts of how far I have come. Quitting is not in my vocabulary, but how can I move on. I'm all alone now, and it's scary. My worst fear is failure. I was raised to win. My life is getting no easier. I've dropped my old life, and struggled in the world of reality, but will I get better things? See new smiles? Happy faces? Or will I stay trapped in a world of hate, failure, disappointment and death? Nobody I guess knows, but I'll try. I've hit rock bottom. I was shot down, beat down, put down. But can I heal up, stand up, raise myself up? Will it ever end? How many homies will leave me this year by the hands of another nigga? How many homies will be torn apart? How many letters will go through the mail to my boys in prison serving time? I live in both worlds. No matter how far I walk, will I always walk the borderline of my past and my future? Can I escape? No. I'm trapped for life.

May the lord be with you for being so kind to someone who wasn't shit. I could never say enough but—Thank you,

Cara-mel

Cara was penniless. On a monthly income of $1,150, Cathy didn't have extra money to send her. I sent Cara a $25 money order every two weeks; otherwise she wouldn't have had money in her commissary (inmate "bank") account to buy personal hygiene items, such as shampoo and conditioner, and treats that make jail life a bit easier.

Cathy told me that Cara was trying to arrange a professional ("pro") visit for me and Phil Olson, my colleague and friend, a sociologist at the University of Missouri–Kansas City. Olson is an expert in community development. For 30 years he has studied KC local communities and been involved in community development. When Cara moved to 5403 Smart, I took Phil to her apartment and introduced him to her, Cheri, and Carmen. He was interested in their life-styles as a reflection of community disorganization. Phil, like me, wanted to help Cara and was willing to be Cara's local contact person.

I called Phil and told him the story of the bust on Smart. He wanted to visit her right away. I told him about the pro visit option. He called Cherry and talked to the official who oversees pro visits. Pro visits are contact visits, intended for attorneys, not college professors, where an inmate and his or her attorney sit together at a table and review the inmate's case. Most visits are noncontact visits, where an inmate and his or her visitor sit on opposite sides of a thick plexiglass partition and speak over a black phone.

Phil told the pro visit manager that he and I were helping Cara get through high school and into college, and despite her current trouble, we were standing by her. Phil visited Cara and called me afterward to say that Cara was terrified and in tears. After Phil's first visit, Cara called him regularly, and he then would call or e-mail me.

The weeks passed, still no word on the disposition of Cara's case. I began to think again about paying the $1,500 bail and getting her out. I felt it was inappropriate for me to make such a decision without consulting Cathy. I called her. She said Cara's spirits were good. She was busy every day and was attending GED classes, Alcoholics Anonymous, and Narcotics Anonymous, and had been appointed as her housing unit's lead inmate (a housing unit is two-tier residence unit; each unit has a lead inmate who oversees daily activities, such as sanitation and meal distribution). As long as she could be the boss and in the middle of the action, she'd feel better.

A week after Phil's first visit, I received another letter from Cara. It was brighter than the first one.

Mark—
I received your money order along with your letter today and I wanted to thank you very much for all your concern. You told me [in your letter] not to buy bud [marijuana] w/it (well . . . actually I kinda wish I could) but to be for real: I'm attending the JAM program, it's a drug program [lasting three weeks]. I'm gonna graduate, and when I get out stay away from bud, brews, and hopefully even my Newports. The temptation isn't as hard here as it will be out there, but why not do it all in one swipe (changing my whole life)? My physical withdrawals from cigarettes are gone. Believe me I still get cravings but I can do it, right? Oh yeah! I go to GED classes up here 2x's a week for one hour. But starting Monday, I'll go to pre-GED three hours everyday. Cool huh? That's 17 hrs a week at school (and I'm in jail). I go to JAM three hours everyday. So, I'm going to sign up for choir and I go to church on Sunday.

Mark—I talked to Phil a few days ago and I feel like I might of kinda raised my voice. He didn't act like he was offended but could you tell him if I did, I am sorry. I was really frustrated on my case and kinda jumpy. You two and my mom are my hope for now, and always.

Mark—I'm so scared. I wrote Chucky and Sammy telling them I must move on to better things, that I was sorry. I loved them all, but I keep getting pulled down because of how they lived. I feel like I'm not a true friend, but now I must think of me, right?

Thanks for being there for me and being my friend. One day I'll be able to pay you-n-Phil back, even if it means just living right. Love always,
Cara-mel

The final week of March was approaching, and there was no word on when the grand jury was scheduled to convene. Phil and I talked and decided to call Cara's public defender instead of hearing news from Cara, Cathy, and April. I told Phil that calls from us to the PD would indicate to her that Cara has so-called community support from legitimate folks.

I called the PD's office several times but never got a call back; perhaps, I thought, the PD's office didn't have a budget line for out-of-state calls. Phil persisted and talked to the PD. He explained his and my involvement in Cara's life and said we'd go to court on her behalf.

Phil was impressed with the PD's knowledge of Cara's case and with her personal concern for Cara's well-being. This convinced me that the PD was not a "two-minute" lawyer, a disinterested and overworked public servant who meets a client two minutes before court convenes. I called Cathy and told her that Phil and I felt good about the PD. Cathy felt better.

The PD said Cara was in very serious trouble, but the police didn't have "hard" evidence of her involvement in Northeast's drive-by shooting. Cara's fingerprints weren't on the weapons. Also, the PD said that the police witness, Joe, the ex-con drug addict who was shacked up with Carol the Gang Mamma, wouldn't be a credible prosecution witness.

The KCPD's game was obvious: they got Joe to snitch on Cara and TJ and, in turn, overlooked the illegal drugs in Joe and Carol's apartment. Joe had been in a tight spot, facing parole revocation, so he put Cara and TJ in jail to keep himself out.

Detectives wanted Cara to name T-Man's killer. The cops were really after Afro or Chucky D, both well known to the KCPD. They'd release Cara if she'd point the finger at a killer. Her options were: snitch on T-Man's killer (although Cara insisted then and throughout this research that she knew nothing about that shooting); admit she had tampered with the weapons used in the drive-by shooting (her alleged tampering with evidence was that she had carried guns from her apartment across the hall into Joe and Carol's, where they were found by the police); or stand trial for armed criminal action.

I still hadn't heard from Cara about a visit. Phil gave me the name of the pro visit manager. He'd allow me to have a contact visit, but he knew Phil and I were scamming him. I drove to KC to visit Cara.

It was the end of March. KC was awakening from the winter and about to blossom. The weather was warming quickly, grass was turning green, and the Royals' opening day was the next week.

I drove to Cherry and parked in an underground parking lot across the street and to the east of the jail. Parking there was cheap. Parking lots and businesses near jails are a microexposure of the American class structure. In the underground parking lot, old junkie cars driven by inmates' visitors park next to new BMWs and Ford Tauruses driven by those who earn their living by prosecuting or defending kids like Cara and TJ or by keeping them imprisoned.

I arrived at Cherry early and walked around. Street folks' seedy bars dot the blocks around Cherry, and so do bail bondsmen, upper-scale eateries, and Friday-afternoon get-together places for the urban elite. I've seen little in most of these folks' behavior to suggest that they feel they have a stake in improving neighborhoods like Fremont and the juvenile justice system.

I entered the jail and walked to the visitor's check-in desk in the lobby, gave the young man my name, and he searched for it on the pro visitor's list. It was there; I was amazed, but then he couldn't find Cara's name on the inmate roster. "She's not here," he sad. "Oh yes, she is," I told him. He looked again and discovered he had overlooked her name on the roster, printed with a ribbon that should have been changed months ago. I stashed my coat, wallet, keys, and coins in the lobby lockers and waited while someone called upstairs to tell Cara I was on my way. I sat in the lobby on the hard plastic bench seats next to women and children awaiting their turn for a visit.

It has always hurt me to see children in jails and prisons. If I had my way, minors wouldn't be allowed inside a correctional institution, ever. To these children, visiting the jail has become as familiar as meandering in a grocery store or going to the post office. There is no surprise on their faces. They know where to find the few plastic toys tossed into a corner for them to play with and are familiar with the check-in routine. There's no sadder sight than seeing a child in a jail visiting room.

"Flesher," called the officer, mispronouncing my name. Now I had to go visit a child in a jail cell. I didn't like this one bit.

The elevator dropped me on the ninth floor. The stainless steel door opened into a sally port. There were a living unit and visiting rooms to my left and to my right. I pressed the stainless nipple on the wall in front of me, alerting someone in a control booth to open the sliding door that separated me from the visiting room. Through a speaker in the sally port, I heard "to your left." The steel door cranked open with a high-pitched squeal. Even the doors suffer on Cherry.

The pro visit room was 10 by 10 and dotted with stainless-steel-topped tables, three feet in diameter, surrounded by short, stainless-steel-topped stools. I sat down and waited. On the far left was a steel door with a plexiglass window five feet above the gray-painted concrete floor. On the right was the incoming sliding door through which I had walked.

The squeal of the visitor's door distracted me from my thoughts about what I'd say to Cara. A little girl, maybe four, walked in. Her hair was pulled into cornrows, and she wore a pretty blue dress and sneakers. The round-faced girl looked like a kid on her first day at school. Next to her was a social worker in her midtwenties. She was comfortable in the visiting room and with the child. I knew she'd been doing this kind of work for a while.

This curvy and lean young woman had perfect teeth and flawless tanned skin, was an inch over five feet, and had long wavy brown hair that draped below her shoulders onto her upper back. Her hair shone and reflected the light cast down from incandescent lights in the ceiling, and it cascaded over a beautiful, multicolor sweater, the sort I've seen in the windows of the expensive shops on the Plaza. Tasteful leather shoes, a full-length skirt that matched the sweater, and an engagement ring whose diamond was as big as my nose completed her jail ensemble.

The inmate door opened; a frail woman walked in. Another rock cocaine addict, I thought. I silently conjured this woman's story to test my power of prediction. I guessed she was a habitual rock addict. The baby in the visitor's room was the outcome of sex with an anonymous guy who gave her rocks or cash for rocks in exchange for sexual intercourse and oral sex. This youngster, I guessed, had been picked up by social service authorities after the woman was busted for possession of cocaine or for hooking on a street corner east of The Paseo at 2:00 in the morning.

Cara's face appeared in the inmate's door. She looked awful. Her eyes were droopy and sad, and the lids were half closed. I hated seeing her in Cherry's orange overalls. The steel door slid open; I stood up.

"Caramel," I said and reached out to hug her. She fell into my arms. I hugged her as I do Aaron and Emily when they've had something unpleasant befall them. Her body relaxed and leaned into me, her head on my left shoulder, her arms loosely folded around my back. I squeezed her, rubbed her back lightly, and patted her. She cried.

We sat down. She sobbed and hung her head. Tears dripped from her pale cheeks onto the stainless-steel table top, creating half a dozen puddles. I reached over and took her right hand and sandwiched it between mine, saying nothing.

"Oh, Mark, I'm so scared."

"I know, Caramel, I know."

Ten minutes passed before she could talk. She needed to talk about her legal case and the injustice leveled against her by the police for "listening to that fuckin' snitch Joe and dat bitch 'ho'e Carol. Dem motherfuckers put me here, and I ain't gonna forget it. Fuck, Mark, I'm scared. I could go to prison, and I ain't did shit."

She said that her PD had talked to her about a plea bargain and probation, once the grand jury made a decision. Cara's reaction was predictable. "Fuck dem, I ain't did shit, and I ain't copping to nothin' neitha." I knew once she was on the street again, I'd be able to convince her to take the plea.

"Caramel, if you stand trial, the prosecutors'll make you and TJ look like Bonnie and Clyde. Don't fuck with them. Get out of this mess in the easiest way."

"Fuck dem. I ain't doin' it. I'll go to trial."

The social worker and the little girl walked out of the room before I did. The social worker told the preschooler to hug and kiss her mommy. The kid followed orders. The mother hugged the child with the same affection that a staggering drunk uses to hang on to a tree as he's urinating.

Before I left, I tested my prediction about the woman and the child. The woman, Cara said, was on the pipe and had been riding with her pimp at 3:00 in the morning. She had her little girl in the back seat. The child awakened and cried; the crying annoyed the pimp. He told the child's mother to get rid of the kid or he'd cut off the woman's rock supply. The pimp stopped the car in the middle of a downtown KC street and the mother opened the car door and abandoned the child. Mom and the pimp drove off.

Cara's arrest and my own growing paranoia about the KCPD kept me looking over my shoulder as though I were a teenage drug seller. It was the day before Easter at 2:00 in the afternoon. Easter is a good time to take a breath of fresh air, enjoy the early spring, and feel alive. The day was beautiful and the blue sky was broken only by billowing white clouds. The air was clear and cool, and it felt good to be alive.

I dropped a quarter into one of the two pay phones at the northeast corner of the parking lot two blocks uphill from Cathy's Van Brunt apartment. Cathy had moved there a few months earlier. I called Bernard and left a message on his pager's voice mail. I asked him to meet me in the parking lot adjacent to Popeye's Chicken. I knew he wouldn't show up, but that didn't matter to me at that moment. I simply felt the need to reach out to him, to stay in touch with one of the more elusive kids on the street. He's elusive for a good reason. He's always being chased.

Bernard, Northeast TJ, Afro, Chucky D, and the other hardcore kids have been hunted as if they had a bounty on their heads. Cops want them as trophies, and the only direct association the majority of citizens have with gang kids is driving by Cherry. Kansas Citians believe that Bernard and Cara are feral humans. Nothing could be further from the truth. But taxpayers' error in judgment is good for the juvenile justice business.

The business of gang policing and juvenile custody requires employees. As the number of imprisoned kids increases, employees are added. These workers process arrested kids into correctional facilities, watch over them inside, and provide services, such as education and medical and dental care. If citizens feel scared and politicians feel threatened by citizens' fear, police departments are charged with the responsibility of "cleaning up" the street. That euphemism means arresting and imprisoning more kids. In the end, kids like Cara are commodities that represent a certain number of jobs in the juvenile justice system, employees' retirement checks, and purchases made with salaries, including boats, summer vacations, and house mortgages. And taxpayers pick up the tab.

In the last half of the 1800s slaves were sold in an area of KC a few blocks north of the Plaza. Today Missouri trades in teenagers who have disobeyed the community's rules.

Staying in touch in a genuine way was important to me and is also the key ingredient in gang ethnography. Once I got to know these kids, I needed to be a good companion, not just a researcher. More times than I can remember, I didn't open a notebook or turn on a tape recorder. As I grew to like these kids I didn't want them to feel I was only using them as "research subjects." I thoroughly enjoyed their banter and some of their outlook on life. Most of all, I appreciated their irreverence for things that mainstream life tells them they are supposed to do and care about. Wouldn't I like to say "fuck it" and do whatever I want to do without worrying about what people will think? Well, they do. But, I wondered, do they act this way out of courage or out of fear? Are these kids disobedient, as mainstream folks think, or are they acting out a need to survive in the only way they know how?

I was standing in the parking lot next to Popeye's, across the street from and south of a bar sporting a huge handpainted sign above its open door:

COUNTRY'S INN. COME ON IN AND FORGET . . . YOUR PAIN.

To the east, on a narrow street that runs parallel to Van Brunt, a few white guys were selling fruits and vegetables on the sidewalk. To the south, on the west side of Van Brunt, a white preacher and black parishioners celebrated Easter by calling to neighborhood folks to attend church. The preacher had set up a microphone and speakers on the sidewalk. From this outdoor pulpit he praised the Lord, hour after hour. No one left Country's Inn to pray.

On April 8 at 8:00 in the evening, the phone rang. Cathy had never before called me. Cara had been charged with tampering with evidence; TJ, with armed criminal action and first-degree assault for the robbery of the athletic jackets; Chris, 19, TJ and Bernard's eldest brother, was already serving a 12-year state sentence for armed criminal action (a drive-by shooting).

Cara had called Cathy after the grand jury hearing. Cathy reported the conversation to me: "Cara said, 'The judge looked at me like I was a killer.' I told her, 'She [the judge] looks at everyone like that.' Cara doesn't understand. She's still young."

Cara then began having nightmares and writing about them. Cara expresses feelings and emotions clearly in prose but has a harder time doing it in speech, because her anger muddles her articulation. Cara kept a journal of jail poems. The following is one she wrote after the indictment:

Reality

There're chances you take, and chances you don't
Places you'll go, and places you won't
there are dreams to follow and failure ahead
Life beyond meaning and death beyond dead
There're babies that cry in the dark of the night
Mommas to cuddle them and say its alright
There're men with guns, the bullets no names
Innocent children dying in their games
Women who want children but seem to only fail
Mothers on trial for the children they killed
The use of a knife against one's throat
No need for this; just wanting his coat
Black is the sky, the dreary night
In the alley screams of another fight
Glass breaks against the wall—
blood on his hands—the other one falls
The screaming of a mother's cry
Hanging on the phone, her son gone in a drive-by
Reality is all you know—where else can you go?
Will you live or will you die?
or will you be lucky for a second try?
Convicts stand behind thick walls;
doing time for what went wrong
Some are guilty this I know—
but some are innocent and
must be let go
But who's to make that awful choice?
and go along with the same ol' course
The things you feel the things
you've seen are very real to you and me
Distance between us grows and grows
Tomorrow is the guess that nobody knows
Be careful of what you choose

It was now the middle of April. Cathy, Phil, and I waited to hear about the next step. Would Cara be offered a plea, or would prosecutors take her case to trial?

I talked to Cathy every two days and got reports about Cara, and Cathy forwarded Cara's messages to me. The longer Cara stayed in jail, the less frequently she called Phil. I kept writing and sending money orders. Cara stopped writing.

One night in mid-April I called Cathy. She told me that Cara had had an especially powerful dream that awakened her in the middle of night. Her journal was next to her bed, and she recorded words spoken to her in the dream.

In her dream Cara was killed by an unknown assailant, and Chucky D avenged her death by murdering Cara's killer. In the following poem, Chucky D speaks to the dead Cara:

The Killing of Three Hearts
He must have thought I'd let him walk
To brag what he did—to talk his talk
But he should have known what he did to you
You should have seen that face of his
One way be begged me to let him live
He said he was sorry for what he did
Cried like bitch—whined like a kid
I looked him straight into his eyes
I seen that he had started to cry
My smile widened, my anger flared
His life I would take and wouldn't care
He dropped to his knees, begging me please
"Whatever you do, don't hurt me"
"You took away my love, and now she's gone
Her life is over, I'm all alone
My better half can't talk to me
The way we use to that hurts me, G
It'll take your life, as you took hers
You'll get dissed, just what you deserve"
His heart was beating awfully fast
The hatred I felt to kick his ass
I wanted him to feel what he did to you
So I kicked and hit him till he turned blue
I seen the blood flowing out of his mouth
My pain was easing, but I still had doubt
I'd never be able to laugh w/you
So now what was I supposed to do
I grabbed him up by his throat
Blood was draining down his coat
His eyes were swollen, his nose was broke
With his own blood, he began to choke
My mind went blank and all turned black
I knew that I couldn't journey back

The phone rang in the middle of Saturday afternoon, April 20. It was Cara. She was at Cathy's on Van Brunt and had arrived home on April 19. She bubbled, and I heard Cathy talking to me in the background, trying to be heard over Cara's exuberant voice. "What happened, Caramel? How did you get out?" I asked.

Cara said her attorney had requested another court hearing with a different judge. She got it. The judge reviewed the facts and saw that there was no hard evidence against Cara, and the only witness was ex-con Joe. Cara said that the judge ordered her immediate release, and given the nature of the fuzzy evidence against her, the judge, said Cara, remarked that her case had been mishandled. By default, the judge had also eliminated the cops' T-Man squeeze play on Cara. A plea bargain was now imminent.

Cara was thrilled and felt a sense vindication, but she still wasn't off the hook. The final disposition of the case had to be worked out between Cara's PD and the prosecutors.

The next Thursday I visited her for the weekend. When she opened the door to Cathy's apartment, a big smile creased her face. She still looked like Cara, but a lot healthier than I had ever seen her. She wasn't exhausted; she'd been eating three times a day; she'd been sleeping at night; and she hadn't used drugs for 43 days.

Now on home confinement, she wore an electronic monitoring device on her ankle and had to report to her probation officer weekly. Cara said the PO told her that she would be allowed to work but she had to go back to her mother's. She was housebound. Over the first few weeks, she felt like a free woman. Then home confinement became restrictive, and she began to worry about how she'd pay the $896 dollars she owed the court for the victim's fund, court costs, house arrest fees, lawyer's fees, and room and board at Cherry, at $20 a day for 43 days. Her PO set up a rough payment schedule and gave Cara deadlines to pay her debts. Cara fought this every step of the way.

Cathy sat on the couch, Cara on the love seat, I in a stuffed armchair along the wall between the kitchen and bathroom. April wandered back and forth, listening but uninvolved.

"Fuck dem," Cara howled. "They throw me in dat fuckin' jail for 43 days and feed me shit and treat me like shit, and they want me to pay for it. Fuck dem."

From her bedroom April injected, "Yeah Cara, you tell 'em, girl. Fuck them, huh? Well, they'll fuck you. You're lucky you're out."

"Watch your language, girls," Cathy said in a mother voice. She glanced at me, I at her, and we nodded agreement as parents.

"Cara, you are lucky . . ." Cathy started, but Cara cut her off. I cut off Cara before she began ranting.

"Caramel," I said in my father voice, "if you don't make some effort to pay something, they'll revoke your probation and you'll be back in jail and have to pay even more. Look, just call the PO and talk to her about it. Be nice, don't scream and call her a bitch or a niggah or a mothafucker, you hear me?" I looked at Cathy waiting for her to tell me not to use such language.

"Yeah, listen to him, Cara," Cathy said pointedly.

Cara laughed. She looked at Cathy and me as if she had two parents. "Now I gotta fight two of you, shiyt," Cara said, smiling.

Regularity returned to Cara's life. Cathy enjoyed having her at home, even though her tiny apartment was packed with people and she and Cara snapped at each other more than Cathy liked. Cara staying at home didn't mean she'd stay out of trouble though.

Cathy and April slept in the bedrooms, Melanie slept on one couch, sometimes with her boyfriend on the floor below her, and Cara had the other couch. Taco Bell became Cara's full-time obsession again, and she seemed to be doing well. Tranquility set in, because the electronic monitoring device and the threat of jail kept her home and off the street. She was also ordered not to have contact with a long list of Northeast boys who had been arrested in the Smart bust, including Bernard and TJ.

TJ stayed on Cherry. Sammy had his charges lessened and disappeared into the crevices at The Spot. Bernard not only talked to Cara; he also came by to visit her when Cathy was at work. While there, they'd arrange three-way calls which allowed Cara and Bernard to talk to TJ inside Cherry. I got in on it too. Oh, the wonders of technology.

Talking to TJ wasn't the only thing Bernard and Cara did. They also smoked weed, lots and lots of weed. Because Cara hadn't been arrested on a drug charge, she wasn't required to have regular urine tests.

Cara's presence back on the street was a social magnet. Kids flocked to Cathy's like Royals' fans to the beer counter at Kaufman Stadium. Cara and Bernard met Wendy, Cheri, Steele Bill, and Glen, as well as Glen's drug-smoking, drug-dealing companions, at Cathy's house when she was at work.

Steele Bill and Glen were full-time marijuana sellers. Weed was never in short supply. Cara enjoyed having Steele Bill around the house. Cara and Steele Bill had been together in the late summer of 1995, and that August Cara had lost his child. Steele Bill and Cara started to move closer again.

Steele Bill's girlfriend, Janet, was nearly six months pregnant now. Bill balanced time with Cara and Janet, but because he relied on Janet's duplex as his residence, he wasn't ready to jeopardize a place to sleep and a source of food by getting too close to Cara. Had Steele Bill and Cara slept together again, the Fremont gossip network would have sent that news to Janet in microseconds, and a war would have ensued. Steele Bill and Cara negotiated a relationship, for now at least, based on marijuana.

Within days of Cara's release from Cherry, the social scenes I had witnessed on Fremont and 13th and at 5403 Smart were being re-created at Cathy's when she was away. Kids smoked weed on the enclosed back porch, bought and sold weed in April's room, and when April was there, she smoked too. The phone started ringing at all hours, and in the wee morning hours, kids banged at the door. This was driving Cathy crazy.

The chaos of late April slowly subsided in May. The clandestine meetings at Cathy's apartment ended because she laid down the rules. She was absolutely fed up with incessant phone calls and knocks on the door at 1:00 in the morning. Cara worked every day, but her hours switched from the night shift of 8:00 in the evening to 4:00 in the morning to regular day hours or late afternoon and evening hours. With this schedule Cara was free to answer the phone and the door late in the evening.

Cathy's rules were house law. Cara couldn't run away from home without going to jail. Cara conformed, because the memories of jail and the fear of 60 months or more in prison terrified her. Cathy was pleased; tranquility set in again, at least temporarily.

Most of the month of May was calm. Cara was going to work and following court orders, up to a point, and there had not been a plea bargain offered yet by the prosecutor's office. But Cara got into trouble again between late May and mid-June.

Cara worked at Taco Bell on The Ave. She caught a bus to work and got a ride home, usually with some Fremont or Northeast kid who was hanging around protecting her. Recall that it was common for these boys to watch Cara and Wendy. They'd sit at the tables for hours; however, Cara was now also being watched by a fellow she'd never met, a boy named Drez.

Drez watched Cara hour by hour and tried to talk to her. "I tol' him to fuck off." But he had a car, which made Cara's life easier. He was annoying and obnoxious, Cara said, but she started dating him anyway. When that happened he became jealous of other boys who talked to Cara, but he was insanely jealous of Cara's relationship with Chucky D.

Cara talked continuously about Chucky D and how much she loved him and the wonderful life they'd have when he got out of prison. Drez's jealousy led to anger and then to violence. He began to hit Cara. She'd go home with black and blue marks on her arms and shoulders. Cathy questioned her about the injuries. Cara defended Drez. Cathy tried to protect Cara by telling her love isn't hitting your partner. Cara saw Cathy's advice as an attempt to control her. Cara's relationship with Drez was the lightning rod for old anger between Cathy and Cara. Outbursts echoed off the walls.

"I caused the hitting most of the time," Cara explained to Cathy.

"It doesn't matter who caused it, Cara," Cathy said in a mother voice. "Hitting should never be part of love. He beat her up, Mark, look at her arm," said Cathy, pointing at Cara's black-and-blue wounds.

Cara's injuries looked like those caused by repeated pounding with a blunt object. In the heyday of Fremont, Wendy and Angie and other girls had had similar injuries.

"I pushed him," Cara tried to explain, "and punched him in the eye. He was just protecting hisself from me. Sometimes love makes you do stupid shit, know what I'm sayin'? He said he was sorry. He does a lot of good stuff for me too. He drives me around."

Drez would appear at Cathy's unexpectedly, to see if Cara was dating another boy. He was driving Cara and Cathy crazy. One day Drez's harassment ended with a phone call. Cara and Cathy told me about it.

Drez showed up at Cara's. Cara opened the door while she was on the phone with Chucky D. Drez got furious, snatched the phone out of her hand, and told Chucky D that if he didn't stop calling Cara, Drez would kill Charlene.

Cara heard that and grabbed the phone from Drez. Chucky D told Cara to put Drez back on the phone. Drez listened, said nothing, handed the phone to Cara, and walked out. Cara never heard from him again. Chucky D had told Drez that he knew where Drez stays and what kind of car he drives, and that if he didn't leave Cathy's, he'd die that day by the hand of Eddie Solo.

Drez disappeared, but he left Cara pregnant. On July 2, 1996, at five-and-a-half weeks, Cara miscarried. She said an RH-factor incompatibility had caused the miscarriage. In the weeks between the positive pregnancy test and the miscarriage, Cathy and Cara announced to everyone the impending birth.

Cathy was at first shocked but then said, "If it's gonna happen, it's gonna happen, so I'll be a grandma again. What can I do about it? She's young, but I was young too."

Cathy announced to co-workers that she would soon be the grand-mother of a "mixed baby." Mother and grandmother seemed excited. Neither of them, however, was disappointed or saddened by the mis-carriage.

On Fremont babies come, babies go. This was Cara's third pregnancy in two years. Pregnancy and miscarriages, and 15- and 16-year-old girls giving birth, raise no one's eyebrows on Fremont.

The following is a childbirth tally during the 21 months I hung with Fremont kids (this list doesn't include miscarriages): Joanne gave birth to Charlene, Chucky D's daughter, and became pregnant a third time with a child fathered by one of Chucky D's cousins. Teresa gave birth to baby Kevin and within weeks became pregnant again with another one of Kevin's. Christina, Lucky's stepsister, gave birth to their first daughter. Rosa had Afro's daughter. "Too Small," a charming and quiet 16-year-old, had Cain's second child sometime in late 1996 (he had no contact with his first child, who was cared for by its mother's mother). Angie had Wayne's child, Olivia, in early 1997. Janet delivered Steele Bill's baby in September 1996.

Cara was forced to remain at Cathy's apartment, and wandering off to Fremont or Northeast wasn't as easy, but she still did it. I would give Cara a week's notice, she would tell her PO that her out-of-town "uncle" would be in KC for the weekend, and the PO would give Cara permission to leave home.

Cara fled the confines of home with gusto. To her, physical confinement was also emotional confinement and someone's attempt to control her, and these were punishments worse than Cherry.

During the time I hung with Cara, I also saw folks on Fremont, but I wouldn't tell Cara when I did it, whom I saw, and what I was doing, especially if I wandered off to see someone like Janet. Cara and Janet "hated" each other, because they vied for Steele Bill's affection and because Janet had dated Chucky D in 1994.

When I became close to Fremont girls, they used me in "palace intrigue." Then when I hung with Northeast boys, I had to be careful to balance my time between them and Fremont kids, in order to avoid jealousy.

At first I didn't understand the dynamics of this, but then it dawned on me: I had become a valuable legal resource. By June 1996, I had been on Fremont a long time and had, since January that year, earned a good reputation among Northeast kids. To these kids, "Mark Fleisher" equaled McDonald's, Pizza Hut, Gate's Barbecue, and Texas Tom's greasy food, grocery shopping, rides around the city, counsel when they got into trouble, cigarettes, commissary money, and companionship. But I never became an ATM machine.

Only at the end of the research did I pay for interviews, and then I offered cash only to Cara and to Wendy because they were in a tight spot. Before the Fremont bust I didn't pay anyone for an interview. I never paid a Northeast boy, nor did I pay anyone hanging around Fremont or 5403 Smart.

I paid Cara twice and Wendy once—$20 for interviews lasting between an hour and a half and two hours. I paid them only because they asked me to give them money outright. I wouldn't do that, and wanted them to recognize that my money was part of a negotiation: cash in exchange for time and information.

Although I paid Cara and Wendy only a few times, Cara often asked for money, as if I paid her an allowance, and she asked in a clever way. She'd call, we'd chat, I'd ask her how she was feeling and about her job; about Cathy, April, and Melanie; about Wendy, Cheri, Jackie, and Mike (Wendy's father); about her new boyfriends; and she'd give me a rundown on street happenings from Northeast and Fremont. Then she'd turn the conversation either to the money she owed the court or, after she purchased an old Ford Escort in May 1996, to the cost and urgency of car repairs.

Once she was in hot water over nonpayment of court fees associated with home confinement, and I sent her $100 dollars to get her out of trouble; I also told Cathy that I'd sent Cara money for that purpose. I never gave her money to fix her car. I had told her not to buy it, and afterward I wouldn't support her decision with my money. She knew it and stopped asking.

Once in the summer of 1996, Cara called me in the middle of a Thursday afternoon. I was at home writing about the Fremont Hustlers. She called from a pay phone in midtown KC near Cherry. She and Cheri were off wandering and waiting to meet Cheri's newest boyfriend, whom Cara didn't like because he beat Cheri. Cara said Cheri wanted to say hi. I knew this would be a request for cash.

"Hi, Cheri, you doing OK?" I asked.

"Well, not really."

"Why? What's up?"

"My ma lost her job last week and now she can't pay the utility bills, and we don't have no electricity and no phone and no food."

"Is your mom looking for work?"

"Yeah, but she cayn't find none."

"Well, Cheri, why doesn't your mother go to a government office and ask for help, food stamps, something?"

"Well, she hasn't been feelin' too good lately."

So it went, until I told Cheri I'd see her on my next time to KC. Cheri's mother, a 39-year-old die-hard rock cocaine and speed addict, wastes cash on drugs. Janet had hired Cheri's mother to work in the convenience store Janet managed, but, Janet said, Cheri's mother either didn't show up for work or didn't work when she did show up. Janet had hired Cheri's mother only because Janet and Dante, Cheri's sister, are best friends. Janet eventually fired Cheri's mother, which alienated Cheri. Janet then hired her own father to replace Cheri's mother, because he needed a second job.

Cara was offered a plea bargain in the second week of June. A guilty plea to a D-class felony on evidence tampering would be expunged if Cara successfully completed two years' probation; if she failed probation, she'd go to court and face a prison term. Or, she could hire a private attorney and stand trial. The plea sounded like a winner to me and to Cathy, but Cara dug in her heels and screamed.

On a Saturday morning a few days after Cara had been offered the plea bargain, Cathy, Cara, Melanie, Melanie's boyfriend, and I sat in Cathy's living room and discussed Cara's options. April wandered between her bedroom and the kitchen and bathroom, looking and listening and saying nothing.

By this time Cara hadn't yet forgotten about her anguish on Cherry. She was feeling free and feisty and wanted to fight the world. Cathy had rented the movie *Twister*, which was playing in the background. A fitting movie, I thought, to match Cara's mood.

"Fuck dem, I ain't gonna do it," Cara howled. "Why should I? I didn't do dem things they say I did. Mom, didn't you teach us not to lie? If I take the plea I'll be lying. Now dat ain't right, is it, Ma?"

"But Cara, if you go to trial, you don't know what'll happen, do you? They'll say bad things about you, and the jury won't know who you are; they'll only know what the prosecutor says about you," Cathy said in the low calm tone of an advisor.

My turn. "Your mom's right, Caramel. Look, people in KC are afraid of gangs and gang kids and gang crimes. The newspapers and television have scared the hell out of them, and you're one of the people they're scared of. If you stand trial, you don't know what the prosecutor will say. You hung on Fremont and with Northeast boys, you haven't been to school since you were 14, you been shot in a walk-by shooting in gang territory, everybody in town has heard about the Fremont Hustlers, and they'll say you were a big part of all of it.

"Now if I get called to testify, which I'm likely to be, I can say that Fremont was just a bunch of kids hanging out; some of them may have sold drugs and some may have done bad things, but do you think anyone on the jury will believe me? Cara, they'll hang you, send you to prison, and none of them will lose a minute's sleep over it."

April walked into the living room, took a Newport off the coffee table, and stood in the kitchen listening.

Cathy agreed with me. "He's right Cara. They'll turn you into a crazy monster." Cathy looked at me and at Cara and said, "Of course, we know you *are* a crazy monster, but we don't want them to know it."

Cathy laughed, I smiled, Melanie nodded. April's silence expressed her feelings.

Cara lit a Newport. "Thanks, Mom, thanks a lot."

Cara took the plea bargain. Cara's ordeal had begun months earlier at 5403 Smart, and now it was just about over. I waited for the onset of the next ordeal.

The weekend ended; I drove home. On June 15, the day before Father's Day, I received a Father's Day card from Cara. The weekend after Father's Day, I drove back to KC. I wanted to see Janet. I didn't tell Cara that I had breakfast with Janet. I knew Cara would feel that, by seeing Janet, I was disloyal to her.

Janet, then 19 years old, was five-one, usually 110 pounds. She has light brown hair, a wispy voice, a bright smile. On June 21, 1996, she was six months pregnant. Her due date was September 19. I hadn't seen her for a few months. I had stayed away from her because of her conflict with Cara.

Janet's midteenage years were dominated by the Fremont hustle, drug use, hanging out, and drug selling. Janet sold weed, but her main enterprise was dank. Between the time we met in July 1994 and June 1995, she had separated herself from Fremont, saying that she wanted to finish high school and get a job and "get out of it." "It" is the hustle of the street.

Janet's clean and tidy one-bedroom home is off The Ave, only about six blocks east of Cara's Smart apartment. Janet's parents live a few blocks away.

Janet is a pleasant young woman who, I thought, needed some support. I called her every six to eight weeks. She wasn't directly into the drugs and gang scene anymore, but her association with Steele Bill linked her to Cara. I wanted to stay in touch with Janet. I like her and didn't know whether my calls and visits were helping her, but I felt as though I was doing something to support her effort to pull away. Trying to stay straight isn't easy, as Cara's turmoil on Smart has shown.

Janet's proud of her home and job and income, and still feels good when her customers recognize her from "The Geraldo Rivera Show." Recall that in June 1994 she and Wendy had been panelists on a show about girl gang members; they were flown to New York City and stayed in a Times Square hotel for a few nights. They loved it. Someone on Geraldo's staff had found Wendy hiding in a KC safe house run by a local church. Wendy said she had sought protection because someone was out to kill her in a jealous dispute over drugs and money. Because Janet and Wendy were tight, Wendy brought Janet to Times Square.

"People still remember me," Janet said with a smile on her face. "They walk into the store and look at me like they know me and say,

'Weren't you on . . . ?' It feels good to be remembered for something good
I done."

By the summer of 1996 Janet didn't sell drugs anymore, nor did
she use them now that she was pregnant, although she liked to hang
on weekends with Fremont kids. Cara said Janet still smoked weed and
drank, but she looked too healthy to be doing it. Cara's assertions were
anger talking.

At 9:00 on a hot and humid Saturday morning, I picked Janet up at
her duplex, and we drove to her favorite breakfast restaurant, Denny's
in Independence, just two blocks north of the exit off I-70. We sat at the
counter. I made sure that she had plenty of food. She drank a large glass
of orange juice and ate a plate of scrambled eggs and pancakes with lots
of syrup, bacon and hashbrown potatoes, buttered toast, and water. Janet
had sworn off caffeine too.

We ate and chatted about the "ol' days" on Fremont, her job, her
impending childbirth and plans for baby care, and her relationship with
Steele Bill, the baby's father. Janet was largely on her own, she said, when
it came to baby care. Her mother worked full-time and was busy helping
Janet's 22-year-old sister tend to her two children.

I knew from earlier conversations with her, and from conversations
with Wendy and other girls, that Janet and her mom fought like hell most
of the time. That's why Janet sold drugs and hung full-time on Fremont.

Janet had no idea about how she would care for her baby and work
long hours from 7:00 A.M. to 6:00 P.M. Monday through Friday and six
hours on Saturday. Steele Bill offered no assistance, she said. "I thought
he'd be a good father. I need him now and he's not here." Steele Bill wasn't
staying with her at that time. He had disappeared. She thinks he's in St.
Louis "doing his things." Despite his absence, Janet said she and Steele
Bill had a one-year anniversary coming up on June 26.

Janet said her $1,200 monthly gross income wouldn't be sufficient to
pay for her and the baby's needs. She, like all the other Fremont teenage
mothers, would join the ranks of welfare recipients. But to be sure, she
didn't get pregnant to collect welfare checks and food stamps. She got
pregnant because she had unprotected sex. "You get free birth control
pills and condoms. I was going to get pills, but then I got pregnant."

The restaurant's servers and cooks looked like folks you'd see in a
prison. Many of them had skin with the texture and color of gray clay that
had been decorated by prison tattoos on forearms and backs of hands.
The short-order cook, whose top half I could see behind the counter, had
a gang tattoo just below his left ear.

Janet said Denny's and other such restaurants in the area hire pro-
bationers and parolees and folks from alcohol and drug rehabilitation

programs. Denny's reminded me of eating breakfast in a prison chow hall.

A pause interrupted our slow-paced conversation. Janet looked into her pancakes as if she were reading Tarot cards. Casually she turned toward me. "You have kids, right?"

"Yeah, a boy and a girl, 14 and 17."

Softly she uttered a question that caused me to vibrate with apprehension. "What would you do if your daughter was like us [Fremont girls]?"

I was speechless and stared at the short-order cook's gang tattoo.

"Well, what would you do?" she asked again, looking squarely into my eyes.

The question terrified me. I said nothing and then finally answered, quietly and truthfully, "I don't know."

"It's a bitch, ain't it?"

She finished her pancakes and said she needed to rest. Denny's was filled with cigarette smoke, and it felt good to breathe outside air tainted only by diesel exhaust blowing from stacks on 18-wheelers rolling by on I-70.

While we drove back to The Ave through the traffic, she didn't say much, just pleasant chit chat. I walked her into her duplex. The cool air inside the air-conditioned rooms brought energy back to my body sagged by the humidity. The humidity was the worst thing about hanging on Fremont; that's why both the kids and I enjoyed cruising in the Acura. But as soon as they got inside, they lit joints, and the secondhand weed smoke always made me nauseous.

We stood for a moment in her living room while she wrote my 800 number and access code in her phone book. I had given it to her many times. I knew I'd never hear from her. These kids never expect adults to do nice things for them and never expect adults like me to return to see them. Why should they? We hugged goodbye.

A few days after I got home from the weekend of June 22, Cara called me. Steele Bill had been staying with "a couple o' dudes in Overland Park, just chillin'," and two guys run in his house and tried to slash his throat and cut him across the arm, leg, and did get him some in the throat, but not much." Steele Bill had fought off his attackers. The reason for the assault, said Cara, was a drug rip-off, but she wouldn't say any more about it.

The weeks rolled along in the rest of June and July and were uneventful on Fremont and at The Spot. Afro grew marijuana and sold weed and rocks. Everybody else stayed off the corners to avoid police scrutiny. The

Spot was quiet and still felt the sting of the March arrests. Bernard stayed behind closed doors too; he faced seven court dates on different charges, including escape from a local treatment center. The days were calm for Cara and Wendy as well. When there's a hammer held over a network of kids, they all feel the pressure. But when only one of them is in trouble, no one cares.

The court advised Cara that her home confinement would end on August 19, or 120 days after she was released from Cherry. Cara managed her days carefully, abiding by the rules—well, some of the rules. Good thing there were no drug tests. The best part of her two-year probation was that there would be no drug tests at all.

A calm life left her bored. "Mark, this is bullshit; I'm going crazy. All I do is work and go home."

"Hey, Caramel, what does your mother do everyday? She goes to work and comes home. This is what citizens do, young lady. Your ol' partners come over."

"Yeah, they do. We smoke, but I cayn't go nowhere wid 'em, Mark. I'm trapped at my ma's."

"Choice is yours, Caramel," I said in my father voice, "trapped here or jailed on Cherry."

"Yeah, yeah, yeah, I know, OK. Hand me a Newport," she said in a low scratchy voice.

Time dragged; the same old stuff happened. Cara worked at Taco Bell. Bernard sneaked into Cara's back door after parking his car behind Cathy's apartment house. Wendy started to hang around Cathy's apartment and spent nights on a couch. Cathy didn't like Wendy around the apartment. It signaled trouble. Wendy and Cara are old drug partners and like to party. They are both control freaks, want the same thing at the same time, and are quick to fight over it. These girls have the organizational skills to build a criminal organization, but they'd both want to be the leader. When it comes to doing something they want to do, they are determined and energetic. Just don't tell one or the other to do anything without her consent. If you do, they'll tell you to "go fuck yourself."

Fighting for control has always been the Achilles heel in their relationship. They scream when one feels the other has taken the advantage. Cathy and Cara do it too, but Cathy knows when to stop. When Wendy and Cara fight, it's relentlessly, and eventually they split up and won't speak to each other for months or until one of them has something the other one wants. Then the seeker comes crawling back, as Wendy did.

Over the summer of 1996, Wendy needed a place to hang out and to reconnect to old Fremont partners, because staying up north with Angie had cut her off from the street. Wendy now came easing back into Cara's life, until Wendy got a "sugar daddy."

Wendy was 16 when she met her father, Mike, but she didn't want to see him. Over the summer of 1995, I had asked her about her father, and she said he was worthless. Wendy now discovered that Mike had a lot of money, and she decided she needed a father. It sounds cold, but it's true.

"Shiyt, she heard he hit it rich, and that bitch straight picked up that phone and called Mike," said Cara.

Wendy smiled. "Mark, hanging out and doing drugs and banging is fun, know what I'm saying? I was doing it, dog, know what I'm saying? I just got fucked up and tired of it."

Mike had been struck by a car while riding his motorcycle. The car was owned by the Kansas City Chiefs, and the driver worked for that organization. Mike got a settlement, Wendy said, of about $200,000, but he lost his lower left leg, which was replaced with a prosthesis. Mike was an ATM and appeared in Wendy's life at just the right moment.

I like Mike. In the old days at Wendy and Jackie's drug house and even before then when I called Jackie, I'd hear about Mike. The man I heard about and the man I grew to enjoy were very different men.

Jerry, Jackie's brother, the paranoid and jittery ex-con commercial burglar, said Mike is a "real fuckin' thug." Mike, said Jerry, would go to bars and get drunk and beat the living hell out of guys. He said, one day Mike killed somebody and went to prison. Jackie didn't confirm the details of Jerry's version of Mike's story, but she too said he used to be a "bad ass."

I met Mike at his garden apartment in Raytown, a suburb of KC about 20 minutes east of the Plaza, on a Saturday afternoon in early July. Cara went with me. She gave her PO the out-of-town uncle story. When I got to Cathy's, I had Newports for Cara, nonmenthol Virginia Slims for Cathy, and a dozen of LaMar's Donuts, the best donuts in North America. LaMar is a rich white guy who hires mostly minority folks to cook and serve his fabulous donuts. The folks who work at LaMar's look like those who cook and serve at Denny's off I-70 in Independence.

The original LaMar's is a converted 1950s gas station. It's in midtown KC, four blocks east of the intersection of Linwood and Main. Early on any weekday or weekend morning you'll wait in a long line, sometimes extending out the tiny interior of the place and into the parking lot. You'll stand under the heavy roof that was constructed 40 years ago to keep folks dry while they pumped gas. The line moves quickly and it's friendly. On weekends it's really busy, and LaMar hires an off-duty KC cop to stand inside to dissuade robbery. The cop wears a uniform and carries a big weapon like a 9-millimeter. In this neighborhood the cops and kids have the same artillery.

LaMar's chocolate-covered chocolate and glazed blueberry donuts and foot-long glazed twists attract folks of all colors to a neighborhood where suburbanites wouldn't go were it not for the fabulous confectionaries. Even in this neighborhood with drug houses around the corner, folks in business attire or in a tasseled-shoe weekend look don't appear nervous. Donuts must have a tranquilizing effect.

The phone rang as the girls ate donuts. Cathy doesn't eat sweets; she's diabetic. Cara, April, and Melanie do. I answered the phone. It was Wendy. "Wha's up?" she said. This expression isn't a question. It's what sociolinguists call phatic communion, or the stuff folks say to one another that doesn't expect a truthful answer. "Wha's up?" is equivalent to "How are you?" I told her that Cara and I would be at Mike's soon.

We pulled into the parking lot of a middle-class garden apartment complex. No junk cars parked around, no junkies hanging around, no kids dishing dope, no soda cups and beer cans and bottles shattered on the lawns, no shot-out street lights.

It was brutally hot and humid, but the blue sky was bright and clean. We located Mike's apartment, parked and walked up the slight incline on a well-maintained concrete sidewalk unmarred by cigarette butts and graffiti.

Sitting on a folding lawnchair, smoking a cigarette, and reading a magazine was a woman in her late thirties to early forties. We said hi. She knew Cara, and while they chatted, a man walked up the sidewalk. He wore tight blue jeans and sneakers and a Harley Davidson short-sleeved T-shirt. Street and prison tattoos told his story. He was my height, five-seven, and should have been my weight, 145 pounds, but he had a beer belly that pushed his heavy leather belt and its massive buckle downward, angling them toward the sidewalk.

Wendy heard us outside and came to the door. "Dad," she said, "this here is Mark. He's a writer doing a story on us Fremont kids."

We shook hands and looked each other squarely in the eye. "Nice to meet ya," I said. He nodded, took a drag on an unfiltered Lucky Strike, and bent down to tap off the ash into the plastic ashtray that lay next to the woman's lawnchair.

"So what are you kids up to today? No trouble, I hope," said Mike in a father voice. "Mark, did Wendy introduce you to Tammi?" Mike asked. I shook my head. "Wendy, you know better than that. Where are your manners?" Her head dipped and she looked embarrassed. No one else, I mean no one, ever spoke to Wendy that way without a fight.

Mike's not the guy to pick a fight with. He has outlaw biker tattoos on his arms as well as ink tying him to white supremacists. He looks like guys I've seen hanging around Prison Ministries offices. They're cut out of the same cellblock mold: middle-aged, tattooed ex-cons wearing gold chains and gold nugget rings and watches and bracelets bought in past lives with coke money.

Tammi and I shook hands. Her fingers lightly wrapped around mine with too little force to lift a beer glass. "Go on in if you want to," Mike said. We did. Tammi stayed outside.

Mike's apartment was spotless and nicely decorated but not to my taste. Above the dining room table was John Wayne painted on velvet. Two new three-cushioned couches lined the walls. A new 31-inch TV and a VCR faced the couches on the opposite walls. Two bedrooms were filled with new furniture. Mike and Tammi's was tidy; the other had the teenage-girl look.

Mike jumped on the phone and returned calls to people who had left him messages on his new answering machine. He talked about his upcoming wedding to Tammi scheduled for July 13.

Wendy stood in the bathroom with a curling iron in one hand, a can of hairspray in the other. Cara leaned against the door jam, chiding her, "Come on, biytch, let's get the fuck out of here. I need a smoke." She meant a joint.

"Gimme a fuckin' minute . . . ," Wendy paused and looked out the door to see if Mike heard her say *fuck*. "He doesn't allow no cursin' in the house."

"Wendy, let's go," pushed Cara.

"Biytch, I got to have my shit tight. I'm seeing Gleyn tonight," she purred, putting down the hairspray. She reached into the small upper center pocket of her Oshkosh overalls, pulled out a condom, and waved it in Cara's face, smiling a satisfied grin.

"Biytch, I kick yo' fuckin' ass," said Cara in a low tone, nearly a whisper.

Wendy finished primping and combing and smearing stuff on her face. "Now," she announced, "my shit's tight."

"Ugly biytch," Cara slammed her.

"'ho'e mothafucka," Wendy defended herself.

All was well, for the moment.

I shook Mike's hand as he talked on the phone and said a pleasant "Nice meetin' ya" to Tammi. She looked up and nodded, saying, "Don' get in no trouble now, you two."

"No way," said Wendy. "Mark be takin' care o' us. Right, Mark?"

We weren't out of the parking lot before Wendy lit a joint she had in her overalls and took long deep drags and passed it to Cara. Cara offered me a hit, knowing I don't smoke. She was being polite. In a moment, the girls' eyes shone like headlights, and smiles creased their faces.

The girls wouldn't let me slide down the windows, which would have let in the hot humid air. They wanted cool air. But I was feeling the nauseating effects of the secondhand weed smoke.

The girls smoked and laughed and talked with my tape recorder perched between the parking brake handle and my seat. We drove to a nearby Wendy's for hamburgers. We walked in and, before Cara could raise hell, I cautioned her in my father voice, "Now be good, Caramel. Don't tell the kids behind the counter they should serve us faster. Relax."

"Nah nah nah, I work hard to give people good service, and when I'm paying for it—well, when *you're* paying for it—I want good service too."

"That's the point, Caramel, *I'm* paying for it, and it's OK if they're slow."

"Stand back, Mark, I'll take care of it."

They ordered hamburgers and french fries and huge cups of soda. I got a Diet Pepsi. "Aren't you eating, Mark?" Cara asked.

"You're buying and you're not eating," Wendy followed up.

"That damn weed made me sick to my stomach. I just want a drink," I said.

"Yeah, Mark, you don' look so good," Cara said, laughing.

They got the orders. So far so good. Cara led us to the only available table. It was dirty. Oh no, I thought, here she goes. Cara must take control.

"Look at this shit. We pay a lotta money, and them motherfuckers don' clean and wipe the tables. Stay here, don' move." She walked to the counter, pushed her way through customers waiting for food, and yelled, "Hey, is the manager here?" He walked to the counter. She reminded him that she had paid $10 for lunch and the only available table had garbage on it. She always added, "I work fast food too, and I never let this happen." The manager apologized, and she returned with a rag and wiped the table. Then she let us sit.

Grumbling about the confrontation is Cara's next step. Wendy and I sat and stared at her. Wendy tires quickly of Cara's tirades. "Girl, shut the fuck up and let me eat. You be givin' me inDIEgestion. Biytch."

Two things were on today's interview agenda. From the back of the waistband of my jeans I pulled out my notebook and took out my little tape recorder and began to ask about nuances of speech. We got into terms related to gender—*biytch, pussy, killa pussy, bomb ass pussy, the shiyt*—and paradigms for their use and social nuances about status and role relationships and rapport. Girls regularly use terms that describe their own or other girls' sexual attractiveness. The expressions *bomb ass pussy* and *killa pussy* refer to a girl who is attractive and sought by the boys. *The shit* refers to a girl's sexuality, her genitalia, and the sex act. "Give 'em da shit," says Wendy, "and them mothafuckas leave ya."

These gender terms led to yet another discussion of sex and birth control and why these girls do and don't use birth control like pills and condoms. For more than a year I heard them and other girls too, as well as boys, talk about sex and pregnancies and babies. I had a hard time understanding the casualness they show about sexual intercourse and pregnancy and open discussion of sex acts.

On my second afternoon on Fremont, Poodle had sat on the ragged, three-cushioned, overstuffed couch with broken springs and told Cara and Wendy the following tale: "I woke up the next morning all fucked up from drinking and smoking all night, and he was next to me. I looked at his hands, and his fuckfinger had blood all over it. That mothafucka musta fingered me when I passed out, that pussy."

At that time, I couldn't believe my ears or understand why a girl I'd met 24 hours earlier would tell this tale to a stranger who had a tape recorder running right in front of her face. I was nonplused; Cara and Wendy weren't, and then they too began to tell sex-play tales.

I wanted to know, in plain English, what these girls thought about sex and pregnancy. Recall the list of girls who've been pregnant and had babies, and remember that together Cara and Wendy have had six pregnancies by six different boys.

Wendy began with a cliché . "You don't have no one so you look for someone who'll love you."

I wanted to get past clichés, so I told Wendy exactly how I felt about such statements. "I don't believe it. That doesn't make sense. If you wanted a baby you'd take care of yourself and wouldn't party, but you don't take care of yourself and you do party. You also don't make enough money to take care of a baby, do you?"

Wendy sat quietly.

"How much do you make at KFC?" I asked.

"Three-fidy, somethin' like that, every two weeks."

"And on $350 every two weeks you're gonna pay day care, medical expenses, rent, utilities, transportation, and food. Wendy, you're a businesswoman. You know money. You know it won't work if you have a baby."

"I wanted a baby with 'Fro and carried it till six months," Wendy noted. She was 16 then.

"Then who?" I asked.

"Right after 'Fro was Earl's baby. I didn't want that one," she said. She was 18 and carried that baby a few months.

"Then Glen. I wanted that baby and lost it after three, four months." She was still 18.

"In two years you had three pregnancies, two you wanted, one you didn't," I recounted.

"Yeah."

"Well, why'd you get pregnant when you didn't want to?" I asked.

Cara butted in. "That's all bullshit, biytch," she said assertively. "You like gettin' fucked up and fucked. That motherhood shit, fuck dat. You'll end up like Joanne; dat bitch be slackin' off on her motherhood, know what I'm sayin'?" They nodded agreement.

"She be tellin' ya she's in love and wants babies. That be bullshit," Cara continued. Wendy looked at her and at me like the proverbial cat that has the family's parakeet in its mouth.

"Bitches get high and get fucked and don' think about nothin' else. Shiyt, ya go ta parties smokin', drinkin', you don' think about birth control or goin' to buy condoms. That ain't the way it is."

"Hey, Mark, boys say dat bitch," Wendy pointed with her chin to Cara, "got some bomb ass pussy and they all want some, and she give it to 'em." They roared.

Cara had the final word, "Now what the fuck you gonna do with a baby, biytch? Babies, babies are about some real nice niggah who you'd done one night," Cara said calmly.

"Condoms, why don't you use condoms and spare yourself the trouble?" I asked.

"I'm stupid," Cara said.

There were many afternoons like that one, from mid-June to mid-July, and always the secondhand marijuana smoke nauseated me. I was glad my university didn't drug test me.

By late July, Cara had planned her mid-August escape from home confinement. We discussed the purchase of a car many times, and she didn't listen to me. I told my daughter, Emily, the same things I told Cara. Cars are expensive to buy, expensive to repair and maintain, expensive to insure, and if you can do without one, do without one.

"Phil said he'd take me to look for cars down on Prospect. He said he knows some guys there who'll give me a good deal and even a loan."

"I understand, but their loans are usually expensive. The interest rate is high," I said calmly.

"Interest rate?"

"That's the money it costs you to borrow money. So if you buy a $2,000 car, you might pay $2,500. The extra money is interest. Tell me why you need a car, Caramel."

"Wendy and me been talkin' about gettin' our own place, out in Raytown near Mike's. We can get somethin' nice out there and then we'd get away from all dem silly ass mothafuckas up on Fremont and over on The Spot," she explained.

"You mean they won't find you? They found you on Smart, now didn't they, Caramel?"

"Dis time, it'll be different. Me and Wendy already done talked about it. We won't tell anybody but Cheri and maybe a few others where we be stayin'. And I talked to Chucky and he said he might be out in August, and if he is we're gettin' a place, just me and him together, and fuck all dem other raggedy ass mothafuckas up dere. They ain't done shit for us 'cept bring him and me down. They jealous o' what I got. Fuck dem."

I didn't like the sound of this scheme. Phil took her out looking at cars three times while I was in Illinois. He and I e-mailed and discussed her need to buy a car. He too tried to convince her to take the bus or work at the Taco Bell that's two blocks downhill from Cathy's. But she wouldn't budge.

If she's going to buy a car, I thought, I'll try to get her into school. She had talked about finishing her GED at a local community college. April had done it, and Cara thought she could do it too. April's a different kid. She sets goals and completes things. Cara bounces like a ball in a pinball machine, lighting up each time she bounces into something bright and colorful and then bouncing off to something else. The only positive thing she's stuck with has been Taco Bell. She's devoted to work. She's immediately rewarded, earns cash, feels successful and, except for the March 6 bust and her stay on Cherry, her Taco Bell job had kept her going in the right direction.

Midweek, midafternoon, Cara called with the big news. "Phil and I found a car, a great car too. He talked to the dude for me and got a good price, and the dealer's gonna give me the loan."

"Interest, Cara, interest. How much?"

"Mark, it's only $150 for a year. See the car's jus' $3,000, and I put down $500 and pay $100 every two weeks for a year. Good, huh?"

"What kind of car is it, Caramel?" I asked calmly, trying not to show disapproval. I knew Cara by now, and the harder I pushed, the further she'd withdraw.

"It's a 1986 Ford Escort."

"Automatic or stick?"

"Stick? What's stick?" she asked.

"Shift transmission, you know, with a clutch."

"Yeah, yeah, that's it."

"Can you drive a stick?" I asked, still calm.

"Uh-uh, but Wendy, she said she'd teach me."

"How much is insurance?"

"I don' know. It's a great little car, Mom," she caught herself, "Mark."
What a Freudian slip.

I waited for her request for cash. She had no money for a down
payment. Phil knew the owner of the used car lot, or I should say,
extremely used car lot. Cara was to have her 1986 Escort with no down
payment, and—this is the best part—the owner told Cara that, if she
needed repairs, he'd do them at a discount. She would soon discover
that her car needed repairs every two weeks. That's when she'd call me,
and even though I felt sorry for her financial predicament, I wouldn't
send money.

"So tell me again, what will your bills be and how will you pay for this
car?" I wanted to hear how she'd make car payments, rent an apartment
with Wendy, pay car insurance, and most of all handle the court payments.
I reminded her that she owed nearly $1,000, and if she didn't pay and the
PO got pissed off, back to jail she'd go.

"Fuck dem," she grumbled. "I ain't doin' shit no more, and if they
wanna throw me in jail, fuck dem. I don' hang out up der no more, I ain't
smokin' much, I go to work, pay my biylls, and if they wanna bust my
ass, fuck dem."

Rational thinking wouldn't work at all, I thought, to convince her to
avoid thousands of dollars of additional debt on a salary of, maybe, $800
a month if she worked very long hours. Watching Cara and Wendy try to
pull off the street with low-wage jobs was painful. Seeing how these girls
resolved or didn't resolve their economic plight is a "laboratory experi-
ment" in youth-gang socioeconomics. What's more, these girls had more
than an economic problem to resolve. They had old gang companions who
would never let them go as long as they had an apartment and money.

Mike and Tammi's wedding had gone off as planned on July 13, but on
July 14 a complication popped up. Wendy told me the tale.

The Saturday-afternoon ceremony and reception were fun, with lots
of food and friends, ex-cons and straights, in attendance. The next day,
the newlyweds were leaving for a week in Minnesota, to visit the lakes,
go fishing, take it easy. Mike said he had no warrants now and it felt good
because he could go anywhere without getting arrested.

Early Sunday morning, Mike got a call from two pals who attended
his chapter of Alcoholics Anonymous. These guys needed to talk to Mike

ASAP. They met him at the AA hall. It was bad news. They told Mike that Tammi had had an affair some number of months before the wedding, and they didn't know if they should tell Mike. They were afraid he'd start drinking again, or worse—Mike had used heroin too. In fact, when he was younger, Mike sold 12 kilos of weed a month and used the profit to support his heroin addiction. But now Mike's pals felt they couldn't keep Tammi's affair a secret. This is an example, I thought, of why the expression "better late than never" is stupid.

Mike took the news calmly. He went home and told Tammi to get out of his apartment. He gave her his brand new American car as a going-away gift and had the marriage annulled.

Wendy said, "Man, I don't understand my dad, no more. He shoulda whipped the shit outta dat bitch, but no, he gave her his fuckin' car. He coulda give it to me."

The next time I saw Mike, I didn't have the heart, or the courage, to ask him about Tammi and the wedding. It's always best not to pop open a septic tank unless you want to live with the smell.

In the late summer of 1996, TJ was still being held on Cherry. There was no good news in his case. He faced charges for armed criminal action (a drive-by shooting in the early-morning hours of March 6) and first-degree criminal assault (the athletic jacket robbery). The bad news was that TJ's case was transferred to adult criminal court, even though he was 16 years old.

Wendy was staying at Mike's and working at KFC on 350 Highway in Raytown. Cheri stayed at her mother's and sometimes slept at Cathy's. Janet was working long hours and sharing her duplex with Steele Bill; however, the two of them fought so often and so ferociously that he sometimes left her. That's why Steele Bill wasn't at Janet's duplex when we had breakfast together. When he fled, he didn't call Janet, and she worried about him.

On occasion he'd stay at Cathy's, but she didn't like him there. She was troubled about his influence on Cara. "I'm afraid, Mark, that when Cara's off home confinement she'll head back out there and do it all again," Cathy lamented. When Steele Bill didn't sleep on Cathy's couch, he stayed on Fremont at Plumber Mike's or Smoker Mary's.

Afro controlled the drugs on Fremont and dished rocks and weed. He and Rosa were staying with Joanne. Duck came up to Fremont and bought rocks from Afro and resold them at a profit in other neighborhoods.

House of Pain and his brother Cain were still hanging out and selling drugs. Cain had a job working in underground storage caves, north of the I-435 and I-70 interchange. He worked because he needed cash for a used car. House of Pain worked part-time too, for the same reason. These boys stayed at home with their parents. There was no need to work too hard.

Cara hated, I mean absolutely hated, Cain. "I'm gonna smash that mothafucker's face with a tire iron," she said one day while we were standing on Fremont. Cain is known for hitting girls. One day he ran down the street and punched the mother of his child in the mouth because she had said something he didn't like. He once smacked Cara and split her lip. Cara told Chucky D, and he put Cain on his "work" list, that is, his violence agenda.

School started after Labor Day. Cara was planning to move to Ray-town with Wendy, and I wanted to push her toward school, but she wasn't interested in public school. April had had trouble at East High, up the street from Cathy's apartment, and said she didn't like being hassled and pushed around by groups of "black bitches." Cara's history in public schools was also bad. She hadn't been in school since she was 14.

Cara listened to me tell her about the DeLaSalle Education Center, in Midtown KC. I had first heard about DeLaSalle from folks at Kansas City's well-known grassroots organization called the Ad Hoc Group Against Crime. At Ad Hoc in 1993, the gang outreach worker, Calvin Neal, a product of KC's worst gang neighborhoods, introduced me to a fellow named Terrence, known on the street as T-Bone, who had just joined Ad Hoc's Gang Outreach Program.

T-Bone was 17 then and had been a member of the Harvard Park 6-Deuce Brim, a Blood set. We sat at a table in a back room at Ad Hoc. He wore a flowered silk shirt with the top three buttons open, exposing his nearly hairless chest, which was adorned with a gold chain, a reminder of his rock-selling days.

Over the next several years T-Bone and I became friends. At his wedding on August 27, 1994, a bitterly hot Saturday afternoon, I was the only white guy and the only guy who hadn't been to prison. The church reminded me of Prison Ministries.

Five days later, T-Bone's new wife, Teresa, gave birth to a charming little boy. T-Bone and Teresa rented an apartment and furniture and played house for a month, before married life became unbearable for them. She returned to her father's house on Troost, in what's now a high-crime area of south KC. T-Bone shared an apartment with a fellow gang outreach worker, Yusef, who'd just been released from a 15-year federal sentence, which had included 10 long years behind the 40-foot wall at the United States Penitentiary, Leavenworth, Kansas.

Yusef had also been a KC gangbanger but now in his early forties was straight and mellow and on parole. Over the next several years T-Bone and Yusef and I became friends, and, together, they visited me twice in central Illinois. Yusef had to get his federal parole officer's permission to leave the city and the state. I'd send them $50 for gas money and issue one fiat: "If you need money call me, but don't rob gas stations or banks on your way to my house." We'd laugh together.

T-Bone's history was worse than Cara's. Reared in a drug house off Prospect by his cousins in the rock business, he pulled out of the Harvard Park Bloods only after being shot three times in the back. Ad Hoc found a home for him at DeLaSalle, which then had a small, residential, drug-treatment program. That program is defunct now, no funding. T-Bone sobered up, graduated from DeLaSalle, and become a star in the KC community, and in 1995 he was recognized as KC's outstanding youth.

I thought, if DeLaSalle and its executive director Dr. Jim Dougherty straightened out T-Bone, Cara may find salvation there too. What I didn't count on was something simple: Cara had to want to be in school as much as I wanted her to be there. I called and made an appointment with my friend Jim Dougherty. He was on a family vacation, but when he returned I called again and asked for a big favor. I arranged to meet with him and introduce him to Cara.

Driving downtown, I praised DeLaSalle, told Cara how smart I think she is and how, with Phil's connections, she could be a college student at UMKC. She sat quietly, smoking a Newport, saying nothing. This is atypical of Cara.

Coming to DeLaSalle was more difficult for Cara than I had imagined. I guessed she'd be nervous; after all, she hadn't attended school in five years, and kids are anxious when they go to a new school, but Cara's reaction surprised me.

"Mark," she paused, "I'm scared, I mean really fuckin' scared. I ain't been to school in a long ass time, and what if I fail?"

"Fail?"

"I ain't been to school in a long time and ain't so good in math. And anyways, I don' have no new clothes, I don' have sneakers; all the other kids are gonna laugh at me."

I was floored. This tough kid all of a sudden was worrying about Nikes and jeans. I never expected it, but I should have. My daughter, Emily, worried about such things; why wouldn't Cara?

"DeLaSalle is a kind place, Caramel." I told her T-Bone's story, and she calmed a bit.

"Look, I promise, if you like it there and want to stay, you and I will go to Metro North and buy you Nikes and jeans and everything else you need, OK?"

She smiled and nodded agreement.

Metro North is a massive enclosed shopping center about 15 miles north of downtown KC. I lived two miles north of there when I worked for the Federal Bureau of Prisons. It was at Metro North in 1995 that Bernard and his Northeast boys chased down a carload of Southside boys who had insulted them and, as Bernard says, "had a little thing" with them. Bernard didn't like a Southside boy calling him a "pussy mothafucker," so he opened fire on the Southside kid with a 9-millimeter. No one got hit, Bernard told me, because he was high and aimed badly. He and his partners were arrested, and Bernard was charged with unlawful use of a weapon. The court gave him probation and ordered him to attend school. Those years, Bernard says now, were awful. "I was nothin' but a straight menace."

When we reached DeLaSalle, Cara and I met Jim in his office. He was in great shape and had run a marathon since we had last seen each other a year and a half earlier. We chatted and refreshed our acquaintanceship. Jim and I had met through my wife. She and Jim met in a statistics lab at UMKC while each sweated through his or her doctoral dissertation.

Jim was friendly and kind to Cara. He has saved dozens of kids like her. They chatted, and I got out of the way. Even though there were dozens of kids on the waiting list to attend his school, as a special favor to me, Jim put Cara at the top of the list. I told him I was very worried about her and summarized her personal and her family history. He saw urgency as well.

He offered her a tour. The school was empty, except for a few kids sitting in the library, reading. One boy, age 19, put down his history book and shook my hand. The boy said he had a court date coming up in two weeks; it was a sentencing hearing. He too was a gangbanger, a Crip from a neighborhood close to Ad Hoc's office on Troost. Jim wished him luck and asked the boy if he could do anything for him. I reminded the young man to dress nicely, no sagging pants and gold, and to be sure to say "sir" to the judge. Jim, Cara, and the boy smiled and nodded.

Walking down the hall, Cara saw a man coming toward us; she turned her back to him and bent over at the waist and covered her face. "Cara, you OK?" I asked. She turned back and stood up and looked at the man, who was now in front of her.

"Remember me?" she said. Embarrassment spread across her face.

"Yes, Cara, I do," he said solidly.

"I was afraid you would." She covered her face with both hands. "Remember when I threw a folding chair at you?" she asked, knowing the answer. "I was pissed, huh?"

"Cara, when you were 12 you were always pissed," he said. "Of course I remember." Tom gave her a light hug and welcomed her to DeLaSalle.

Cara, as you recall, was in a treatment center at age 12. Tom was her case manager. Now he supervised the DeLaSalle new student familiarization program. He outlined all the school's rules, reminded kids that no one wore "colors" to school, and that respect for one another and quiet voices were keys to success there. DeLaSalle graduates kids who go on to attend community and state colleges and join the workforce. This school's chess team, composed of dropouts and former gangsters, rivals the chess teams from the best schools in Missouri.

Cara was happy when we drove off and excited about school. She talked about finishing her GED right away and then completing her high school diploma and going on to college. That made me feel good. If, I thought, my face-to-face relationship with Cara, as well as financial assistance and access to resources like Phil Olson and Jim Dougherty, couldn't redirect her lifecourse, what would?

Cara's home confinement ended on August 24. By then Wendy and Cara had already found a two-bedroom apartment in Raytown off 350 Highway. Wendy worked across the street at KFC, earning about $346 every two weeks; Cara earned about the same. Rent was $365, and because Cara had a car, Wendy agreed to pay utilities and they'd split the rent.

The week that Cara's home confinement ended, the residence on the northeast corner of Fremont and 13th was shot up. House of Pain didn't talk about it. Cara said, "It was some niggahs that did it who he tried to jack or get over on."

Rumors said that Chucky D was hustling Teresa's 17-year-old sister, Netta, and that she had eaten heroin and developed stomach ulcers— "sores," the kids called them—and had picked up a sexually transmitted disease as well. She was being treated at Truman Medical Center, where the Fremont kids give birth and are patched up. Truman recently sued Cathy for $7,221, an amount that's approximately one-third of her annual income, for the cost of Cara's August 1994 walk-by injuries.

Life was changing again; none of it was good. August 24 brought an end to Cara's home confinement and a reunion with Wendy. Cathy and I agreed their reunion wouldn't lead either of them toward anything positive. Wendy talked about finishing a GED, but I knew she wouldn't do it. Cara was scheduled to attend DeLaSalle, but I knew in my heart it wouldn't work as long as she roomed with Wendy.

10
Wrong Side

Cara called me on September 1, the day she and Wendy moved into the Raytown apartment. She was excited and optimistic about staying out of trouble. I asked for the phone number and address and said I'd be over soon. Cara transferred to a Taco Bell near the Blue Ridge Mall, which is on the left on the way into KC on I-70. Wendy was easy walking distance from KFC across the street, 100 yards away, but she always had to be driven.

The first weekend in September, I visited Wendy and Cara. I got there on Thursday night, September 5. Twenty-four hours earlier the Raytown police had showed up at their door for the first time, but the girls weren't sure why. "Fucking racists out here, that's why?" said Wendy. "Mothafuckers in these apartments seen niggahs walking here and figured they was gonna get robbed."

The police frightened the apartment complex manager, and Wendy and Cara got a warning: If the cops came again, they'd be evicted. Cara called the manager "a fucking 'ho'e bitch" and said, "They always be pickin' on us."

Mike heard about the police visit and calmed the outraged girls. "Calm down. You might not know it, but the landlady's reaction is normal. Regular folks don't have cops at their door and drug sellers wandering in and out."

Life in Raytown was the same as it had been on Fremont and at 5403 Smart and on Van Brunt after Cara's release from Cherry. Wherever Cara goes, trouble drags behind her in the form of street leeches. Steele Bill, Glen, Bernard, Snoop, and a fellow who I'd not seen before showed up regularly in Raytown to sell Wendy weed. She'd buy some for personal use and repackage and sell the rest and recover nearly her entire investment. At least that's the way it starts. The girls said they "have to get high," there's nothing else for them to do. But as weeks wore on, Wendy and Cara smoked more and sold less weed.

At its most expensive, weed cost Wendy and Cara $100 on Friday and Saturday; they used most of it themselves and in sharing joints with the leeches. Cheri, Bernard, and other Northeast boys would call and come over and get high. The miles between Fremont and The Spot and Raytown didn't separate Wendy and Cara from the kids who they said are "niggahs who drag us down." The talk of separation was, in the end, just talk.

Mike called Wendy every day and visited her regularly too. He knew she and Cara were getting deeper into drug use and being sucked back into street life. One Saturday morning, Mike knocked at the door and had with him a new girlfriend, a biker chick dressed in cowboy boots and black Levi's three sizes too small. Her beer belly hung over a brass Harley belt buckle. She sported a worn out and faded heart tattoo on her left shoulder, visible below her black, skintight, short-sleeved shirt, which had a pack of Lucky Strikes rolled into the right sleeve.

"How ya doin', Mark?" he said rhetorically.

"Good, Mike, nice seeing ya again." I meant it. His pleasant manner and good sense of humor covered a troubled past, which he hinted at only on occasion. When he was Wendy's age in KC, he was drinking, doing drugs, selling heroin, fighting in bars, and was a "bad motherfucker," he said. Now this bad motherfucker said he had been working on an associate's degree from a local community college, but a learning disability caused by a severe beating had made formal education difficult. In 1990, Mike said he was in downtown KC, three blocks from a shelter where he was staying, and a few "black guys" wanted the hat he was wearing. They fought and Mike lost because, he said, he was "shit faced."

Mike shows no signs of alcohol and drug addiction. He's genuinely concerned about Wendy's well-being, and I called him often to check on Wendy and Cara without their knowing about it. He had a more accurate and honest opinion of the girls' progress with independent living than they were willing to admit.

While I sat with Wendy and Cara in their apartment over the course of one Saturday morning, Mike showed up. Steele Bill and Snoop strolled in, then Glen, and finally Jackie called and walked in. Everyone but Mike had come to do business, drug business.

Jackie's car had broken down about a mile and a half away, and walking in the late summer heat nearly killed her. When she walked into the apartment, it took me a minute before I recognized her. I knew the voice, but the face and body didn't match it. Back on Fremont, she had been a gaunt rock addict. When her court-ordered drug rehabilitation program ended, she stopped smoking rocks, because she was still on probation and had to work. Off the rock pipe, her weight ballooned and her body assumed near-dirigible proportions.

She was on her way to Wendy's to buy weed when her car broke down. She still smoked weed, and the guy she was living with—a "raging alcoholic," Wendy said—enjoyed weed as well. I never met him. I drove Jackie to her dilapidated, brown, 1987 Ford station wagon to lock it and leave a note asking the police not to tow it.

"Jackie," I said, "my car's older than yours and runs great. Next time buy a Honda."

"Fuck that," she exclaimed, "I can't afford a Honda or anything else that runs good."

Jackie walked out of Wendy's with a pocket of "good shit," enough for six joints, which repaid an old cash debt. Jackie and Wendy and I drove to the Stadium Inn, a 1950s wood motel-home to drunks, hookers and pimps, and drug sellers and users. Jackie said she was pregnant and working at a coffee and bagel store in downtown KC, in the same shopping complex as the one in which Janet worked. Jackie's employment wasn't voluntary. It was court-ordered, a condition of her probation and a follow-up to her drug rehab.

Jackie said she had regained custody of chubby-faced Robert, now 10 years old. She was proud of Robert. In his foster family, she said, he had stopped "cussing," gambling, and smoking cigarettes and weed, and was now earning A's and B's. I hadn't talked to Robert since August 1995, but Wendy and Cara too said Robert "looked good, for once."

As Jackie told me about Robert, I bit my tongue. The news of her pregnancy was bad enough, but now she had her hands on Robert again. I told Cathy about Jackie's pregnancy and Robert's return to her. Cathy sat nonplused. "Why would a social worker let her have Robert? Pregnant, Jackie, look what she did to the two kids she has; now she's bringing another child into the world. That makes me sick."

I didn't talk to anyone at the agency, but I too wondered, why would a social service agency return Robert to Jackie and remove him from a family in which he had stopped using drugs, stopped gambling, had gone to school and earned good grades? Why would a social worker return him to the person who bought him a one-hitter for his ninth birthday? By what rational process would a social worker recommend giving a child to an alcoholic drug addict shacking up with a raging drunk? Whoever made that decision, I thought, needs a midnight visit from Chucky D and northeast demons like Eddie Solo.

DeLaSalle's classes would begin on September 16, and I wanted to be sure to see Cara before them. Wendy also had a traumatic event coming up. I drove back to see them and arrived at their apartment on Thursday night, September 12.

In August 1995, Wendy had been arrested for the possession of marijuana and placed in a high-risk offender program. If she were to resist and fail to meet the conditions of her probation, she would be back in jail. That's precisely what she faced on Friday, September 13, in municipal court in downtown KC. Late on the 12th we discussed her options.

"It's all bullshit, you know, Mark. I'm working every day, payin' my biylls, and stayin' the fuck outta trouble. I could turn my paycheck into rocks and make thousands, like I done on Fremont, but, uh-uh, I don', and now them mothafuckers wanna put me in jail. Well, FUCK dem.

"See, selling drugs makes you lots of money, and with money you gots lots of time on yo hands and then you get into trouble, but now I working and, shiyt, I even got Bernard a job wid me at KFC. You know I'm in management training, and they let me lock up at night, and soon I'll be carrying keys. Good, huh?"

"Very good, Wendy, you should be proud, but you have to go to court, or your ass will be in jail, girl."

"Fuck it, I ain't going."

Cara interrupted. "Shiyt Wendy, if you don' go to court and you get yo' fat ass thrown in jail, I lose all my shiyt, girl, do you hear me? How am I goin' to pay rent and utilities and all my otha biylls and go to school and work wid you in jail? I gonna lose everything. Why me again? This shit is always happenin' to me," Cara cried.

The phone rang. It was Mike. Wendy listened and spoke quietly with no obscenities. "Mark's here, Mike. He says he'll take me to court. OK, here he is." She handed me the phone.

"Pain in the ass, ain't she, man?" Mike said, in a less-than-fatherly tone.

"Sure is, but I got it under control. No sweat. I'll pick her up, take her there, walk her into the court, and sit there and wait. If they revoke her and put her in jail, I'll call you. Maybe we'll let her ass rest in a jail awhile, huh, Mike?" I said smiling and staring at Wendy, who was inhaling off a fat joint Cara had rolled after her tirade.

"I hear ya, man. See ya later, Mark, thanks," Mike said.

"Sure."

The court date was scheduled for 10:00. I picked up the girls at 8:30, plenty of time to drive downtown, park, and get inside.

Neither had eaten. We stopped at a 7-Eleven on 350 Highway for muffins and sodas. With a full stomach, I thought, Wendy might be less likely to growl and grumble and strike out at the world. I was wrong.

They finished eating, and Wendy asked Cara if she had a joint with her, because she wanted to smoke before court.

"No, no, no," I insisted. "Smoke before going to court on a marijuana possession charge? Are you fuckin' nuts?" I howled.

"Mark, watch your language," Cara said. Wendy and Cara laughed out loud.

"OK, Mark," Wendy said, "I'll smoke after court."

"Keep it up, girl, and I'll tell your ol' man," I said. That brought Wendy back to reality, not because Wendy feared him, but because he promised to buy her a car if she stayed out of trouble and kept going to work.

We parked a few blocks from Cherry and walked the rest of the way to the courthouse. Wendy was audibly upset.

"What if he throws me in jail today? I have no bail money," she said with fear in her voice.

"Be nice, tell the judge you did your best, you have a job, and don't curse at him and give him attitude, your hear me? Be nice. This guy controls your future. Understand?"

"Yeah, yeah, yeah, but I fuckin' hate it when people tell me what to do."

Cara jumped in, "Hey biytch, gimme a cigarette."

"What? What did I just fuckin' say, bitch?" Wendy responded. Cara and I laughed, and Wendy cast a ferocious look at us. I'm glad she didn't have her 9-millimeter.

We cleared security. Inside the courthouse, the halls were filled with tattooed clients, well-dressed attorneys, the KCPD hanging around on the public dole, leaning against halls and talking to each other. I was dressed in a sweater and Dockers, and folks looked at me as though I were a PO.

Riding the escalator up to the second floor, Wendy started another tirade, which continued as we walked past clients, cops, and lawyers standing outside courtrooms.

"I gonna tell that motherfuckin' judge to suck my dick," howled Wendy.

"Biytch," said Cara calmly, "you don' have a dick." We laughed, Wendy said nothing. I tried to calm her and give her final advice before walking into the courtroom.

"Wendy, don't tell the judge to suck your dick. Even if you had a dick you wouldn't tell a judge to suck your dick, you hear me, girl? Call him Your Honor or Judge, but don't tell him to suck your dick, and don't call him bitch or motherfucker.

I asked a few questions. "Now this is about a marijuana possession charge, right?"

"Yeah," said Wendy.

"Tell me something. There are no other charges against you other than simple possession of weed—nothing like intent to distribute or anything really serious?" I asked.

"I have community service, too, I didn't do," she said.

"On the marijuana charge, you got probation with community service?" I asked.

"Nah, nah, I got 100 hours of community service on larceny." Wendy said.

"Larceny? What the hell does larceny have to do with the marijuana?" I was lost, but this is precisely what happens when interviewing these kids. They are involved in so many court cases and bits and pieces of street action that I had to ask lots of questions to get even close to an entire picture.

"I got community service in August '95 before the house got busted. You didn't know about it. I didn't tell you. Me and Angie [Lang] went into Drug Mart. I had her baby, and she had the baby bag. We shopped and shit, and then she took the baby before we left the store, and I had the bag. We walked out and some dude stopped us and said I had shit in the bag. I told him, 'Go fuck yourself, mothafucker, I ain't got shit in here but shitty diapers.' They took us inside, and there was two bottles of shampoo in that mothafucka. Angie, dat bitch, done it. I took a guilty plea and 100 hours of community service, and if I do the community service OK, the larceny will be expunged. See?"

I stared at her, "What a tangled web we weave . . ."

She interrupted, "Fuck you, Mark."

Cara roared.

We walked into the courtroom. "Sit there," I said, "and say nothing until the bailiff calls your name, OK?" She nodded; Cara looked bored.

"All rise." The judge walked in; we sat back down.

"Wendy Shaw," called the bailiff. She was the day's first case. I whispered, "Be good, or be in jail."

She stood in front of the bench, looking like a little girl called to the principal's office. The judge read some paperwork. "You haven't done your community service?" he asked.

"No sir, but . . ."

He interrupted, "Case continued until October 11. See the community service office downstairs."

We walked out of the courtroom and Wendy was furious. "That mothafucker. I had to get up early and get all dressed up for that shit. Continued till October. Fuck him. And now I have to go see some shitheads in a community service office. Fuck it, let's go. I cayn't be doin' no community service. I got work and biylls to pay. Fuck it."

"'Fuck it,'" I repeated. "No way, Wendy, we're going to the community service office now, or next month your ass is in jail. Do you want the car Mike's getting you or not?"

She stopped screaming. "The office be on the first floor," she said.

A patient woman in the office listened to all of Wendy's excuses for failing to do community service. "You have to do it now, or you'll face a jail term. This is a last-chance program, Wendy," she said calmly.

"But, . . ."

I interrupted Wendy. "That's good advice," I said to worker. "What do we have to do now?"

Community service was administered by a pastor in a church on 27th and Benton, close to Fremont. We found the lady who kept track of community service hours, and Wendy had a calm conversation with her. Wendy heard that, if she attended religious services on Sunday, those hours would count toward community service. Cara suggested going to church together. "You two in church," I said, "who' you kidding? You're going to get up early on a Sunday morning and drive down here to attend church? Let's be realistic, OK?" The church lady gave Wendy her phone number and told her to call back in a week to 10 days, because it'd take that long to get the paperwork from the court. We walked out.

"I need a smoke," said Wendy. Off to Fremont we went. On the way up there, we drove past an ATM and, out of nowhere, the girls told me a tale about Jerry, Jackie's brother.

Once, maybe twice, a year he had called me since we met in June 1994. I held my breath until he hung up. He is a bizarre, angry man with a grudge as big as Kauffman Stadium. Jerry thinks the world should forgive him for being a thief, because he hasn't stolen anything in a while; at least, that's what he told me.

Wendy said, "That mothafucker, what an asshole. He called a few months ago and said he got the keys to all the soda vending machines in the area. Me and him went around and robbed them and split the money 50-50. I did the fuckin' robbing; he sat in the car.

"Then that mothafucker, he wants me and Cara to go with him to rob ATMs. He said he got the tools to open them so we could grab the bucks. We went out and got gloves, hats, and masks, and spray paint to paint over the camera. He wanted us to do the robbin', and he said he'd sit in the car around the corner. Know what we told him? 'Fuck you.' "

"Good decision, ladies, or you'd be in federal prison till you're 95 years old."

"No shit?" Cara said.

"Yep, no shit. The feds won't fuck with ya. They'll throw your young asses in prison and the game's over."

"You know, huh?" Cara said.

"How does he know?" Wendy asked.

"'Cause he used to work for 'em, biytch," Cara noted.

"Oh, yeah, that's right, now I remember," Wendy said.

On Fremont, the girls found Buddha, the elder brother of Shawn, who, according to Cara and others, had sexually molested Chucky D's daughter. The girls also said, when Chucky D gets out, Shawn better find a good hiding spot. Wendy walked inside Buddha's house with him, Cara went to visit Joanne and Charlene next door to the south, and I hung with some boys who I'd not seen before. They weren't local Fremont kids. They were Buddha's companions.

Wendy walked out with a smile on her face and said she'd been to court.

"Who hasn't?" said one of the boys.

"Fuck," commented another, "we're all on probation."

I saw Afro and his brother Duck out in the street near the car parked by Buddha's parents' house.

"Wha's up, 'Fro? Yo, Duck, whatcha doin'?"

"Got a thousand?" Afro asked me.

"A thousand what, 'Fro?" I played dumb.

"Dollas, mothafucka, dollas."

"For what?"

"A half ounce. Give me a thousand today and I give you three [thousand] day afta tomorra."

Wendy walked over, and Duck asked her if she wanted to go have sex. "Fuck you, you fat ugly mothafucka," she said to him.

He smiled. "Baby, come wid me over dere. Lemme show ya what ya missin'," said Duck in his most seductive voice.

"Ugly bitch," said Wendy. "Let's get outta dis mothafucka, Mark."

"Yo, 'Fro, how's your daughter?" I asked.

He shrugged, "I don' know, don't see it."

It was time for lunch. Gate's, on 12th off The Paseo, was only five minutes away.

"Hi, may I help you?" shouted the counter lady. The food's so good; the greeting, so obnoxious. Whoever thought of "Hi, may I help you?" needs a visit from Chucky D. When I'd take the kids to Gate's, they'd be served a lot of food and would take home leftovers and stash them in the refrigerator. These leftovers were always the only food in there.

Cara had barbecued beef on a bun; Wendy had the same, with french fries and onion rings. Cara wrapped her leftovers, and the next evening, Saturday, she ate them at 8:30 after eight hours at Taco Bell.

Wendy had Saturday off. We spent it together. Since the drug house bust, she and I hadn't spent any time alone until that day. I picked her up at noon.

"What would you like to do?" I asked her.

"Let me show you the elementary school I went to," she said. We drove around Raytown, found the school, and parked next to it. She reminisced and told me about her first day of school. Then we drove around chatting and listening to the 103.3 JAMS. I asked her where she'd like to have lunch. She chose a small Chinese restaurant in a strip mall.

"Me and my grandpa used to eat here all the time when I was little," she said. Grandpa was Jackie's father. Wendy didn't know any of Mike's relatives. That day Wendy told me that Mike has two daughters with two other women and that she hasn't met her half-sisters and doesn't want to. As we finished picking food from the Chinese buffet, Wendy said her grandpa was "drunk all the time." She said neighbors called the family the Crown Royals, after his favorite drink, Diet Coke and Crown Royal. He committed suicide, Wendy said.

After lunch, we drove to Fremont and hung out a bit. Wendy said, "I don't like it here no more. I lost everything here."

I wanted to find Cheri, because it had been a few weeks since I'd seen her. We drove to her house, and she was horsing around out front with some younger neighborhood kids. Van Brunt was lush at this time of year and overgrown with trees. The sun shone and warmed the air, and it was almost easy to miss the poverty on the hill where Cheri lived.

Cheri joined Wendy and me, and we drove to Raytown. When we got inside the apartment, Wendy rolled a few joints, played CDs, and jumped on the phone to return calls listed on a caller ID which was built into a custom-order GTE phone she had bought for $200. It was her pride and joy and the centerpiece of the apartment.

Wendy smoked and gossiped, and I pulled Cheri aside and we went for a walk. It was early in the evening and the air was cooler.

"Staying with your mom?"

"Yeah for now," she said in the voice of a little girl.

"For now? What do you mean? Where you going?" I asked. We walked on the shoulder of 350 Highway. I put my right arm around her shoulders as I do when I walk with Emily and Aaron.

"I wanna join Job Corps but I'm too young, so my ma has to sign, but she cayn't 'cause she gots to go downtown and she gots no car and no money for the bus. Anyways she's been sick a lot lately." "Sick" means she'd been using drugs a lot.

"I'll drive her down there, you know. Let me know when, and I'll pick up her and you, and we'll go together."

"Well, my auntie says she'll sign for me and just tell 'em that she's my ma."

"I don't know that you want to do that, Cheri. That's probably illegal, you know. If you get caught doing it, they might throw you out of the program or never let you in. It's better to let me drive your mom."

"But my auntie says she will sign. I know she'll do it. Thanks, Mark. It's nice to see you again."

Later that evening Bernard drove to Raytown to visit the girls in a car owned by one of his many girlfriends. Cara had been home for a while by the time Bernard arrived, and the girls were flying high on weed. The apartment was lit by a dim red light in the kitchen and smelled and looked like a bordello.

Cheri liked Bernard. Years earlier they had had a brief affair, but charming Bernard has had brief affairs with lots of girls, although he still has no children. That was an amazing fact, I thought. It was obvious that tonight Cheri wanted to return to the old days. She and Bernard danced to slow love tunes; Wendy chatted and laughed on the phone; Cara puffed on weed and grabbed the phone now and then and danced by herself, eyes closed and drifting off to someplace only she saw.

Bernard pushed Cheri against the wall and pressed his body hard into her. She smiled and laughed as he kissed her neck.

"Give 'im some of dat bomb ass pussy. Give it to 'im, biytch," Cara called out and broke the mood.

"Mind your own fuckin' bidness," Cheri cried as Wendy and Cara laughed.

"See dat biytch dere?" Cara said to me. "The only time she has safe sex is when she don' have no sex at all. She be a dumb little biytch."

Cheri heard Cara and came roaring to her own defense. For a few minutes she stopped bumping and grinding with Bernard and told me about her last boyfriend.

"He liked me, Mark, real bad," she slurred. "We was arguin', and he threw a full fucking beer can at me and hit me in the nose," she said, pointing to a spot on the bridge of the nose. I saw a small scar. "I ran to the kitchen and grabbed me a butcher knife and cut his mothafuckin' ass seven times. And he still wanted to be wid me." She smiled and retreated to Bernard, who gladly welcomed her into his arms.

In a few minutes she paused and sat next to me again. "I'd like to be someone else," she said, "and live a glamorous life."

Cara overheard. "Biytch, you have multiple personality, isn't that enough?"

The Fremont Hustlers as I had found them in the summer of 1995 no longer exited, but the Fremont kids still did, and they continued to refer to themselves as the Fremont Hustlers. I had spent time thinking about how and when I'd end this research. I told myself that I was too enmeshed in these kids' lives simply to pull out and never return or call them. That, I felt, wouldn't be fair to them, and I like them and wanted to stay in touch.

I was satisfied with the full range of experiences I had had with them. I had seen everything I came to see: drugs, guns, drug houses, and a lot more that I hadn't expected to see, like the misery at Teresa's and the horrible lives of Fremont girls and their babies. I knew by now that the most interesting tale to tell about Fremont involved the girls, not the boys. But I still wanted to get very close to a functioning youth gang composed of violent young males. The Northeast Gangstas fill that bill.

This night, I thought, was the beginning of that research. A little after midnight, Bernard was high, and before he ran off with Cheri, I took him into the hallway as I was leaving for the night, nauseous after hours of secondhand marijuana smoke, and talked to him straight up about hanging at The Spot with him. I knew TJ, Dusty, Snoop, Chris, and others too, but there were dozens of Northeast kids, and, with his brother Chris in prison, Bernard was their young charismatic leader.

"Fremont's pussies," he said. "Come over to Northeast, we're bad mothafuckas."

"Will you introduce me to all your boys?"

"Yeah."

"I wanna know about the drug operation, the guns, the whole deal; otherwise I'm not interested," I said honestly.

"No problem. You been good to TJ. Anything you want, you get." We shook hands and embraced. I got his pager number and gave him my 800 number and access code.

On September 17 at 10:55 P.M. Cara called. She was high and in tears, nearly breathless from sobbing.

"'Member the other night when you was talking to B out in the hall?" she said quietly.

"Yeah, sure."

"You told B you wanted to hang out up at The Spot, right?"

"That's right, Caramel, you knew I wanted to do that. Is that a problem?"

"No, it's not a problem."

"So why are you so sad?" I asked.

"B said you're not going to come see us anymore, me and Wendy," she sobbed.

"Oh Caramel, that's not true. You know I wouldn't leave you guys. I told B that, when I come over to see you guys, I wanna spend time at The Spot too. I'm not trading them for you. I wouldn't do that."

"Really?"

"Really, Caramel."

Cheri was staying at Wendy and Cara's apartment, at least for the moment. She yelled to me from the background that Janet had had her baby on the 16th. Cheri was excited and said the baby looks like Steele Bill. I asked Cara if I could speak to Cheri. Cheri said she'd visit Janet in the hospital, even though Cheri was very angry at her for firing Cheri's mother. She didn't visit Janet. Cheri's excitement and good intentions were the effects of weed. Cara didn't want to talk about Janet's baby. Steele Bill had been spending more and more time at Wendy and Cara's.

Cara had started DeLaSalle on September 16. Because I didn't want to be pushier than I already was, I didn't call her that night to see if she had attended school, nor did I say anything about it when she called me in tears the evening of the 17th. I waited for her to raise the subject. She didn't.

No other word from Cara for more than a week, and I didn't call her. On September 26 at 3:50 P.M., she called again in tears.

"Mark, I gonna quit school," she sobbed. "I have to quit school."

"Do you?"

"I have no time to sleep. The last two nights [September 24 and 25] I worked from 4:00 [P.M.] to 5:30 [A.M.], and I have to be at school by noon."

"Talk to your manager about a transfer to a downtown Taco Bell and a shift in hours. Tell him you're in school. I'll bet he'd help out. When I come over, we'll talk to him together, OK?"

She continued with reasons why she couldn't go to school, even though she was excited about the results of a pre-GED test she had taken on September 17. She said she had passed everything except math. "Not bad, huh?" she said proudly.

"That's very good for a kid who hasn't been in school in five years. There's no reason why you would have passed math, Caramel, you need to be in school for that."

I encouraged her and asked her to think about my work suggestions and to let me know how I could help her. I waited for her to call me; I waited for weeks, no word. That meant she had quit school and didn't want to tell me about it.

I visited the girls over the first weekend in October. I needed to tell Cara that her decision to quit school was OK and that I wasn't angry. She expected me to be angry, she later said; that's why she didn't call me. Anger she understands; acceptance is tough for her to grasp.

Cheri went home for a while and stayed with her mother, who got a job repairing TV cable boxes, but that job didn't last long.

To Wendy and Cara, life in Raytown, away from "dem niggahs on Fremont," as Wendy said, was new and exciting and wonderful. The wonder of independent life was momentary.

Cara is well organized, Wendy isn't. Wendy earns money and spends it, as she did on Fremont in the heyday of the drug house. Cara prepared a budget every month, even though she didn't stick to it. Long hours at minimum wage earned her about $315 every two weeks, or $630 a month. The following is Cara's October budget:

Cara's October 1996 budget	
Car seat for Billy	60
shoes for April	60
get my hair done	65
get my pictures taken	30
go buy some clothes on The Ave	100
go get me some shoes	60
sent Jack	100
give moms	100
send both TJs	20
give EHD	90

The girls' financial arrangement was a 50-50 split of the $365-a-month rent. Recall that Wendy paid utilities, and Cara provided the car and gas for their mutual use. Note that Cara prepared a deficit budget totaling $685. She didn't include her half of the rent or the cost of gas and food, but the budget is filled with gifts, including cash for Jack. The only listed expenditures she actually made were for the car seat, a gift at the birth of her eldest sister Mary's second child, and a money order to Jack.

"Shoes for April" was a kind thought, but that's all. Recall that April had quit school. Cara tried to bribe April into returning to school with a pair of Nikes. It didn't work for two reasons: Cara didn't buy April the Nikes because she ran out of money. April wouldn't have gone back to school even with new Nikes.

By this time in October, Janet was struggling financially and emotionally. Steele Bill split his time now between Janet and Cara. When he stayed with Cara, he didn't tell Janet, and vice versa. Cara was pleased with this arrangement and felt in control. Janet knew about Cara and Steele Bill's growing relationship. Cheri was the link in the information network between Raytown and Janet's duplex off The Ave. Cheri told her sister Dante, Janet's closest companion, about each time that Steele Bill walked into Cara's. Then every time Steele Bill showed up at Janet's, there was an explosion. Even Mike said he knew about Cara's "nigger boyfriend."

Mike's only objection to Cara and Wendy's living arrangement was, as he said, "all them niggers around the place."

Such explosions between Janet and Steele Bill forced him further and further away from her. When he drifted off and stayed with Cara or at Smoker Mary's or Plumber Mike's, Janet used infant Briana to coax or threaten him home. Janet said that, unless Steele Bill stayed with her, she wouldn't let him see his daughter. Janet wouldn't even let him remove photographs of Briana from the duplex, because she was fearful that he'd show them to Cara.

The anger between Janet and Steele Bill flowed outward and into other relationships that linked with Cara. Cheri stopped visiting Cara and wouldn't talk to her, because Dante was angry at Cara. Mind you, Cheri "hated" Dante, but they united over a sudden and mutual dislike of Cara. Wendy got pulled into this too. She had been close to Dante and years ago had tattooed on her upper left biceps the name "Pooter," one of Dante's two nicknames. (Dante's other nickname is "MoMo.") Wendy slowly withdrew from Cara, and they began to fight more often and more intensely.

Their aggression focused on marijuana and money. During this first weekend in October, Cara didn't want Wendy to join us on our customary cruising to Fremont and The Spot, nor did Cara want Wendy to eat with us. I respected Cara's wishes.

On Saturday night Bernard knocked at Wendy and Cara's door just minutes before Northeast TJ called from Cherry. TJ was still awaiting a trial date on charges for possession of a weapon and armed criminal action. This was his first arrest, he told me; Bernard and Cara confirmed it. His bond was $50,000, which required a $5,000 bail, an excessively punitive amount, I thought, to ask poor people to pay on a case with little evidence (a drive-by) and another with no witnesses (a robbery). The kids who lost their jackets had no intention of testifying against TJ in open court.

Cara, Wendy, Bernard, and I talked to him. I said I'd come down to visit if he would put me on his visiting list. I asked if he had commissary money, and he didn't, so I said I'd send him a money order each month. He also asked for these magazines: *Low Rider, Source, Black Tale,* and *Ammo,* or any firearms magazine. Guns and girls are the obsessions of gang boys.

Driving home on Sunday, I knew the love-hate relationship between Cara and Wendy had swung to the hate end of the scale. It always does eventually. I knew too that Cara's relationship with Steele Bill would lead her down a path she'd been down before. Cara, I thought, would have been safer on Cherry with TJ.

I called Wendy on the evening of October 11, her next court date. She had appeared in court earlier that day and was fined $100 for not completing her community service and her probation was continued. Mike paid her fine.

Later, on October 24, I called Mike and asked him how the girls were getting along and chitchatted about Wendy's court case.

"They're fighting again," he said.

"Fighting about what?" I asked, as if I didn't know.

"You know those two. They don' need anything to fight about, they just fight."

Mike said he had told Wendy he'd buy her a car as a reward for being promoted to manager at KFC. He told me Cara and Wendy had moved into separate bedrooms. Wendy took her stereo out of the living room and put it into her room and wouldn't let Cara use it or the GTE phone.

"Don't tell them girls I told you any of this," Mike said.

"It's our secret," I assured him.

A car is what Wendy needed to pull away from Cara. With her own car, Wendy wouldn't need Cara's, and in the end, she wouldn't need Cara either. After all, Wendy contacted Cara only because Wendy had become isolated up north with Angie the Shoplifter, and when she broke away from there, Wendy needed a place to stay. She used Cara for that, and she also used Cara the Gatekeeper to reconnect to the street. Add to that Wendy's link to Pooter, and the Cara-Wendy split was inevitable.

I called Cara repeatedly over the next few hours and didn't find her at the apartment. I called Cathy's to ask her if Cara was OK, and low and behold, Cara answered the phone.

"Fuck that bitch. I'm moving outta dere," she said.

"Why?" I asked. I didn't tell Cara that I had spoken to Mike.

"Wendy smokes too much. She spends all her money on weed and cayn't pay the utilities. Fuck her."

Later that evening I called Wendy at the Raytown apartment and didn't tell her I had talked to Cara.

"Dat bitch ain't payin' her biylls, she smokin' all my shit, and she quit her job. I'm jus' gonna lose the apartment, and I'm movin' back into Mike's for a while. Anyways, he said he's buyin' a big house with a pool someplace up north."

I called Cara again.

"I'm worried about you, girl. Sure you're OK?"

"Yeah, I'm OK. When you comin' over?"

"Soon. Oh," I asked nonchalantly, "how's work?"

She paused, I heard her drag on a cigarette. "OK," she said slowly.

"You still working on 350 Highway?" I asked.

"Nah, I decided I didn't like the way the manager was treating me. He's an asshole, so I'm going back to my old store on The Ave."

"That's a long ass ride everyday from Raytown to The Ave, isn't it?" I asked, pushing her a bit more.

"Yeah it would be if I be staying out at Raytown, but I'm moving back in here with my ma for a while. She said it was OK till I get my own place. Fuck all them on Fremont. They be jealous because I have more than they do."

Wendy and Cara split up and hated one another and vowed never to speak to each other again. Old news.

Mike called at 11:00 that evening.

"Mark, Mike."

"Hey wha's up, Mike?"

"You didn't tell them girls about the talk we had before?" he asked.

"Nope, not a word, and I talked to both of them tonight too," I said.

"Yeah, I know, Wendy called me and said you talked to her."

"We cool?" I asked.

"Yeah."

"See ya soon, Mike. Thanks for calling."

This conversation with Mike reaffirms cardinal rule number one: Never say anything to anyone that you don't want repeated to everyone.

Northeast TJ sent me a letter acknowledging the money order I'd sent him. I received it on October 29. The letter as he wrote it follows:

Dear Mark,

Wass up? Me just chillin, waiting on a Court Date. Thanks for the money you sent. When will be the next time, you will come back to Kansas City? Because I would like for you to come up here and talk to me about my case, to give me some advice. My lawyer make's me nervous because I dont know what in the hell he's doing. And you already know about the law. If you can make it then try to get in as a *Pro visit*. Show them that you writes 'n shit and they might let you in like that. Well my words are kinda short. I just wanted to say *Thank You*.

"Take Care" . . . . . "God Bless" . . . . .

TJ

TJ's long stay on Cherry bothered me. In this letter and others he sent me, he sounded lost in the juvenile justice system and had no one to steer him through its complexities. I felt a bit guilty too. I don't know it for sure, but I felt that my involvement in Cara's case, on charges as serious as TJ's, might have motivated an overworked public defender to reach out a bit more to Cara and perhaps work a little harder to free her. Phil had called and spoken to the PD many times, and I had called too, though she didn't return my long-distance calls. Perhaps, I thought, Phil's concern showed the lawyer that Cara had community support, which is a vital element in deciding how to proceed on a kid's or an adult's case. Cara had clear support, and in this way she was different from Fremont TJ, Northeast TJ, Bernard, Chucky D, and the others who passed through Cherry and KC's juvenile and adult courts. If I had called on TJ's behalf, I chided myself, maybe he would have been better treated.

I visited TJ on Cherry on November 1. I called the jail and found out that his visiting time was from 11:40 to 12:00. I took the elevator to the third floor, the same elevator I had taken to visit Cara last March.

TJ and I had a noncontact visit. I didn't want to bother lying about a pro visit. Sitting on one side of the thick plexiglass and talking over a black phone still hot from use by a previous visitor would have to do.

This young man's face usually sparkles when he laughs, but it was dulled by nine months on Cherry. I preferred seeing the TJ who smoked a joint in the cold parking lot next to Pizza Hut on The Ave and told fighting and drive-by shooting tales to a table full of Northeast Gangstas while Cara watched with adoration in her eyes. TJ and Cara felt and acted toward each other like siblings.

We chatted about his cases, and he recounted, as Cara had when we visited on Cherry, the details of the street robbery, the one where Dusty and the other boys stole the athletic jackets, but said nothing about the drive-by he'd been charged with. Staring into TJ's eyes, listening to the deliberate words that described his sins, I felt like a priest in a confessional.

I asked him about the day the cops had picked him up on those charges. He told me the same story about police deception in the interrogation that every kid on the street has told me. It made me so angry, I was about to call the ACLU. Cops are violating the constitutional rights of kids, and the kids don't know it. Because these kids have no one on the street to support or even visit them, they get screwed. Sure, if TJ and Dusty and Cara do illegal things, the system has the obligation to prosecute them; however, the system that prosecutes them also has the obligation to protect the rights of juveniles. The KC detectives who chase and arrest kids, I thought, need to be chased and arrested by federal authorities and interrogated about their treatment of penniless children.

TJ said the same detective who arrested him had also arrested Cara. There's a detail of cops who track down and bust kids; I've heard about them for years. TJ said the detective told him that if he didn't request a lawyer and if he told the truth about the sidewalk robbery of the athletic jackets, he would be released with no charges filed against him. TJ said it was early in the morning, he was tired, and he believed the detective. As soon as he told his tale, TJ said, the detective threw him in jail.

Even TJ's court-appointed lawyer was abandoning him. TJ didn't have a PD, as Cara had, but rather a private lawyer on contract to the court. This attorney had little time for TJ. This boy's family couldn't afford to bail him out or hire a private lawyer. The family had put themselves in debt hiring a private attorney to help out Chris's case. Chris, now doing time in a Missouri prison, had escaped even more serious federal prison time, said Bernard, because the private lawyer had "got him off federal charges on drug conspiracy." Even if TJ's family had been able to bail him out, they'd have had to hire a private lawyer, because the court does not provide an attorney for offenders on bail.

TJ hadn't talked to his court-appointed lawyer in months, he said. Early on, he told me, his lawyer had accepted his 95¢ collect calls. TJ claimed that his lawyer's secretary wouldn't accept calls if the lawyer was out of the office, and then she'd lie and say the lawyer was out when he was in. In either case, there wasn't much of a defense being prepared. He said the lawyer wanted him to accept a plea: 120 months on the robbery and 36 months on the aggravated criminal assault, with sentences to run concurrently. Given Missouri's sentencing guidelines, TJ would be in prison for 85 percent of the 120-month sentence.

"The time's going by fast," TJ said quietly. "At first the days they went by slow, but now it's OK and time is going by fast." Each day he gets an hour of recreation and two hours to make phone calls, and he has a single cell.

TJ was readying himself for prison. "I don't wanna go to no pen, but Boonville'll be all right. I'd get used to it, you know, learn the system like I did here. I could do it." I hope he won't have to get used to it, I thought.

"When you go to trial, let me know. I'll come over and be in the courtroom." He smiled. I like TJ. That's the least I could do for a kid who said I am "the coolest white dude he ever knew."

Our time passed quickly. TJ thanked me for the visit, the money orders, and my concern. "God bless you," he said over the phone when he stood up. Then he walked back into the steel and glass cellhouse.

Cara called me at midnight on Tuesday night, November 12. Bernard had just told her that TJ had been assaulted. There was sadness and panic in her voice. The call was short, she was at Taco Bell, but she filled me in. TJ had been standing in line to get dinner when someone came up behind him and smacked him in the back of the head with a hard-plastic food tray. When he fell, the assailant dropped onto him and beat him with his fists. TJ was taken to the jail hospital.

The next time I saw Bernard I mentioned the assault. "Who did it?" I asked.

"We know," he responded in a clinical way.

"You gonna let him make it out of his teenage years?"

Bernard stared at me. "As long as I have court dates, he's OK."

When Cara and Wendy split up, Wendy stayed in the Raytown apartment. She felt good about her freedom from Cara and her ability to pay her own bills. Wendy had been promoted to manager and felt good about the responsibility of opening and closing the store.

Wendy got Bernard a job at her store. Bernard didn't look for work voluntarily. He was on probation and had to work and attend school. He attended school some of the time; now he needed a job.

It was a long drive from The Spot, or wherever Bernard crashed for the evening, to Raytown, and I wasn't sanguine about Bernard's longevity at KFC and school, for that matter. As it turned out, Bernard got into serious trouble on his second night at KFC. A co-worker said something to him which he found insulting, and he threw scalding water on her back. He was fired on the spot and charged with assault, and another case was added to the list of future court appearances.

With a car and a higher-paying job, Wendy broke off her three-year relationship with Glen. "That niggah, he gots no money, no car, and I'm tired o' him." She found a new beau, one of Angie the Shoplifter's former boyfriends, a southside gangbanger.

Cara moved in with Cathy, but the mood at Cathy's wasn't happy. Cara was growing frustrated, and everyone paid for it. The PO insisted on the repayment of $892 in court-ordered financial obligations, including per diem jail costs, restitution, victim's compensation, and the lawyer's fee. And Cara's probation required on-site GED classes at the downtown probation office. Given Cara's lack of skill at sticking to a budget, repaying nearly $900 in six months, as she was required to do, would be virtually impossible. I knew she'd send cash to Jack and Chucky D before meeting her obligations to the court. Cara fought the court and did it by claiming the court's hold on her was unjust and overly punitive.

This is the way Cara always responds to external control. But now Cara felt the court's pull and had to perform by someone's else's rules or face either a stint on Cherry, or a probation violation and more fines, or take a ride to prison. And on top of that, Cathy wouldn't let Cara turn the apartment into a flophouse and didn't want the phone ringing at all hours and kids knocking at 2:00 in the morning. Steele Bill was hanging around Cara a lot and on occasion spent the night. Cathy and I saw her relationship with him as a harbinger of evil.

I called Cathy's two or three times a week. Cara would be gone, either at work or just off somewhere, Cathy said. The frustration in Cathy's voice was palpable. I knew Cara wouldn't, or couldn't, stay there much longer, because Cathy was doing what all mothers do: offering direction, rules, counsel, in short, all the things that Cara rejects.

Over the weekend of November 15 I visited Cara. Life at Cathy's was calmer than I had anticipated. It took them a few weeks to adjust to one another before the tension lessened.

KC was cold, and when the weather is brittle, gang kids stay inside. Cara and I wandered around and visited Fremont, hung out at Joanne's, and cruised The Spot, chatting with whomever was around.

This weekend Cara said Joanne was angry at Chucky D and, because of it, wasn't paying attention to 13-month-old Charlene. By now Chucky D hadn't seen his daughter in seven months. Sequoia, Joanne's first daughter, fathered by Charles B, Cheri and Dante's brother, had a "disease in her private areas," Cara said, because Joanne "wasn't paying no attention to her neither."

I also heard that Janet was growing angrier at Steele Bill. He spent more time with Cara, less with her. Janet continued her tactic to leverage Steele Bill's attention by withholding Briana. Next week was Thanksgiving, and Janet said Steele Bill couldn't take his daughter to visit her grandparents in south KC. Cara was disgusted with Janet's attitude and said, "She's always doggin' on that man." The split between Steele Bill and Janet pleased Cara. Steele Bill was close to being hers.

I was becoming weary of Cara's continuous pressure to fight compliance. My patience was growing thinner, and I began to wonder when I'd pull out of this scene and declare a symbolic end to my Fremont Hustlers' fieldwork. Ethnography can't just end after six months or a year or two years; there has to be a natural break. I needed to reach a point at which I could feel comfortable about separating from these kids and one at which I could feel that I had everything I came for and could write a "thick" narrative which includes a representative sample of incidents and events and problems and achievements experienced by these kids. I knew, at least I was hopeful, that time would come soon. I would know it when it happened.

On Thanksgiving morning around 11:00 I called Cathy's. She was preparing a turkey. April and Melanie were talking and laughing, and Cara sounded good too. Steele Bill and Briana were joining Cathy and her daughters for dinner. Then Cara and Briana and Steele Bill would visit his parents.

Over the week prior to Thanksgiving, Cara had moved into Cheri's house across the street. Memories of past feuds faded when Cara needed a place to sleep and Cheri's house was available. Cara and Cathy felt good about it; so did April and Melanie. Cara still had the ability to take a happy family situation and turn it sour. Cara's being across the street seemed to make them all more content. Cara even admitted to me on the phone, "I like Moms."

Wendy spent Thanksgiving with Mike. She had moved from Raytown to an apartment on The Ave, well east of 5403 Smart. With a new boy on her arm, a job, a car, and Mike the ATM, Wendy said, "I'm doing good."

Cara rented Cheri's mother's unheated attic. It cost $150 a month. Cheri's mother rented this awful dark space to Cara and also charged Cheri rent. Cara said she'd pay Cheri's rent, because Cheri wasn't working. I asked Cara about that financial deal many times, and she told me, "Cheri's looking for work." I reminded Cara that Cheri never exhausted herself looking for work and, when she got a job, her poor performance and attendance led to a quick dismissal. In fact, the only jobs Cheri had ever had, Cara had got her at Taco Bell. Cara's and Cheri's rent subsidized Cheri's mother's addictions.

The weather turned brutally cold, and my phone started to ring.

"Hiiy, Mark."

"Caramel, what's up, girl, stayin' warm?" I asked the ethnographer's "fishing" question.

"Fuck, Mark, they ain't no heat up in dat fuckin' attic."

"Are you OK?"

"I gots lots of blankets, but Mark it be cold. I work all day and come back here and it's cold."

"Did you talk to Cheri's mom about heat?"

"Yeah, but they ain't no way heat can get up in dere 'cause they ain't no ducks. She said she be gettin' a heater—you know, one of dem little ones—for up in here, but she ain't did it yet," Cara said with urgency in her voice.

"Caramel, she isn't going to buy a heater, you know that. She smokes the rent."

She paused, then said quietly, "Yeaah," sounding like the helpless kid she is.

"Where are you now, at your mom's?" I asked, knowing the answer, because I could hear the TV in the background.

"Yeah."

"Ask her if you can move in till spring. That'll be better for you. It's warm; pay your mom the $150 you pay Cheri's mom and stay home. Let your mom take care of you, Caramel. It'll be OK, you'll see. Just don't be smoking on the back porch."

She laughed. "Yeah, I know. But what if she say no and don't want me around?"

"She won't, Cara. It's zero degrees outside, and you're freezing inside. Your mom won't say no. Just talk to her nicely, OK?"

"OK."

"You need money?" I asked. "You paying off the court? That's serious biz, Caramel. They'll throw your ass in jail again, and your debts will just get bigger. Face this one or you'll do time, Caramel."

"I know. I talked to my PO, and she said I can do the GED classes at Penn Valley [Community College], and I said I'd send $100."

"You have a 100, or do you need 100? I'll send it to you, you know that. I don't want you to go to jail again."

"I gots it, Mark. Thanks though, OK? I love you."

"I love you" floored me. She'd never said that to me before.

"I'll see you soon. Call me, OK?"

"Yeah."

That evening I called Cathy. It was just a "Hi, how are you?" call, but I had to say something to her about the unheated attic Cara was renting. Cathy said he knew about it and thought Cara's decision to stay there was "dumb but just like Cara." Cara was welcome to go home for as long as she liked, as long as she followed house rules.

Cara moved back to Cathy's. I called a few times a week for the next few weeks. Cathy was happy with Cara's behavior, and there were no boys banging at the door in the middle of night, no stalker threatening to beat Cara, no drug deals in the back room, no cops at the door. Peace, at least temporarily.

On December 18 at 10:15 p.m., Cara called with the big news: she was five weeks pregnant with Steele Bill's baby. My first thought was, "Oh, here we go again. Will this crap ever end?"

11
Miscarriage

I took seriously the impending responsibilities as a grandfather. When Cara said, "You're the only dad I've ever had," I felt pushed into a role I hadn't asked for, but when I thought about it, I realized I surely had asked for it.

I wanted to visit Cara right away, but I had already promised my family that I'd stay home over Christmas and New Year's 1997. So when Cara told me about her pregnancy, I said I'd visit her at the end of January.

Cara and I talked at least every three days. I wanted her to see a doctor and a social worker and to call her PO about the pregnancy. The PO was still squeezing her about repaying court-ordered costs and, I thought, the PO might lighten the pressure on Cara if she knew Cara was six weeks pregnant.

Without question, I wanted to reach out and control Cara's future, more now than ever. But I had learned that pressure and control will cause her to flee. As hard as it was for me, I had to let her feel as if I were shaping but not controlling her path.

"Next time I see you, I'm giving you $400," I said. "You'll need lots of things, and this should help." There were now so many things hanging over Cara's head that I felt the need to relieve some of the burden. Cathy didn't have extra money. I was the only person Cara knew with enough cash to make a financial difference in her life at that moment. If money would solve the easier problems, I thought, then I'd pay the bills.

On January 10 at 8:30 in the evening, Cara called and told me that Phil Olson at UMKC had called and invited her to participate in a Saturday-morning, semester-long, undergraduate, experimental course called "Diversity," a class about urban life, poverty, class, and race. She was excited about earning three college credits, and at the same time the fantasy of finishing high school and attending college resurfaced.

Phil thought it would be a good opportunity if Cara met minority and nonminority students at different education levels. This course would have students from East High School, several community colleges, and UMKC in the same room, sharing assignments and talking. I reminded him about Cara's initial excitement over DeLaSalle and then her array of excuses for quitting. I told him that I was not sanguine about Cara attending more than a few classes. He said I was too pessimistic. On Saturday, February 1, 1997, the course began. I told Phil she'd attend, even if I had to wrap Cara in duct tape and kidnap her.

The middle of January was busy with panic phone calls from Cara. She had kept her pregnancy a secret until December. I asked her why she did that. I thought it had something to do with the dynamics between Cara, Wendy, Cheri, Janet, Dante, and Steele Bill. Cara was superstitious. "I didn't wanna say nothin' till I was sure I was gonna keep it."

News of Cara's pregnancy had spread through the network in microseconds once Cheri heard about it. Then hell broke loose, and Cara's companions abandoned her, again, and for the same reasons they had abandoned her before. On January 17, Cara called me at 11:00 in the evening and sobbed so hard she was breathless.

"Hello," I said.

Without a warning Cara yelled, "I hate them. They're motherfuckers."

"Who? What are you talking about?" I asked.

"They found out I was pregnant, and now they won't talk to me." She cried and cried.

"I hear you Cara, tell me more."

"When I had shit I let 'em use it. I didn't keep none of them motherfuckers out of my place on Smart when they didn't have no place to go. Fuck them."

Cara recounted the same tale I'd heard many times about social alienation from her own companions, and this time I felt her anguish. I wanted to know about Steele Bill's whereabouts. I knew that, as Cara's stomach swelled, so would the distance between her and Steele Bill. His inattention to Janet was the best prediction of what he'd do with Cara, but Cara's self-deception kept her from seeing it. She'd conveniently forgotten that Steele Bill had abandoned her, pregnant and penniless, in August 1995. Chucky D took his roll of twenties out of his rear pocket and paid the Truman bill. Truman accepts drug money but was unwilling to be patient with a repayment plan for Cathy.

"Where does Steele Bill stay? With Janet, or you, or where?"

"He been stayin' wid Smoker Mary, and I'm worried about Biyll stayin' up dere wid dem smokers," Cara said.

"Where's his stuff, at Janet's?"

"Nah, all his stuff's in my trunk."

To my eye, Steele Bill had already abandoned Cara. In a conversation weeks earlier, Cara and I had talked about her moving into an apartment or perhaps HUD housing. Poodle and Robin, Cara's former caregiver, lived in government-supported apartment complexes which were well maintained and safe. But Cara said that she and her sister Melanie were talking about rooming together. Even though Melanie has no criminal history and has never run the street, she has a history of low-wage jobs. Two bad jobs, I thought, won't help Cara's financial situation. And I imagined Melanie and Cara and Cara's baby becoming a magnet attracting all the street leeches.

"You still thinking about moving in with Melanie?"

"Nah, she got a place up north."

"With who?"

"A friend. But I called Phiyl, and he said he'd take me to where I need to go to get HUD housing. What'm I gonna do about an address? If I tell 'em I live here, they'll add up all the incomes of everybody, and I won't qualify [for HUD housing], 'cause my mom makes, ah, 245, something like that, a week," said Cara, and from the background Cathy yelled, "1150 a month."

"Yeah, but you don't live with your mother and your sister. You're just staying there till you get your own place. Tell them you live at Cheri's."

"I talked to Cheri's mom. She's nice. She said she'd help me wid this. I told her I haven't forgotten about her [to pay her a month's rent], and she said dat was cool." What choice did Cheri's mother have? I thought.

"Caramel, you hang in. I'll be over soon."

"I'm here waiting for ya."

On January 21 at noon Cara called.

"Hello."

"Hiy." I heard panic in Cara's voice.

I paused. "What's wrong?"

She sobbed. "I hate Biyll. I don' wan' not'in' to do with him no more."

"What's going on, Caramel?"

"He told Janet he ain't been seein' me. He's been denying my baby and telling folks my baby ain't his. And he's not defending me in front of Janet. He told her that my baby ain't his.

"Yesterday, I made him go with me to Janet's. I hate him. She insulted my baby. She said, 'Your baby's gonna be ugly,' and he didn't do nothing. She's a bitch. She said he spent the night at her house last night. I hate him. I gonna make him pay child support, and I tol' him that too."

"What'd he say?"

"He said, 'Oh well.' I hate him. He ain't done shit for me."

On January 30, I called Cara at 1:00 in the afternoon and put a message on her answering machine. "I'm leaving now and I'll be there at 8:00."

She knew I stayed with my friend John. I gave her John's phone number. From the time I left home until I arrived, Cara called John's house twice, once at 4:00 and again at 7:00, asking John's girlfriend, Karen, if I had arrived.

I arrived at John's and called Cara. She was speeding with the excitement of spending that evening with Little Man, Steele Bill's best companion. Her voice quavered at the thought of seeing Little Man and having the money I had promised her.

After saying hi, the first thing Cara asked was, "Am I still getting that money?"

"Of course," I replied.

"Yeah, good. I gotta pay $100 rent to my mother, 100 on the phone bill, and Melanie don't have a job, and she has no money for cigarettes and no money to do her laundry."

Little Man had just finished a three-year state prison sentence on a drug distribution and weapon's offense conviction and was staying until March 1 in a halfway house a block east of the new Lynwood police station off Troost. Little Man's halfway house was one of two on the block. These wonderful old wood houses with shutters and dormers look odd with tattooed men in stocking hats pulled over the tops of their ears, standing on the wrap-around porches, smoking cigarettes, and staring at folks walking and driving by as if these civilians had invaded the parolees' territory.

Little Man and I spoke on the phone several times that weekend, and we planned to get together. He was leary about me, but Cara vouched for me. "He's OK. He's been around a long time. He's a mothafucka like you, asshooollle."

Little Man was wiping cars at a downtown car wash, which is the first employment stop for many ex-cons fresh out of prison. Car washes pay little, so Little Man had hooked up with a dealer in less than a week and was dishing drugs at the car wash. "A guy's got to make a living," he said. If I were faced with a choice between wiping cars for tips in the bitter winter air or selling weed, I'd sell weed.

On January 31 I made the long drive to Cathy's. I gave her two cartons of Virginia Slims and handed Cara four crisp $100 bills, or as she'd say, biylls. "If I'm going to be a grandpa, we need to take care of our baby, right?"

Cara waited for Newports, too. "You're pregnant and shouldn't smoke," I admonished.

"I'm cuttin' back," she said. "I'm not smokin' no weed."

"So you think smoking cigarettes but no weed is healthy. You have to stop smoking everything. You're messing with my grandchild." I smiled at her. Cathy and I nodded agreement. Cara reached for a Virginia Slim.

Over this weekend we all had fun. Cara and I cruised the old spots and ate at Texas Tom's on The Ave and sat at Cathy's talking and laughing and watching Saturday afternoon movies on the Lifetime channel.

On Saturday night I took Cathy, Cara, and Steele Bill, who were once again back together, to Gate's for dinner. This was my treat to Cathy. Spending $40 on a meal, as I did that night, is not something Cathy could do without facing a shortfall later.

At first, Steele Bill didn't want to go out to dinner. He was hanging out with his three sisters at a rental house in Grandview, a suburb south and east of downtown KC. His three sisters are single mothers and rent a small two-story house, affordable with government benefit checks and extra money from unknown sources. Cara, Cathy, and I drove to Grandview to pick him up.

The ride took 30 minutes, and it was controlled warfare all the way. Cara and Cathy talked and grumbled nonstop. Cathy told Cara that the next time she got pregnant to be sure she fell in love and got married first. Cara retorted by saying that marriage wasn't important to her. "I really love Biyll. I love him deeply, but I don' wanna get married. I'm not ready to do that."

"You weren't ready to get pregnant either. He's got another girlfriend and sleeps with her, and he made you pregnant. Does that makes sense to you?" Cathy was getting hot and animated.

Cara was quiet for a moment. "The only thing that matters is that Biyll's a good father to his child. I know he'll be a good father."

I bit my tongue. But Cathy continued, "I just wish it were with someone you love, Cara."

I interrupted and asked Cara for directions. I had heard Cathy and Cara's arguments escalate into screaming bouts too many times to hear it again. In the past, Cara would scream at Cathy, and Cathy would tell Cara to leave if she couldn't control herself. A pregnant teenager shouldn't run off. I did my best to keep the campfire from burning down the forest.

We arrived. Steele Bill was waiting for us. He and Cara slumped into the backseat of my Illinois State University car and asked me to turn up the radio. They chatted quietly, leaning their heads toward each other, and listened to 103.3 JAMS. Cathy and I made small talk about the weather and the road conditions. The car filled with cigarette smoke from Newports and Virginia Slims. The stickers on this state car's windows and dashboard announced, "We appreciate your cooperation by not smoking." I envisioned the university's physical plant director chewing me out for allowing passengers to smoke. We all swim in someone else's fishbowl.

At Gate's Cara devoured a double-decker barbecued beef sandwich with french fries and onion rings. Cathy consumed a homemade sausage as long as a cop's nightstick. It was cooked slowly and basted with Gate's sweet yet tangy barbecue sauce. Steele Bill drank a Sprite from a glass large enough to soak your feet and ate french fries. Cara teased him about being skinny and not eating too much, and he took the teasing well. Steele Bill is a shy fellow but impatient, stingy with his drugs, and unwilling to accept anyone's insults.

Babies create an odd social tie between the baby's father and the baby's maternal grandmother, especially when the baby's father and mother have no plan to marry. Such a situation is worsened when the baby's maternal grandmother-to-be knows that her daughter's lover is sleeping with another young woman who recently gave birth to another child of his. The American kinship system has no terms for such relationships, albeit they are a common occurrence in neighborhoods such as Fremont and Northeast. Perhaps it's time to attach words to these relationships and pay attention to them.

We finished dinner and drove to Cathy's. Steele Bill slumped in my chair, the one between the kitchen and bathroom doors, and acted as if he were alone in the room. His shy nature emerged in this uncomfortable social scene.

I sat directly across from him. He dropped his head to the right, lifting his left shoulder as if to protect himself from Cathy, who sat to his left on the couch. Cara smoked Virginia Slims despite Cathy's and my howling at her, and we chatted about the future. We pretended Steele Bill wasn't there; he did the same.

Cara got bored and nudged Steele Bill. She had to drive him all the way back to Grandview. I said goodbye to Cathy and walked to the street with my right arm around Cara's shoulders. Her left arm encircled my lower back. I told her I'd be back in four days on Thursday, February 6.

"Take care of yourself," I said. She stopped walking. We turned toward each other and hugged, as we always did when I left. I squeezed her tightly; her body felt like a child's against mine.

On Wednesday, February 5, at 9:00 in the evening, Cara called.

"Hiiy," she said quietly.

"What's wrong?" I heard a problem in her voice.

"Nothin'."

"I know somethin's up. What's up?"

Pause. "I went to the hospital today."

"Why?"

She had bled and suffered cramps and drove herself to Truman. The doctor, Cara said, reported that she had lost two pounds in the last month. She scheduled a visit to the hospital's nutritionist and another check-up in a few days.

"Did you tell Bill about this?" I asked, knowing the answer.

"Biyll didn't call me today. Wait till he does, I'm gonna tell him, 'See what can happen in just one day?' "

On Thursday afternoon, February 6, I returned home from campus and found this message on my answering machine. "Mark, this is Cara. Call me before ya leave, 'K?" I had planned to drive to KC that day. I called back right away. KC was about to get a major snowstorm, and I thought she had called to tell me about it. She wasn't home, so I left a message on her machine.

As I was packing, the phone rang. "Hiya." Cara's voice was cheerful, light, and airy, and it emitted a sense of relief. I knew what had happened.

"What's up? You OK?" I asked.

Without hesitating she said, "I lost the baby."

"What happened?" I asked.

She'd had cramps and felt ill and had driven herself to Truman. The fetus had lost its heartbeat.

"How do you feel now?"

"Okay."

"What's the doc say?"

"He said he'd operate on me on Monday, and I should take it easy."

"Monday? Did he say why he wanted to wait four days to remove the fetus?"

"Nah."

"Look, I'll see you tomorrow, right after I visit TJ in jail."

"Ya gonna visit TJ again?"

"Yeah."

"Tell him I love him, 'K?"

Seven days earlier Cara and Melanie had been planning a baby shower. Cathy was excited about the thought of a grandchild. Cara seemed happy and claimed to be pleased about her impending motherhood. I had suggested to her in early January that she might think about an abortion, but she insisted that, if she was old enough to have sex, she was old enough to be responsible for her behavior. An idealistic and unrealistic notion.

I could feel Cara's relief filter through the telephone lines when she told me the fetus' heart had stopped. I knew what this meant. It wasn't good. The intense economic pressure of impending motherhood would have forced Cara to change her day-to-day lifestyle, I thought. With the fetus gone, the economic pressure was lifted, and she could stumble ahead, one day at time.

Over the late evening and early morning hours the snowstorm, predicted to drop a 12-inch blanket on the metro KC area, did little more than wet the ground.

On Friday, February 7, I visited TJ on Cherry at 11:00 and then drove through icy wind and snow showers to Cathy's. I knocked on the door. No one answered, but when I turned, ready to walk away, Cara yanked it open. A clear plastic hospital band was wrapped around her right wrist. She held the phone in her left hand and a cigarette in her right; she was talking to Little Man at his halfway house. A young woman sat in my chair with a smile on her face and two preschool boys leaning against her.

Cara looked worn-out and pale. She had delivered the dead fetus between the time I had talked to her the day before, Thursday afternoon, and now, Friday at 1:00. Thursday night she and Steele Bill, his sister Lilly, and Little Man had gone out partying, even though she knew a dead fetus lay inside her. Before midnight Cara had started to bleed, and she drove herself to the hospital. The others continued to party.

"I got dere and had blood runnin' down my legs. God, it was so awful. I felt like shiyt."

Cara had called Cathy at about 12:30 A.M. But with the phone on the coffee table and the door closed to her bedroom in the back of the apartment, Cathy didn't hear it ring. Over the next several hours, Cara slowly delivered the dead fetus. She was alone.

"I tried to remember your friend's [John's] phone number," she said to me, "but I couldn't get all the numbers. Boy, did it hurt. Six hours, Mark, six hours of cramps and pain. Oh fuck, it hurt."

When she couldn't reach me at John's, she called the police in the hope that they could rouse Cathy or April.

"I called the police to get my mom, 'cause I needed clean clothes. They came over here twice and banged on the door, and no one woke up." At 5:00 in the morning Cathy's alarm sounded, and soon after, Cara called her again. Cathy drove to Truman and then went on to work.

"So how are you?" I asked.

She didn't respond quickly. That was unusual. "OK. A little sad, but relieved too. Know what I mean?"

"Sure, I know."

One corner of the living room was piled high with empty boxes that had once held baby gear, a small seat, a multipurpose chair, and a swinging-rocking device. Cara had had them on layaway at Wal-Mart and had picked them up and assembled them a couple days after I left a week ago. Now we had to return all the stuff.

Cara and I chatted. She introduced me to Lilly, who had just turned 18. Her two children scampered around the house while she talked on the phone to a boyfriend. Demetrius, the elder, was four; Lamarcus, the younger, nine months. The four-year-old's father had been killed in a shooting on the street. The baby's father was alive and "helps out," Lilly said, with the baby. Lilly collects welfare checks and food stamps but doesn't work. When she smiled, the gold implant in an upper incisor glistened.

Lilly's boys are cute. I grabbed my camera, which I had in my fieldwork bag, where I kept my notebooks, tapes, tape recorder, extra film, aspirin, pens, pencils, all the stuff an ethnographer needs. I should have carried condoms to give away too.

Demetrius saw the camera and stuck his face right in front of the lens. Cara growled at him get away. I took his picture many times and his little brother's, and Cara's and Lilly's too. I put down the camera and reached for the boys. Demetrius was starving for affection. I laid him across my legs and pulled his thin body close to my chest and put my cheek against his and squeezed him. He squirmed and wiggled and giggled but lay relaxed in my arms. I felt so badly for him and Lamarcus. I could predict their future, as well as Amy's and RoniRo's.

I excused myself and walked out. I had to leave. I was annoyed at how Cara and Lilly treated the boys, and I couldn't stand watching it another moment. I knew for sure the end of this fieldwork was coming soon, but I had to find the right moment.

I drove off and thought only about the little boys. I could still see Lilly gripping and squeezing Demetrius' upper arm so hard that he cried and slumped over on the floor, because he had noisily interrupted his mother's conversation. All the while Demetrius cried and tears ran down his cheeks onto his lips, Lilly smiled, oblivious to his pain, apparently more concerned about the attention she wanted from the boy on the phone than about her son. Maybe, I thought, the boy on the line would be the father of this teenager's third child.

On Saturday, February 8, I arrived at Cathy's to pick up Cara at 8:15 to shuffle to Phil Olson's diversity class. Cara lay asleep on the floor in front of the television. Melanie was awakening on the couch. Cathy was sitting at the kitchen end of the couch, smoking a Virginia Slim and drinking from a half-full cup of black coffee.

"Want a cup of coffee?" she asked me. I declined. Cathy was disgusted with Cara's behavior. She wanted her daughter to attend Phil's class and asserted, "If Cara's well enough to party, she should be well enough to go to school."

Cara opened her eyes. "Oh, Mother, leave me alone. I just lost a baby yesterday."

"Yeah," said Cathy, "and you went out partying last night."

That was my cue to leave. I told Cathy and Cara that I'd return after Phil's class. I walked out without any hesitation, before my desire to improve Cara's education caused Cara and Cathy more trouble.

Cara and I had planned to return baby furniture that afternoon. I arrived at 1:30, and we loaded my car with a plastic high chair, a play crib, an infant seat, and smaller boxes of baby paraphernalia that wasn't sold when my kids were infants. We drove into the northland 15 miles, piled the boxes into two shopping carts, and wheeled them into Wal-Mart.

Cara had purchased some of this stuff, had put other goods on layaway, and had made a few payments. I knew she'd have a hard time explaining the combination of layaway and purchases, but I made sure she had her receipts.

Two blue-haired ladies in their sixties couldn't make sense of Cara's rapid-fire tale of baby furniture purchases. Cara showed the ladies her receipts and told them, "I just lost my baby." They looked puzzled and walked off to consult with a manager. Cara turned to me, "If they fuck with me, Mark, I'm going off on them ol' bitches."

"Calm down. Nobody's fuckin' with you. It's confusing, you know. You bought some stuff, and had some stuff on layaway, paid cash to layaway. It's confusing. Give them to chance to understand it."

"They don't wanna fuck with me."

"Relax, Cara-mel, relax. If you go off on 'em, they'll get pissed and you'll get screwed."

"What? It's my fuckin' money." I'm sure she meant to say that it was my money.

"It may be your money, but they have it. So be cool."

The blue-hairs eventually sauntered back to the return counter and had it figured out; they handed Cara a short stack of twenties and some coins. We now walked to layaway. She started growling again about the customer service agents, the hassle she thought they had given her, and what she'd do if the layaway agents did the same thing. There was no trouble.

Cara had $220 in her hand. What would she do with it? She apparently never thought of returning it to me. I didn't ask for it. This, I thought, was an experiment in social networks, equivalent to tossing red dye into a glacial stream and tracing its flow.

She first bought a CD. Then she bought me a Diet Pepsi at McDonald's and herself a cheeseburger and a Coke. We strolled out of Wal-Mart and crossed the parking lot, talking about Chucky D. Cara had been concerned that he would be upset by her relationship with Steele Bill.

"He's OK with it?" I asked.

"Yeah, he says he is, but I know he doesn't like it. We're gonna be togetha when he gets out."

"When's that gonna be?" I asked. Chucky D's parole date changed each time I asked Cara. When he went inside in November 1995, his release date, Cara had said, was in early 1996, which then changed to late 1996. Cara called me at midnight once, sobbing and crying and absolutely distraught, to tell me that Chucky D had received an 80-year sentence, which within three days changed to 18 months. I had no idea what Cara was talking about and how she got her information. Reality, I had learned, never influenced Cara's thinking.

"Early next year [1998]," she said, as if she knew.

"What's he gonna do?"

"I tell ya, Mark, we're leaving this fucking town. There's nothing but trouble here."

"Where ya gonna go?" I asked.

"Far away from here. Maybe Chicago. You live there, right?"

"South of Chicago 120 miles. Central Illinois."

"Nice there?" she asked calmly.

"Yeah, it's quiet."

"Sounds nice. Can I visit you?"

"Anytime, Caramel. You can come home with me sometime. Would you like that?"

"Yeaah," she purred.

"No smoking in my house though."

"I'd go outside," she agreed.

"Where's Chucky D gonna work? He has to get a job, you know, and he can't afford to sell dope at the car wash with Little Man. If he gets busted again, he'll go down for the fourth time, and they'll throw the key into the river."

"I know, but, shiyt, he be a lazy mothafucka, you know daat."

I began to tease her now, and she didn't know it.

"Well shit, Caramel, let's get him a job doin' what he does best."

She laughed. "What's dat—fuckin'?"

"Well, maybe," I laughed. "But I was thinking about killing. You know Chucky D likes to hurt people."

"Yeah, he does."

"And he's good at it, right?"

"Yeah, he is."

"So, there's the answer, Caramel. Let's hook him up with the KC Mafia. You know, there's Mafia all over Kansas City. Ever been in the Sicilian part of town?" I asked.

"Think we could?" she asked in a businesslike fashion.

"Here's what we do. When he gets out, we'll find somebody to hook us up to the mob. Sound good?"

"Yeah, sounds OK."

"Till then, he can contract on his own and do hits for guys around town. He must know folks who need people hit or know folks who know folks who need work done. He's good at it, leaves no footprints. He can charge, maybe, five grand. How's that?" I asked, still teasing her.

"Really, five grand a hit?"

"Yep, one hit a month, you guys be living good. New car, house, clothes, fat sacks of weed," I jested.

"No shit."

"No shit. He can get him a cold gun. There's guys all over the streets downtown selling cold guns. You can buy any gun on the streets. So whadya think, Caramel, is this a business plan that fits Chucky D's personality, or what?"

"I talk to Chucky the Man."

"Don't tell Chucky D the Man this was my idea."

She smiled. "Why?"

"In case it doesn't work well, I don' wanna be on his hit list."

"I don' blame ya. Dat boy's evil."

We got back to my car. She unwrapped and ate a small cheeseburger as we drove and tossed the yellow wrapper out my car window. I wondered why she felt it was necessary, or even OK, to do that.

We got back to the city and headed to Eddie Solo's drug house. Eddie, Cara said, had the necessary paperwork to send Chucky D a money order that would be added to his commissary account. Cara wanted to send Chucky D $20.

Solo's drug house was open only in the daylight hours. That cut down on the likelihood of busts. He stayed in the northland with "respectable people," said Cara. Eddie wasn't there; his partner was running the store. Cara gave him a $20 bill and instructions. "I'll beat yo fuckin' ass if you fuck wid my money." This fellow, Eddie's alleged accomplice on the gambling casino killing, smiled at her.

We then drove back to Cathy's and chatted and watched a black-and-white movie on television. Cathy had nearly a dozen public library books stacked on a kitchen chair—her weekend reading, she said.

"Call B," I told Cara. She paged him once, then once again. Ten minutes or so later, the phone rang.

"B said he'd be here in a few minutes. He's up the street at Popeye's." That's across the street from Country's Inn, the bar that invites folks in to ease their pain.

We waited for him outside. Cathy knew that Bernard and Cara weren't supposed to meet.

"Every time I see him, he be in a new ride," Cara said.

I asked her, "Does he own the cars or borrow 'em?"

She said, "Borrow 'em, I guess, from some dumb bitches dat he be fuckin'."

Bernard pulled up. "Who's car?" I asked.

"A bitch's," he said. Cara smiled warmly at him.

He pulled into the small parking lot behind the apartment complex, hidden from the view of folks and cops cruising north and south on Van Brunt.

We sat in my car and chatted. Bernard wore an expensive Kansas City Chiefs leather applique jacket, a style which reminded me of applique I had seen done by Native Americans on the northwest coast of the United States. It was a beautiful and expensive jacket, the kind I've seen for sale in upper-scale shops on the Plaza at the Sharper Image.

"Hey, I wanna get a twenty," Cara said. Bernard smiled.

That evening Cara was planning to party with Lilly, Steele Bill, and Little Man, the same group she had partied with two nights earlier when she lost the fetus.

We drove in my car to a house a few blocks west. Bernard ran inside for a moment and came out with a twenty stuck inside his jacket pocket, and we drove back to the apartment house's parking lot. Cara sat in the front seat, tossing seeds and twigs out the window, and then rolled a fat joint.

"Nasty shit you got me, B, ya mothafucka," she joked. She lit it and took a deep drag, and then Bernard took a hit and offered it to me. I refused.

"Maaan, you used to smoke wid us," he said to me.

"Nah, that wasn't me. You must be thinkin' about some other bald white dude you know." Bernard laughed, Cara smiled.

I got out of the car to avoid the nauseating marijuana smoke. The three of us stood in the cool air. Bernard and Cara shared the joint. I took pictures of them.

"Now there's no date printed on those pictures, right?" asked Cara.

"Nope, no date."

We laughed about the months I'd spent on Fremont, talked about TJ and the likelihood that he'd go to prison, joked about the feud between the Northeast and Fremont, and then Bernard returned to a conversation we'd had earlier.

I liked Bernard. He had an electric smile and boundless energy, and he looked like the sort of boy you'd want your daughter to date. But would you? Would a nice boy try to kill other kids with a handgun, as Bernard had at Metro North? Would a nice boy call himself a straight menace? Can he be trusted? He looks respectable and safe, but is he? Gang kids never look like the things they do. How does a teenager look like a killer, a burglar, a carjacker? How can we tell who these kids really are?

"Don' forget, Mark, you said you'd write a book about me."

"OK, but I have to stick a tape recorder in your face. There can be no bullshit, you know, right?"

Floating on weed, Cara interrupted and slurred. "Dis mothafucka's been 'round a long time, more than a year and a half, and he asks about everything, B."

"I know. Dat's cool."

Cara asked me the time.

"It's about 6:30, Caramel. Why, is it time for a urine test?" I joked. She laughed, "Mothafucka, don't be sayin' dat shit."

"Where ya goin'?" I asked her.

"Partying. I gotta pick up Little Man, Lilly, and Biyll," she said with a smile, her eyes polished and glossy like a marble in the sunshine.

She joked a bit more with Bernard and me and turned and ran up the blacktop driveway's slight slope. Just as she was going out of sight behind the corner of the apartment house, she stopped, swiveled on one leg, and looked over her shoulder. Our eyes glued together. We smiled at each other, and I felt some recognition that she knew our relationship as we had known it over the last 21 months had ended.

She yelled to me, "Call me, 'K?"

I smiled at her. "I will, I'll talk to you later. Be careful." She ran away.

Cara's pause in the driveway and our brief exchange of words whose meaning extended beyond the simple sentences were the moment I had waited for, the moment when I would know that my Fremont research was symbolically over. It has now ended, I thought.

Bernard and I turned toward each other. He took a deep drag on the last half-inch of the joint. He exhaled and the hot smoke lay in the cold air like fog.

"Write a book about me," he said. His handsome young face shone and his eyes glowed like bright lights on a country road.

I nodded OK. Inside I said to myself, There's no way I can do this again.

Bernard and I embraced, my arms wrapping around his supple leather jacket. I climbed into my Acura, checking the backseat to be sure there were no sacks of weed left behind, and backed up a few feet and stopped. I lowered my window and stuck out my head in the cool February dusk.

"Yo, B," I shouted as he slid into the black Buick, "stay away from the drug man." That had been my customary goodbye phrase to the Fremont and Northeast kids.

He looked over and gave me the smile of a million-dollar man. "Yo, Mark, I *am* da drug man."

We laughed. I waved goodbye.

12
Pregnant Again

When I drove away from Cathy's apartment on the evening of February 8, I started a gradual social and psychological withdrawal from Fremont and Northeast and Cara's life. I called Cathy at the end of February and chatted about work and her daughters and grandchildren. Cara and Steele Bill, she said, were sharing a studio apartment Wendy had just vacated.

After Wendy had moved out of the Raytown apartment on 350 Highway, she rented a studio apartment on the east end of The Ave, in Independence. Within two months she tired of living alone and moved into an apartment on the northeast side, with Jackie, chubby-faced Robert, and a friend of Jackie's from Alcoholics Anonymous.

Nearly four months passed, and I hadn't heard from Cara and didn't call her. If she wanted something, she'd call me. I told myself it was time to stop meddling in her affairs.

On June 26 at noon, out of the blue, Cara called. She didn't say "hiya" but instead launched into a rapid-fire question-and-answer session about domestic abuse. She asked me what I thought might happen to a guy who beat his girlfriend, but not too severely. Steele Bill had whipped Janet, I knew it. I asked Cara if she was talking about him, and she reluctantly said, "Yeah. But she's a bitch and egged him on and came after him with a stick." Janet, if you recall, is tiny; Steele Bill is six-one.

I wasn't sure what to tell Cara and Steele Bill. I asked if he was on probation and if he had prior arrests for domestic abuse. Cara said Steele Bill had once hit Janet ("da bitch deserved it"), but he hadn't been arrested for it. I suggested that, if Janet's injuries weren't serious, if he hadn't used a weapon—a board, for instance, such as the one Wayne had used to beat Poodle—and if he appears in court, and if he is respectful and behaves himself until his court date on August 22, he may receive probation or be court-ordered to attend a domestic violence program. I also said that Steele Bill's fate depends on Missouri laws, KC's procedures in such cases, the mood of the Jackson County state attorney's office, and the judge's opinion about big boys who beat small girls.

I cautioned Steele Bill about in-court behavior and appearance. I told him not to disrespect the judge, to wear a suit and tie, and to forget the gold. I warned him not to lose control and tell the judge to "suck my dick," as Wendy had threatened. Steele Bill said, "No, I won' tell 'im to suck my dick. I'll tell 'im to kiss my ass."

In reality, I thought to myself, Steele Bill should be duct-taped and thrown into a closet until retirement age. I bit my tongue. After all, I will return to KC's streets, and given my paranoia over the KCPD, I don't need to feel apprehensive about Steele Bill's behavior toward me. Discretion is the best part of valor, so I took a politically correct middle-road.

"Thanks, Mark," Cara said abruptly, as if this had been our first conversation over the 1-800-criminal justice advice hotline. "I gotta jump off dis phone now."

Cara had never been comfortable talking about herself, happenings on the street, or just gossip in front of Steele Bill. In a sense, she assumed his shyness.

On July 16 in the middle of the afternoon, at 3:30, I was proof-reading my manuscript for *Dead End Kids* and was reading the chapter "Miscarriage" when the phone rang.

"Hello," I said, expecting to hear the voice of a student.

"Hiya." It was Cara. Trouble, I knew it.

"Caramel. How are ya? It's been a long time. You OK?"

"Guess what, Mark?" I knew what she'd say. "I'm pregnant."

"Really. How far along are you?"

"A month. The doctor said a month. I just heard today. Yeah and the nurse said she'd 'splain to me about O-negative blood and why I lost that other baby and 'bout vitamins and all that stuff."

Her reference to Drez' child, naturally aborted because of an Rh-factor incompatibility, reminded me of a disturbing time in her young life. Had she kept that child and had Drez not been terrified of Chucky D, I can't imagine the nightmare that would now be Cara's life.

"The father's Steele Bill, right?"

"Yeah," she said with sadness in her voice.

"Where is he? You guys are living together, right?"

"Nope. He stays wid me only two or three times a week."

Big surprise, I thought. I heard noise in the background. "Where are you?"

"At work. Me and Wendy and Cheri's all working at KFC on 350 Highway." This is the store where Wendy had worked and aspired to be a manager in the fall of 1996, when she and Cara shared an apartment in Raytown.

"So are ya happy about the baby?" I asked, as if I didn't know her answer.

She paused; I heard her take a deep breath. "Yeah, kinda." We chatted about her general health, and she said she'd signed up for Medicaid and joined the WIC program and was looking for a one-bedroom apartment.

She sounded energetic and determined, at least for now. But how she copes with the incessant pressure of pennilessness and pregnancy and miscarriage and yet another pregnancy and planning an indefinite future by herself without becoming loony is a mystery to me.

"Has Steele Bill been helping ya with money?" A dumb question. Why did I ask?

"No. But he said he's getting a job at Pizza Hut."

"That's nice," I said.

"Yeah and April's been a real pain in the ass about this. She angry, dat bitch, and my mom's really pissed." She paused.

"How's Chucky D gonna feel about it?" I asked, just to move the conversation away from April and Cathy.

"He's gonna be pissed," said Cara in a declarative way. "He was pissed the last time, but he was cool about it. I don' know what he'll say now, but he won't like it. When ya coming over?"

"I'm busy now, but I can come over sometime in the first two weeks of August. OK?"

I heard her drag on a cigarette before she said in a voice as soft as cotton, "OK, see ya then. I love you."

I hung up the phone and wrote a draft of this brief chapter, then scanned the manuscript for *Dead End Kids,* revisited the last 24 months of Cara's life, and looked into her future.

13
A Look Back

In June 1995, when I drove to Wendy's house on Fremont Avenue, I found the prospect of doing research with its kids, whom the KCPD called one of the most active gangs, a once-in-a-lifetime opportunity. Simply the thought of hanging out with the Fremont Hustlers electrified me and at the same time filled me with apprehension. By February 1997 when I watched Cara run off to party with Steele Bill, Lilly, and Little Man, I was drained, untrusting, and paranoid. Perhaps those feelings mean I did the ethnographer's job well.

Ethnography exceeds the collection of observations and interviews, allowing a fieldworker to become enmeshed in a community and at the same time to acquire a sense of how "natives" feel and react. The truth is, however, at the moment that Cara ran up the driveway and I waved goodbye to Bernard, it didn't matter to me how well I had done the ethnographer's job. I desperately needed to find peace and put physical distance between myself and the chaos of these kids' lives.

A distance of 450 miles between them and me didn't ensure me peace, anymore than Wendy and Cara's physical distance from their friends had kept them out of trouble. The street had seeped into my bones and filled my synapses and automatically slid into my dreams. Whether or not I wanted it, I carried inside me the images of Amy and RoniRo in the company of Teresa and Kevin; of Fremont Hustlers selling rock and weed in an improvised drug house; of Cara pale and exhausted and running off to smoke weed and party 24 hours after delivering a dead fetus; of teenage girls' black-and-blue bruises on arms, legs, and backs inflicted by angry boys; of nine-year-old, chubby-faced Robert pleading with me for money to buy weed. All these things and much more happen within a few miles of state and federal government workers who can protect preschoolers from harm, keep teenage girls safe, and at least offer young workers an opportunity to find a job.

It's easy to say that Wendy, Cara, and Bernard, as representatives of gang youths in Kansas City, are threats to the safety of that city's communities and must be locked up and thrown away forever because citizens feel threatened. What can we say about government workers whose deliberate disregard for and neglect of children and adolescents put these kids at great risk? What can we say about police officials whose only purpose is to arrest and imprison adolescents as if they were zoo animals? Don't police officers have a legal and a greater moral and ethical obligation to protect children and adolescents under age 17 or 18 whose environment is injurious to their welfare? What should moral adults and taxpayers say to the KCPD and police departments in general when patrol officers' disregard for children's and adolescents' well-being drives up the cost of the juvenile justice system and wastes the lives of children?

The kids I did research with in Kansas City are a sample taken from two of KC's most notorious gangs. Only a handful of those kids are serious threats to the safety of community folks or other gang members. Chucky D, Afro, Dusty, and Eddie Solo will probably not find an alternative to street crime. But we don't know that for sure, do we? Bernard, Fremont TJ, Northeast TJ, Caramel, Wendy, Poodle, House of Pain, Snoop, and the others are decent kids who have endured both economic and social poverty and been pushed to the streets by forces they don't control. The paradox of the Fremont Hustlers' gang network is that it allowed these kids to survive on the street but at the same time it and their quest for survival inevitably drew them to illegal acts and, on occasion, to violence.

Among all the Fremont and Northeast kids, Cara's social history is the most disturbed for the longest time. To me, Cara is a special girl. Her energy and zest for life are endless; her sense of humor sparkles. Years ago I was hopeful about her future. I now realize my hope for a bright future for her was largely self-deception. I believed that Cara could "make it," and I wanted her success to be linked to my help. I needed her success more than she did. In the end, her agenda superseded mine.

Cathy has tried to keep Cara out of harm's way. She knows the long-term value of education and has repeatedly talked to Cara about high school and college and encouraged her to participate in Phil Olson's Saturday morning class. Cara has had more opportunities than April to acquire an education, but Cara chose a different and a destructive path.

Cara's path was set in her earliest years, perhaps by age six, when professionals said she had an "anger problem." The etiology of her anger doesn't matter anymore. What matters now is that she is still angry and is still victimized by anger and by the bad decisions it engenders. Cara has never, to my knowledge, physically harmed anyone in any angry tirade. She has been her only victim.

Cathy's family history shows that destructive life courses permeate a family's future generations deeply and invisibly. Cathy's life course and her daughters' too were foretold 40 years ago, when Cathy's mother made bad decisions. Families are rivers of good and bad decisions flowing from one generation to the next. Despite the force of Cathy's family history, I believed that I could open doors and offer Cara opportunities which she wouldn't have had without me. However, these opportunities frightened her and drove her further from the goals I sought for her.

She acquiesced to my plans for her future, and I mistook that consensus as desire. I should have realized this, because I know that Cara has survived on the street through compliance to outsiders' pressure. She was pregnant five times by age 20, and she can't say no to kids who overuse her hospitality. To my requests, however, she could say one thing, do another, and still walk away without any direct harm. Had I been able to pull her away from the street and its leeches and to support her financially and emotionally, Cara might have had a chance to learn to protect and support herself. But no matter how involved I became in her life, I always drove away and left her alone and at risk of becoming someone's victim.

Children need decades of economic and social support, and if adults offer that support, children learn how to venture their way in the world and how to protect themselves. But even under the best conditions for learning responsible independence, adult children, college graduates, for instance, must be able to retreat to a safe and economically secure household. Cara, Bernard and TJ, and Chucky D didn't have a family "bank account," a fallback plan, a safe and secure retreat. Kids who are reared in families like Teresa's and in neighborhoods like Bernard's seem to have one chance to launch themselves onto a safe and steady lifepath. Like a missile blasting into orbit, these kids either achieve that lifepath the first time or veer off on a dangerous trajectory. When communities like Kansas City do little to offer social and economic support, along with a safe and healthy early life environment, Amy and RoniRo and Charlene and others like them will likely end up as teenagers sleeping in drug houses like Wendy's.

Waiting to offer support until adolescents are Cara's age is an ill-designed approach. Bits and pieces of education administered in jails and detention centers will never be a panacea for delinquency and youth gangs. Education functions as a child's "guidance system" only if it's initiated at the very beginning of the life course and then operates full-time and smoothly and effectively for 20 years or more. Education operates best if a child is enmeshed in a financially and socially stable social unit of any shape, such as a group home or an orphanage, whose adults are linked to the mainstream economy.

By the time Cara was offered a full-time education in the safe and secure environment of the DeLaSalle Education Center, education had no personal or practical meaning to her and no place in her life. With or without a GED, she would earn the same low hourly wage at Taco Bell. With or without a GED, her future can be best predicted by looking at the companions she has choosen. With Cara surrounded by Steele Bill, House of Pain, Joanne, Wendy, Cheri, Fremont TJ, Snoop, Dusty, Afro, Northeast TJ, and Chucky D, what future would you predict for her? Cara chose Steele Bill and Taco Bell over DeLaSalle, UMKC, Phil Olson, and me. Those were her choices and her conception of personal freedom and adulthood.

Gangs like the Fremont Hustlers and Northeast Gangstas are monuments to economic failure in households, neighborhoods, and communities. We can't repair such multitier economic failure by offering Cara a GED and a job at Taco Bell. Families will become economically sound units when legislators reallocate correctional funds from their use for prison cellhouses that we don't need to neighborhood economic development projects instead. We must insist, however, that government bureaucrats facilitate community development projects that make sense to neighborhood residents. Legislators' plans may frighten local residents, as my plans frightened Cara.

Poverty frightens the politically powerful and the well-educated. Poverty does not make people stupid, irresponsible, evil, or immoral. Rather, a persistent lack of resources causes folks to think and act in the moment and to develop survival strategies that bring immediate financial rewards, like slinging weed. Acting in the moment is contrary to the education model of social change, or an education plan of deferred gain. The rich and the well-educated argue that the completion of elementary, middle, and high school and then college and maybe graduate or professional school, too, will offer a student a significant social and financial reward. That sounds nice, but in reality a starving child will die in the quarter century it takes to achieve such a reward. Cara said it clearly: "When you gots money you don' wanna lose it. When you poor you don' give a fuck."

Economic development that acts simultaneously on families and neighborhoods will have a good chance of altering individual behavior. A program that would teach kids how to rebuild old cars could act at these two levels.[1] Kids could learn a profitable trade that they would enjoy, and low-income households could buy a reasonably priced and reliable car, which could transport them to work outside impoverished neighborhoods to places where there are good jobs. Cara's $3,000 Ford Escort blew a head gasket, she said when she told me about her fifth pregnancy, and now she must buy yet another old and costly car that will take her to a minimum-wage job.

In the KC metro area, the best jobs aren't on the northeast side. Good jobs are in Johnson County and downtown KC. But Fremont and northeast residents are isolated by inadequate transportation. Even if these residents have job skills and a willingness to work, getting to work on buses is arduous, especially for single mothers and single mothers-to-be like Cara. A dollar here, a dollar there, may not mean much to folks who spend $3.00 on cappuccino, but a dollar means a lot to folks who work 80 hours and more every two weeks to earn $365. And the issue that exacerbates the financial problem of too little income is drug use. Drug use and cigarettes, too, erode these kids' financial lives, not to mention the other numerous ways they erode life, because they cost a lost of money that might be used for other purposes. Wendy and Cara could have stayed in a nicer apartment had they not spent so much on weed. Had they not smoked weed and sold weed and had weed available to their companions, they might have been able to cut the social ties to the other kids with whom they remained in trouble. Saving an extra $100 or $200 each month might have enabled Cara to buy a nicer, more reliable car.

Local neighborhood employment at places like Taco Bell is simple and unambiguous and offers a pay check every two weeks, but the big winners of minimum-wage laborers are corporate executives. Cara and Wendy worked for pennies; Taco Bell executives have stock options. To minimum-wage employees, "Taco Bells" are financial dead ends as well as career dead ends. Whoever said working 10-hour shifts from 7:00 in the evening to 5:00 in the morning is morally superior to selling weed and rocks never worked 10-hour days, month after month, and earned $10,000 to $20,000 a year. Slinging drugs is more profitable and more fun than slinging tacos. The morality of such a choice—to sell tacos or to sell drugs—is an issue debated only by the politically powerful and the well-educated.

We know that personal change must come from inside first, but even then someone on the outside must help. I tried my best to reshape Cara's behavior and offer her opportunities she'd want to grasp. But in fact I tried to remake her life into one which was more to my taste. I failed, and all I can do now is lend my support if she chooses to contact me.

If legislators, community leaders, and neighborhood residents work together, I am optimistic that the lives of Kansas City's urban gang girls and their daughters, as well as Cara's unborn child, will be more than dead-end jobs, miscarriages, romantic fantasies, and failed love affairs.

14
Gang Girls, Gang Babies

"What would you do," Janet asked me during my research, "if your daughter was like us?" In response to Janet's question, I recommend a two-step program of supervised residential centers, designed for adolescent and young adult, gang-affiliated females ("gang girls"), with special care given to pregnant gang girls and young mothers. I discuss below the rationale and details of this recommendation.

You should decide on your own answer to Janet's question, remembering that youth-gang intervention is a real-life struggle among public and private community agencies, gang and drug detectives, high- to low-income families, and flesh-and-blood adolescents and children whose life courses hang in the balance.

Dead End Kids shows: that young women are just as important as young men in the social dynamics of a youth gang; that poor young women get themselves ensnared in cycles of victimization and self-defeating life-styles and, despite their talk otherwise, engage in behaviors which perpetuate their own victimization and poverty; and that unless we intervene in the lives of gang girls, in material ways, they and their children will suffer.

Youth-gang intervention works best when it's immediate, face-to-face, and at street-level.[1] I use *street-level intervention* to mean the neighborhood delivery of a number of services to gang-involved adolescents. My proposal for supervised residential centers is an example of street-level intervention.

A contrasting alternative is centralized service delivery. This service delivery system requires gang kids to travel to a location where services are available, such as a family planning office, a high school or community college, or a job-training site.

Fremont research shows that centralized services are ineffective with gang kids, because they don't have cars to go downtown; they don't take buses; they don't go. Recall that I had to drag Wendy from Raytown to the

210

downtown Kansas City municipal court to attend her probation violation hearing.

Transportation is just one problem. Many cities have territorial gangs, and in those communities, adolescents are fearful about traveling into an opposing gang's territory. Champaign, Illinois, is such a place; gangs there have territories, services are centralized, and most gang members don't travel alone outside their territory because of fear of violence, especially at night. I interviewed a number of midteenage Vice Lord Ladies, a female gang linked to the predominantly male Vice Lords, who reside in a Champaign public housing project where egregious violence, including murder, has occurred. We discussed families and teenage motherhood. I asked a 16-year-old girl why she and her companions don't use birth control pills or condoms. "Yeah, there's a family planning office," she said, "but it's way down there, and we don't go down there."[2]

Community Mobilization[3]

Fremont research describes a discontinuity between the actual problems in gang-affiliated adolescents' lives and the remedies offered by social and law enforcement agencies. Simply put, the local juvenile justice system doesn't give Fremont kids what they need when they need it. Instead, the community response to deviance and disobedience is stereotyped and ill-designed.

Federal juvenile delinquency policy states that "sound policy for juvenile delinquency prevention seeks to strengthen the most powerful contributing factor to socially acceptable behavior—a productive place for young people in a law-abiding society."[4] Such a policy is difficult to implement through programs administered by large and separate local-level government agencies.

Government programs may do well at controlling behavior external to families, such as disorder on the street through community policing;[5] however, the fundamental operational unit of social and emotional dysfunction in children lies inside the family. A social service or law enforcement agency can't intervene effectively in socioeconomic processes embedded in a family's transgenerational history. No one helped Cathy; Cathy and Cara suffered.

Government agencies do well at providing centralized social, educational, and medical services. Ironically, however, such service delivery often occurs best inside correctional facilities, where managers can be held accountable for service delivery and where the quality and delivery of services are embedded in an organizational system that's prescribed and protected by the U.S. Bill of Rights and federal courts.[6] Service delivery on the street requires a different organizational mechanism, because a community's social, educational, medical, and vocational service agencies usually aren't well integrated. And on the street, law enforcement dominates, particularly in the case of youth gangs, and gang kids are arrested and jailed long before a community agency reaches them. Once inside the juvenile justice system, kids get lost and pushed further aside.

This indicates that communities must achieve a balance between law enforcement and service delivery, preferably before arrests occur. If this is to happen, a carefully modeled community organization must be created from a community's social, educational, medical, and vocational agencies and its private businesses, the last of which would offer entry-level employment to young workers. Communities with this shared goal can provide a full range of services to preschoolers like Amy, RoniRo, and Charlene and to adolescents like chubby-faced Robert and Cara.[7]

Mobilizing a community's agencies and developing an operational model to deliver services at street level won't be as easy as program delivery inside correctional facilities. However, every crime-control expenditure has an opportunity cost. *Opportunity cost* means an assessment of how much it will cost now and in the long term to ignore the creation and implementation of a program.[8] In this case the question is: If communities don't act on behalf of delinquents, gang members, and gang members' children, how much will such inaction cost the community and its residents in the future?

Community mobilization can be relatively inexpensive if communities plan properly and invest their resources in the programs that offer delinquents and gang kids something they want.[9] We can continue to allow community agencies to work separately without a shared goal and common strategy to deliver services to children and adolescents. But if we continue with the status quo, there's no guarantee that local-level government agencies, such as a probation department or a school, can ever do more than they're now doing. Cara, Wendy, Little Man, Bernard, Chucky D, Afro, Rosa, and the others dropped out of school or were expelled; while on probation, Cara received almost no assistance in two years, and Wendy received none. When the link between a young offender and a government program is that ineffective, why do we support it? Financial and personnel resources locked away in local community correction agencies can be refocused and retrained to meet kids' needs on the street.

Family Intervention

The term *gang* is a shorthand cue for set of pernicious social and economic processes in communities, neighborhoods, and families. To some degree,

Cara's destiny was determined by the nature of her grandmother's and mother's families. When I learned that Cathy had been a teenage mother and Jackie's father was a raging alcoholic, I better understood Cara's and Wendy's behavior. It's too late to remedy those family dynamics. However, we still can rescue kids who are in families like Wendy's and in neighborhoods like Fremont.

Chubby-faced Robert sitting on the porch of Wendy's drug house smoking Newports and joints at age nine left little wonder in my mind about his future, unless someone were to remove him from that porch and protect him. He needed to be put on a safe path, but Jackie was incapable of putting him on one. However, he was on a safe path for a short time. You'll recall that he stayed with a foster family after the August 1995 bust, and according to Wendy and Cara, he was doing well. He attended school, didn't "curse," and had stopped smoking cigarettes and weed. But social service workers gave him back to Jackie, and by August 1997, he was "mean, real mean," Cara said. By his 12th birthday on August 16, 1997, Robert and Jackie were again smoking weed together and were literally homeless. They bounced between households and for a while stayed with Cara in her studio apartment on The Ave, which she had rented in April that year. The local social service bureaucracy had failed; Robert's fate was sealed.

After the August 1995 bust, Jackie received drug and alcohol therapy and parent training. But teaching and preaching didn't do her any good, nor was Robert a beneficiary of Jackie's alleged new parenting skills. Robert would have benefited most by staying with his foster family. Someone in Kansas City thought otherwise and dropped him back into the pit of poverty, drugs, and neglect.

Cara's family history reveals that, inside disturbed families, parents as well as kids suffer and that well-meaning parents like Cathy are powerless to change their family's life course. Interventionists can't reach back to alter life histories or repair damage inflicted on families by yesterday's alcoholism and violence. Community intervention can, however, mend today's disorganized families and save children from physical, social, and emotional pain by putting them on a path to social and economic security.

Youth-Gang Intervention

Fremont research shows that a youth gang's social life is an intricate set of economic transactions which have social effects. The underlying socioeconomic principle is this: When kids perceive a gain by doing one thing instead of another, they move in the direction of the gain. When there's a perception of greater gain in selling drugs than in doing school work, drug selling wins. The principle operates in purely social transactions. When there's greater gain in hanging out with a gang than in avoiding it, the gang wins. When a girl perceives greater gain in having a relationship with an abusive boy than in having no boyfriend, there's victimization of teenage girls.[10]

Likewise, delinquency and gang intervention can operate on the same socioeconomic principle of gain. Generally speaking, youth-gang intervention is a struggle over money: gang kids earn cash by selling high-profit drugs like rock cocaine, all the while that hundreds of millions of dollars are spent by federal, state, and local crime-control agencies to suppress or prevent gang-related drug selling and other crimes linked to gangs.

The dynamic process central to gang intervention is like tug-of-war: communities must convince gang kids like Wendy that there's greater long-term gain in sticking with an "eight-to-five," usually blue-collar, low-wage, shift-work job, which they don't want to do, than in continuing a relatively easy, albeit risky, drug-selling–hanging-out lifestyle.

If kids gradually accept this economic shift, they'll eventually acquire a sense of the underlying philosophical and moral shift in lifestyle orientations. Gang life is predicated on immediate economic gain from drug and other crime profits and social gain from the agency of rulelessness. Mainstream life is oriented toward the future, and social and material gains are slower but steadier, more reliable, and less risky.

The irony is that communities have more to lose than gang kids do in failed intervention and a great deal more to gain in successful intervention. If communities can convince kids like Wendy and Cara to trade a profitable unlawful job for a less-profitable lawful one, then the community expenses attached to gang crime (drug selling, burglary, carjacking) and gang-related social problems (child abuse and neglect, drug addiction, teenage pregnancy, truancy and dropping out of school) will diminish gradually for the majority of community members as gang members pull away from the street and lead their children toward mainstream lifestyles.

The unlawful-to-lawful shift in income production and the social changes it effects over multiple generations are what I mean by *youth-gang intervention*. This is a difficult shift to encourage and even more difficult to accomplish. Fremont research shows that gang kids do engage in this economic transition even on their own, and that doing so results in less crime and less serious crime. With the stimulus of the August 1995 Fremont drug bust, Cara's and Wendy's lives over the subsequent 18 months illustrate that point.

Successful gang intervention depends on offering gang kids the un-lawful-to-lawful socioeconomic trade by showing them exactly what they have to gain. Some community members may feel this is "coddling young criminals." But remember that taxpayers fund intervention and crime-control policies, and they have the most to gain and to lose. The truth is, without the consensus of gang kids, gang and delinquency intervention always loses, crime soars, costs skyrocket.

Legislators and community officials who hurl threats at gang kids will get only a sore throat. Afro and Chucky D aren't moved by preaching or screaming. Cara too is a hard sell. She saw no immediate benefit in a DeLaSalle education and a GED, so she quit. She had a job at Taco Bell, and a GED wouldn't have added one cent to her income. Like most teenagers, Cara didn't connect more education today with economic gain in the year 2005. What's more, Fremont kids are too cynical to believe that history and algebra lessons will ensure a "better tomorrow." Even my college students don't believe that.

What moves Cara and Wendy to act? The answer is simple: immediate material gain, including money, food, clothes, and shelter. Improvements these kids can see, touch, and possess will pull them off the street. Only after they are sheltered and protected will most of them pay attention to less tangible aspects of their lives. These kids aren't stupid; they know when they're better off in one situation than in another. The trick is to involve them socially and emotionally in their own intervention to the same degree they have been involved in their own destruction.

Community mobilization and a carefully designed system that, first, improves the quality of life and, second, integrates that improvement with educational and vocational training can help remedy the effects of social and economic poverty.

Gang-Girl Intervention

I advocate the implementation of supervised residential centers designed for gang girls like Wendy and Cara. Gang boys won't be overlooked (outlined below is a neighborhood-based intervention for boys), but their intervention can be simpler than girls', and more delinquent and gang boys are already exposed to intervention.

In 1995, 74 percent of juveniles arrested were boys under age 18.[11] While in detention centers and jail, these offenders receive social, psychological, and educational and vocational services. If young men like Chucky D are exposed to such programs and subsequently choose gang life over straight life, then America's culture of personal choice should let these young adults accept the responsibility of that choice.[12]

True, a culture of choice is open to girls too, but gang girls pose a special intervention obstacle: babies.[13] Rosa, Teresa, Janet, Joanne, and Dante have preschool children. Doing little more than classroom education has no immediate material effect on their lives and doesn't improve their children's lives either. In short, inadequate intervention for gang-girl mothers and their children has a high opportunity cost. If communities focus on gang boys and ignore gang-girl mothers, their children are likely to reside in homes like Teresa's or Northeast Carol's, the self-proclaimed Gangsta Mama. If police arrest gang-girl mothers and imprison them, who will care for their children and what will be the conditions of care?[14]

Gang-girl intervention is crime control. Pulling gang girls off the street may, over time, weaken the fluid residential pattern of gang boys and, at the same time, stabilize female-headed households. Cara, Janet, Wendy, Poodle, Rosa, and Joanne, as well as adult women, including Taffy, Jackie, and Northeast Carol, provided a stable residential system which gang boys like Chucky D used to sustain a drug-selling street lifestyle.

Fremont research shows that a baby is an effective link between its mother and father only when the father perceives some material benefit from such an attachment.[15] Cara's link to Steele Bill resulted in three pregnancies, and in the duration of those pregnancies, she received no financial and little emotional support. Janet's association with Steele Bill mirrored Cara's. He abandoned Janet and Briana, gave them little financial support, caused Janet emotional trauma, and twice assaulted her. In August 1997, Steele Bill was sentenced to four months in county jail for domestic abuse. As long as the mothers of the children of gang boys have apartments and houses, these boys will have a place to hang out and sell drugs.

Cara's experience with the imprisoned Chucky D shows that a link between a gang boy and girl doesn't depend solely on proximity.[16] Such a social tie depends in part on a girl's fear of being alone or harangued or beaten by a rejected gang suitor or his emissary.

To ensure that these girls and their children are safe, communities must encourage them to leave the street. One thing is certain: communities should never count on gang boys to assist their pregnant girlfriends or their babies' mothers. Encouraging girls to abandon the street will disrupt boys' residential patterns, protect girls from abuse and another pregnancy, and shelter gang girls' children.

Fremont research also shows that gang girls neglect their children either because of apathy engendered by drug addiction or because of a lack of resources to provide a safe environment. When these young children are neglected for any reason, they end up as Charlene did, sitting on TJ's knee in Cara's apartment at 5403 Smart, breathing cigarette and marijuana smoke, listening to gangster rap, and surrounded by young gangsters.[17]

The intervention option with the lowest long-term cost is to locate young gang-affiliated mothers somewhere that they can be given options that increase their gain and protect their children. Let's remember that we're focusing on adolescents who are 14 to 17 years old; kids this age don't plan well for the future and have no realistic idea about social and economic issues embedded in rearing children.

Finding young mothers and teenagers like Cara, who may not be pregnant today but will be tomorrow, might be the most difficult challenge of an intervention program that targets teenage girls and young mothers and their children. This subpopulation is hidden inside youth gangs, and we're unsure about the number of youngsters (mothers, children) who require services. The percentage of youth-gang members who are adolescent and young adult females isn't well defined.[18] The number of young women who aren't hardcore gang members but nevertheless are affiliated to some degree with gang boys is also unknown. The number of children whose mothers are gang girls and fathers are gang boys is unknown. The number of gang boys who have abandoned children is unknown.[19] And the quality of childcare delivered by gang-girl mothers or members of their extended families is unexamined in the gang literature.

Notwithstanding the ill-defined nature of this subpopulation, there are reasonable ways to reach out to gang girls. Finding them at school seems the easiest way, but Fremont research shows that hardcore girls who are most often pregnant and most involved in crime don't go to school.[20] With this in mind, we can name a number of options. Communities can wait for them to be arrested. In 1995, 26 percent of juvenile arrests (adolescents under age 18) were females; although waiting for an arrest may be too late, this approach is better than doing nothing. Communities can reach out to juvenile females who seek medical care for pregnancy and related medical concerns at public hospitals. Communities can enlist the help of grassroots agencies.[21] The Ad Hoc Group Against Crime (Ad Hoc), a long-standing privately and publicly funded outreach agency in Kansas City, Missouri, does an effective job of contacting kids in high-crime and gang neighborhoods. Ad Hoc's outreach workers are former gang members and adult offenders who have worked with neighborhood organizations, intervened in neighborhood household disputes, supported law enforcement efforts to stabilize high-crime neighborhoods, and saved dozens of young girls from sexual victimization by male gang members.

However, gang and drug detectives have the potential to be the most effective outreach workers. The dominant police role in Kansas City is crime suppression. That's important, especially with kids like Chucky D; however, there's more to policing than making arrests. Juvenile gangs and drug detectives have a moral, if not a legal, obligation to protect children from abuse and neglect and exposure to dangerous environments. Young children like Charlene, Damone, and Briana don't have to be black and blue for us to know they're in trouble; as long as their mothers are tied to boys like Chucky D and Steele Bill, these kids are going to be in unhealthy environments.

The mother-child tie is a critical juncture, because it affords communities an intervention opportunity, which may slow the genesis of the next generation of young gang members and delinquents. Fremont research shows that a community's opportunity cost can be high when a gang or drug detective walks away from neglected children and adolescents and does nothing to intervene.

Supervised Residential Centers

Resources reallocated from juvenile and adult correctional budgets can support two types of supervised residential centers designed for adolescent gang-affiliated girls with or without children.[22] The simpler center is a "safe house–working dormitory"; the more complex center is a "group home" for young mothers.

Residential centers should be located outside high-crime inner cities but close to high schools, community colleges, and jobs. A residential intervention offers girls an immediate change in the material conditions of their lives and gives them an opportunity to achieve independent living.[23] And if you recall, residential and financial independence is a dream of Fremont girls.

Formalizing local-level residential placements under federal oversight with financial contributions from counties, states, and the federal government, as well as corporations who'd hire these young women, would benefit everyone.[24] Federal oversight may better ensure equity in the distribution of resources to the poorest communities. I am fearful that state- and local-elected officials may succumb to the pressure of voters who feel that repairing potholes, building a community swimming pool, and constructing a $60 million state prison are better options than supporting impoverished gang-affiliated girls and their babies.

Community leaders must ensure that the bureaucracy managing these residential centers is streamlined and consumes proportionately little of the allocated resources. Most important, supervisory staff should be trained managers who've passed careful background checks, including criminal history investigations, to ensure the physical and emotional safety of girls. Residential centers would be outstanding training centers for graduate students studying social work, criminal justice, family dynamics, and psychology.

Generally speaking, supervised residential centers would operate on a consensual management model, which engages girls' cooperation with their social support and material gain. House rules and sanctions for violations should be a core underlying operational element, but threats of punishment must be kept in the background. Girls' program involvement and consensus in meeting house rules must be an outcome of their recognition of social support and material gain. Of course, there will be rule violations, but unless these are instances of serious violence, patience must be the order of the day until girls learn how to live in a rule-ordered environment. Gang boys must be kept out and curfews established. When gang boys discover that girls at residential centers have nothing of value to offer them, they will disappear.

Residential centers would meet three specific objectives: (1) to shelter and protect girls; (2) to provide education, job training, and job placement; and (3) to ensure a healthy start for gang girls' children. If gang girls aren't pregnant or already mothers, simple interventions, such as job training and placement, coupled with time to adjust to a new style of life may be all that's necessary to redirect them. Cara took a few months to adjust to life outside Fremont after the August 1995 bust, but once she did, she worked every day. However, both the intervention complexity and the opportunity cost increase dramatically when a teenage girl is pregnant or has a child. At that point, intervention must be designed for the immediate and long-term needs of mothers and children.

Fremont girls and their babies are illustrations of what happens when kids are reared on the street with inadequate adult supervision. If kids like Carmen, the girl whom Cara took under her wing on Smart, have no parents or adults who'll care for them, communities should become "surrogate" parents.

Safe House–Working Dormitory

The working poor suffer.[25] An annual income of $10,000–$20,000 forces these wage earners to reside in cheap apartments in rundown neighborhoods far from good jobs in the suburbs. Cara's story shows what can happen when a single young woman who earns approximately $700 a month decides to share an apartment. True, she could have found a smaller, rattier apartment somewhere and lived alone, but that's not what a teenage girl actually does. True, she could have found a roommate other than Wendy and kept the door closed in the face of drug-using and drug-selling companions like Steele Bill, Glen, and Wendy's mother, Jackie. But these girls don't do that either. There's a lesson here: Communities should design programs on the basis of what gang girls do, not on what we wish they would do.

The first goal of safe houses–working dorms is to safeguard young girls by stabilizing them with housing, food, and safety in a communal residence.[26] A communal lifestyle is an essential element in successful intervention. Dormitory life is more than housing. Girls need to have emotional security as well as social stability. Recall how the Fremont girls huddled together in Wendy's room in the drug house and guarded their cherished private space. These girls are scared of failure and have had few experiences in the mainstream world. Recall how Cara felt before she entered the DeLaSalle Education Center. Despite the bravado and street rhetoric,[27] these girls are frightened, inexperienced children who need guidance and a group of companions to offer social and moral support.

The success of safe houses–working dorms may encourage more girls to leave the street. Cara's and Wendy's experiences on the job show that one girl can pull another one or two into the workplace. Cara and Wendy helped Bernard and Cheri find work, and even Steele Bill worked for a few days. The same energy and commitment these girls show toward drug selling can be diverted into staying straight if we provide them with basic support while they learn how to manage on their own.

In a safe house, a girl can achieve stability and security. In this setting, she can be offered psychological and substance-abuse counseling. Kids who've been on the street need time to relax, settle down, learn to interact in positive ways, and most of all, "stay clean." A lifestyle of hanging out and using drugs keeps kids up all night and wears them out. Recall that some Fremont kids disappeared for a week or two when they retreated to a safe spot to rest. Jail sometimes acts as a safe house. Cara's frantic street behavior calmed in about a week after her arrest in March 1996. Even her letters expressed a different attitude about her past and her future. Cara's experiences on Cherry, and TJ's too, show that, once a young person adjusts to confinement, he or she adapts well and feels comfortable. Cara ate regularly, slept all night, kept busy at productive activities all day, received drug and alcohol treatment, attended religious services, and went to school.

At Wendy's drug house, at Cara's 5403 Smart apartment, and at Wendy and Cara's Raytown apartment, these girls' lives were monolithic, unproductive, and self-destructive, despite their working every day. By contrast, a safe house can be the first step in a multidimensional program delivery system and an alternative less costly than jails and detention centers.[28]

Programs must include more than educational and counseling programs. Recall that Fremont kids have virtually no social ties of value to anyone outside the gang. Girls' ties to family members are strained, and a daughter-mother tie is valueless if the mother is a rock cocaine addict and an alcoholic. Wendy's link to Mike gave her social and emotional support, but his ties to members of Alcoholics Anonymous could do little to improve Wendy's income.

A safe house can change a gang girl's social network by adding the ties she needs to the mainstream.[29] Once girls sense that they're gaining more than they're losing, most of them will likely move to employment.

The second goal of safe houses–working dorms is to prepare girls with workplace skills. This can be accomplished with a careful assessment of a girl's strengths and weaknesses and the development of a detailed case management plan. For these girls, preparation for the workplace means more than acquiring job skills. They need basic social and language skills as well, because these have been cut short by inadequate family socialization, delinquency, and periods of isolation in detention centers and jails.

Fremont research has shown that these kids don't know appropriate workplace speech and behavior. Recall that I taught Wendy and Cara how to shop for groceries; recall the public conversation they had about buying flavored douche; recall their socially inappropriate use of words like *niggah, motherfucka,* and *bitch* in places like McDonald's and Pizza Hut; recall that Bernard tossed boiling water onto a co-worker's back because she "pissed him off"; recall outbursts like Wendy's in front of the QT on Truman in the summer of 1995; and recall that verbal dueling and aggression are core features of street life.

In August 1997, Cathy told me that Cara's Taco Bell supervisor would recommend her for a promotion to store manager if she'd learn how to "get along better" with everyone. This meant she had to learn how to speak in public without screaming, yelling, and insulting co-workers and customers. Beyond vocational training and public speaking, these girls must be taught how to defend themselves from predators like Chucky D.

Safe houses–working dorms are places where girls would receive vocational and social training and reside while they are working full-time at entry-level jobs. Girls would pay a portion of their income as room and board and do chores around the house. When these girls are stable and well trained in a variety of workplace skills, out-placement services could assist them in finding a decent apartment and a better job.

Group Homes for Young Mothers

Communities must face the issue of helping girls through pregnancy and the early years of motherhood.[30] A low-paying job can't adequately support a young mother-to-be or meet the expenses of motherhood. Cara was socially and economically stymied in her fourth pregnancy: Where would she live? How would she earn enough income to meet her growing financial responsibilities? Fremont research shows that gang girls live with economic and social poverty, and pregnancy makes that worse. Pregnant girls lose companions. Recall that Cara's closest companions abandoned her when she announced her fourth pregnancy; recall also that Wendy abandoned Angie the Shoplifter when her infant drove Wendy crazy.[31]

What residential options are available within the personal social networks of pregnant, gang-affiliated girls or new mothers? The answer is, few. Cathy's apartment was too small to house Cara and her child as well as Melanie, April, and Cathy. Cara was stuck; the spontaneous abortion got her off the social and economic hook. If Cara had carried her child to term, her economic difficulties would have been magnified beyond a point where she or Cathy could have handled them.[32]

With a job earning minimum wage and no social ties to anyone who can economically support her, a pregnant girl or young mother is stuck on the street, forced to use welfare, and often is driven to open her doors to gang boys. When Cara was planning the future during her fourth pregnancy, recall that she wanted to reside in a "nice neighborhood," but she couldn't, because such apartments require a damage deposit and the first and last months' rent. She would have needed about $1,000. Access to federally supported housing requires a criminal background check. Cara submitted an application to reside in the same federal housing complex as the one Rosa and Poodle lived in, but Cara was denied access. Her rap sheet listed "aggravated criminal assault."

Despite Cara's financial limitations, I had planned to take her apartment hunting and to pay her apartment deposits and get her settled with furniture and other necessities. Even then, however, she would have been over her head with financial obligations and couldn't have satisfied them on her own.

Fremont research shows clearly that a pregnant teenage girl's life slowly and inevitably worsens.[33] She's compelled to overcome: the reality of economic and social poverty and impending homelessness; social alienation from her family and perhaps also from her companions (as Cara faced); recurring battles with her baby's father over financial and social support and his desire to "be with" other girls (as Janet faced with Steele Bill); and the physical and emotional discomfort of trips by bus to public health hospitals and long waits there, if she chooses to receive medical care. What's more, pregnancy puts social and financial pressure on the adult females in the mother-to-be's family. Often that pressure strains an already difficult relationship even more. Recall that before Janet had Briana, Janet's mother said she wouldn't help Janet care for her baby.

Community inaction in regard to this array of social problems has a catastrophic opportunity cost. The children of Fremont girls are the next generation of gangs like the Fremont Hustlers. Without community mobilization, I'm not sanguine about the prospects of a safe and healthy life for Charlene, Damone, Briana, Amy, RoniRo, and the other babies and preschoolers whose mothers hang on Fremont and 13th.

The single most important issue with the highest opportunity cost in youth-gang intervention is protecting babies and preschoolers.[34] In houses like Teresa's, Amy and RoniRo are reared in economic and social, as well as moral, poverty.[35] Engulfed in such a household, do Amy and RoniRo have a reasonable opportunity to elude drugs and gangs? Only in a community's care will children like Amy, RoniRo, and Charlene be protected.[36]

In a group home, day care and an early-life program for children can get them off in the right direction while young mothers work and return home to a clean and protected environment where they learn how to help one another. Kansas City has new, low-income, single-family houses as well as apartments located in safe neighborhoods near downtown employment and along bus lines. When young women with and without children acquire more job skills and earn better incomes, they can be assisted in finding low-income housing and more sophisticated employment.

Transportation

Reliable transportation carries everyone to work, except the poor. Public transportation from high-crime inner-city neighborhoods to work sites is expensive, time consuming, and inconvenient, and, of course, buses don't often carry low-income workers to the best jobs in the suburbs. Even if Cara and Wendy had jobs in Johnson County paying $12 an hour, they couldn't afford to reside in the suburbs. And there is no public transportation to take workers from inner-city neighborhoods to Johnson County.[37] If there were such buses, they'd take hours to go from the northeast side to Overland Park.

Private transportation is problematic, as well. Recall that Cara and I disagreed over her purchase of a rundown car. Cara's 1986 Ford Escort was a money pit and drained her weekly income faster than the car's engine lost oil. Each time her jalopy needed one of its frequent repairs, it cost $200–$300. On an income of $700 a month, a $200 car repair is an enormous cost. After Cara's car blew a head gasket in July 1997, we discussed her transportation options, and finally she has come to understand that a better job can buy a better car—but she can't get a better job.

Transportation is a persistent problem for workers who don't earn enough income to buy a relatively new and reliable used car. If residents in these areas had reliable transportation, they may be able to obtain better-paying jobs in Johnson County and other suburban areas.

Professor Bernard's proposed used-car-rebuilding program located within inner-city neighborhoods may be a productive idea. Such a program would offer low-income workers reliable transportation at a relatively low cost and would afford young men and women an opportunity to learn the skills of a well-paid occupation. Imagine local businesses, a community college, and the courts joining in a cooperative venture in which nonviolent drug offenders on probation are given an opportunity to train as car mechanics instead of doing time in jail or wasting time on probation. A local business might donate space in a warehouse; a major automobile dealership or community college might lend trained mechanics to instruct young students; a tool manufacturer might donate the necessary equipment; and a university's business department might offer the services of faculty members who would teach students how to develop a business plan. The outcome of such a venture would be an inner-city, on-the-job training program in auto repair and rebuilding. Such a program could be extended to parolees as well.

A car-rebuilding program could be organized as a nonprofit service organization. Citizens donating older cars would receive a charitable tax deduction. Repaired and rebuilt cars sold to local residents at the cost of the repairs would benefit workers and add to their household income, boosting the local economy. Everyone wins.

Poisonous Environments

Cara and Wendy are trapped in poverty or at best on the margin of poverty, and no one seems willing to get close to them, except the police. I'm not optimistic about federal- or state-level political support necessary to accomplish substantial material change in the lives of impoverished kids, let alone gang-affiliated adolescents. Some taxpayers prefer to ignore these children's pain; others prefer to build multimillion dollar prisons to house kids like Chucky D, as if doing nothing or the wrong thing has an opportunity cost lower than a prudent investment in community mobilization and the long-term salvation of children.

Substantial material changes will occur only when mayors and city councils acknowledge the immorality and inhumanity of confining children and adolescents to the inner-city. To see preschool children sleeping in filthy drug houses, teenage girls prostituting themselves on the street corners, adolescents drugging themselves to dull the pain of daily life, teenage boys killing and maiming one another, and kids being arrested and imprisoned as easily as we swat flies, Americans simply have to drive through an inner city. Down those streets, flowing unimpeded, is a poison that deadens young minds and souls. Unless communities act to remedy the social and economic neglect now heaped onto inner-city children and adolescents, the outcome will be so dreadful, it will exhaust our energy, consume our resources, crush us under its weight, and leave us gasping for breath.

15
Street Ethnography
Methods, Ethics, and Politics

The anthropologist is an instrument of cultural translation that is necessarily
flawed and biased. We cannot rid ourselves of the cultural self we bring
with us into the field any more than we can disown the eyes, ears, and skin
through which we take in our intuitive perceptions. . . . Nonetheless, . . .
we struggle to do the best we can with the limited resources we have
at hand—our ability to listen and observe carefully, empathically, and
compassionately.
                    —Nancy Scheper-Hughes, *Death without Weeping*

Dead End Kids is an ethnographic study of delinquents who were also
members of a youth gang. This type of research is known as street
ethnography, or the study of people whose lives are played out on the
streets of a community. Street ethnographers are most often interested
in people who break the law, which immediately makes street research
difficult.

People who do unlawful things usually don't want us to watch them,
don't want to talk about it openly, and are difficult to find through
conventional means. These folks don't have telephones or permanent
addresses or full-time jobs, nor do they receive junk mail. They haven't
left any proverbial footprints that social scientists can easily find. On the
whole, these people are called a *hidden population*, which is defined as
"a subset of the general population whose membership is not readily distinguished or enumerated based on existing knowledge and/or sampling
capabilities."[1] In other words, we can't mail them a survey or call them,
because we don't know where they are. This means we have to go to them.

Despite the difficulty of studying hidden populations, street ethnographers have amassed a large literature about "the street" and the activities
of hidden-population members. There are general studies of inner-city
communities,[2] criminal activity and criminal lifestyles,[3] drug use and
distribution,[4] sex,[5] alcoholics and panhandling,[6] and youth gangs.[7]

Standard social scientific practices would be ineffective to study
drug sellers, burglars and thieves, and street gangs; after all, there's no
place where we can find the names, addresses, and telephone numbers
of all rock cocaine sellers or adolescent gang members in Kansas City,

Missouri. Street ethnography is a perfect technique for researching a hidden population.

Generally speaking, an ethnographer goes off somewhere to a so-called fieldsite, stays at a fieldsite (Fremont) a long time, gets involved in many situations there (drug selling, violence, arrests), deals with emotional stress induced by pressures at the fieldsite (the stress of witnessing child abuse), figures out how to keep going in the research without compromising his or her soul or scientific integrity, and returns home to write about it. This research process turns an ethnographer into a participant and an observer at his or her fieldsite.[8]

Participant observation is the main technique of ethnography, and through it ethnographers are able to collect so-called ethnographic data. These data are observations, words, and experiences derived at the fieldsite. Observations include what "natives" (people who are indigenous to the fieldsite) do among themselves. Words include the things natives say to one other and to the ethnographer, as well as written documents, such as Cara's letters, poetry, and dream diary. The fundamental building blocks of ethnographic description and analysis of life at a fieldsite are the words natives speak to ethnographers, both in casual conversations and in interviews (natives who give us information are called informants).

Words are easy to collect; however, an informant's words are an ethnographer's most difficult data to interpret. Words don't exist as objective entities; rather, words carry meanings that are derived from the speaker's experiences as well as from the culture of the community. Participant observation helps an ethnographer to interpret informants' words by establishing the social context in which they were spoken. If an ethnographer stays at a fieldsite long enough, he or she develops an understanding of what natives say, how they say it, why they say it, and how words reflect community social life and culture, as well as an understanding of informants' unique perspectives on community life.

An ethnographer's experiences as a participant in a fieldsite are important data. Among all participation experiences, two are vital to record: natives' reactions to the ethnographer, and the ethnographer's reactions to natives. The quality-of-life scenes inside Teresa's house are descriptions drawn from direct participation.[9] Donna's (Teresa's sister's) explosive reaction to me as I sat inside the house told me that she knew RoniRo and Amy were being neglected and abused right in front of my eyes.

Direct participation has led me to conclude: that youngsters must be protected and removed from households like Teresa's; that pregnant teenagers must be protected and kept away from male predators; that youth-gang life isn't pleasant, healthy, or ultimately profitable for adolescents; and that nothing in gang life is worth preserving, except the kids.

Ethnography and Theory

The aim of an ethnographic investigation, whether its fieldsite is a gang neighborhood, a jail or prison, or a community of warriors in highland New Guinea, is the use of ethnographic data to achieve an "insider's," or a native's, view of his or her community. Natives' words are guides to their descriptions, conceptualizations, rationalizations, justifications, and explanations of community reality. While ethnographers' aim is to explore natives' subjective, or ethnographic, reality, we also try to achieve an objective scientific analysis of ethnographic data.[10]

Doing ethnography and conducting social science aren't mutually exclusive activities.[11] Ethnographers systematically describe what natives do (their actual behavior) and precisely record natives' discussions about what they do (their explanations). These data are then interpreted using an existing objective standard, or a theory of behavior, or they are used to create a theory of behavior, which is then offered as a way to interpret natives' behavior. Such a theory is then "tested," or used by other researchers, and is modified and retested.[12]

I've used a theory in both ways. In *Warehousing Violence,* I interpreted ethnographic data describing daily life inside a maximum-security federal penitentiary using consensus theory of organizational behavior. In *Beggars and Thieves,* I interpreted ethnographic data using the existing theory of low self-control and, at the same time, built a theory from ethnographic data, calling it a defensive worldview.

Dead End Kids formulates a materialist, or economic, explanation of informants' behavior.[13] This theoretical approach is akin to cultural materialism, although its adaptation here has been simplified. I used an economic/materialist theory to interpret these ethnographic data, because cultural materialism creates an awareness of two complementary perspectives on human behavior that are congenial to ethnographic research. These approaches focus on an economic basis for human behavior as well as on a linguistic approach to interpreting informants' speech within an ethnographic context.

Dead End Kids' economic theory of youth-gang behavior is explicit in the ethnographic data; however, my explanations aren't always similar to those of the Fremont kids (I discuss below this contrast in interpretation). The contrast between the natives' and the researcher's view of community life is fundamental to an anthropological perspective on behavior: natives don't always understand why they do what they do, and natives' statements about their behavior are sometimes contradicted by their actions. It is a primary mission of the ethnographer to reconcile the differences between the researcher's and the natives' perspectives.

The acid test of ethnographic research, as well as the theories generated by it, is whether ethnographic findings from one fieldsite are consistent with findings from a similar fieldsite. Such a comparison of ethnographic findings tests the reliability of our methods[14] and the validity of our data as they are generalized to other fieldsites.

Dead End Kids compares closely with gang fieldwork in other cities. Decker and Van Winkle's research in St. Louis was based on hundreds of hours of interviews and observations in gang neighborhoods. Fremont research findings are very similar to Decker and Van Winkle's, as well as to those reported by Klein.[15] We agree on dozens of key issues, including the role of violence in gang life, reasons for gang membership, problems of exiting a gang, and the role of female gang members.

Such agreement suggests that a fieldwork method used independently at separate sites in different cities can yield consistent and accurate findings if researchers are similarly skilled at data collection and analysis, have a comprehensive knowledge of a research topic on which to base their interview questions and observations, and have informants who know what they're talking about.

Informant Selection. Every street ethnographer faces a major obstacle: how to choose informants. If an ethnographer doesn't pick the best informants, the research findings will be problematic and of limited use.

Comparing an ethnographer's use of informants to a survey researcher's use of respondents illustrates why we need to find the right informants. A survey researcher may collect data on 20 variables about welfare reform from 1,200 respondents chosen in a probability sample. An ethnographer, however, will collect data on hundreds of variables from a few or dozens of informants and hang out in low-income neighborhoods to watch how people respond to policy changes. In the end, an ethnographer has a lot of data about welfare reform and how it affects life inside households and low-income communities, as well as thousands of observations of actual behavior linked to this specific topic. Together, interviews and observations create crucial insight into what's really going on at a fieldsite with respect to a specific research issue.

If we rely on data from a few informants, then we must know explicitly how we select the individuals who become our informants.[16] I had to be sure that Cara and Wendy were the right informants, because otherwise *Dead End Kids'* view of the Fremont Hustlers as a youth gang would be distorted, and my findings would be incompatible with those of other gang research. If I had errors in my data, irrespective of how those errors originated, the research findings wouldn't be useful. The effectiveness of my intervention proposals depends entirely on a correct analysis of why a youth gang forms, how it operates, and how it can be supplanted. If I incorrectly interpreted the cause of the gang problem, then intervention would be less effective.

Picking an informant is like selecting a spouse: if you get it wrong, life will be unpleasant. The fact is, picking an informant must be much more precise than picking a spouse. Ethnographers usually have only one chance at picking the best informants, because we run out of time and money. What does it mean to have a "good" or the "right" or "best" informant?

A good informant is one who can answer questions and knows what he or she is talking about; however, before I can pick informants, I have to know which topics I'm investigating and a lot about each one, or else I won't be able to assess an informant's competence. For this reason, an ethnographer enters a fieldsite only after studying everything available about his or her research topic.

Investigating a youth gang means exploring drug use and selling, inter- and intragroup violence, boy-girl relationships, sex, birth control, pregnancy, adolescent parenthood, and kids' relationships with parents and with the police, among other topics. With this list of topics, I needed a number of really good informants.

When I showed up on Fremont and saw the extent of Wendy's involvement as a central player in the Fremont Hustlers, I knew she'd become a key, or primary, informant.[17] Key informants are "people who you can talk to easily, who understand the information you need, and who are glad to give it to you or get it for you."[18]

Of course, when it came to drug selling, Wendy was my first choice as a key informant, and best of all, she was more than willing to cooperate. But Wendy wasn't the only drug seller on Fremont, and she graciously introduced me to Chucky D. Here were Fremont's main drug sellers, both of whom were willing to talk into a tape recorder about the drug business. And of course, I got to sit around Wendy's drug house and watch the drug business unfold in front of my eyes.

Wendy knew everyone on Fremont, everyone knew her, and during the day, she had hundreds, maybe thousands, of separate interactions with dozens of people who were members of the Fremont Hustlers and with other neighborhood folks too. Wendy was an ethnographer's bonanza. Whenever I needed to know something about anyone, I asked Wendy. Or I'd just hang around her and listen to conversations she had with the folks who approached her. Being near her was like standing at Heaven's Gate—eventually everyone arrives there.

Cara didn't become a key informant until early 1996, but before then, she'd been a very good informant. Cara, like Wendy, knew everyone, but Cara is special for another reason: her verbal skills are excellent, and her emotional life usually doesn't cloud her vision. Wendy is angry, and her anger often clouds her interpretation of social life. Instead of talking about people she was angry at, Wendy would call them obscene names, make grossly judgmental comments, and dismiss any questions I had about them. Cara is much less judgmental than Wendy, and, like her, Cara was active in the network of Fremont kids as well as in other neighborhoods' gang networks. Cara was freer to move around the city, because until the bust, Wendy was tied to the drug house. Together, Wendy and Cara linked me to every major player in the Fremont Hustlers, and every major player eventually found his or her way to the two of them.

Dead End Kids includes interviews with lots of gang kids, but most of them weren't good prospects as key informants. Wendy and Cara are bright kids and were central in the group's social life. The truth is, other Fremont kids aren't as insightful or energetic, or as willing to be open and honest as Cara and Wendy were. Chucky D was a bright informant who knew gangs and street life, but unfortunately, for him and for me, he went to prison. And that fact is a real danger in street ethnography and a danger for which a fieldworker must be prepared by having a lot of informants and a number of key informants. Had my research depended entirely on Wendy and Chucky D, I would have been in trouble when he went to prison and she went into hiding.

Strong ethnography depends on good informants who live interesting lives. Most Fremont kids are dull, rather boring adolescents who live uneventful lives. Afro, House of Pain, Cain, Greenbean, and the other boys, as well as girls like Joanne, Rosa, and Janet (while she hung on Fremont), are stagnant; they hang out and sell drugs and do little else. Their lives would have generated a dull ethnographic account which did little more than tell the world how boring it is to be a delinquent drug seller.

With key informants like Cara and Wendy, why does *Dead End Kids* focus on Cara? Simply because Wendy disappeared after the bust and couldn't be found. No one on Fremont knew where she was; she had cut off all communication and didn't even call Taffy. I couldn't interview and hang out with someone I couldn't find; here again is a problem of doing research inside a hidden population.

After the bust, Cara returned home to Cathy's apartment. I had the phone number, and we visited. But over the fall of 1995, Cara was laying low and griping about being bored and penniless. Once she got a job and moved to 5403 Smart, her life became rich with ethnographic events. At that point, I decided that *Dead End Kids* would tell her story. It wasn't until Wendy began to hang out with Cara after Cara's release from Cherry in the spring of 1996 that the duo of Wendy and Cara emerged and their lives perked up.

I was lucky to have Cara as an informant. When she moved to 5403 Smart and hung out with TJ and the Northeast boys, I knew she'd eventually get into trouble. Those boys had a street reputation as raucous characters, and they fulfilled that reputation. This isn't to say that I was pleased to watch Cara and the Northeast boys get into serious trouble; I wasn't, but Cara's choice of companions and the effects that choice had on her life are powerful data.

Picking key informants was only the beginning of my informant-selection problems. From the onset, I planned to find gang kids' parents who I could hang out with over a long period. Cara and Wendy were ideal connections to parents. Wendy introduced me to Jackie and then later to Mike. Cara's relationship with Cathy was rocky over a number of years, but Cara never abandoned her mother, as Carmen had done. Cara also led me to Carol, Northeast's Gangsta Mamma, but Cara's arrest caused Carol to flee, and I couldn't find her.

Locating parents is difficult. Gang kids hang out together, but gang kids' parents don't.[19] Fremont kids' parents, even those who lived on Fremont Avenue, never talked to each other on the phone or on the street and never walked into each other's houses, even if they lived a few houses apart.

Asking a kid for an introduction to his or her parents may not help you get to parents. Kids may not want to help, because most gang kids, especially those who were hardcore Fremont, have poor relationships with mothers and fathers. Many kids have no relationship with their fathers. Cheri had no recollection of ever having seen her father, but she talked about receiving letters from him, though, in fact, she never did. Recall that many kids' parents kicked them out of the house, as Carmen's mother did; some had a violent relationship with a parent, as Poodle did; others had an on-again, off-again tie to a parent, depending on whether the kid needed the parent, as Cara and Cheri did; others were kicked out of the house and told not to return, as Wayne's parents did to him; and some had parents involved in criminal activity, such as Rosa's family, and didn't want a stranger nearby.

Even getting a parent's phone number might not help. Poodle gave me her mother's phone number; she got it from her brother Roger, because he and his mother still got along fairly well. I called and talked to Poodle's mother many times, but on those occasions that I set up an interview and knocked on her door, she was never home.

In short, a kid may be a poor gatekeeper to a parent, and surely parents feel no obligation to speak to a researcher simply because the researcher hangs out with, or even helps, their kids. Jackie and I chatted face-to-face a number of times, but she refused to be interviewed. I learned more from Jackie over the phone in the months before we met than I did while I hung out in her house. She was tough and resistant, probably because she was a raging cocaine addict and, in the summer of 1995, had no time for anyone or anything but selling and smoking rocks.

It's extremely difficult to cultivate a key informant relationship with a gang kid's parent. But you can try by avoiding the assumption that a kid will facilitate a tie to his or her mother or father, which means you must cultivate an independent relationship with the kid's parent. Kids' parents are potentially exceptional resources, but whether they'll talk openly and truthfully about their kids' gang behavior and delinquency is problematic. Put yourself in the situation of being the parent of gang kid: Would you tell a stranger about your child's most awful behavior, or speculate about how you might have contributed to your son's or daughter's drug addiction and violence?

Ethnographic Error

Fieldworkers' problems with gang kids' parents highlight many of the seminal issues in ethnographic fieldwork and in the interpretation of interview data. Participant observation gets us into hidden populations, but once there, many things can go wrong, and interview data can have errors. *Error*, in this case, pertains to the possibility that the interview data an ethnographer collects from informants may be twisted, idiosyncratic, or contain outright lies. Researchers shouldn't begin the ethnographic enterprise assuming that informants are friends who will help them at all costs. As in any relationship, trust, openness, and honesty take time to create and even more time to build and sustain. Remember, too, that each person at a fieldsite, the researcher included, has his or her own view of the world. It's the principal role of the ethnographer to listen to informants, watch them behave, and then fashion a picture of a fieldsite that's balanced and honest. That skill takes years of practice and a true sense of how the natives and the ethnographer influence each other.[20]

Ethnographers must control for error. We do this in part (a) by creating strong rapport with natives, especially key informants; (b) by becoming explicitly aware of idiosyncratic (unique to the speaker) and contextual (embedded in the interview situation) factors that affect informants' speech; and (c) by cultivating a strong sense of how to interpret what informants say within the sociocultural and economic context of their lives. Below I explore rapport, influences on speech, and the inter-pretation of speech.

Rapport. Michael Agar, a pioneer of street ethnography, wrote that in doing ethnography "one person [the ethnographer] . . . wants to learn something from a second person. A human relationship is established, for however brief a period of time. Despite the fact that this relationship exists, insufficient consideration has been given to it and its implications for the kind of information obtained."[21] It's within the interpersonal relationship between the ethnographer and the informant that research happens. The quality of research depends on what informants tell us, and in large part, what informants say depends on the rapport between them and the researcher. After all, how many of us tell our deepest secrets to someone we don't like?

Rapport refers to how well an ethnographer gets along with infor-mants.[22] Fieldwork is like dating: the longer you hang around, the more you talk and the better the relationship. If good rapport exists between the ethnographer and the informant, they share the communication process between them. A good ethnographer doesn't dominate conversations with an informant or determine the topics to be discussed, the place where conversations occur, and how the conversations end. In any relationship, if one member has "control" over the conversation and the social situation in which it occurs, the outcome of that conversation will likely be biased by the member's dominant status. As in any such case, especially by mem-bers of hidden populations who are subservient to police, lawyers, and judges, informants' statements will reflect a subordinate role. Superior-subordinate interviews may yield data biased by the ethnographer's con-trol. In the end, these data will consist of "plastic," or stereotypical, albeit sometimes clever, responses that informants dish out to researchers. Such responses don't reflect what an informant knows or how he or she feels about the interview issues. When an informant feels cornered, he or she won't speak honestly or openly.

Rapport protects the integrity, or the reliability and validity, of con-versational data. Good rapport has a positive effect on interpersonal relations, strengthening the bond. An informant then opens up and talks honestly with genuine conversation. During this process, the researcher learns how to ask questions properly and get needed information without controlling the informant.[23] Recall how the content and style of my conversations with Cara changed as we shared her life's problems and became closer. Our conversation about Chucky D working as a "hit man" wouldn't have happened early in our relationship. And of course, her asking me to be her baby's grandfather indicated a close relationship.

Calculated talk about creating rapport may sound somewhat manipulative: an ethnographer goes to a fieldsite and creates rapport simply to
hear natives talk openly and honestly about their world. Well, that's the
job ethnographers do. If you think it's manipulative, collect data some
other way, but don't go overboard in judging us. Building rapport and
gathering data in the context of a continuous, long-term relationship are
one thing; coercing and ripping off information, then using it to harm
informants, are another. Good ethnographers protect informants with
full disclosure of the research purpose and may even use informed consent
statements in the field.

There was no doubt about who I was or what I was doing on Fremont.
Every kid on Fremont and every other street kid and adult I chatted with
or interviewed knew I was a researcher and writer. I hid nothing. If you
reread the ethnographic narrative you'll see that I kept my notebooks
open and my tape recorder in full sight. If kids didn't want to talk, they
didn't, and I had to work around it. It's just that simple.

In the end, informants have a choice, and they exercise it. Building
rapport encourages them to talk, and talk is what we go to a fieldsite to
hear. But no matter how long we hang around, no matter how good our
rapport, informants always know we are researchers. I asked Afro dozens
of questions about drugs and drug income over a period of months during
the early stage of my research, and he looked into my eyes, smiled, and
walked away without saying a word.

Building rapport also means that ethnographers are drawn closer to
informants, who may then benefit from that relationship. Recall how I
helped Cara: I helped her because I felt close to her, not because I felt an
obligation to her for being a key informant. I didn't help other kids to the
same degree. While I got the information I wanted, she also got something
that went beyond hamburgers and cigarettes. I was standing at her side
when she needed a "father." That too is an effect of rapport building.

Influences on Speech. Words, whether spoken or written on surveys, are
instruments of elicitation. If we use the wrong words, use words in the
wrong ways, or aren't aware of how rapport or social setting influence
informants' words, then we either won't get the data we want to get or
won't know how to interpret the words informants speak.[24]

Conversations occur between a researcher and an informant, and
there are a number of factors that influence what informants say to
researchers. These are sociolinguistic factors (social and situational influences on speech) embedded in the interview situation. A speech situation
is the specific context in which a conversation or interview occurs. It's
axiomatic that environment influences behavior: people who grow up

on Fremont behave differently from those who grow up in Overland Park. Similarly, the "environment," or context, in which speech occurs influences what informants say. If we are unaware of how context affects informants' speech, then we're likely to misread what we're hearing. And that can be a serious mistake if we use informants' words as the basis for crime control policies but don't know the difference between plastic and genuine comments. I've already discussed how rapport influences conversations, but there are a number of other issues to raise.

Informants' speech can be influenced by stimuli other than questions. Generally speaking, speech is sensitive to social situations and to an informant's perceived relationship with the researcher. Changes in speech and its sensitivity to either a social or an interpersonal situation is called code switching.[25] *Code* refers to an informant's speech. *Speech* is what an informant says (content) and how he or she says it (style). *Content* refers to the topics an informant chooses and the depth of information he or she provides to the ethnographer. Stylistic changes in speech include alterations in the way an informant speaks. For this discussion of ethnographic method, I'll focus on speech content instead of speech style, because a researcher can broaden an informant's array of topics and depth of information by being aware of sociolinguistic factors. But it takes special training to record stylistic alterations in informants' speech, and most likely, street fieldworkers are far more interested in what gang members say than in how they say it.

For the sake of definition, speech *style* refers to vocabulary choice, precision in speaking, grammatical construction of sentences, and other such issues. One example will suffice to illustrate this point. When a student is called into a professor's office about missing assignments, the student will likely speak formally (less slurring, better sentence construction, no use of obscenities). Compare that sample of speech with how he or she speaks later at the local pub when telling the tale about the trip to the professor's office. The difference between these two samples of speech is style.

Anthropological ethnographers like myself are trained in descriptive linguistics and sociolinguistics, and we pay careful attention to how speech is issued. If you return to the text, you'll find that I was careful about illustrating how an informant uttered words such as *bitch, motherfucka,* and *niggah* and the specific context in which those words occurred. I noted details such as how long I'd known the informant at the time of the conversation and some facts about our relationship. These descriptive facts are sociolinguistic variables. Every gang researcher wants to know basic facts about a gang community environment in which gang crime occurs, facts such as race, ethnicity, and income levels. Every fieldworker should know about sociolinguistic variables, and likewise, every reader should ask for these variables, in order to interpret informants' statements correctly.

Fieldworkers want to improve their informants' interview productivity. That is, we want informants to tell us more in less time. We have limited time in the field and need our informants to talk a lot about many of the things they know about. Their "speech content," or the topics they choose to discuss, is influenced by their quality as our informants, by sociolinguistic variables, and by their perceived role in their relationship with the researcher. If fieldworkers aren't aware of how or what signals code switches, then we lose interpretative power or misunderstand what informants say.

Codes switch from one social situation to the next. The speech that is the outcome of a shift in social situation is called a speech register. Gang members speak at the corner of Fremont and 13th in a way different from how they speak standing in front of a judge. If a gang researcher does an unstructured or semistructured interview with a gang member in a detention center, the researcher is likely to get more-abbreviated responses, less detail, and vaster omissions than if he or she were interviewing the same gang member with the same questions while sitting in a drug house.

Simply knowing about these differences will affect how a researcher interprets what an informant says. For instance, I did a structured interview with a gang member in Champaign, Illinois, who said he'd joined a gang because he had nothing to do after school. That's a plastic response, and I certainly don't believe it, but it's predictable given the social situation. We were sitting in a nice clean office while I asked questions and he answered them (recall the above conversation about superior-subordinate relationships). A week later, sitting on a curb in the same gang member's neighborhood, we chatted back and forth and, springing from that casual, uncontrolled conversation, the teenage Vice Lord talked about why he had joined. This time I didn't have an interview booklet in my hand, and he wasn't sitting at a desk. Our personal relationship hadn't changed over the week; we hadn't talked or seen each other; thus, I can't claim that rapport influenced his speech. This time, however, he said he had been thrown out of school for fighting, failed most of his courses, used drugs, and had cousins and siblings who were Vice Lords. Which interview data do you believe—data collected in the office or on the curb?

Codes also switch when an informant perceives a change in the nature of the relationship between himself or herself and the ethnographer. The speech outcome of a perceived shift in social relationship between the informant and the researcher is called metaphoric code switching. This code switch overlaps with the idea that rapport influences speech content, but it's more complicated. At the beginning of my Fremont research in June 1995 I was an outsider, a college professor, and largely a stranger to everyone. Kids talked to me about nonsensitive topics and some even apologized to me for speaking words like *mothafucka* in front of me. Months later in March 1996, when I visited Cara on Cherry, I was her friend, a companion, a friend of the family. By the time the research ended in February 1997, Cara had appointed me her "father" and her baby's grandfather. If you review the speech in *Dead End Kids* and the content of conversations with Cara over time, you'll hear metaphoric code switching in speech content. This is common sense. Conversations between Cara and a stranger, Cara and a friend, Cara and a family friend, and Cara and her surrogate father are very likely to differ in content as well as style.

Ethnography lets us capture a broad sample of speech taken from different social settings as well as different metaphoric contexts established in the relationship between an ethnographer and an informant. In the summer of 1993, I interviewed for the first time a kid named T-Bone, the Harvard Park Blood I met at the Ad Hoc Group Against Crime. We sat in a back office by ourselves. T-Bone didn't know anything about me, except that I knew his boss, Calvin.

T-Bone sat up straight and proper while he talked about the Harvard Park Bloods, and I didn't interrupt him. He said his fellow gang members were his "family" and they "loved" one another. I had been in these situations before, and I knew his speech was plastic. A year later at his apartment early one Friday morning he talked again about his relationship to the Harvard Park Bloods. This time he said, "They're motherfuckers who'll try to fuck ya. Ya cayn't trust 'em." Which speech data reflect the truth? Between our first meeting at Ad Hoc and our conversation a year later, our relationship had changed; we'd gone from total strangers to friends. He called me at home, we chatted about his girlfriend and upcoming wedding, and I invited him to speak at a gang conference I organized at Illinois State University.

During our 1993 conversation, I asked T-Bone about his family. He told me that he had come from a loving family and had a wonderful mother. In the summer of 1994, he invited me to his wedding. Weeks before the wedding, while we were driving around Kansas City in his car with rap music blaring from the stereo, he told me he hated his mother. He recalled being beaten, and he said she didn't care if he wandered the streets. If fact, he spent his early teenage years selling drugs and staying in a drug house operated by his cousin. By age 13, he was a die-hard drug addict; by age 14, he was a Harvard Park Blood; at age 17, he was shot three times in the back in a gang shooting. At his wedding, I watched carefully and saw that T-Bone and his mother ignored each other and didn't speak. Did T-Bone have a loving relationship with his mother?

Interpretation of Speech. Ethnography isn't a slave to natives' explanations, because it's more often the case than not that natives don't understand the complexities of their communities as well as we'd like to think they do. The fact is, many times natives' explanations are simply wrong as objective statements, and we must be able to identify and sort ethnographic responses from objective ones and understand the difference between them. Cara once told graduate students in Professor Olson's seminar on urban issues that the need to protect themselves from the KCPD had caused Fremont kids to become a gang; once they had become a gang, she said, they were isolated and compelled to sell drugs and do violent things to protect themselves from other gangs.[26] Students nodded their heads at Cara's self-serving gang-formation story, and I'm sure some went off telling companions that, if it weren't for the KCPD, there wouldn't have been any Fremont Hustlers. Nothing could be further from the objective truth.

Natives' explanations are sometimes harder to label as folklore than Cara's gang-formation story is. If an adult researcher asks a 14-year-old gang girl about why she's pregnant, how many explanations does a young girl have in her linguistic repertoire that can protect her integrity? She can say, for instance, "I'm a whore and sleep with every boy," or "I was high and didn't think about using a condom," or "If I don't have sex with my boyfriend he'll beat me," or "The only time I feel good is when I'm having sex," or "My father had sex with me and now I'm afraid to say no to any man," or "I want a baby to love me." Such comments lead an ethnographer to ask: Do an informant's statements have psychological or social reality, or are these simply instrumental remarks that are conditioned by the social context of the interview itself?

Hanging around the Fremont fieldsite taught me that midteenage girls have babies because they and their boyfriends don't use birth control. Recall the interviews with Cara and Wendy about pregnancy and birth control; these girls had gotten pregnant more often than any other Fremont girls. But why, I asked myself, are girls in their midteens engaging in adult sexual behavior? Why are adults, like Jackie and Cathy, lackadaisical about their daughters' sexuality and pregnancy? Is there a relationship between adults' disregard for teenage pregnancy and the fact that so many teenagers get pregnant? What influence do female peers have on the sexual behavior of one another? What effect does male and female gang members' sexual behavior have on inter- and intragender social bonding?

The analysis of Fremont girls' sexual behavior links sex to the socio-economic relationship between a baby's young parents (recall my analysis of the socioeconomics of sex in chapter 14, "Gang Girls, Gang Babies"). The maintenance of the father-mother relationship depends on the baby. Thus, the adaptational dynamics of the male-female group would be askew if Fremont girls were to begin using birth control or refusing to have sex.

I seriously doubt, however, that any Fremont kid would agree with my analysis of the economic and social value of "gang babies." But that's fine. Ethnography doesn't demand that natives agree with an ethnographer's explanation. The trick is to describe carefully how a native's words were influenced by speech variables within the natural context of the fieldsite, to be sure we can sort ethnographic reality from contextually conditioned responses.[27] Doing that will add clarity to data interpretation.

One gang girl's account of sexual behavior may reflect an ethnographic consensus, which means that her opinion is similar to the opinions of others in her community (this is the basis for using key informants). Ethnographic consensus notwithstanding, informants' explanations may not necessarily be consistent with an objective explanation of adolescent sexual behavior. Wendy and Cara told me about their own multiple pregnancies, but what they said was different from my interpretation of their sexual behavior within the socioeconomic behavior system of the Fremont Hustlers. In the end, however, ethnographers are left on their own to judge the veracity of informants' statements.

Interpretative clarity is essential for two reasons. First, to build the science of gangs, we need good (valid, reliable) data and precise interpretation, which require an explicit understanding of the contextual speech variables that may have altered the data. Second, intervention programs are predicated on what informants say. If we, as interventionists or consultants to these programs and to legislators, use informants' words as our explanations for natives' behavior without truly understanding what we've heard, we are setting the stage for an intervention disaster.

The most challenging interpretation in gang research may be the speech of gang kids' parents. People in hidden populations hide information. With this in mind, there's no commonsense reason to believe that the parents and relatives of gang members will have an honest discussion with a stranger. Researchers' declaration to parents made with written or verbal informed-consent proclamations, such as informant anonymity, aggregate data analysis, and data security, mean little to informants who earn income illegally and don't trust anyone for any reason. Informed consent makes us feel better, but that's about it. If gang kids' parents choose to be interviewed, it's because they want money if we pay for interviews[28] or because they perceive some benefit to them, even if that benefit is "getting over" on a researcher or doing the interview quickly and getting the stranger out of the house. Deception, twisting the truth, concealing information, and creating folklore about themselves, their companions, and their lives are the nature of street culture. Let's not be naive and believe we're hearing the whole truth and nothing but the truth.

I disbelieve parents who disclaim knowledge of their children's gang activity. *Dead End Kids* shows that a kid's gang activity is only the tip of a family's dysfunction. Ethnographic data show the indicators of kids deeply involved in a youth gang: These kids sell and use drugs; get suspended and expelled from school for fighting with students and teachers; are arrested over and over again by the police; are likely to be injured seriously enough in gang violence to be hospitalized; and don't sleep at home at night. Surely parents hear pagers buzz, phones ring, and banging at the door in the wee hours of the morning. If parents don't hear or see these things, why not? They might be drugged up and asleep or away from the house most of the time, or their kids aren't gang members of the ilk of Cara, Wendy, Chucky D, and Bernard.

Delinquency and gang research shows that gang kids' lives display a clear pattern of delinquency before and after gang affiliation. Parents who pretend not to see what their kids are doing are either stupid, or active criminals, or totally irresponsible, or ideal illustrations of broken social bonds, or manipulative, or protecting their own economic interest in their kids' criminal involvement, as Jackie did.

The common parental response to outsiders' queries about their children's gang involvement is their "social distance" from their children. Recall when Cara and Wendy used the social distance defense, they moved to Raytown in order to move away from Fremont and Northeast companions and thus stay out of trouble. Cathy claimed biological distance. She argued that Cara's behavior problems are a byproduct of her genetics, not Cathy's parenting or the influence of the men Cathy had married, so she used biology to distance herself from Cara's problems.

The following is a snippet from an interview with a gang girl's father who used the ploy of social distance: "We don't hate the kid. But at the same time, I basically don't really want her around me as long as she's affiliated with this. It's caused problems in the family—her gang affiliation and the babies and stuff like that. It's caused problems between me and my wife."[29] These are good data about the weakness of the parent-child tie and its role in delinquency. Fremont data show that neglectful and abusive parents, like Carmen's, Poodle's, and Cheri's, push their kids away, and when asked about it, these parents try to convince outsiders that they've done the best they can for their kids and that their kids' behavior has nothing to do with them. Teresa did this with her adolescent son; Poodle's parents did this with her. Such parents think that separation from their children (in word or fact) is supposed to convince outsiders that the parents disapprove of their kids' behavior.[30]

Generally speaking, wouldn't it be embarrassing for a father or mother to tell a stranger that he or she simply doesn't give a damn about his or her children, or that he or she benefits financially from his or her child's criminal activity? What's more, many parents once were or still are gang members and have an active interest in protecting themselves.[31] Despite our need for total research disclosure and honesty, members of hidden populations are not inclined to provide this and have no reason to trust us. Lying to us, they think, keeps the police away from their door.

Ambiguity and deception are woven into the fabric of gang members' family lives. Participant observation is a gang researcher's salvation. When the statements of informants really don't meet the canons of simple common sense, the researcher must dig for data to distinguish the behavioral facts from the verbal folklore. This means hanging around and watching and listening.

In the interpretation of problematic interview data, it's a conceptual error to assume that gang members' families are like the proverbial "average family" except for the gang affiliation of a child. Social life is never the way it appears or sounds at first glance. To be sure, a fieldworker has a much easier time hanging out with and interviewing gang kids on the street than understanding how a gang lifestyle and children's gang affiliation fit into a family's history and dynamics.[32]

If researchers haven't established good rapport with gang kids' parents, there's little hope of going beyond plastic responses. Establishing rapport with them is tough. With an ethnographer and gang teenagers, there's a sense of a parent-child relationship inherent in the bond between them. If the researcher is pleasant, these kids may derive pleasure from the relationship itself; after all, many gang kids are starved for adult affection, and a researcher's return to a fieldsite month after month is a sign of affection.

With gang kids' parents, however, researchers must go beyond the link to the kids and find other common ground and a reason to visit these parents at home or on the job. I established separate relationships with Cathy and with Mike and enjoyed their company. Cathy enjoyed talking about old movies and books; Mike enjoyed discussing his involvement in Wendy's life and his own recovery from alcohol and drug abuse. Mike's participation in Alcoholics Anonymous made it easier for me to establish rapport with him and for him to talk openly to me.

However, when a researcher interviews parents about their kids' gang behavior, those questions carry an implicit sense of judgment, especially when spoken by a "university professor." Keep in mind that members of hidden populations don't look at university researchers as we look at ourselves. We may not see anything special about us, but they do. They see a sharp distinction in social class and income, and that immediately puts social, emotional, and cognitive distance between these interviewees and researchers.

Gang kids' parents perception of us generates a metaphoric distance, which must be overcome before a researcher will get good data. You can hear the social distance. Parents often apologize for or avoid using obscenities in casual speech, or are embarrassed by their children when they use obscenities or raise conversation topics that parents think are inappropriate for us to hear. Making spontaneous phone calls with no research agenda, offering cigarettes, sitting around watching television, sharing a cup of coffee or a meal, telling jokes, sitting and not asking questions, and simply listening to what parents say without interrupting or being intrusive with follow-up questions are mechanisms that go a long way to break down the metaphoric barriers between the researcher and the gang kids' parents.

No published gang or crime research includes an explicit description of how interview data are influenced by a given social situation and the metaphoric relationship between an informant and a researcher, as well as by dozens of other communication issues. If you reread *Dead End Kids,* you'll see that carefully built into every conversation are those variables needed to further understand an informant's speech content. I have described the physical setting, any bystanders, the time of day, the informant's emotional state, the informant's use of drugs or alcohol, the month and year of the conversation, and the degree of rapport with the informant, among other variables.

We should be as explicit in identifying such variables as we are in establishing links between behavior and poverty, race, and income. One thing is certain: data collected with a structured survey instrument aren't by their nature more scientific than data collected in casual conversations on street corners.[33] So-called in-depth interviews of 60 minutes are neither in-depth nor usually insightful and surely aren't useful if our research purpose is to understand the complexities of social life in a human community where speech is the primary vehicle of interpersonal interaction.

Gang research has no theory of speech and speech interpretation. If our intent is to study "surface" data,[34] then quick-and-easy structured interviews are fine. In such a case, no matter how sophisticated our data-collection instrument, sampling strategy, and statistical analysis, the outcome will always be an inadequate representation of the complexity characterizing the sociolinguistic world of natives. Each informant is capable of an infinite number of expressions, and each expression carries complexities of innuendo, metaphor, and symbolism. These complexities are easy to gloss over in a research project with limited time and funding; however, researchers must try to attend to the details of social dynamics that influence informants' speech.

Better Interviews. A number of simple suggestions can improve the quality of face-to-face interview data.

- Short interviews are best. A number of short interviews with the same informant are better than one long interview. Each time the researcher sees the informant, the nature of the social tie changes, and eventually, if the researcher is an open and friendly person, the informant should relax and offer better speech data.
- Watch for boredom. Researchers may be comfortable with sitting for a long stretch and thinking and talking, but street people, especially gang kids, aren't. They don't sit still for too long, and they'll get bored in 45 minutes. If you keep them pinned down, they'll just offer up perfunctory answers. Humor helps. When I sensed that an informant was tiring of questions, I changed the topic to something that was more interesting to him or her. Such conversation flexibility shows indirectly that you aren't controlling the situation and that you respect an informant's desires.
- Change interview settings. Do interviews in different social settings. Interviewers should avoid offices and sitting behind desks. Don't wear white lab coats or white shirts and ties. This attire can ruin rapport. White shirts and ties make interviewers look like judges and lawyers, and that's not such a good idea if you're interviewing kids like Chucky D.
- Be hospitable. Offer informants a soft drink, let them smoke, give them a chance to relax before and after the interview, especially if you're going to do more than one interview. You may find, as I have, that the best data are elicited in casual conversations after a 45-minute interview ends. I use 60-minute tapes, 30 minutes on each side. When the tape runs out, it's time to quit, unless the informant wants to continue talking.
- Be sincere. Informants know you're a stranger, so just be a genuine and sincere outsider and enjoy informants' company. It's remarkable how adolescents feel the social situation and know intuitively if the researcher cares about what they're saying.

• Be precise and patient. Use vocabulary correctly. Ask informants short, precise questions which have reasonably simple answers. Remember that gang kids haven't benefited from the practice of responding to questions, except in an interrogation. If an informant feels embarrassed or threatened, the quality of the data will change, probably for the worse.

Speech, Politics, and Ethics

Establishing rapport with informants and genuine closeness to them are distinctive outcomes of ethnographic research whose ethical and political implications are significantly different from each other. Rapport is an instrument; genuine closeness isn't. An ethnographer can establish and maintain excellent rapport with informants and still be distant or aloof or, worse yet, indifferent about his or her informants' fate.[35] Bourgois has an opinion that touches this issue: "College-educated intellectuals are usually too elitist or too frightened to be capable of treating unemployed, drug-addicted, violent criminals with the respect and humanity that ethnographic methods require for meaningful dialogue to occur."[36]

If it's to work really well, ethnography must be a continuous, long-term, meaningful dialogue between a researcher and his or her informants. Unless an ethnographer is made of stone, creating such a meaningful dialogue means that his or her life will be influenced by informants, probably more than the reverse.

Bourgois' research expresses such a dialogue, and I have no doubt that he became genuinely close to his informants. This happened to me on Fremont and in my two other long-term ethnographic studies. Feeling genuinely close to the Fremont and Northeast kids like Cara and Bernard made creating *Dead End Kids* especially difficult at times, because I had to decide if I'd publish data on family abuse and crime, which might contribute to law enforcement intelligence investigations of the Fremont Hustlers or other KC gangs.

My role as an ethnographer of a youth gang shouldn't facilitate police intelligence, but how can I write about a youth gang without, by definition, offering a narrative about street crime? I've published Fremont's gang-oriented drug distribution scheme knowing that Wendy and Chucky D will have been out of business for years by the time this book hits the shelves. The same applies to Afro and my descriptions of his ongoing operation; by the time I was writing up my research, he had been arrested for yet another shooting. Had they not been busted, however, I would have faced a serious ethical and legal dilemma: Should I describe cocaine distribution at a particular spot when the dealers and runners (street-corner sellers) are still active? What are the implications of my knowledge of Fremont's drug distribution for them and for me? Might I get arrested? If so, what would I say on the witness stand?

On the basis of my experiences, I feel that, as rapport evolves into genuine closeness, ethnographers have a more difficult time creating a balanced portrait of informants' behavior. I use the word *creating* intentionally. Ethnographers collect data, but there are fewer rules for assembling those data into a picture of life at a fieldsite than for guiding objective statistical analyses of self-reported data.

On the street, informants are free to withhold or twist information about legal and illegal things they do, but if I hang out long enough, I'm likely to see them do the illegal or legal things they say they don't do. Nevertheless, to contribute to the science of gangs and, in this case, to youth-gang intervention, I tried to create a balanced narrative. But if I were to disclose too much "raw" information, readers would likely say that I sensationalized my research and thus created a biased snapshot of the street. If I were to reveal too little, readers would likely say that I protected my informants or became their advocates and thus created another kind of biased picture. In the end, we're damned if we do and damned if we don't, but this is the nature of creating and publishing street ethnography in America's political environment.

In *Beggars and Thieves* and in *Dead End Kids,* I wrote about the touchiest topics—child abuse and neglect—and brought readers inside families to show this abuse and neglect, as well as alcoholism, drug abuse, and spouse abuse. In publishing material about sensitive topics, I use a rule of thumb: If a behavior is characteristic or representative of the lifestyle within a community or the families who compose it, I'll write about it. If child abuse had occurred once in one Fremont family, I would have labeled it idiosyncratic or anecdotal and overlooked it. One case of child abuse out of hundreds or thousands of parent-child interactions wouldn't be a sample representative of family interactions in that fieldsite.

In *Dead End Kids,* the behaviors I described are representative of typical themes, such as parental neglect and abuse, parental and adolescent drug use and crime, adolescent interpersonal violence, and joblessness among Fremont youth-gang members and their families. These representative ethnographic data describe the lifestyle of the youth gang called the Fremont Hustlers as well as the individual lives of its kids. The validity of my descriptions is demonstrated objectively by comparing Fremont findings with other gang research.

In today's world, it simply isn't good enough to write about street life without offering thoughtful opinions about how to fix the problems we see. At that point, we have a serious choice; we can hide inside the university community and pretend that parents are loving and warm and only beat, punch, slap, kick, and molest their children on rare occasions, or we can be honest. If we are honest, then we must be willing to publish what we see. If we do that, we must be tough-skinned enough to accept criticism without flinching and running away when times get tough.

Street ethnographers must assume a moral stance and report and interpret touchy subjects, even if that means offering judgment about our informants' behavior. This may not be politically correct, but given the destructive nature of street life, hiding behind scientific neutrality or political correctness is immoral. If I were to see child abuse and write, "Gang-girl mothers commonly neglect their children and put them in situations which are physically and emotionally injurious," and then drop the topic as if to say, "It happens a lot; therefore it's OK," I'd be a foolish, ivory-tower academic who shirks his moral responsibility.

As an observer of poverty, abuse and neglect, and adolescent self-destructiveness, my first moral obligation is to protect young victims. How I do that is problematic, particularly while doing research inside a potentially dangerous street scene. If I inform local authorities and report cases of child abuse and neglect, there's a chance that social service agents won't respond or, worse yet, will respond poorly. Chubby-faced Robert was under the care of the local social service system, but that system failed him. Amy and RoniRo needed protection too. I could have called the police or social service officials. I knew if I were to do it, there was a strong possibility that nothing would be done to protect these preschool children. In fact, I did ask a companion in Kansas City to report what I had seen inside Teresa's household. The phone call was made to the proper authorities. Nothing happened. In such a case, what is the ethnographer's next step?

On a more general scale, there are contrasting ways of handling sociopolitical issues. Bourgois interpreted the behavior of a key informant, Caesar, as atypical within the Puerto Rican community in East Harlem, New York. "Caesar . . . [embodies] the social injustice of a nation that systematically chews up its most vulnerable citizens and spits them out onto inner-city streets where their desperate celebration of suffering terrorizes themselves, their neighbors, and their loved ones."[37]

In Kansas City, I saw an entire community neglect its most helpless residents, poor children. On Kansas City's streets, there are dozens of lost children like Carmen who are victims of neglectful families, juvenile justice incompetence, and community indifference. Poverty and unemployment influence the neighborhoods in which these kids' parents reside, and in turn, those disorganized neighborhoods and these kids' parents have detrimental effects on the kids. Poverty has a cumulative effect, and that burden feels the heaviest on the shoulders of the youngest and weakest children. Fremont kids are hungry for food and for attention. Kansas City's only response has been to chase them further from the mainstream.

Social and economic change must necessarily occur within the dominant political context. Even when that political context is hostile to intervention-minded social scientists, we must not abandon the fight. *Dead End Kids'* policy recommendations look down toward the street, because I know that communities can remedy the problems that contribute to youth-gang formation. And if communities do their fair share, then the social injustice Bourgois brilliantly described in *In Search of Respect* can be eroded, household by household, neighborhood by neighborhood.

The single most important challenge to interventionists isn't learning how to remedy youth crime or identify its causes and effects; seven decades of gang and delinquency studies have generated a rich research and intervention literature. Rather, the researcher's greatest challenge is learning how best to bring his or her research to lawmakers' attention, irrespective of their political orientation, in a form that's useful to them.

Old dusty, albeit prestigious, academic journals and tomes are superb for earning tenure and promotions, conning salary increases, and securing grants, but how many influential state and federal lawmakers read our journals or could truly understand them if they did? How many university researchers would feel satisfied publishing op-ed essays in major newspapers or political magazines instead of in "major" journals? While we publish and save ourselves from perishing, our informants perish in the ghettos we leave behind.

Bourgois describes his role as an ethnographer this way:

> . . . I hope to contribute to our understanding of the fundamental processes and dynamics of oppression in the United States. . . . I also want to place drug dealers and street-level criminals into their rightful position within the mainstream of U.S. society. They are not "exotic others" operating in an irrational netherworld. On the contrary, they are "made in America." Highly motivated, ambitious inner-city youths have been attracted to the rapidly expanding, multibillion-dollar drug economy during the 1980s and 1990s precisely because they believe in Horatio Alger's version of the American Dream.[38]

Fremont research showed me that a "made in America" youth gang is more than a group of kids who commit crimes. A youth gang is a tangle of morality and immortality, control and anger, fury and passion, love and hate, responsibility and irresponsibility, and fearlessness and paranoia. Fremont kids' behavior is a twisted knot of paradoxical themes. Cara never missed a day at her job at Taco Bell or arrived late to work. She worked overtime until 4:00 or 5:00 in the morning and never pilfered a penny. Such a level of responsibility in a teenager who once preferred smoking weed to doing anything else shocked me. However, Cara didn't have the patience to attend school or the foresight to use birth control. Even Chucky D and Afro smiled, laughed, and showed care and warmth toward fellow Fremont members. But neither one of them cared for their own children, and both, if you recall, exhibited terrifying violence.

Dead End Kids stresses the paradoxical nature of Fremont kids' behavior for a specific reason. Legislators formulate crime-control policies on simple dualities: good versus bad, right versus wrong, legal versus illegal. Lawmakers then ask us to believe that these dualities really exist in our communities. Simple dualities may exist for legislators, but they don't exist for me or at Fremont and 13th and The Spot. Out there where households are impoverished and kids are hungry, there is no clear path to righteousness, no firm stand on morality, no index of goodness, no uncompromising grasp of what's lawful and unlawful. When you're poor, the future is bleak, morality is a blur, and affiliating with a gang may be the only rational economic and social option in the neighborhood.

Fremont research shows that a monolithic crime-suppression policy that leads to arrests of more, as well as younger, gang members and sentences them and their fathers, cousins, brothers, and sisters to prison terms of 10–40 years for nonviolent drug offenses is unquestionably the wrong policy if our goal is to resolve the causes and conditions breeding alienated children who merge into youth gangs.

The nuances of the political interpretation of ethnographic data will depend on an ethnographer's experiences in the field, personal inclinations, political propensities, and silent motivation for spending years on the street among a hidden population. Before I answered Janet's penetrating question, I reminded myself that I drove away from Fremont and 13th Street and left Amy, RoniRo, and Charlene inside a forgotten neighborhood and ramshackle houses in the company of drug-addicted, sometimes out-of-control adolescents and young adults. I asked myself, How best can I serve these children, their young parents, the neighborhood, and the city of Kansas City?

I don't make laws or control funding levels for inner-city socioeconomic development or crime control. However, I have written this book to tell the world what it's like inside one small inner-city neighborhood in America's heartland. I will be content if *Dead End Kids* convinces one state or federal lawmaker to pay more careful attention to the smallest, poorest citizens in America's most marginal households.

Street ethnographers may not be able to alter the quality of our informants' lives, but we can show readers the young face of poverty and misery and the dead end that awaits children, adolescents, and adults inside America's cities. It's our moral obligation to engage fully in the arguments over how to remedy poverty, repair neighborhoods, and improve the lives of the youngest people who inhabit the poorest households. To hide behind the white coat of science is immoral and irresponsible, and it contributes to social injustice and oppression in America. If we aren't actively engaged in restructuring our poorest neighborhoods, who is?

Notes
Index

Notes

Introduction

1. Anne Campbell, *The Girls in the Gang,* 2d ed. (New York: Basil Blackwell, 1991), classifies gang girls. A "straight G" is the equivalent of Campbell's "tomboy" category (p. 245): "girls who try to succeed on male terms."

2. Mark S. Fleisher, *Beggars and Thieves: Lives of Urban Street Criminals* (Madison: University of Wisconsin Press, 1995).

3. Scott H. Decker and Barrik Van Winkle's *Life in the Gang* (Cambridge: Cambridge University Press, 1996) is an outstanding long-term, systematic, single-site field study of inner-city gang life. This research in St. Louis, Missouri, mirrors in every important detail my findings in Kansas City.

4. G. David Curry, Robert J. Fox, Richard A. Ball, and Darryl Stone, *National Assessment of Law Enforcement Anti-Gang Information Resources,* Final Report (Morgantown, W. Va., 1992), p. 22.

5. Malcolm Klein, *The American Street Gang: Its Nature, Prevalence and Control* (New York: Oxford University Press, 1995).

6. G. David Curry, Richard A. Ball, and Scott H. Decker, *Update on Gang Crime and Law Enforcement Recordkeeping: Report of the 1994 NIJ Extended National Assessment Survey* (Washington, D.C.: National Institute of Justice, 1995).

7. Jeffrey Butts, *Offenders in Juvenile Court, 1993, Juvenile Justice Bulletin* (Office of Juvenile Justice and Delinquency Prevention, Washington, D.C. (July 1996): 2.

8. See Cheryl L. Maxson and Malcolm W. Klein, "Street Gang Violence: Twice as Great, or Half as Great?" in *Gangs in America,* ed. C. Ronald Huff, pp. 71–100 (Newbury Park, Calif.: Sage, 1990); Irving Spergel, *The Youth Gang Problem* (New York: Oxford University Press, 1995), pp. 33–42.

9. Kansas City Gang Task Force Report, Kansas City Police Department, 1993.

10. John M. Hagedorn, *People and Folks: Gangs, Crime and the Underclass in a Rustbelt City* (Chicago: Lake View Press, 1988), pp. 23–24; and Malcolm Klein, *Street Gangs and Street Workers* (Englewood Cliffs, N.J.: Prentice Hall, 1971), pp. 15–19, discuss the role of the media in exaggerating and twisting public perceptions of gangs.

11. This and the next section were suggested by Professor James B. James, New York University, School of Law. Professor Jacobs suggested that, because the book is a complex sociological narrative with an array of characters and underlying concepts, it might be useful to offer a reader's guide to *Dead End Kids* and a list of major characters. These were very good ideas.

Chapter 2. Fremont Hustlers

1. Kansas City has territorial and nonterritorial gangs. Fremont Hustlers and the Northeast Gangstas are two of the city's few territorial gangs. A territorial gang "claims" some block or neighborhood as their "turf." Fremont defends the corner of Fremont Avenue and 13th Street in a neighborhood no one in KC really cares about. A nonterritorial gang is a group of adolescents and/or adults who move between neighborhoods, sell drugs and commit other crimes, and stay just ahead of the police.

A 1992 Kansas City Gang Task Force report published a listing of entities KC police called gangs (the number of members in each gang is shown in parentheses): Gangsta Disciples (44), Crips (162), Bloods (129), and other (29). Gangster Disciples include the Silver City Gang (4), Insane Disciples (6), and Black Gangster Disciples (34). Crips include the 25th St. Posse (15), Southside Posse Crips (20), 43rd St. Crips (24), 33rd St. Crips (6), Rollin' 60s Crips (12), 35th St. Crips (10), 24th St. Crips (14), Rollin' 40s Crips (9), 12th St. Gangster Crips (26), 51st St. Gangster Crips (17), and Macken Gangster Crips (9). Bloods include the 21st St. Bloods (4), 60th St. Bloods (4), Westside Latin Counts (6), Banda Loca (15), 69th St. Dogs (5), 57th St. Road Dogs (7), 33rd St. Latin Kings (18), 23rd St. Hardcores (22), Eastside Latin Counts (32), and Malditos (16). Other gangs include the 9th St. Dogs (20) and Gracemore Boys (9), which are affiliated with Eastside Latin Counts.

Fremont Hustlers and Northeast Gangstas don't appear on the 1992 Gang Task Force report, because they didn't emerge and become recognized by the KCPD until sometime in 1992 or 1993. I discuss later the emergence of these youth gangs.

The gang names Crips, Bloods, and Gangster Disciples shouldn't be misunderstood as necessarily indicating a gang connection between Kansas City and the Crips and Bloods in Los Angeles and Gangster Disciples in Chicago. Crips and Bloods originated in Los Angeles in the early 1970s, Gangster Disciples in Chicago some 40–50 years ago (Mark S. Fleisher, *Warehousing Violence* [Newbury Park, Calif.: Sage, 1989] discusses the origin of the Crips and Bloods). In KC, I didn't know or hear about a gang member who had grown up in Los Angeles or Chicago and traveled to Kansas City in order to spread his or her gang to that locale. There are, however, adolescents and young adults in Kansas City who spent their early years there, later moved with their families to Los Angeles or another west coast city, where they joined the Crips or Bloods, and then returned to Kansas City.

2. The Fremont Hustlers reside in the extreme northwest corner of the East Blue Valley census tract, identified in the 1990 Census data as Area 007,

Neighborhood 006. The boundaries of East Blue Valley are 12th Street (north), 17th Street (south), Belmont Avenue (one block west of Fremont), and Winchester Avenue (east). The 1990 census data show that the East Blue Valley population of 2,387 was predominantly white (85 percent; 9 percent black). Average annual income for persons was $9,238; among the 945 households, 18.8 percent earned less than $9,999, 26.6 percent earned from $10,000 to $19,999, and 11.2 percent earned over $40,000. Among the 617 dwellings in East Blue Valley, 74.7 percent were valued to be worth less than $29,999; 1.6 percent were valued over $60,000. Among the 1,531 residents older than age 15, 42.8 percent had less than a high school diploma.

Until approximately 20 years ago, this area of Kansas City was home to workers in the Sheffield steel industry, whose dilapidated factories stand east of Fremont and within easy walking distance of residents and former employees (Dr. Phil Olson, University of Missouri Kansas City, personal communication). When the steel mills closed, workers migrated out of this area and economic decay set in. Housing data show that 68.7 percent of East Blue Valley householders moved into this area after 1970.

3. Cara told me that the "Rolanda" show paid $500 to the Fremont Hustlers for participating in the film. Paying Fremont means they gave the money to Wendy, because the film was shot at her house. Cara also said, "They tol' us what ta say. They wanted us to sound like gangstas', know what I'm sayin', so they told us to say stuff and talk about violence 'n shit like dat."

4. Irv Spergel, *The Youth Gang Problem* (New York: Oxford University Press, 1995), chapter 10, is an outstanding synthesis of theoretical perspectives on youth-gang formation.

5. The origin of the terms *Folks* and *People* is unclear, and most tales are apocryphal. The terms themselves connote a link to neighborhoods and households, as in "that's where the real people (or folks) are." Conversations with state and federal prison officials over the past 15 years, as well as my experience working in the United States Penitentiary (USP) at Lompoc, California, where I became familiar with inmate self-classifications (east coast versus west coast; Los Angeles versus San Francisco), imply that a Folks-People classification is likely to be an artifact of prison life.

Prison conflicts over drug distribution, for instance, often caused heated conflict between inmate groups. Four inmates on one side of a dispute may ready themselves to fight 12 inmates on the other side, the smaller group asking companions for assistance in return for a cut in the drug action. A newly formed larger inmate group is often composed of street gang members from local neighborhoods in cities. Such a simple affiliation may be the origin of the Folks-People classification. The diffusion of these terms and the informal affiliations implied by them would spread quickly from prisons to the street with the release of inmates and then back to other prisons upon parolees' rearrest.

I can only speculate that such a system of social segmentation had simple beginnings. Today, however, gang members have elaborated the symbol systems, and claiming to be either Folks or People is a trendy thing to do, as Wendy's behavior suggested. People symbols are oriented to the left side (hats turned to the left, for instance) with a five-pointed star, and they use the slogan, "All is well." The dominant People gangs originated in Chicago and include the Latin Kings, Vice Lords, P-Stones (Black P-Stone Nation), Inmate Unknowns, and P.R. (Puerto Rican) Stones. Now even the Bloods, a gang born in Los Angeles, are People. Likewise, Folks symbols are oriented to the right side with a six-pointed star, and they use the slogan "All is one." Folks gangs are also Chicago groups and include the Black Gangster Disciple Nation (Gangster Disciples), Maniac Latin Disciples, Satan Disciples, Spanish Cobras, Ambrose, and the Crips, the last being one of the two most dominant Los Angeles street gangs.

At the street level, young gang members don't know the meaning of the People versus Folks classification, although they are familiar with the terms. My 1997 fieldwork in Champaign-Urbana, Illinois, found some 3,000–4,000 gang members, most of whom were Gangster Disciples, Vice Lords, Black Gangsters, P-Stones, and Mickey Cobras. In this community, Vice Lords engaged in fistfights with P-Stones and shot and killed them, even though both groups are People. Likewise, the Gangster Disciples warred against the Black Gangsters. However, these gang members got huffy when I referred to their groups as gangs and to them as gang members. They preferred the terms *organizations* and *members of organizations*.

6. No member of the Fremont Hustlers expressed an interest in protecting local area businesses (cf. Martin Sanchez-Jankowski, *Islands in the Street: Gangs and American Urban Society* [Berkeley: University of California Press, 1991]).

Chapter 3. Inside

1. Richard A. Ball and G. David Curry, "The Logic of Definition in Criminology: Purposes and Methods for Defining 'Gangs,'" *Criminology* 33(2) (1995): 225–245, offers an excellent discussion of gang definitions.

2. The vast gang literature is synthesized nicely in Irving Spergel, *The Youth Gang Problem* (New York: Oxford University Press, 1995); and Malcolm Klein, *The American Street Gang: Its Nature, Prevalence and Control* (New York: Oxford University Press, 1995).

3. Gang researchers have systematically sought theories to explain gang formation. Frederick Thraser's 1927 study, *The Gang* (Chicago: University of Chicago Press), was the first serious research on gangs, and since then gang researchers have created a number of categories of theories linking gangs to poverty, socioeconomic strain, social class (low class, underclass), social disorganization (neighborhood, community), family disorganization, racism, and abnormal personality development.

Despite the search for gang theories or integrated theories of delinquency and gangs, gang researchers haven't looked into the literature on cross-cultural adolescence or on adolescent development. Thus, the focus on gangs has largely been to explain gangs' deviant aspects, with researchers virtually overlooking the universal sociocultural aspects of adolescent social processes. The fact is, most of what we call gang behavior is not especially interesting as a research phenomenon, because it's so commonly a part of adolescent culture. Kids' wishes to hang out with kids like themselves, kids' use of symbolic means (graffiti, clothes, jargon) to sort one group from another, kids' aggressiveness, the impermanence of membership in kids' social groups, kids' rebelliousness against adults, including their families, aren't unique phenomena. Cross-cultural adolescent research has shown that male adolescent aggressiveness is related to increased peer contacts (see Alice Schlegel, "A Cross-Cultural Approach to Adolescence," *Ethos* 23, 1 [1995]:24). Is it really a surprise, then, to find that large groups of American kids (a gang) do more of something (commit crime) than smaller (delinquent) groups?

Bonnie Miller Rubin ("Today's Teens Have Plenty of Picks to Clique," *Chicago Tribune*, National section, Sunday, September 14, 1997, pp. 1, 17) points out that adolescents in large high schools stratify themselves into ranked homogeneous subgroups (skaters, preps, hip-hop, ravers, postgrunge, goths, and stoners); that some kids pretend to be members of a group they really don't belong to (wannabes); that kids shift between groups; that there's conflict between groups; that the school as the adolescent community is fragmented by these subgroups; and the parents are concerned about their kids being in the "wrong" group.

An overemphasis on criminological theories and on adolescent male delinquents seems to have clouded our vision about adolescent delinquent females. Meda Chesney-Lind and Randall G. Shelden's excellent study of girls' delinquency (*Girls: Delinquency and Juvenile Justice* [Pacific Grove, Calif.: Brooks/Cole, 1992]) is narrowly focused on delinquency theory (ecological, strain, differential association, control, labeling) and doesn't cite studies on girls' sociopsychological development or research on nondelinquent-female relationships among themselves and with males. If we don't understand a full range of cross-cultural adolescent female behavior, how are we to pinpoint those behaviors which are unique deviant responses to a range of family and environmental stimuli? In short, we don't understand how much of what we're measuring in female (and male) delinquent and gang behavior is within the range of predictable adolescent behavior in complex urban settings. Why is this such an important issue? Unless we know which adolescent behaviors are natural (and will terminate with adolescence) and which are effects of controllable negative stimuli (family disorganization, for instance), then we won't be able to develop truly effective intervention strategies.

Perhaps the true uniqueness of a "youth gang" is how communities respond to it. Generally speaking, decades of research show that kids in gangs are marginal in school and have been injured by family disorder, among other things. That marginality and injury don't preclude these kids from engaging in universal adolescent sociopsychological processes (homophilous groups, stratification, ranks, aggression); however, so-called gang members act out these processes in an unconventional venue, the street, which alarms adults and engenders a law enforcement (control) response instead of a parental (supportive) response. As an anthropologist observing this scene, it's alarming to watch American adults castigate and alienate their own youth and further injure already victimized adolescents. It isn't youth gangs that should bother America's lawmakers, but rather the dominant culture's response to America's most vulnerable children. America's aggressive and punitive reaction to youth gangs as "community evil" marks the abusive nature of our society.

4. Fremont Hustlers fit a common operational definition of gang as a group involved in illegal activity (Finn-Age Esbensen and David Huizinga, "Gangs, Drugs, and Delinquency in a Survey of Urban Youth," *Criminology* 31 [1993]: 565–569). I prefer the definition in Scott H. Decker and Barrik Van Winkle, *Life in the Gang* (Cambridge: Cambridge University Press, 1996), p. 31: "an age-graded peer group that exhibits some permanence, engages in criminal activity, and has some symbolic representation of membership." The notion of age-grade is important, because we know that gang members in their late teens and early twenties commit most of the violent acts (Spergel, *The Youth Gang Problem*, pp. 33–36). Thus, older gang members in consort with young boys and girls pose a serious problem in the socialization or coercion of young members to be involved in violent acts. How age distribution influences violence in male gangs and in mixed male-female gangs, like the Fremont Hustlers, has not been carefully studied.

5. Malcolm Klein, *Street Gangs and Street Workers* (Englewood Cliffs, N.J.: Prentice Hall, 1971), includes a comprehensive discussion of gang cohesion and leadership. Fremont findings support Klein's and show that external pressures, including poverty, family dysfunction, unemployment, and schools' inadequate responses to difficult kids, have a stronger effect on group cohesion than internal forces, such as a code of conduct and ethos.

6. Few publications focus specifically on females in gangs and female gangs. See, for instance, Lee Bowker and Malcolm Klein, "The Etiology of Female Juvenile Delinquency and Gang Membership: A Test of Psychological and Social Structure Explanations," *Adolescence* 18 (1983):740–751; Joan W. Moore, *Going Down to the Barrio: Homeboys and Homegirls in Change* (Philadelphia: Temple University Press, 1991); Carl Taylor, *Girls, Gangs, Women, Drugs* (East Lansing: Michigan State University Press, 1993); Anne Campbell, *The Girls in the Gang*, 2d ed. (New York: Basil Blackwell, 1991).

Also see Ruth Horowitz, *Honor and The American Dream* (New Brunswick, N.J.: Rutgers University Press, 1983).

7. Using the roster elicited on my first day on Fremont, I wrote each of the names of the 72 Fremont Hustlers on its own three-by-five card. I gave the stack of cards to each girl and asked her to sort the cards into as many piles as necessary, as long as each pile had more than one card (see H. Russell Bernard, *Research Methods in Anthropology* [Newbury Park, Calif.: Sage, 1994], pp. 249–252). After each informant had created the piles, I asked why she had grouped those people together.

Pile sorting is useful, but there are a number of difficulties in structured interviews with gang kids in noisy apartments. First, kids want to help each other put cards into piles. I had to tell bystanders to stay quiet. Second, kids see names on cards and start to tell stories about those kids. This is wonderful, but it distracts the informant from the task. Third, kids see names that disturb them. Enemies, former lovers, dead homeys, snitches, and others distract both the informant and the bystanders. If she is upset, either the informant wants to stop the pile sorting or she gets into arguments with bystanders about the names on the cards. Fourth, sorting 72 cards takes time and effort, and then enduring my questions takes even more time and effort. In the end, an hour interview becomes 90–120 minutes, or the kids just abandon the task out of boredom. Fifth, kids have other things going on at the same time. Distractions are endless. Phone calls, buzzing pagers, people knocking at the door, and other kids getting high keep the informant away from the job. Sixth, pile sorting requires good rapport with informants and a fully open channel of communication. I did this pile sorting eight months after arriving on Fremont. Kids are suspicious, and without good rapport, they're likely to conceal good data by glossing over kids who are "really in the shit."

In the end, however, pile sorting gave me insights into the internal classification of the Fremont Hustlers through the eyes of three of its longest-standing active members. With these data, I decided who would likely be the best kids to interview next and whom could be passed by.

8. Labels such as "core," "peripheral," "associate," "wannabe," or synonyms of these labels, were not used by informants.

9. I elicited these categories in March 1996 and asked Cara to sort the cards as social groups had existed during the gang's 1994–95 heyday. Social dynamics are continuous; thus, these categories should be viewed as a temporal snapshot. I recorded notes about the kinship relationships within each group, and in some cases between groups, and also noted violent incidents (perpetrator or victim) or other unique characteristics for each kid, as Cara reported them.

10. Fremont girls are in Anne Campbell's (*The Girls in the Gang*) "bad girls" category. "They are not tortured by dreams of upward mobility and have a realistic view of their chances of success in society. They have not done well in school, and when they have money, they spend it. . . . Like the boys in the neighborhood, they enjoy excitement and trouble, which break the monotony of a life in which little attention is given to the future. They like sharp clothes, loud music, alcohol, and soft drugs. They admire toughness and verbal 'smarts.' They may not be going anywhere, but they make the most of where they are" (pp. 7–8).

To be sure, Fremont girls aren't chattel, that is, possessions of gang boys. These girls are staunchly independent, although many have customary adolescent boy-girl relationships. Gang boys are more aggressive than girls and frequently try to control them; in such a case, girls play a passive role. Boy-girl pairings often display violence, as I describe and discuss later. In some cases, a girl will perceive her victimization at the hands of a boy as his affection for her, but I don't think this is unique to gang-affiliated adolescents.

I'm unconvinced that girls, like Cara and Wendy, who have been physically hurt by boys actually believe their own words ("He hit me because he loves me"). If anyone knows about violence, it's these kids, and they know from experience at home that violence isn't love. The public talk equating physical violence and interpersonal affection is a girl's culturally defined rationalization for her inability to escape such a horrible situation. If a gang girl pulls away on her own, her boyfriend will likely beat her more severely. To escape an abusive relationship, a girl needs a new suitor who's stronger and more violent than her current abusive boyfriend. This is how Chucky D and Afro succeed in relationships. No one challenges them, and girls can, in a sense, "hide" behind them. In relationships with them, however, girls pay a price, and that price is obedience and sex.

The most realistic way to escape from these boys is to become pregnant. Once real-life responsibilities face Afro and Chucky D and other Fremont boys, they flee and find new girlfriends. Although pregnant girls don't say it directly, they believe their pregnancy will soften their abusive boyfriends. Later I discuss pregnancy, sex, and boys' financial and social irresponsibility.

11. Anthropologists have reported that social groups with a special purpose, such as a fraternity, commonly have a rite of passage, or initiation, for the prospective members. An initiation rite is the public transformation of social status from, in the case of a gang, a non–gang member to a gang member. Such a rite of passage serves an additional function. It is also a rite of social intensification, which draws group members together and further bonds them on a collective occasion.

It's no surprise to find that a youth gang has a rite of passage. The number of gangs requiring a rite of passage is unknown, although folklore about such rites is plentiful and often apocryphal. Folklore has it that such rituals may include, for instance, being beaten by fellow members or being forced to commit a violent act. Even if such rites of passage occur, it'd be very difficult to know if these are idiosyncratic events or a core feature of gangs as a uniform expression of marginal adolescent culture. By an idiosyncratic event, I mean an event that is initiated by a violent boy like Chucky D and his violent companions, who use new members as a means of satisfying their own bloodthirst (see Decker and Van Winkle, *Life in the Gang*, p. 184). In any case, a violent rite of passage certainly isn't unique to innercity gangs. In my college years, fraternities "paddled" initiates, and many still do, although paddling is members' "secret" knowledge.

Gang initiation stories have become so exaggerated that on occasion they reach the news and engender public fear. Over the winter of 1993–94 in central Illinois, local news stations broadcast that gangs were engaged in an egregious violent initiation. It was reported that gang members would drive around at night with the headlights on high beam. When an oncoming car, usually driven by an elderly person, flashed its lights signaling the high beams, the gangsters would turn around and follow the elderly driver to his home and then rob, beat, or kill him. A colleague in the California Youth Authority in Los Angeles told me that such a tale was broadcast on the news there at about the same time it appeared in central Illinois.

While doing Fremont research, Kansas City newscasts reported a violent and bizarre "new" gang initiation. A prospective gangster, the story went, would hide underneath a car in the parking lot of a KC shopping center at night, and when the driver (usually a woman holding bags) stood next to the door to unlock it, the gangster would slash at her ankles with a knife, pull her to the ground and rob her and steal her car. Such an event never occurred in Kansas City. Cara, Wendy, Afro, and Chucky D chuckled when they heard that tale. Chucky D said, "What da fuck d'ya wanna do dat for? Ya getcha clothes dirty and dey ain't no money in it."

12. Social groupings are static representations. To be sure, daily Fremont life isn't static. Pagers helped me to track changing social ties. When a kid gave me his or her pager number, it was a sign of rapport. Old fashioned "low-tech" street ethnography isn't sufficient to keep up with kids who have cars, pagers, and cellular phones, and who shift residences every week or month. "Pager" ethnography helps. I learned to use their pagers and caller identification to my advantage. Kids who know one another's pager numbers, how often kids page one another, whether or not a kid returns a page, how quickly pages are returned, who borrows a pager from whom and then puts his or her own outgoing message on that pager are good data. Boy-girl relationships are traceable with pagers. A girl might carry her boyfriend's pager, and a boy might lend his pager to a girl he wants to sleep with.

Pager numbers are sensitive information. I never had a problem collecting information about drug selling or kids' sex lives, but when I asked for pager numbers and numbers listed on caller identification machines, I often had problems. Even after a long and close association with Cara, she was judicious in giving me caller ID numbers. Their numbers were valuable, and they told me who was contacting whom and how often. Once I had that information, I could ask about the content of the calls and move into the most intimate aspects of kids' social ties.

13. The fundamental gender-linked difference between Fremont girls' and boys' response to one another is this: girls think about relationships as moral contracts; boys don't. Beyond the street rhetoric of the gang, girls' implicit construction of relationships, especially with boys, includes fairness, reciprocity, and equality. A girl expects that, if she pairs up with a boy and has sex with him, then he will treat her fairly and be responsive to her and to their children. In what they perceive to be long-term relationships, girls feel an inherent responsibility toward the boys with whom they are involved, but the boys feel neither reciprocity nor fairness nor equality. This conflict between girls' and boys' underlying conception of the nature of interpersonal relationships is the source of boy-girl physical and emotional abuse. A baby has an important role in the unwritten moral contract between its mother and father, from a girl's perspective. I discuss this issue later.

14. See Cheryl Maxson and Malcolm Klein, "Differences between Gang and Nongang Homicides," *Criminology* 23 (1985):209–222.

15. See Scott H. Decker, "Collective and Normative Features of Gang Violence," *Justice Quarterly* 13, 2 (1996):243–264.

16. Dank sticks are prepared by dipping cigarettes into an ounce (28 grams) of formaldehyde cut, or diluted, with 7 grams of fingernail polish remover or, if it isn't available, brake fluid, paint thinner, or everclear (drinking alcohol).

17. See Mark S. Fleisher, "On the Streets of America," *Natural History* 106, 6 (1997):44–53, for a photograph of the Fremont Hustlers and their weapons.

18. I've interviewed dozens of teenage gang members from Chicago who said they know of incidents in which a glance, a momentary stare, a bump has caused

fights and even killings. Assuming there's truth to these claims and violence did occur, I argue that such an explosive reaction from a gang member has little to do with the gang and much to do with the gang member's personality. A youth gang is a perfect place for such kids to act out violence.

Chapter 4. Families

1. I wish to thank Moira Beach, administrative assistant to the chair, and secretary of the Earth Sciences Department, SUNY–Oneonta, for bringing to my attention this passage.

2. I heard similar stories from inmates at the USP Lompoc. These prisoners said they received letters, regular visits, and Christmas and birthday gifts from their mothers and fathers. Record checks showed they received no such visits or packages. The "kind parent" fantasy extends to imprisoned lovers, who upon their release will care for Fremont girls. It's a pervasive idea. Wendy talked for nearly a year about "her boy" who, once released, would return to Fremont and take her away from, as she said, "all the crazy shit up in here." He was released and returned to his mother's home in a public housing project and was then rearrested within a month and sent back to prison. During that time he didn't call or visit Wendy.

Angie talked continuously about an imprisoned lover, Aaron, who'd rescue her upon his release. Cara also had a fantasy lover, Jack, who I'll discuss later.

3. See Mark S. Fleisher, "Ethnographers, Pimps, and the Company Store," in *Ethnography at the Edge*, ed. Jeff Ferrell and Mark Hamm, pp. 44–64 (Boston: Northeastern University Press, 1998).

Chapter 5. Dark Side

1. Meda Chesney-Lind and Randall G. Sheldon, *Girls: Delinquency and Juvenile Justice* (Pacific Grove, Calif.: Brooks/Cole, 1992), has a summary of issues in regard to girls and delinquency. For an excellent study of serious delinquents, see James A. Inciardi, Ruth Horowitz, and Anne E. Pottieger, *Street Kids, Street Drugs, Street Crime: An Examination of Drug Use and Serious Delinquency in Miami* (Belmont, Calif.: Wadsworth, 1993).

2. Fremont's unlawful behavior included status offenses (crimes linked to a person's age, such as truancy) and felonies, such as drive-by shooting, burglary, possession of stolen property, carjacking, robbery, battery, possession and sale of illegal drugs, and allegations of murder (see Cheryl Maxson and Malcolm Klein, "Differences between Gang and Nongang Homicides," *Criminology* 23 [1985]:209–222).

The only crime committed as the outcome of a consciously designed social arrangement was illegal drug selling. This was "gang crime," and on occasion, as I described, drug selling engendered neighboring gangs' competitive aggression and violence toward all Fremont Hustlers. The other crimes were neither motivated by the majority of the Fremont Hustlers, nor did the group benefit by those crimes.

These crimes were "personal" and effected trouble only for the perpetrators. (See Irving Spergel, *The Youth Gang Problem* [New York: Oxford University Press, 1995], pp. 179–180, 309–312, for definitions of a gang-motivated and gang-related crime.)

Fremont's gang structure was at first difficult to recognize, because the kids didn't talk about how it was structured and operated. These internal statuses were unlabeled. Recall that Fremont had no formal leader and lacked gang-internal status labels, such as "sergeant at arms," "treasurer," "secretary," "lieutenant," "captain," which have been reported by researchers and law enforcement officials for adult criminal organizations, such as the Gangster Disciples (see *Gangs: Public Enemy Number One,* Chicago Crime Commission, 79 West Monroe, Suite 605, Chicago, Ill. 60603).

Wendy had face-to-face influence among Fremont kids, because her house was Fremont's main drug spot; thus, she controlled the most valuable property. Steele Bill, the gang's drug connection, resided inside Wendy's house. Even with social influence, no one called Wendy—or Afro or Chucky D, the other two major players in the drug business and Fremont's defenders—the boss, shot caller, or leader. There was no gang leader either inside or outside the drug hierarchy.

With no leader, no internal police force, no rules, there were no so-called violations. In gangs such as the Gangster Disciples, Vice Lords, and Latin Kings, which have internal status differentiation and high gang-generated income, there are strict rules, and members are "violated" for breaking rules. Violations are physical punishments. These range from minor offenses, such as failing to heed the orders of a superior, to serious ones, such as ripping off the gang's drug-related income. Corresponding violations range, respectively, from a "mouth shot" (being punched in the mouth) to being shot through the hand or leg or beaten to death with baseball bats.

3. Gang researchers have commonly reported drug selling within a hierarchical structure. See, for instance, Jeffrey Fagan, "The Social Organization of Drug Use and Drug Dealing among Urban Gangs," *Criminology* 27 (1989):633–669; Felix M. Padilla, *The Gang as an American Enterprise* (New Brunswick, N.J.: Rutgers University Press, 1992); Martin Sanchez-Jankowski, *Islands in the Street: Gangs and American Urban Society* (Berkeley: University of California Press, 1991); Carl Taylor, *Dangerous Society* (East Lansing: Michigan State University Press, 1990).

4. Bruce A. Jacobs, "Crack Dealers and Restrictive Deterrence: Identifying NARCS," *Criminology* 34, 3 (1996):409–431, reported that rock cocaine sellers in St. Louis self-report monthly sales of $2,300 per respondent (p. 412). Jacobs, a field researcher, couldn't directly verify the accuracy of such self-reports, nor could I. However, young drug sellers are teenagers, and if they have cash, they spend it on cars, athletic shoes, shirts, jewelry, leather jackets. If a drug seller is earning money, he'll buy new possessions, wear them a few times, and often give them away to companions and relatives. Good observation can offer indirect validation of drug income.

5. Fremont wasn't a cohesive organization in the sense of a minicompany

with a chain of command and formal rules of appropriate and inappropriate behavior. Fremont was a haphazardly assembled social unit composed of deviant adolescents who shared social and economic needs and the propensity for resolving those needs in a similar way.

The August 1995 bust showed the Fremont Hustlers' internal social units: a small unit was the gang, and a large unit was the delinquent group (see Mark Warr, "Organization and Instigation in Delinquent Groups," *Criminology* 34, 1 [1996]:11–37). Social instability in delinquent groups has been identified by a number of scholars. See, for instance, Malcolm W. Klein and Lois Y. Crawford, "Groups, Gangs, and Cohesiveness," *Journal of Research in Crime and Delinquency* 4 (1967):63–75; Robert J. Sampson and John H. Laub, *Crime in the Making: Pathways and Turning Points through Life* (Cambridge, Mass.: Harvard University Press); Lewis Yablonsky, "The Delinquent Gang as a Near-Group," *Social Problems* 7 (1959):108–117.

The bust affected the gang and the delinquent group in different ways. Fremont's gang was eliminated when Wendy's house was boarded up and then burned; she then went underground, and Chucky D went to prison. However, the bust failed to damage Fremont's delinquent group. Fremont kids who had sold drugs as part of the Fremont gang continued to sell drugs as members of the Fremont delinquent group.

When the gang ended, the raucousness ended at Fremont and 13th Street, and so did intergang gang-motivated violence. However, the bust pushed drug selling farther from the street, and it became a quieter, stealthier, and more low-key business.

6. Fremont's postbust fragmentation supports my earlier claim (see chap. 3, note 5) that group cohesion depends largely on group external forces rather than on internal forces of cohesion, and further supports Klein's 1971 argument, as well (Malcolm Klein, *Street Gangs and Street Workers* [Englewood Cliffs, N.J.: Prentice Hall, 1971]).

7. See Mark S. Fleisher, "Can We Break the Pattern of the Criminal Lifestyle?" *USA Today: The Magazine of the American Scene* 125, 2624 (May 1997):32, for a photo of Afro's makeshift marijuana greenhouse.

Chapter 6. Misery

1. See James Garbarino, *Raising Children in a Socially Toxic Environment* (San Francisco: Jossey Bass, 1995). See pp. 27–32 for the argument about family and child rearing and their effects on children's lifelong adaptation.

Chapter 8. The Arrest

1. Westside Kansas City Mexican street gangs have gang mamas, too. Jose, a former member of the Mexican Mafia, told me about a number of households like Taffy's and Carol's on KC's westside Mexican community. Jose said he knew a westside household in which the kids spent their days indoors, to avoid the police

who had truancy warrants for their arrest. These kids slept and smoked weed and drank beer. In one such household, Jose said, the mother of a 16-year-old gang boy was sleeping with her son's 15-year-old homeboy.

Chapter 13. A Look Back

1. This car rebuilding program is the idea of Professor H. Russell Bernard, Department of Anthropology, University of Florida. See more discussion on this proposal in Chapter 14.

Chapter 14. Gang Girls, Gang Babies

1. See Irving Spergel, *Street Gang Work* (Reading, Mass.: Addison-Wesley, 1966); and Malcolm Klein, *Street Gangs and Street Workers* (Englewood Cliffs, N.J.: Prentice Hall, 1971).

2. See Shay Bilchik, "The Office of Juvenile Justice and Delinquency Prevention: A Federal Partner in Meeting the Mental Health Needs of Juvenile Offenders," *Focal Point* 11, 1(Spring 1997):17–20.

3. A further discussion of community mobilization and gang intervention can be found in Irving Spergel, *The Youth Gang Problem* (New York: Oxford University Press, 1995); Irving Spergel and G. David Curry, "The National Youth Gang Survey: A Research and Development Progress," in *Gang Intervention Handbook,* ed. Arnold P. Goldstein and C. Ronald Huff, pp. 359–400 (Champaign, Ill.: Research Press, 1993); Arnold P. Goldstein and Fernando I. Soriano, "Juvenile Gangs," in *Reason to Hope,* ed. Leonard D. Eron, Jacqueline H. Gentry, and Peggy Schlegel, pp. 315–333 (Washington, D.C.: American Psychological Association, 1994).

4. *Federal Register* 62, 125 (June 30, 1997):35251.

5. See George L. Kelling and Catherine M. Coles, *Fixing Broken Windows* (New York: The Free Press, 1996).

6. See, for example, Mark S. Fleisher, "Management Assessment and Policy Dissemination in Federal Prisons," *Prison Journal* 76, 1 (1996):81–91; Mark S. Fleisher and Richard H. Rison, "Health Care in the Federal Bureau of Prisons," in *Classical and Contemporary Issues in Corrections,* ed. James Marquart and John Sorensen, pp. 347–354 (Los Angeles: Roxbury Publishing Company, 1997).

7. See Robert J. Bursik, Jr., and Harold G. Grasmick, *Neighborhoods and Crime* (New York: Lexington Books, 1993); Spergel, *The Youth Gang Problem,* p. 154.

8. *Opportunity cost* also means that the cost of one program lowers spending on another one. If a community allocates resources to community mobilization projects, fewer local-level resources may be available to fix potholes, construct a new swimming pool, or hire a new police officer. A community may have to choose between building a new swimming pool and fixing potholes or helping gang-affiliated minority children.

9. Spergel, *The Youth Gang Problem,* pp. 172–174.

10. Jody Miller (Department of Criminology and Criminal Justice, University of Missouri at St. Louis), "Gender and Victimization Risk among Young Women in Gangs," paper presented at the 1997 National Research and Evaluation Conference, Washington, D.C., supports the Fremont findings that girls are victims of intragang violence.

11. *Juvenile Arrests 1995, Juvenile Justice Bulletin* (Office of Juvenile Justice and Delinquency Prevention, Washington, D.C.) (February 1997):2.

12. The socioeconomic community void into which kids like Fremont TJ, Little Man, Chucky D, Wendy, Cara, and others drop when released from institutional care is the single most important weakness in the institutional approach to delivering programs to juveniles and young adults.

13. Alice Schlegel's cross-cultural research on adolescent sexuality ("A Cross-Cultural Approach to Adolescence," *Ethos* 23, 1 [1995]) shows that the "sexual activities of adolescents are tolerated or prohibited depending on the consequences of these activities for the adults who are responsible for them" (p. 23). Fremont gang girls who become pregnant (as Wendy, Cara, Angie, Joanne, Dante, and Janet did, for instance) have a strained or broken relationship with their mothers and receive little or no maternal supervision past age 10 or 11. A Fremont girl's pregnancy or childbirth has few consequences for the girl's mother. Young gang fathers walk away with no material consequences for them, their mothers, or any of their relatives. Recall that Janet's mother told her she wouldn't assist Janet after the birth of Briana. The mothers of many gang girls have little concern if their daughters are sexually active, pregnant, or have given birth. A danger lies in the link between these gang girls and their daughters, should these young mothers come to feel similarly about the sexual behavior of their daughters.

14. Joan Moore, *Going Down to the Barrio: Homeboys and Homegirls in Change* (Philadelphia: Temple University Press, 1991).

15. If you recall, all the Fremont girls' babies were illegitimate. However, these girls never raised that issue in our conversations. That fact was simply unimportant to them. Alice Schlegel's cross-cultural research on adolescent sexuality ("A Cross-Cultural Approach to Adolescence") shows that, when children are an economic asset to a community, legitimacy isn't problematic (p. 21).

16. An important point is shown here. When Cara tried to pull away from gang ties, the ties followed her because she had valuable resources. What's more, Cara and Wendy, for instance, knew each other years before they were Fremont Hustlers, and kids who have few companions don't easily relinquish them. Scott H. Decker and Barrik Van Winkle, *Life in the Gang* (Cambridge: Cambridge University Press, 1996), pp. 262–264, offers a similar observation in regard to St. Louis.

17. See Joan Moore, "Bearing the Burden: How Incarceration Weakens Inner-City Communities," *Journal of the Oklahoma Criminal Justice Research Consortium* 3 (August 1996):43–54.

18. See Anne Campbell, *The Girls in the Gang,* 2d ed. (New York: Basil Blackwell, 1991); G. David Curry, "Responding to Female Gang Involvement," a paper presented at the 1995 Annual Meetings of the American Society of

Criminology, Boston; Moore, *Going Down to the Barrio;* and Jeffrey Fagan, "Social Processes of Delinquency and Drug Use among Urban Gangs," in *Gangs in America,* ed. C. Ronald Huff, pp. 183–219; nearly 50 percent of respondents in Fagan's study were female (p. 214).

19. I served as an expert witness on behalf of two Traveling Vice Lords in a federal case in Chicago. At the time of their arrest, these defendants—one age 19, the other 22—had five children by five young women. Had Cara's pregnancies reached term, she would have had five children by three fathers at age 20. Consensual sex isn't considered to be sexual victimization, but we need a careful examination of intragang sexual dynamics and a comparison of pregnancy frequencies between gang- and non-gang-affiliated female adolescents and young adults.

20. Educators are the commonest source of reports on child neglect and abuse (Howard N. Snyder and Melissa Sickmund, *Juvenile Offenders and Victims: A National Report* [Washington, D.C.: Office of Juvenile Justice and Delinquency Prevention, 1995], p. 37).

21. Robert L. Woodson, "Reclaiming the Lives of Young People," *USA Today: The Magazine of the American Scene* 126, 2628 (September 1997):56–59, offers a brief summary of grassroots delinquency intervention in a number of cities.

22. See John J. DiIulio, Jr., "Saving the Children: Crime and Social Policy," in *Social Policies for Children,* ed. Irwin Garfinkel, Jennifer L. Hochschild, and Sara S. McLanahan, pp. 202–256 (Washington, D.C.: The Brookings Institution, 1996). Also see James Q. Wilson, "In *Loco Parentis:* Helping Children when Families Fail Them," *Brookings Review* 11 (Fall 1993):14, for a discussion on "out placing" children in institutional care.

23. See Richard B. McKenzie, "Orphanages: The Real Story," *Public Interest* 123 (Spring 1996):100–104.

24. DiIulio's, "Saving the Children," pp. 230–232, has an excellent summary of the costs of crime. In pondering the cost of a proposal such as this one, let's not forget that every girl who doesn't commit a crime today or tomorrow is saving us far more in tax dollars than an intervention program like this one might cost. Remember, too, that without direct intervention, gang-girls' children will likely commit crimes in the future, and those offenses will be more costly than today's.

25. John Hagedorn, *People and Folks,* argues strongly for the causal role played by poverty in gang formation. William Julius Wilson, *The Truly Disadvantaged* (Chicago: University of Chicago Press, 1987), discusses the development of an urban underclass and the effect of job loss on family disintegration and crime.

There is no question that class structure, poverty, and racism (as mechanisms blocking economic opportunities) have had an effect on gang formation and street crime; however, most inner-city minorities aren't criminals and don't live in poverty (DiIulio, "Saving the children," p. 248). Fremont ethnography shows that the principal operational unit of social and economic poverty is the household. A careful study of households shows that the parents and other relatives of gang members make conscious socioeconomic choices that often lead them to crime instead of less risky options. The effect those decisions have on children's well-being shouldn't be overlooked.

26. Allowing girls to reside together in a safe environment where they are treated with respect and decency should have a positive effect on their behavior. Cara's life shows that even a highly rebellious girl is willing to conform, especially if she is treated well. Fremont girls value independence and enjoy operating in a social sphere where they aren't always at a humiliating disadvantage, as they are among gang boys. Encouraging independence in a decent environment may well be the trick necessary to engage gang girls in accepting a lawful lifestyle.

27. See Campbell, *The Girls in the Gang,* for a discussion of street speech and its functions.

28. Peter W. Greenwood, Karyn E. Model, C. Peter Rydell, and James Chiesa, *Diverting Children from a Life of Crime: Measuring Costs and Benefits* (Santa Monica: Rand Corporation, 1996), shows clearly that reasonable, effective prevention is less expensive than imprisonment.

29. Gang boys commit more crime and more serious crime than girl gang members do, but no one has determined how much less crime boys might commit without the direct or indirect participation of gang girls. Thus, to determine the opportunity cost associated with gang girls' residential centers, we must consider how much money would be saved on crime costs if the size of a mixed-gender youth gang were reduced by removing girls. As a corollary, we should also consider this question: Would altering a youth gang's gender structure by removing girls decrease its violent and nonviolent criminal activities, thus decreasing its cost to a community?

30. Decker and Van Winkle, *Life in the Gang,* pp. 81–82, shows that youth gang girls attract young boys to gangs, and that poor young mothers must rear their children in inner-city neighborhoods, increasing the likelihood that these girls will join gangs. Once young mothers are entrenched in a gang network, their children are very likely to be reared within a gang setting.

Young women rearing children in impoverished, high-crime environments is a tragedy beyond the scope of gang research. Poor teenage gang girls having babies are special cases of teenage pregnancy, worthy of focused attention. The Fremont Hustlers were a "first-generation" gang, but the children of its young mothers are at high risk of delinquency. Recall the aggressive behavior of Teresa's eldest son, who was 11, and his propensity toward preying on the younger chubby-faced Robert. Teresa and her sisters and their children illustrate how alcoholic parents contribute to multigenerational delinquency.

31. Recall that in the chapter "Inside," note 13, I noted that girls perceive an inherent contract in relationships, a contract that focuses on reciprocity, fairness, and equality. Cara's relationships with other Fremont girls and with Fremont and Northeast boys illustrate that contract. However, extraordinary strains of street life seem to affect how these girls act out this inherent contract. When life on the street gets socially and economically stressful, these girls respond in atypical ways. I think that abandoning one another at times of high stress is an example of such a response. At some point, these girls must think of themselves and their own

well-being before others'. Within residential centers, we are likely to find that, when the stress of street-based economic pressure is lifted, these girls respond well to one another and their children and do well in the workaday world.

Fremont girls' life courses are atypical compared with mainstream adolescents, but Fremont girls' responses to their social world aren't atypical, except in cases of violence. The Fremont research recorded a few instances of girl-to-girl fights, but there were no instances of girls committing a serious or moderately serious violent act that required a victim to seek a physician's assistance.

Aggressive behavior is an outcome of harsh socialization. However, harsh socialization coupled with gang life has left harmful imprints on these girls' perceptions of the social world. The primary examples of this are: social connections are often painful; interpersonal conflicts are difficult to resolve and often lead to anger and violence; girls and boys are dependent and need "mothering"; boys who have been mothered by girls don't reciprocate to show kindness; boy-girl, boy-boy, girl-girl relationships are often fleeting and unreliable. In residential centers, these issues can be specifically treated in order that girls adapt well to mainstream life as well as to motherhood.

In addition, gang life illustrates that girls have special skills applicable to the workplace. Wendy has exceptional leadership skill; Cara has a strong social intelligence and empathy with others. Traditional classroom vocational training might overlook these special talents. In residential centers, girls' special talents could be recognized, developed, and then marketed to employers.

32. Alice Schlegel, "A Cross-Cultural Approach to Adolescence," shows that daughters are most aggressive and competitive when the mother is the only permanent member of the daughter's household. Likewise, when children are reared among many women, there is less aggression and competitiveness and improved mother-daughter relations. Boys reported similarly: multigenerational families suppress boys' competitiveness, but larger peer groups encourage boys' aggressiveness and competitiveness (pp. 23–26).

33. An interesting discussion of adolescent female sexuality can be found in J. D'Augelli and A. D'Augelli, "Moral Reasoning and Premarital Sexual Behavior: Toward Reasoning about Relationships," *Journal of Social Issues* 33, 2 (1977):46–47; and L. Kirkendall, *Premarital Intercourse and Interpersonal Relationships* (Westport, Conn.: Greenwood Press, 1961).

34. Greenwood et al., *Diverting Children from a Life of Crime*, shows that parenting programs and financial incentives to remain in school are effective and cost efficient. Residential centers perform similar functions and offer better control.

35. Philippe Bourgois, *In Search of Respect* (New York: Cambridge University Press, 1995), makes the compelling argument that theories of family violence alone are insufficient to explain adolescent and adult criminality. He argues: "Structural problems of persistent poverty and segregation, as well as the more complex issues of changing gender power relations, are rarely addressed in public discussions. The most immediately self-evident policy interventions, such as offering affordable, developmentally appropriate day care for children of over-

whelmed or addicted mothers, are not even part of most policy debates. Similarly, effective drug treatment facilities, or meaningful job training and employment referral services, remain off-limits to women who live in poverty" (p. 260). I agree. My proposal here protects adolescent mothers and their children and at the same time provides drug treatment, work training, and job placement on a manageable small scale.

36. In reported cases of child abuse and neglect in 1992, 52 percent of all maltreated children were female; 49 percent were neglected, 23 percent were physically abused; in 81 percent of all cases, parents were the perpetrators, and in 12 percent, the perpetrators were other relatives (Snyder and Sickmund, *Juvenile Offenders and Victims*, pp. 38–39).

37. Decker and Van Winkle (*Life in the Gang*) have similar observations about the underclass population in St. Louis, Missouri. "Manufacturers, retailers, and service industries have migrated out of the city—especially from those neighborhoods where our subjects live [gang members]. . . . Public transportation to places outside the city limits is slow, infrequent, or unavailable, and inner-city residents find it difficult to follow jobs out to the suburbs or across the rivers" (p. 221).

Chapter 15. Street Ethnography

1. W. Wayne Weibel, "Identifying and Gaining Access to Hidden Populations," in *The Collection and Interpretation of Data from Hidden Populations*, NIDA Research Monograph 98 (Washington, D.C.: National Institute on Drug Abuse, 1990), pp. 5–6.

2. Elijah Anderson, *A Place on the Corner* (Chicago: University of Chicago Press, 1978); Elijah Anderson, *Streetwise: Race, Class, and Change in an Urban Community* (Chicago: University of Chicago Press, 1990); Elliot Liebow, *Tally's Corner: A Study of Negro Street-corner Men* (Boston: Little, Brown, 1967); William Foote Whyte, *Street Corner Society* (Chicago: University of Chicago Press, 1943).

3. Mark S. Fleisher, *Warehousing Violence* (Newbury Park, Calif.: Sage, 1989); Mark S. Fleisher, *Beggars and Thieves: Lives of Urban Street Criminals* (Madison: University of Wisconsin Press, 1995); Carl Klockars, *The Professional Fence* (New York: Free Press, 1974); Ned Polsky, *Hustlers, Beats, and Others* (Chicago: Aldine, 1969).

4. Patricia Adler, *Wheeling and Dealing: An Ethnography of an Upper-Level Drug Dealing and Smuggling Community* (New York: Columbia University Press, 1985); Michael Agar, *Ripping and Running* (New York: Academic Press, 1973); Philippe Bourgois, *In Search of Respect* (New York: Cambridge University Press, 1995); Edward Preble and J. J. Casey, Jr., "Taking Care of Business: The Heroin User's Life on the Street," *International Journal of the Addictions* 4 (1969):1–24.

5. Laud Humphreys, *Tearoom Trade* (Chicago: Aldine, 1970); Jennifer James, "Prostitution and Addiction," *Addict Disorders* 2 (1976):601–618.

6. James P. Spradley, *You Owe Yourself a Drunk: An Ethnography of Urban Nomads* (Boston: Little, Brown, 1970).

7. R. Lincoln Keiser, *The Vice Lords: Warriors of the Street* (New York: Holt, Rinehart, Winston, 1969).

8. H. Russell Bernard, *Research Methods in Anthropology,* 2d ed. (Newbury Park, Calif.: Sage, 1994), is the most comprehensive introduction to qualitative research. Bernard (pp. 38–39) makes the distinction between a participant observer and an observing participant. In this research, I was an outsider making observations, and by virtue of spending a lot of time on Fremont and at other fieldsites, I was a participant. When I did fieldwork at USP Lompoc (Fleisher, *Warehousing Violence*), I became a certified correctional worker and a member of the penitentiary staff, and I worked at a job everyday, as other staff members did. In that role, I was an observing participant.

9. See C. Wright Mills, *The Sociological Imagination* (New York: Oxford University Press, 1959), p. 196.

10. A fundamental premise in language and culture is that language has psychological reality, in the sense that an individual's interpretation of his or her world is influenced to some degree by language. Likewise an individual's worldview, or the unconscious manner in which he or she perceives, conceptualizes, and explains his or her world, is structured to some degree by language and expressed through speech. Such a distinctive worldview is what I mean by *ethnographic reality.*

This distinction between the informant's subjective reality and a researcher's objective analysis of that reality is, generally speaking, the basis for the concepts of emic and etic perspectives. James Diego Vigil and John M. Long ("Emic and Etic Perspectives on Gang Culture: The Chicano Case," in *Gangs in America,* ed. C. Ronald Huff, pp. 55–68 [Newbury Park, Calif.: Sage, 1990]), do what they call an emic-etic analysis of Chicano gang data. Emic (inside) and etic (outside) perspectives seem simple enough to use in ethnographic data interpretation, but these concepts are neither simple nor practical in ethnographic analysis without understanding both their historical origin in descriptive linguistics and their theoretical role in cultural materialism. I recommend that prior to using emic and etic analysis of any speech data, a researcher review these references: Marvin Harris, *Cultural Materialism* (New York: Random House, 1979); Benjamin Lee Whorf, "Science and Linguistics," in *Language, Thought, and Reality: Selected Writings of Benjamin Lee Whorf,* ed. J. B. Carroll, pp. 207–219 (Cambridge, Mass.: MIT Press, 1956.)

11. Ethnography yields data amenable to either qualitative analysis or quantitative analysis. Bernard, *Research Methods in Anthropology;* Steve Borgatti, *Anthropac 4.0* (Columbia, S.C.: Analytic Technologies, 1992); and Steve Borgatti, *Anthropac 4.0 Methods Guide* (Columbia, S.C.: Analytic Technologies, 1992), are the best sources on formal data collection and the analysis of ethnographic data.

12. See, generally, B. Glaser and A. Strauss, *The Discovery of Grounded Theory* (Chicago: University of Chicago Press, 1967).

13. Harris, *Cultural Materialism.* Generally speaking, cultural materialists assume that human behavior is most significantly influenced by forces such as modes of production and mating patterns.

14. This is the notion of reliability, which means, if Decker and Van Winkle had asked St. Louis gang members, "Why did you join a gang?" and I had asked Fremont Hustlers the same question, all things being equal, we'd have heard similar answers. Even though the responses may be similar, the next issue in reliability asks, Are the responses to questions accurate? Accuracy is a difficult issue to assess in qualitative work, especially in dealing with criminals and other informants who very likely have information they want to hide. To overcome this shortcoming, we ask many informants the same question and listen to what they say. If the majority of them say the same things, we can be reasonably certain that we have some degree of accuracy, unless, of course, all informants have conspired to lie to the interviewer.

15. Scott H. Decker and Barrik Van Winkle, *Life in the Gang* (Cambridge: Cambridge University Press, 1996); Malcolm Klein, *Street Gangs and Street Workers* (Englewood Cliffs, N.J.: Prentice Hall, 1971).

16. Bernard, *Research Methods in Anthropology,* has an excellent discussion of both probability and nonprobability sampling strategies (pp. 71–101).

17. Whyte (*Street Corner Society*) used a key informant named Doc. My key informant in *Beggars and Thieves* was Popcorn, and in *Warehousing Violence,* I had several, including Pimping Slim.

18. Bernard, *Research Methods in Anthropology,* p. 166.

19. Decker and Van Winkle (*Life on the Gang,* p. 44) also made this field-work observation in St. Louis.

20. Fleisher, *Warehousing Violence,* discusses in detail how the first few months of fieldwork at USP Lompoc were strongly influenced by the culture of correctional officers and then how my mentor, Professor H. Russell Bernard, visited and helped me to work through the bias.

21. Michael H. Agar, "Ethnography in the Streets and in the Joint," in *Street Ethnography,* ed. Robert S. Weppner (Beverly Hills, Calif.: Sage, 1977), p. 146.

22. See Howard Becker, *Outsiders* (New York: Free Press, 1963).

23. See Bruce A. Jacobs, "Crack Dealers and Restrictive Deterrence: Identifying NARCS," *Criminology* 34, 3 (1996):413, footnote 2.

24. This is how speech data influence validity. Validity refers to whether we're measuring what we think we're measuring. The point here is that, if we use words imprecisely or aren't aware of how external factors may influence an informant's speech or responses to our questions, then we compromise content validity or the substance of the category we're investigating.

25. See Basil Bernstein, "Social Structure, Language and Learning," *Educational Research* 3 (1961):163–176; Susan Ervin-Tripp, "An Analysis of the Interaction of Language, Topic, and Listener," *Ethnography of Communication,* ed. John Gumperz and Dell Hymes, special issue of *American Anthropologist* 66, 6 (1964), part 2:86–102; Erving Goffman, *The Presentation of Self in Everyday Life* (New York: Doubleday, 1959).

26. The notion that the gang formed as an effect of an outside threat is a common theme in gang-formation tales. Decker and Van Winkle report it as well (*Life in the Gang,* pp. 64–65).

27. Agar, "Ethnography in the Streets and in the Joint," p. 145, discusses the role played by "natural context" in ethnographic studies.

28. If a researcher needs to collect data in a hurry with a structured instrument, paying for interviews may be the only way to encourage gang members or their parents to answer questions. In such a case, a streetwise gatekeeper should be used in order to find informants who meet the target demographic description. The researcher should be leery of everything they say and should pay the informant only when the interview ends. Otherwise, the informant can answer a question or two and walk away, because interviews are voluntary.

29. Decker and Van Winkle, *Life in the Gang,* p. 55.

30. An outstanding review of literature on parental rejection is Kevin N. Wright, "Parental Rejection and Delinquency: An Examination of Theoretical and Empirical Links," manuscript, School of Education and Human Development, Binghamton University, Binghamton, N.Y. 13902-6000.

31. James Diego Vigil, *Barrio Gangs* (Austin: University of Texas Press, 1988).

32. Decker and Van Winkle (*Life in the Gang,* p. 43) write: "Parents were often reluctant to be interviewed; in general, we found more resistance from relatives than from gang members."

33. Collecting data with a survey, a probability sampling strategy, and a statistical analysis doesn't escape this epistemological issue. In the case of this kind of data collection, ethnographic subjectivity is quantified, but that doesn't get us any closer to objective truth.

34. The study of surface data involves recording the speech of informants without paying attention to the variables in the immediate speech situation that influence what an informant says and interpreting informants' words as if these words were truthful comments.

35. See Nancy Scheper-Hughes, *Death without Weeping: The Violence of Everyday Life in Brazil* (Berkeley: University of California Press, 1992), pp. 23–24.

36. Philippe Bourgois, "Confronting Anthropology, Education, and Inner-City Apartheid," *American Anthropologist* 98, 2 (1996):249. Also see Scheper-Hughes, *Death without Weeping,* for a discussion of social scientists' "refusal of engagement" with and "indifference" to the people we study.

37. Bourgois, "Confronting Anthropology, Education, and Inner-City Apartheid," p. 256.

38. Bourgois, *In Search of Respect,* p. 326.

Index